International Cybersecurity and Privacy Law in Practice

International Cybersecurity and Privacy Law in Practice

Charlotte A. Tschider

Wolters Kluwer

Published by:
Kluwer Law International B.V.
PO Box 316
2400 AH Alphen aan den Rijn
The Netherlands
Website: www.wolterskluwerlr.com

Sold and distributed in North, Central and South America by:
Wolters Kluwer Legal & Regulatory U.S.
7201 McKinney Circle
Frederick, MD 21704
United States of America
Email: customer.service@wolterskluwer.com

Sold and distributed in all other countries by:
Quadrant
Rockwood House
Haywards Heath
West Sussex
RH16 3DH
United Kingdom
Email: international-customerservice@wolterskluwer.com

ISBN 978-90-411-8841-0

e-Book: ISBN 978-90-411-8922-6
web-PDF: ISBN 978-90-411-8962-2

To my family, thank you.

C'est cela l'amour, tout donner, tout sacrifier sans espoir de retour.

– Albert Camus

About the Author

Charlotte A. Tschider is Affiliated Professor with the Mitchell Hamline School of Law Cybersecurity and Privacy Law Program and Owner of Cybersimple Security, an international privacy and security consulting firm serving diverse multi-national clients. She is also a member of the International Association of Privacy Professionals (IAPP) Training Advisory Board, reviewing and editing international privacy educational publications, and a Fulbright Specialist (Fulbright Scholar Program) in Cybersecurity and Privacy Law.

Tschider was most recently Director of Information Security Management for Carlson Wagonlit Travel and has led information technology teams and served as a privacy liaison in various industries for sixteen years, most notably at Target Corporation leading security incident response, risk management, and risk governance. Tschider writes and presents internationally on a variety of topics involving the intersection of law and technology, and has authored publications in the *Oxford Journal of Law and the Biosciences*, the *Tulane Journal of Technology and Intellectual Property*, the *Annals of Health Law*, and *IDEA: The Intellectual Property Law Review*, among others. She has spoken at international conferences on law and technology topics in the global marketplace. Tschider holds a BS and MA in Rhetoric and Scientific and Technical Communication with a minor in History and Philosophy of Science and Technology from the University of Minnesota, USA, and a Juris Doctorate from the Hamline University School of Law, also in Minnesota. Tschider holds industry certifications in IAPP's Certified Information Privacy Professional (CIPP/US, CIPP/E) and (ISC)^2's Certified Information Systems Security Professional (CISSP).

Charlotte Tschider is a member of the American Bar Association's Cybersecurity Section and associated working groups; an active member of the App Association's Connected Health Initiative, a Washington D.C.-based legal advocacy group supporting app developers; a lecturer for the Information Systems Security Association's CISSP certification preparation program; and previously a legal advisor for the Online Web Application Security Project (OWASP).

Table of Contents

Preface

Each year, information is increasingly stored, used, and transferred fluidly for legitimate business purposes. Amid the headline-grabbing reports of state-sponsored hacking and U.S. National Security Agency (NSA) snooping lie everyday consumer transactions where consumers provide information for services or goods: visiting a clinic, applying for a job, buying groceries with a payment card, logging onto a social networking site, and playing a game on a mobile application. Organizations increasingly collect personal information and transfer to other organizations or aggregate data and sell for profit reducing the traceability of personal information and an individual's ability to monitor privacy and security of personal information. Most of the time these activities evidence lack of awareness to privacy obligations or confusion at their complexity.

The fields of cybersecurity and privacy laws have changed dramatically in the past five years. Increasingly more often, attorneys must advise on strategic implementations of new technologies, advise on the impact of certain laws to the enterprise, interpret complex cybersecurity and privacy contractual language as part of contract negotiation, and participate in incident response or data breach activities as trusted advisors and to preserve conversations as privileged. The attorney of the future must complement legal knowledge with a working knowledge of information technology to effectively advise organizations that increasingly collect and process more data, often in an increasingly globalized, regulated world.

The legal field has begun to embrace legal modernization, too. Increasingly more often codes of conduct and professional responsibility include an attorney's duty to protect client confidentiality and to understand how technology might affect that duty. In cybersecurity and privacy law fields, privacy and cybersecurity have begun to converge: with increased data breach frequency, legal obligations have started to change. Where organizations previously relegated "administrative and technical measures" to a generic category, jurisdictions increasingly include specific cybersecurity obligations in privacy laws.

Data breaches, critical infrastructure compromise, and global ransomware attacks have demonstrated the importance of business and legal awareness to potential issues, while new regulations around the world, such as localization requirements in

Russia and the Cybersecurity law in China, have introduced cybersecurity into legal discussions. I began considering the potential intersection of cybersecurity and privacy law in 2008, while working for Target Corporation in the United States. At the time, legal counsel discussed privacy, and technologists discussed information security until the information security team determined legal assistance was needed. I noticed that casual questions turned into repeat involvement: reviewing security policies, drafting vendor agreements inclusive of security terms, clarifying legal obligations, and assisting in incident response matters. Today's privacy and cybersecurity attorney must become a dynamic and nimble leader, who understands the real legal implications of technology choices and relishes the challenge of continuous, immediately applicable, learning.

International Cybersecurity and Privacy Law in Practice balances privacy and cybersecurity legal knowledge with technical knowledge and business acumen needed to provide adequate representation and consultation both within an organization, such as a government entity or business, and when advising these organizations as external counsel. Although this book is written with legal counsel and compliance professionals in mind, other practitioners, such as security personnel, should also benefit from a broader perspective exploring privacy and data protection laws and their connection with security technologies.

List of Abbreviations

2FA	Two-factor Authentication
AICPA	American Institute of Certified Public Accountants
ALE	Annual Loss Expectancy
AOC	Attestation of Compliance (PCI)
APAC	Asia-Pacific region
APEC	Asia Pacific Economic Cooperation
APT	Advanced Persistent Threat
ASV	Approved Scanning Vendor (PCI)
B2B/B2C	Business-to-Business/Business-to-Customer
BA	Business Associate
BAA	Business Associate Agreement
BCM	Business Continuity Management
BCR	Binding Corporate Rules
BYOD	Bring Your Own Device
CAN-SPAM	Controlling the Assault of Non-Solicited Pornography and Marketing Act
CCTV	Closed-Circuit Television
CE	Covered Entity
CIPP	Certified Information Privacy Professional
CISA	Cybersecurity Information Sharing Act
CISA	Certified Information Systems Auditor
CISO	Chief Information Security Officer
CISSP	Certified Information Systems Security Professional
CMMI	Capability Maturity Model Integration
COBIT	Control Objectives for Information and Related Technology

COPPA	Children's Online Privacy Protection Act
CPO	Chief Privacy Officer
CRO	Chief Risk Officer
DBA	Database Administrator
DCS	Distributed Control System
DOS/DDoS	Denial of Service/Distributed Denial of Service Attack
DNS	Domain Name System
DPA	Data Protection Authority
DPPA	Driver's Privacy Protection Act
DR	Disaster Recovery
DRP	Disaster Recovery Plan
EBR	Established Business Relationship
EC	European Commission
ECHR	European Convention on Human Rights
ECPA	Electronic Communications Privacy Act
EDPS	European Data Protection Supervisor
EEA	European Economic Area
EEOC	Equal Employment Opportunity Commission
EMEA	Europe, the Middle East, and Africa
EU	European Union
FBI	Federal Bureau of Investigations
FCC	Federal Communications Commission
FCRA	Federal Credit Reporting Act
FDE	Full Disk Encryption
FERPA	Family Education Rights and Privacy Act
FINRA	Financial Industry Regulatory Authority
FIPs	Fair Information Practices
FISMA	Federal Information Security Management Act
FTC	Federal Trade Commission
FTP	File Transfer Protocol
GDPR	Global Data Protection Regulation (EU)
GLBA/GLB Act	Gramm–Leach–Bliley Act
HHS	Department of Health and Human Services
HIPAA	Health Insurance Portability and Accountability Act
HTTP	Hyper-text Transfer Protocol
HTTPS	Hyper-text Transfer Protocol Secure
IAM	Identity and Access Management

ICS	Industrial Control System
IDA	Identity Assurance (UK)
IDS	Intrusion Detection System
IEEE	Institute of Electrical and Electronics Engineers
IaaS	Infrastructure as a Service
IoT	Internet of Things
IP Address	Internet Protocol Address
IPS	Intrusion Prevention System
IPSec	Internet Protocol Security
ISACA	Information Systems Audit and Control Association
$(ISC)^2$	International Information System Security Certification Consortium
ITIL	Information Technology Infrastructure Library
KBA	Knowledge-Based Authentication
MAC address	Media Access Control address
MAM	Mobile Application Management
MDM	Mobile Device Management
MFT	Managed File Transfer
LAN	Local Access Network
LATAM	Latin America region
LBS	Location Based Services
LUA	Least User Access
NAC	Network Access Controls
NIST	National Institute of Standards and Technology
NSL	National Security Letter
OCC	Office of the Comptroller of Currency
OCR	Office for Civil Rights (HHS)
OECD	Organization for Economic Co-operation and Development
OSI	Open Systems Interconnection Model
PaaS	Platform as a Service
PAN	Primary Account Number (PCI)
PCI-DSS	Payment Card Industry-Data Security Standard
PDPA	Singapore Personal Data Protection Act
PHI	Protected Health Information
PIA	Privacy Impact Assessment
PII	Personally Identifiable Information
PIN	Personal Identification Number

PIPEDA	Personal Information Protection and Electronic Documents Act (CA)
PKI	Public Key Infrastructure
PLC	Programmable Logic Controllers
PPA	The Privacy Protection Act
PGP	Pretty Good Privacy
QSA	Qualified Security Assessor (PCI)
QSV	Qualified Scanning Vendor (PCI)
RACI	Responsible, Accountable, Consult With, Inform diagram
RAM	Random Access Memory
RFID	Radio Frequency Identification
ROC	Report on Compliance (PCI)
RSA	Rivest, Shamir, Adleman (who created the encryption algorithm)
SaaS	Software-as-a-Service
SAS	Statement on Auditing Standards
SCADA	Supervisory Control and Data Acquisition
SCIAP	Safety, Confidentiality, Integrity, Availability, Privacy
SFTP	SSH File Transfer Protocol
SIEM	Security Incident and Event Monitoring
SMS	Short Message Service
SOC	Security Operations Center
SOC	Service Organization Control
SOX	Sarbanes–Oxley Act
SPI	Sensitive Personal Information
SSAE	Statement on Standards for Attestation Engagements
SSL	Secure Sockets Layer (SSL), now replaced by TLS
SSN	Social Security Number
SQL	Structured Query Language
SQLi	Structured Query Language Injection
TCPA	Telephone Consumer Protection Act
TCP/IP	Transmission Control Protocol/Internet Protocol
TLS	Transport Layer Security (followed SSL, sometimes called SSL)
TOS	Terms of Service
TOU	Terms of Use
VoIP	Voice Over Internet Protocol

VPN	Virtual Private Network
WAN	Wide Area Network
WAP	Wireless Access Point
Wi-Fi	Wireless Fidelity
WPA	Wi-Fi Protected Access
XSS	Cross-site Scripting (AKA CSS)

List of Figures

List of Tables

Acknowledgments

It goes without saying that nothing would be possible without the support of so many. To my many wonderful colleagues at Medtronic, Inc., Target Corporation, and Carlson Wagonlit Travel, especially Janine Foster and Matt Fritz: your mentorship, friendship, and education made all the difference. Thank you.

To Professor Sharon Sandeen and Professor Marie Failinger, your collaboration, thoughtful ideas, and endless encouragement throughout this writing process and foray into academia have made the impossible, possible. I can only hope to pay it forward someday. To my students in the Cybersecurity and Privacy Law program and Health Law Institute, thank you for sharing your diverse and varied knowledge and experiences with me, raising many of the issues identified in this book.

I would also like to thank my colleagues and friends on Twitter around the world for your helpful thoughts, ideas, and editing suggestions, especially Jacob Tewes and Lisa M. Brownlee.

Thank you to the Loyola University Chicago School of Law's *Annals of Health Law* for allowing portions of my article entitled "Enhancing Cybersecurity for the Digital Health Marketplace" to be printed throughout this volume.

Thank you to Dr. Rogier Creemers, of Universiteit Leiden, for permitting me to print his translation of China's "Decision on Strengthening Network Information Protection."

Introduction

Cybersecurity and privacy law has emerged as a new and exciting field of legal practice. Not only is existing technology evolving and changing, but new and emerging Internet-connected technologies—such as big data and cloud computing, the Internet of things, expansive mobile device computing, and artificial intelligence—are changing how organizations operate and manage data. Countries have also discovered the challenge of regulating personal information data handling practices and simultaneously neutralizing emerging cybersecurity threats to keep residents and consumers safe.

State-sponsored and other hacker entities disgorge global corporate income, and it is estimated that approximately USD 445 billion dollars of global Internet-generated revenue is stolen annually.[1] High gross domestic product (GDP) countries appear to be targeted by hackers the most: these countries average an estimated loss of nearly 1 % GDP just for e-Commerce fraud.[2] Cybercrime is a growing problem, not only for individuals affected by personal information exposure, loss, or fraud, but for the global economy. The cybersecurity threat and vulnerability landscape has introduced new cyberattack capabilities at an alarming pace, such as ransomware, and has mobilized attackers from all corners of the globe. State-sponsored hacking has also ballooned available financial resources. Previously unaffected industries now face attack as new targets and emerging technologies present new opportunities for compromise.

Organizations increasingly span multiple geographic boundaries, which often introduces new regulatory concerns. Increased technical reach to new customer markets coupled with changing, new, and increasingly extra-territorial application have introduced multi-national organizations to new regulatory obligations.

1. *See* Mark Clayton, *Hackers steal 15 percent of money generated by Internet, study estimates*, Christian Science Monitor (Jun. 9, 2014). Studies estimate that Internet shopping revenue generates between USD 2 and USD 3 trillion dollars per year, and hackers steal around USD 445 billion annually, which includes not only financial crime but theft of intellectual property and confidential information. High GDP countries, like the U.S. are estimated to have lost nearly 1 % of GDP on average.
2. *Id.*; *GDP (current US$)*, The World Bank (2014), http://data.worldbank.org/indicator/NY.GDP.MKTP.

Ubiquitous computing has enabled organizations to collect growing data volumes. Due to the dramatic increase in volume, diversity, and use of data, including personal data, current data protection laws have not anticipated challenges, especially relating to cybersecurity. Importantly, most data protection laws include only partial reference to cybersecurity measures: the classic terminology denotes "technical and organization measures" without providing guidance of what measures might be reasonable under the circumstances.

While in some countries organizations have focused on protecting personal information, organizations also risk substantial financial, reputational, operational, and legal damage by not protecting non-personal, yet highly restricted, organizational data. For example, formal accounting records might require cybersecurity measures to ensure record integrity, a business customer may require cybersecurity measures to protect trade secret information, and nuclear facilities require additional cybersecurity measures to protect citizens. All organizations have some data that are valuable to someone else, either for monetary gain or other nefarious purposes.

In the past five years, organizations have spent substantially more money on data breaches, due to higher breach frequency, larger and more expensive breaches, and legal fallout. Regulatory authorities, consumers, and business customers have become increasingly more active in pursuing financial remedies following data breach or privacy right violations. Gemalto has similarly estimated worldwide compromise of nearly 1 billion records, an increase of 49%.[3] In 2017, the Ponemon Institute and IBM Security conducted a study estimating the average cost of breach at around **EUR** 3.1 million or **EUR** 120 per record (likely diminishing in cost per record for larger breaches), with an average breach size of 24,000 records.[4] Data breaches with at least 10,000 compromised records now occur with a probability of 28% over two years. In 2017, Saudi Arabian, Indonesian, Brazilian, French, and Montenegro organizations have a higher probability of data breach than American companies, at between 41% and 32% over two years.

Not only is data breach more likely than ever before, but also organizations spend a substantial amount of money to recover. Target Corporation data breach, one of the largest breaches in global history compromising payment card data in the United States (U.S.), approached a breach cost of **EUR 172 million**. The alleged cost of banks re-issuing cards (not including fraud) amounted to several hundred million Euro.[5]

Due to these headline-grabbing, high-frequency data breaches, cybersecurity has emerged both connected to and distinct from privacy law. However, the concept of *data protection*, enshrined in the text and title of so many international laws, reflects the need to protect individual rights while also safeguarding information about an individual person. Privacy rights cannot be protected when information about the individual is easily discoverable, changeable, or open to misuse.

3. *Gemalto Releases Findings of 2014 Breach Level Index*, GEMALTO (Feb. 12, 2015), http://www.gemalto.com/press/Pages/Gemalto-Releases-Findings-of-2014-Breach-Level-Index.aspx.
4. IBM, *Cost of Data Breach Study* (2017), https://www.ibm.com/security/data-breach/. The cost of data breaches continues to fall, while the size of data breaches continues to rise.
5. REUTERS, *Target Pays Millions to Settle State Data Breach Lawsuits*, FORTUNE (May 23, 2017), http://fortune.com/2017/05/23/target-settlement-data-breach-lawsuits/.

Privacy law focuses on protecting a natural person, such as notifying users of how information will be handled, obtaining consent prior to processing personal information, giving the user enough information to ensure meaningful choice, and compliance with applicable laws and internal policy. Cybersecurity, however, focuses on protecting an organization's interests, including safeguarding the rights of individuals. Cybersecurity focuses on preventing disclosure and protecting data integrity of proprietary and personal information, to prevent reputational damage of an organization, to ensure continued operation of critical operations, and to build resilience in recovering from attacks and disasters.

I THE ATTORNEY'S ROLE IN CYBERSECURITY AND PRIVACY

Many organizations expanding into new geographic areas find it difficult to both manage increasingly stringent compliance obligations and respond to new challenges. To be effective in cybersecurity and privacy law, attorneys must build three skill sets. First, attorneys must be a translator for the organization. Cybersecurity and privacy laws are continuously changing and updating, and often time-pressured information technology decisions require attorneys to make fast yet informed decisions. Attorneys also must clearly describe legal obligations to a wide variety of audiences, including C-Level executives and engineers.

Attorneys must also facilitate global conversations. Previously, organizations operated in only one country increasingly consider expansion to reach new customers or procure lower-cost services, exposing an organization to new legal obligations and risks. Finally, attorneys must fulfill the role of risk manager, advising an organization on various risk-based decisions, including cybersecurity and privacy matters. In doing so, attorneys must be able to effectively assess and communicate real risk probabilities to advise the business, not only about legal implications, but also business implications of certain decisions, such as technology choices.

Cybersecurity and privacy attorneys must go further than informing organizations about the law; they must also facilitate informed decision-making by collaborating to find effective solutions for legal and risk-based problems. Attorneys are crucial counselors and trusted advisors within any organization, and to effectively support these organizational decisions, attorneys must develop strong technical knowledge to better understand how technology choices affect these legal obligations.

II NAVIGATING THIS BOOK

Although many chapters will interrelate and reference one another, the organization of this book is purposeful. The same or similar concepts may arise throughout the book from different perspectives, such as the philosophy of a concept, the law itself, processes that support the concept, technology that facilitates the concept, and legal methods that protect an organization's interests.

Chapter 1 introduces the reader to privacy law fundamentals and provides a framework for understanding country and regional laws. Chapters 2–6 briefly discuss a cross-section of country laws as they deviate from the Organisation for Economic Cooperation and Development (OECD) and Asia-Pacific Economic Cooperation (APEC) Privacy Frameworks.[6] Chapters 2–6 include portions of laws that illustrate deviation from the commonly adopted EU Data Protection Directive foundation.

Chapter 7 explains privacy program management, or the process of operationalizing privacy programs. In order to accommodate a wide variety of international laws, I will adopt the phrase *information privacy law*, rather than *data protection law*, although for the reader, information privacy law will include data protection laws as they implicate privacy obligations. Beginning in Part II, I will also adopt the word *security* rather than *cybersecurity*, as cybersecurity sometimes translates to technical solutions only, when administrative processes often provide complementary protection.

Part II focuses on developing foundational technical and cybersecurity knowledge. Chapter 8 describes information technology fundamentals, how computer systems function and common system types. Chapter 9 builds on Chapter 8 by introducing security technology, including challenging cybersecurity concepts like cryptography. Chapter 10 connects these concepts back to information privacy and cybersecurity laws. Chapters 11 and 12 introduce cybersecurity programmatic practices that illustrate reasonable administrative measures, while Chapter 13 explores cyberattack dynamics and incident response strategies for responding to data breaches.

Part III combines information privacy and cybersecurity to address appropriate legal strategies to protect organizational interests. Chapter 14 discusses protective legal measures, such as cyber liability insurance and contract negotiation, designed to minimize organizational risk, while Chapter 15 summarizes legal data breach notification obligations and process. Chapter 16 offers strategies for combining privacy and cybersecurity functions within an organization and highlights emerging technology that will require more dynamic and challenging conversations.

---

6. Please note: this book does not provide a complete review of all information privacy laws in the world. Rather, it highlights laws of particular note in each region. Individuals seeking a high-level picture of all privacy laws around the world might consider reviewing comprehensive, survey-based online resources. *See e.g.*, DLA Piper, *Data Protection Laws of the World* (2017), https://www.dlapiperdataprotection.com/index.html.

PART I Information Privacy Law and Practice

CHAPTER 1

Introduction to Information Privacy Law and Practice

Distinctions between private and public life have existed at least as early as Aristotle's writings in the *Politics* and have largely accompanied political conversation for at least as long. However, *information privacy law*, or law concerning information about a natural person, has a relatively recent history. Information privacy laws today focus on safeguarding individual rights and protecting data collected.

§1.01 A BRIEF HISTORY OF INFORMATION PRIVACY LAW

Most privacy scholars track the recognition of privacy "rights" to post-World War II Western Europe. From a European perspective concepts of privacy usually accompanied personal liberties, especially those expressed as human rights requiring protection, rather than exploitation, by government.[7] However, concepts of personal privacy surely existed in various global regions prior to World War II, often with respect to the free exercise of other rights, such as rights to family life, private communications, speech, assembly, free exercise of religion, or freedom from discrimination. Perhaps this explains why the definition of protected or sensitive personal information (SPI) enshrined in international omnibus privacy laws often includes personal or political opinions, union membership, religious affiliation, national origin, race, ethnicity, and health status. Privacy rights enhance and enforce important individual liberties, and although all liberties in all countries are not alike, most countries recognize some individual privacy rights in Constitution or law.[8]

---

7. European Union Agency for Fundamental Rights & Registry of the European Court of Human Rights, Handbook on European Data Protection (2014), available at: http://www.echr.coe.int/Documents/Handbook_data_protection_ENG.pdf.
8. It should be noted that this chapter does not aim to explain all conceptions of international privacy and how they have developed. Rather, this chapter focuses on statutory development of

In 1948, the United Nations (UN) released the Universal Declaration of Human Rights of 1948 on respect for private and family life (UDHR). This Declaration, for the first time, explicitly linked concepts of human, or civil rights, with conceptions of privacy. Following the UDHR, the Council of Europe adopted the European Convention on Human Rights in 1950 and created the European Court of Human Rights (ECHR). The UDHR states, in Article 12:

> No one shall be subjected to arbitrary interference with his privacy, family, home or correspondence, nor to attacks upon his honour and reputation. Everyone has the right to the protection of the law against such interference or attacks.[9]

In 1977, Germany passed the *Bundesdatenschutzgesetz* (following state passage of a similar law in 1970).[10] In 1978, the French government passed the Act No. 78-17 of January 6, 1978 on Data Processing, Data Files, and Individual Liberties. Act No. 78-17 also established the Commission Nationale de L'nformatique et des Libertés (CNIL), which developed a structure for regulatory involvement in France. Both laws thought to have inspired activity by the Organisation for Economic Co-operation and Development (OECD) and the European Council (EC).

When computing appeared on the horizon, countries began to anticipate privacy concerns. In 1980, the OECD created the Guidelines on the Protection of Privacy and Transborder Flows of Personal Data, which informed different regional approaches to privacy and continues to provide the most influential international information privacy framework.[11]

In the late 1970s, the EC began considering the potential impacts of processing information about an individual's personal affairs and adopted the Convention for the Protection of Individuals with Regard to the Automatic Processing of Personal Data ("Convention 108") in 1981, which remains the only international, enforceable legal instrument for signatories today. Convention 108 provided a substantial framework for the Data Protection Directive of 1990 and, more recently, the General Data Protection Regulation (GDPR) of 2016.

The OECD Guidelines recognized personal information as truly central to fundamental human rights recognition in the world. The OECD guidelines also recognized that disparate regulations would hamper the free flow of information, impacting

privacy laws with their roots in the UN Universal Declaration of Human Rights and subsequent European developments that have informed omnibus privacy legislation in EMEA, LATAM, APAC, and NORAM.

9. United Nations (UN), Universal Declaration of Human Rights (UDHR), 10 Dec. 1948.
10. The Federal Data Protection Act (*Bundesdatenschutzgesetz) (1 Feb. 2017)*, http://www.gesetze-im-internet.de/bdsg_1990/index.html (in German, 1990). For an excellent history of German data protection, *see* J. Lee Riccardi, *The German Federal Data Protection Act of 1977: Protecting the Right to Privacy?*, 6 B.C. Int'l & Comp. L. Rev. 248 (1983), http://lawdigitalcommons.bc.edu/iclr/vol6/iss1/8.
11. Organisation for Economic Cooperation and Development, *OECD Work on Privacy* (2017), http://oe.cd/privacy.

financial security and trade relationships. In order to create a common vernacular, the OECD guidelines established concepts of controller, data subject, and personal data within the OECD principles:

- Organizations should limit the collection of personal data (*Data Minimization*).
- Personal data collected should be relevant to the purposes used (*Purpose Justification*).
- Purposes of collection should be specified at the time of collection (*Meaningful Choice*).
- Personal data should not be disclosed, made available outside purposes specified except with consent of the data subject or by law (*Informed Consent*).
- Organizations should protect data with reasonable safeguards (*Confidentiality*).
- Organization should be open about practices and policies with regard to personal data (*Transparency*).
- Data subjects should be able to obtain information that is collected about them (*Access*).
- The data controller is accountable for compliance of themselves and their processors (*Accountability*).

By 1981, the European Union had developed a rigorous approach to privacy protection, adopting two conventions that created a foundation for modern conceptions of information privacy. In 1983, Canada passed its government-oriented Privacy Act and created an Office of the Privacy Commissioner of Canada, adding the Personal Information Protection and Electronic Documents Act (PIPEDA) in 2001.

Both the OECD Guidelines and the European approach paved the way for future privacy law developments in Asian and Latin American (LATAM) countries. In 1987, Australia formed the Australian Privacy Foundation, finding an opportunity to guide data protection in Australia and the greater APAC region.[12] Australia leveraged the OECD Guidelines to champion development of the Asia-Pacific Economic Council (APEC) Privacy Framework in 2004.[13] LATAM countries at the time of writing have not yet formed a consolidated guidelines approach to privacy in the LATAM, although Chile became the first country to pass a data privacy law in 1999 and many countries have followed, with at least two countries, Uruguay and Argentina, receiving a European adequacy determination.[14] Unlike many countries in the world, a large

12. For a particularly complete history of data privacy within the Asian continent, see Graham Greenleaf, Data Privacy Laws in Asia –Context and History (Oxford: 2014), DOI:10.1093/acprof:oso/9780199679669.003.0001.
13. APEC (2004), APEC Privacy Framework, http://inicio.ifai.org.mx/Estudios/APECPrivacyFramework(Oct-2004).pdf. The most recent version was published in available at: https://www.apec.org/Groups/Committee-on-Trade-and-Investment/~/media/Files/Groups/ECSG/05_ecsg_privacyframewk.ashx.
14. Law No. 19,628, Sobre Proteccion de la Vida Privada, http://www.oas.org/juridico/spanish/cyb_chi_ley_19628.pdf.

proportion of LATAM countries guarantee privacy of home and family life in their respective constitutions.

In Africa and the Middle East, omnibus information privacy laws have begun to emerge, although some Constitutions and religious traditions reinforce concepts of personal privacy. Since 2009, the African Union (AU) has sought to improve harmonization between AU countries' privacy laws. In 2014, several AU countries attended the AU Convention on Cyber Security and Personal Data Protection.[15] It is yet to be determined how African countries will reflect privacy commitments from the Convention in country-specific laws, as African regional information privacy frameworks had emerged at least two years prior to the Convention.

The United States (U.S.) has had an inconsistent relationship with privacy protection. Although some personal privacy rights exist through the Fourth and Fourteenth Amendments within the Bill of Rights, no explicit reference to a broad conception of individual privacy was enshrined in the U.S. Constitution. Despite this, in 1890 a famous article penned by Justice Samuel Warren and Justice Louis Brandeis, "The Right to Privacy" expanded concepts of legal tort (legal wrong) to include privacy-related torts, passed for the first time in Georgia as an "invasion of privacy" tort in 1905.[16] From 1890 to 1970, the Supreme Court of the U.S. decided several cases involving privacy of the home, reproductive privacy, and search and seizure, and in 1970, anticipation of a computer revolution initiated a flurry of sector-based laws passed in the U.S.

In 1970, the Fair Credit Reporting Act was passed to protect consumer privacy, and in 1974, the U.S. passed the Privacy Act, which required privacy protection for both government usage of U.S. resident personal information and U.S. government employees, and the Family Education Rights and Privacy Act (FERPA).[17] Since that time, the number of U.S. privacy laws have ballooned, expanding to many industries and specific information uses. However, the U.S. has not passed any baseline, broadly applicable information privacy laws (*omnibus laws*), as found in Canada, Europe, the Middle East, Africa, Asia, or Latin America.

---

15. AU (2014), African Union Convention on Cyber Security and Personal Data Protection, Art. 14 (the Guidelines were originally developed in 1980), available at: http://au.int/sites/default/files/treaties/29560-treaty-0048_-_african_union_convention_on_cyber_security_and_personal_data_protection_e.pdf.
16. Samuel D. Warren & Louis D. Brandeis, *The Right to Privacy*, 4:5 Harv. L. R. 193 (1890). The *right* to privacy can be a bit of a misnomer – no enumerated right in the U.S. Constitution actually uses the word "privacy" or grants any broad civil right.
17. The Fair Credit Reporting Act, 15 U.S.C. § 1681, available at: https://www.bulkorder.ftc.gov/system/files/publications/pdf-0111-fcra.pdf; The Privacy Act of 1974, 5 U.S.C. § 552a, available at: https://www.gpo.gov/fdsys/pkg/USCODE-2012-title5/pdf/USCODE-2012-title5-partI-chap5-subchapII-sec552a.pdf; The Family Education Rights and Privacy Act, 20 U.S.C. § 1232g; 34 CFR Part 99, available at: https://www.ecfr.gov/cgi-bin/text-idx?rgn=div5&node=34:1.1.1.1.33.

§1.02 THE LAW AND PHILOSOPHY OF PRIVACY

Privacy is an intrinsic concept of personal integrity that feeds other legal concepts. For example, privacy is a consideration in law enforcement activities, judicial decision-making, and anti-terrorism efforts. Especially in law enforcement, a tension exists between effective law enforcement and individual privacy rights. Privacy rights of the individual—such as personal property or information stored within an individual's home, car, phone, computer devices or on a person—may be tempered by an expectation of personal privacy. This tension may shift towards law enforcement rights or towards individual privacy rights depending on each country's constitutional limitations and practices.

In judicial decision-making, tensions exist between efficient adjudication of cases and natural persons or business entities. Although in some circumstances discovery, or disclosure of confidential information is tremendously important to provide evidentiary support for a cause of action, judicial systems do not often permit unlimited access to information about a person or business entity without meeting a threshold (such as a warrant, letter, or other legal document). In anti-terrorism or national defense efforts, governments require access to information or monitoring (as in through surveillance or wiretapping) with high expediency, yet individuals still require some individual privacy guarantees. In recent years, with the prevalence of terrorism around the world both domestically and internationally, many countries continuously struggle with the appropriate balance and tradeoffs between more and less privacy.

Privacy expectations may also have a legal relationship with other rights, such as reproductive choices or sexual preference, religious beliefs and affiliations, and health privacy. Where countries recognize civil rights related to individual choices, an expectation of privacy generally accompanies these choices. For example, disclosure of personal information regarding an individual's religious beliefs might lead to negative treatment in other spheres of an individual's life, such as employment and education. Although disclosure could result in concrete personal injury as in discriminatory effect, several privacy laws protect sensitive information disclosure because third party disclosure is per se damaging (i.e., moral damage) when an individual does not choose to disclose.

Each of these considerations illustrates the broad range of privacy laws and how they might apply within a given country. Some countries might recognize substantially more privacy rights with respect to law enforcement and judicial decision-making, but fewer rights with respect to personal information, and vice versa. For this reason, privacy scholars often divide privacy considerations into two distinct practice areas: (1) physical privacy and (2) information privacy.[18] Information privacy law includes collection, access, processing, storage, and transfer of personal information.

Information privacy laws consist of two foundational, connected concepts with respect to the information: identifiability and risks associated with identifiability.

---

18. This book will focus purely on information privacy. For further inquiry into physical privacy, *see* N. A. Moreham, *Beyond Information: Physical Privacy in English Law* 73:2 CAMBRIDGE L.J. (2014), DOI: https://doi.org/10.1017/S0008197314000427.

Personal information is information about a natural person, a human being, which may identify a natural person. The concept of personal information can be difficult to understand and is usually not defined in law, because personal information depends on identifiability of an individual data element (i.e., name) and a collection of data elements, a *data set*. Data elements may be *direct*, or primary identifiers of an individual, such as a name, address, or e-mail. They may also be *indirect*, or secondary identifier, such as food preferences, items purchased, or movies viewed. Usually, a data set includes both direct and indirect data elements. Laws generally identify data elements, either direct or indirect, which require additional protection or limited collection.

Privacy laws are often written broadly, making it difficult to determine exactly which data require protection or limited collection. Laws define personal information broadly because the probability of being identified depends on the data set collected. Consider the following examples:

Example 1: A woman has shopped at a department store in Uruguay for the past five years. For those five years, the department store has retained information about all of her purchases, the time of checkout, and her preferred payment type and payment information, but has not collected her name.
Example 2: A child routinely visits a local clinic in a small town for allergy treatments. The child's name is not retained, but the child is assigned a unique patient number and all treatment information is included along with other demographic information about the child, such as age, weight, and physical description.
Question: To what degree could either of these individuals be identified without a name?

Often, the larger the data set about an individual, the more likely an individual will be identified, even with indirect data elements. However, identifiability is not necessarily a harm in and of itself. Information privacy laws focus on how to reduce probability of harm to an individual, often called a *data subject*, by structuring rules around limited collection and individual choice.

Limited collection usually focuses on restricting or reducing data collection to organizational need, reasonable collection, and it includes, by reference, the concept of data minimization and reasonable data retention. Limited collection is also reflected in privacy law "risk mitigation" techniques, such as limited data set, pseudonymization, de-identification, and anonymization discussed throughout the rest of this book. Limited collection reflects a public recognition that unfettered data collection and retention can lead to individual harm, a centerpiece of almost every privacy law in the world.

Restrictions on use of SPI illustrate the concept of limited collection and risk mitigation. Although some laws expressly categorize data elements as SPI, often laws call out specific data elements of concern and require additional steps be taken, such as reducing data collection, more frequent review of practices with relation to these data (i.e., an audit or assessment), more sophisticated data protection measures, and explicit, informed consent. The concept of *consent*, or legal agreement to some practice, is central to the concept of choice.

Individual choice regarding collection and treatment of personal information provides most information privacy law content today. Individual choice requires transparency, or information sharing that enables an individual to make an informed, free choice. The concept of informed choice bears out in other fields of law, such as required disclosures in contracts, a duty to warn for highly dangerous activities, food labeling, or product safety disclosures. Information privacy law centers on the belief that natural persons, sometimes called *data subjects* (used throughout this book to describe natural persons), should be able to make choices about what personal information can be shared, to whom, and under what conditions. Consent, then, is the mechanism by which data subjects make affirmative decisions about how their personal information will be treated. *See* Figure 1.1 for a map of limited collection and individual choice ("Collection" and "Choice").

Figure 1.1 Collection and Choice

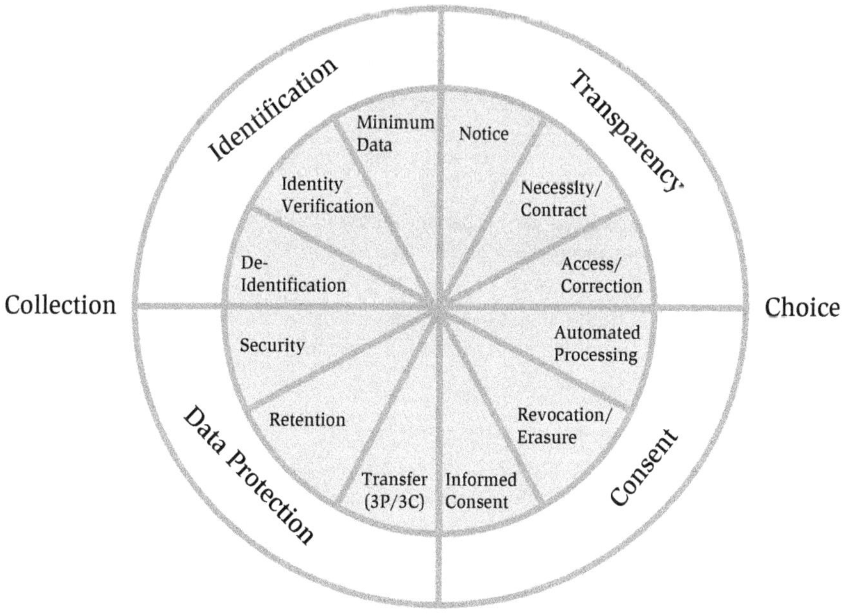

§1.03 TRANSPARENCY AND CONSENT: NOTICE

Informed legal choice consists of Transparency and Consent. Transparency focuses on information disclosure and prior notice. Information disclosure involves an organization providing information to communicate *information treatment* to a data subject, or how an organization will manage and use personal information collected. Disclosure can take several forms: most commonly, disclosure is through a formal *privacy notice*, sometimes called a *privacy policy* displayed prominently on a Website or linked through a Web form.[19] Some organizations include privacy language within terms of use (TOU) document, although this is generally considered a less transparent practice.[20] Organizations may provide other disclosures in addition to a formal privacy notice, such as a banner describing how information might be collected from Website visitors (in the case of cookies, described in Chapter 8) or information about marketing practices, such as a request to send marketing messages to a data subject.

Transparency requires *adequate notice*. Adequate notice refers to the concept of disclosing information that would affect a natural person's choices on whether data is processed, stored, or transferred. Across privacy laws, this may include the justification or reasons for data collection, conditions for transfer, such as third-party use, protections for personal information, or relevant support activities regarding user's rights. When designing privacy notices, attorneys and practitioners must consider what information would be valuable to a data subject in making a decision and what information would inform a data subject of potential risks. Many laws specify the contents of a privacy notice, but most include the following:

- Identity of the organization and multiple avenues for contacting the organization (physical address, phone number, e-mail address).
- Where data is located, if not evident from organization's location.
- Personal information data types collected.
- How personal information will be used, in detail (*purpose specification*).
- Whether personal information will be used by any third parties, and for what purposes.
- Identities or descriptions of third parties receiving personal information, even when providing support.
- Information about security practices.
- Notification of data subject rights (depending on the jurisdiction).
- Details about how the individual will be contacted, or not contacted if the privacy notice changes.

Organizations present privacy notices in a variety of formats: as a singular page online privacy notice, a layered, clickable online privacy notice, a paper notice provided when signing a contract or visiting a location (as in a doctor's office), or a mobile privacy notice. Privacy notices have become lengthy and complex over time

19. This book uses the language "privacy notice," as "privacy policy" can easily be confused with internal organizational privacy policies. However, some organizations may call an outward, consumer-facing document a privacy policy.
20. TOU documents typically provide a substantial amount of information, so it can become very difficult to meet standards of visibility and "informed consent" when information about privacy and data protection practices is buried in 100 pages of text. Most countries require a dedicated privacy notice, except for the U.S., which at a minimum requires visibility standards for statutes like the Telephone Consumer Protection Act (TCPA). Other contractual recovery mechanisms could protect data subjects under some circumstances (unconscionability).

with changes to laws and increasingly complex data use. At the same time, users have very little time to spend reviewing privacy notices that are several pages long, especially via a mobile device, which causes a transparency problem. Organizations should balance appropriate disclosure with readability.

Different notice disclosures may be required, depending on the data collected and the jurisdiction where data subjects reside. Further different requirements for data subject consent may apply depending on the jurisdiction. The primary types of consent include: express and implicit consent. *Express* or expressed consent involves a data subject affirmatively agreeing to information disclosed in a privacy notice. Implicit consent requires data subjects to have an opportunity to understand practices, but does not require affirmative manifestation of agreement. *Implicit consent*, or *tacit consent* relies on an "opportunity to review" model, where a data subject must exhibit some due diligence to ensure an organization's information privacy practices are acceptable.[21]

In *implicit consent* models, the data subject *opts out* of data sharing by either not using or continuing to use the service or by leveraging an opt-out function later (e.g., an "unsubscribe" link in an e-mail). *Explicit consent*, sometimes called *direct consent*, involves a direct manifestation of agreement to a disclosure, called *opt-in*, and can be oral or written. *Written consent* involves paper consent with a signature or virtual consent (electronic signature) on a computer.[22] Explicit written consent, however, does not include preselected or pre-populated consent that is passive in nature, such as a pre-selected check (tick) box.

Consent not only must be informed, it must be *freely given* in many jurisdictions. The goal of freely given consent is to prevent organizations from coercing data subjects into unwanted relationships. Specifically, consent to marketing activities generally should not be combined with consent to provision of standard services, *consent bundling*. Organizations should separate consent for marketing activities from other activities. *See* Figure 1.2 for a Website example of unbundled consent.

21. The challenge with some implicit consent models is that data handling practices often reply before a data subject has an opportunity to review. Cookie banners, for example, provide notice before a user moves forward through a site, but many U.S. privacy notices include a "right to change" provision where the notice may change before any communication is distributed to users. In some cases, no communication is provided of these changes.

22. It should be noted that some countries without contract laws permitting electronic signatures may not interpret *written consent* as including electronic signature.

Figure 1.2 Marketing Consent

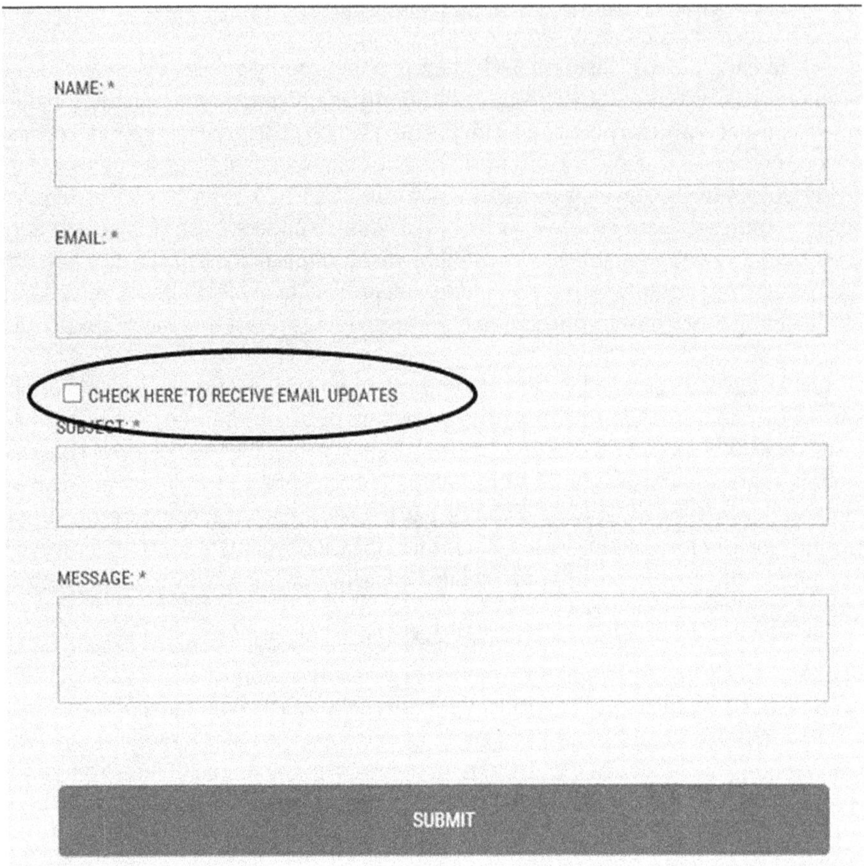

Organizations can also establish notice and consent through other means, such as public availability, necessity, or contract. Public availability, much like confidentiality obligations, eliminates privacy obligations. If data is publicly available, it is not personal information deserving additional protection and therefore may be processed. Necessity generally covers situations involving emergencies or health needs, where information may be processed because the data subject's well-being depends on it.[23]

Previously executed contracts provide the most interesting and dynamic question for privacy obligations, especially in employment scenarios. Organizations typically execute employment agreements, which may include some privacy obligations owed to the individual, depending on the country. When privacy commitments are included

23. Readers should note the difference between "necessity," which permits processing without consent (as in, processing is so necessary, standard rules need not be followed) and "necessary" which is a condition for data collection and subsequent processing with consent (an organization may only collect what is necessary for provision of services, and all rules apply).

as part of the employment agreement, in some circumstances, additional notice, and consent may not be necessary. However, when personal information is used in a manner not contemplated or reasonably covered in the agreement, organizations may still need to provide notice and consent. Consider the questions in Table 1.1.

Table 1.1 Contract v. Notice

Data Type and Use	*Covered in Employment Contract?*
Data transferred to HR system vendor	Yes, necessary for employment
Health data collected for "incentives" program	Notice required, as this is an extra program involving additional data collection
Data transferred to support team in the Philippines	Yes, support activities are part of standard working conditions
Family information transferred to insurance provider	Notice required, as family information is not contemplated in an employment agreement
Self-appraisal information shared with supervisor via a third-party system	Yes, self-appraisals are part of the standard review process

Managing consent for an organization can prove complicated because an organization must inform a data subject of data handling practices prior to receiving consent.[24] For consent to be informed, organizations must provide appropriately detailed disclosures prior to data subject consent. When an organization changes its practices with respect to data collected, for example beginning to aggregate data for reporting or other purposes, new consent to these practices is required under most laws. Some implicit, opt-out models generally encounter fewer issues, but organizations should provide some notice to data subjects of changes, such as sending an e-mail communication or visibly displaying a banner to offer the opportunity to opt-out of new data handling practices.

In addition to the content and process for facilitating privacy notice agreement, it is also important to understand that privacy notices, at their foundation, are a *contract* or *quasi-contract*. In some jurisdictions, privacy notices may be enforced as private contracts, while in others they may not. Privacy notices include some aspects of contract, such as explicit or implied agreement to specific terms based on legal concepts of contract formation. Of course, like all consumer contracts, challenges include the degree to which data subjects read these notices, whether providing a notice without data subject review constitutes "informed" consent, and whether the

24. Notice and consent can prove challenging even for first-time consent, as these models do not match all technologies or potential uses. Despite this, prior notice and informed consent still form the backbone of international privacy law. For an excellent critique of U.S. conceptions of notice and consent in relation to onward third-party transfer, *see* Clark D. Assay, *Consumer Information Privacy and the Problem(s) of Third-Disclosures*, 11 Nw. J. Tech. & Intell. Prop. 321 (2013).

privacy notice is enforceable when *adhesive* or *coercive*.[25] Because privacy notice terms necessarily relate to service or goods provided, in many cases consumers can "take it or leave it," e.g., when receiving a loan or health care.

Adhesive contracting might be more acceptable when consumers have an equal opportunity to pursue alternative goods or services and there is enough competition to allow for consumer choice.[26] However, when alternative goods and services do not exist or when substantial differences in bargaining position between an organization and a consumer could result in coercive practices, organizations should carefully consider their approach. To ensure compliance, organizations should consult local counsel focused on contract matters to determine what, if any, restrictions apply to privacy notices within a country's contract law framework.

§1.04 TRANSPARENCY AND CONSENT: ADDITIONAL RIGHTS

The concepts of transparency and consent also include the ability to choose how information is used: whether an organization may: (1) continue collecting the data (*right of revocation*), (2) may retain data already collected (*right of erasure*), (3) must provide copies of information already collected (*right of access*), or (4) must disclose and allow data subjects to contest decisions involving automated processing (*right of objection to automated processing*).

The right to revocation allows an individual to "undo" a previous consent and stop further processing. To satisfy the right to revocation, organizations must allow for data subjects to revoke consent in a convenient manner. In some jurisdictions, any manifestation of revocation must be honored, including verbal revocation. Revocation does not mean that previously collected data must be deleted; rather, some technical solution or information removal should eliminate future processing. Organizations retaining data for data subjects that have revoked consent must still protect personal information as part of a continuing obligation, regardless of the current relationship between controller and data subject. The right of revocation also carries with it an operational requirement: organizations must maintain a record of revocation associated with a data subject's account so that a data subject's personal information is not

25. For further description of concerns regarding consumer choice, *see* Jared S. Livingston, *Invasion Contracts: The Privacy Implications of Terms of Use Agreements in the Online Social Media Setting*, 21 ALB. L.J. SCI. & TECH. 591 (2011), available at: http://www.albanylawjournal.org/Documents/Articles/21.3.591-Livingston.pdf; Mark E. Budnitz, *Privacy Protection for Consumer Transaction in Electronic Commerce: Why Self-Regulation is Inadequate*, 49 S.C. L. REV. 847 (1998).
26. It is worth mentioning that from an organizational perspective, it is usually organizationally inefficient to manage "consumer chooses" options or to negotiate terms with an individual consumer, so this usually means including expansive terms that may over-reach and put a consumer in a less beneficial position or include basic terms, which restrict organizational use. Organizations that handle SPI and provide discretionary services where a data subject is more likely to be in a less favorable bargaining position should consider more conservative (narrower) business uses for data collected, depending on contract law interpretation within applicable countries.

further processed. The maintenance of a record relating to the data subject, however, can prove challenging for the right of erasure.

The right of the erasure provides that an individual can request data captured about them is deleted. The right of erasure can prove challenging for many organizations today, due to the complexity of technical implementations and desire for data re-use and backup capabilities. The right of erasure provides that information about an individual is completed deleted, but because the right of erasure is, at the time of writing, only recognized in the EU's new GDPR effective May 2018, there has not yet been sufficient time to truly understand what deletion might mean. Most technology configurations provide better options for broad-scale, time-bound deletion (e.g., following a retention schedule), rather than individual record deletion. For example, many databases "delete" data, but the data can be recreated, if needed. Data can also be included in backup tapes with large volumes of other data, where finding and deleting data could prove incredibly difficult. Further, archival copies (sometimes on paper, others on tape that is not meant to be routinely searched) provide point in time information for legitimate operational purposes and historical record-keeping, and routine deletion may prove very difficult. It is not yet known to what extent each of these copies must be deleted.

Erasure requests may also cause collisions between individual requests and legally required retention. Highly regulated industries, such as financial services and health care, may require data retention for a period of time to ensure organizational accountability and provide records for regulatory authority inspection. The European Commission (EC) has not yet clearly articulated where the right of erasure ranks in priority against other laws and protected rights, although non-EU countries will not likely recognize GDPR priority over other local laws.

Access is the ability for a data subject to request information about themselves for purposes of review, correction, revoke consent, or erase records. Some jurisdictions further grant a right of access to view the identities of individuals who have accessed SPI of the data subject. Access, like data deletion, can sometimes prove difficult for similar reasons. Advanced computing techniques allow for data storage in multiple locations and often organizations also transfer data to third parties. Although organizations should have a *data inventory*, or a record of all systems and third parties receiving personal information from the organization, technology in many cases moves too quickly to ensure its accuracy.

Although the right of *correction* more closely reflects identification and accuracy in personal information record-keeping, the right of correction requires access to formal data subject records. The right of correction usually emerges in relation to an organization's adverse decision, such as failure to receive a loan, not receiving admission to an educational program, or not getting hired at an organization as a result of incorrect information.

> **Example:** A data subject, Flavio, received notice that he has not received a car loan because he has too much debt. Not having any debt, Flavio completes a credit check and reviews his bank and credit accounts. After he determines that the debt is not his, Flavio wants to correct information about his debt to purchase the car. In order to correct these records, Flavio contacts his bank, creditors, and applicable credit monitoring agencies to contest these decisions and correct his records.

Without a right of correction, Flavio would likely not have an opportunity to receive a car loan, even though his debt was either a records-keeping mistake on the part of the banks or creditors, or he was the victim of identity theft.

Automatic processing takes the right of correction one step further and permits a data subject to object to automatic processing, combined with a right to access and correction. At the time of writing, only EU residents have automatic processing rights, but it is likely with increased frequency of algorithmic decision-making that additional regions and countries will begin assessing whether data subjects should have some rights when math and machines make life-changing determinations, such as what sentence a convicted felon receives or your loan rate when buying a home.

§1.05 IDENTIFICATION AND IDENTIFIABILITY

The concept of collection practices includes both identification and data protection considerations. Identification involves dual concepts: verifying identity and reducing or eliminating identifiability to reduce risk to data subjects. Organizations also prefer to reduce identifiability for easier data use, transfer, and sharing. When de-identified or anonymized, depending on the jurisdiction, most privacy laws no longer apply.

Identity verification, although not explicitly referenced in most global laws, supports access and correction requests, and also provides data protection by ensuring that the individual contacting an organization has appropriate rights to access or change personal information. Identity verification ensures personal information protection, yet information can be disclosed to the data subject or other previously approved individuals. For this reason, organizations should develop standard procedures that ensure verification prior to information disclosure, especially for SPI.

Reducing or eliminating identifiability reduces risk to a data subject by removing data that could be used to identify a data subject. It also provides maximum flexibility for data transfer and broad usage to organizations. Although the generic process of removing identifiable data elements in a data set is called "de-identification," in that it removes these identifiable elements, de-identification in the U.S. is a term of art requiring very specific data element removal for health care purposes.

De-identification and full anonymization differ in that de-identification generally removes direct identifiers, while anonymization removes direct (primary) and indirect (secondary) identifiers.[27] De-identification and anonymization rely principally on risk determination, or the probability that re-identification of a data subject could occur, causing harm. Anonymization in the EU, for example, requires an *impossibility* of re-identification, a rather high bar also deemed nearly impossible to meet. De-identification in the U.S. under the Health Information Portability and Accountability Act (HIPAA) requires either formulaic removal of certain data elements or certification of low re-identification probability using an actuarial scientist. Most laws around the world accept a de-identification procedure similar to the U.S. model as reasonable. It is not yet known whether the EU will, in coming years, develop a similar procedure that permits more flexible information exchange.[28]

§1.06 REASONABLE SECURITY MEASURES

In line with data reduction and de-identification processes, organizations under most information privacy laws also have an obligation to protect data, including implementing adequate security measures, employing data retention strategies, and managing third party and third country transfers. Across nearly all information privacy laws except for a few laws in the U.S., the Chinese Cybersecurity Law, and the Russian Federal Law on Personal Data No. 152-FZ (OPD), explicit, legally binding reference to security procedures is extremely scarce. Most privacy laws require organizations to employ reasonable or proportionate administrative and technical measures to protect personal information. Administrative and technical measures will be discussed further in Chapter 8.

> Some countries may have local laws requiring additional steps to protect personal information, yet most multi-national organizations do not today recognize or employ these requirements. Unfortunately, most countries also do not provide any indication of what reasonable measures suffice under the law. Part II of this book will be dedicated to exploring the concept of "reasonable" from an information technology perspective.

Retention strategies have two roles within data protection: (1) appropriate retention and management of preferences ("preference management"), (2) record-keeping responsibilities for personal information, and (3) data minimization and data erasure. Retention management, or records retention, ensures that appropriate records are maintained for a period of time specified in the retention schedule. Preference

27. *See* Chap. 9 for a detailed technical account of identifiability.
28. The unfortunate impact of a re-identification impossibility standard is that organizations must provide notice, establish consent, and abide by all other information privacy rights, including rights of access and erasure. Similar to how non-copyrightable information is often remixed and reused, organizations use de-identified data for new and inventive purposes. When data cannot be de-identified, inventive use is not possible.

management requires organizations to retain opt-in and opt-out preferences, other data about the consent or revocation of consent (such as date, time, method), and specifics as to how the preferences apply. For example, an individual data subject may wish to be removed from one marketing campaign, but not another. Organizations should have the systems and record-keeping to manage preferences to a granular level of detail while simultaneously being able to revoke consent for all preferences.

Record-keeping in relation to personal information is also a critical responsibility for records retention functions. Organizations must understand, track, and manage data flow of data between their organizations and third parties, between systems, and geographically. Record-keeping for this purpose usually includes a data inventory, which logs the classification of data (such as personal information) and where technical systems store these data. Strong record-keeping also involves creating and periodic updating of data flow diagrams, which illustrate relationships between systems, such as architecture diagrams that also include details regarding data transfer and storage. Consent revocation, access, correction, and erasure rights all require data inventories and data flow diagrams to support these procedures. Record-keeping also includes designation of primary records in a system. Without a primary "source of truth," that informs other systems, it is likely data subject preferences and personal information will be inaccurate, causing downstream issues. Further, data subject rights involving change or removal will require substantially more effort.

§1.07 IDENTIFYING PARTIES AND PROCESSING

When organizations first consider how information privacy laws might apply, they must determine whether their organization is an applicable party under the law. Under most international laws, organizations that *process* personal information must follow privacy and data protection laws where the organization is located or, often, where data subjects reside. *Processing* can include various definitions, depending on each specific law, but in the main processing means data collection, data transfer, and data storage (discussed from a technical perspective in Chapter 8).

Under some laws, simply accessing data, even when accessed from a remote location, can be included in a definition of processing. Processing often is the deciding factor for whether the law applies because in processing, an organization is undertaking a responsibility, voluntarily fulfilling a duty with respect to personal information. In undertaking this responsibility, certain obligations apply under the law. As described earlier in this chapter, privacy does reflect contract law to some extent, but because organizations also fulfill a duty under the law, privacy also reflects principles of common law tort, such as delict or rabbinic damages. Countries with civil laws may or may not have included codes that include information privacy law duties and recovery.

In addition to processing, information privacy laws in some countries have different obligations for different parties. The most significant difference involves a first party that directly engages with a data subject, and a third party, which has a relationship with the first party. Because first parties have the direct relationship with a data subject and the data subject may not know the identity of a third party, data subjects often cannot enforce their rights with respect to a third party. Further, third parties may have sub-contractors or other parties that do work on their behalf, such as technology vendors. In all practicality, data subjects would have to exert tremendous effort to: (1) determine the identity of all parties processing their data and (2) negotiate the terms for data handling. For this reason, *most* privacy law obligations fall on the first party, which has a direct relationship with the data subject and presumably derives some value from processing the data subject's personal information.

The first party is sometimes called a controller, operator, person responsible, or data user ("controller"). A controller controls the process of data handling, setting the rules associated with the data subject's personal information. For this reason, controllers are responsible for fulfilling all data subject rights, such as providing notice, collecting and retaining consent, fulfilling access and correction requests, and directing the deletion of data under rights of erasure. A controller, unless sub-contracting these responsibilities pursuant to a contract, must maintain the data inventory, run several procedural processes, maintain consent management tools, and manage third parties that are part of data handling or receive personal information. In some countries, the controller role is not defined in law. However, even in countries where controller is not defined, a primary or first party is usually responsible for the obligations of itself and any third party actions.

The third party is sometimes called a processor, sub-contractor, data holder, or third party.[29] A processor acts at the direction of the controller and is responsible for ensuring that any of its third parties also comply with the controller's direction.

§1.08 DATA TRANSFER

Relying on third parties often also means transferring data from the first party to a third party, which can also mean transferring data across geographical, and therefore jurisdictional, boundaries. Data transfer is the most problematic concept today for information privacy, because data transfer requirements differ substantially between jurisdictions. *Data transfer* from a legal perspective is the process of moving personal information from one jurisdiction to another jurisdiction, whether transfer occurs within a controller (e.g., in multi-national organizations) or between a controller and processor. Data transfer has substantial legal implications because cross-jurisdiction transfer invokes a new legal framework, the framework of the receiving country. A legally unbalanced transfer results when the receiving country (regulating the third party) has laws requiring fewer protections for data subjects when more stringent legal guarantees governed personal information at the time of collection.

The GDPR in the EU, Privacy Shield between the U.S. and the EU, and other regional principles such as the APEC Privacy Principles and the African Union

29. We will not be using the term "third party," as it has a specific connotation in information privacy law that does not mean someone who does business on behalf of or at the direction of, a controller. Third parties typically do not act at the direction of the controller, yet nevertheless may receive data subject data. In relation to cybersecurity activities, a third party is any organization without a direct relationship to the data subject.

Convention on Cyber Security and Personal Data Protection, have sought to create harmonization between countries to facilitate international and regional trade. However, some countries do not have privacy laws or lack sufficient regulatory enforcement to be deemed "adequate" by some standards. When controllers contract with processors and processors with sub-processors (and so forth) in countries not deemed adequate, parties write contract language with applicable laws for contractual performance.

Organizations, then, must rely on one of the three options for legal data transfer: (1) transfer to an adequate or sufficiently similar country, (2) transfer to another entity within the organizational structure under internal policies reflecting legal obligations, or (3) transfer pursuant to a contract including terms that reflect legal obligations of the original country. Some countries will also permit transfer pursuant to specific data subject consent. *See* Figure 1.3 for an example of a typical determination for a controller.

Figure 1.3 Enforcing Data Subject Rights in Data Transfer

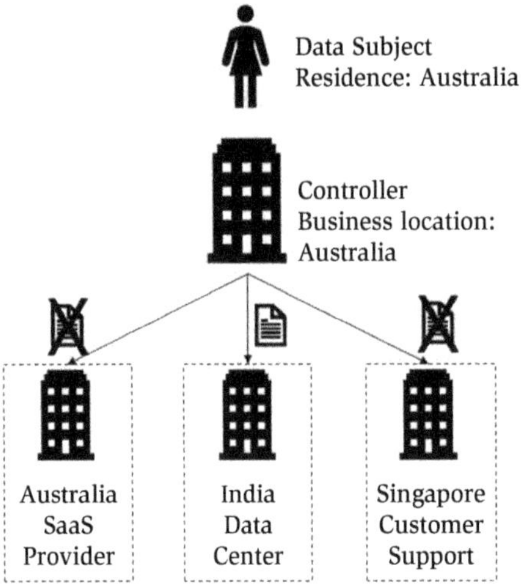

Under an adequacy determination, a controller must review whether the law in the country the third party resides provides an adequate or sufficiently similar legal framework, providing the same protections to data subjects. The country where a data subject resides often has a model for determining adequacy or substantial similarity, usually through an analysis completed by the data protection administrative or regulatory agency for that country and contained in a public register. Although processes to determine adequacy or substantial similarity may differ depending on the country, many countries have a list of countries acceptable for transfer without any additional safeguards.

When third parties reside in "inadequate" countries, the controller must rely on contractual language to legally enforce obligations.[30] In the EU, the Article 29 Working Party (WP, now called the European Data Protection Board (EDPB) under GDPR) historically drafted and approved standard contractual language, which must be incorporated as a whole into contracts without change.[31] In many other countries, the controller must execute contractual terms that reflect that country's legal requirements, such as Australia's Australian Privacy Principles (APPs).[32]

For organizations that have multiple legal entities with offices in various countries, laws may permit data transfer under internal policies and procedures. Usually these requirements include common control or leadership between the entities (rather than affiliation or partnership) and that the organization execute a common framework internal to the organization ensuring common treatment of personal information, regardless of office location. Multi-national organizations will likely find this model beneficial because personal information can be aggregated into common data stores, eliminating costs associated with multiple separate instances of information technology (IT) systems. In the EU, organizations can apply for Binding Corporate Rules (BCRs) approval from a lead DPA, but the approval process often is lengthy and complicated because it requires approval from all other EU country DPAs where contemplated data subjects reside.[33] Other countries may require similar common policies to ensure compliance, although most other countries do not require approval.

Increasingly more often, however, countries have specified complete bars on information transfer for various purposes. Russia, China, Indonesia, Australia, New Zealand, Canadian provinces, and many government agencies currently restrict transfer out of country for types of personal information. This bar is typically called *data*

30. For practitioners new to contract law, contracts provide an excellent means for enforcing obligations between parties in different countries. Although international laws may not recognize obligations or have the means to enforce laws across geographic boundaries, contracts are enforced through the Convention on the International Sale of Goods (CISG, if goods are the dominant part of the sale) and through trade agreements and principles of comity. For the most part, contracts are considered a reliable way to enforce obligations for entities across nation-states, which explains their reference and role within privacy laws.
31. At the time of writing, it is unclear whether existing contractual clauses will suffice, whether new contractual clauses will be drafted by the EDPB, or if a different approach will result. *See* Article 29 Working Party, Model Contracts for the Transfer of Personal Data to Third Countries (2010), http://ec.europa.eu/justice/data-protection/international-transfers/transfer/index_en.htm. Organizations can pursue adoption of alternate contractual clauses, but such clauses will require approval through a review procedure. Article 29 Working Party, Working Document Setting Forth a Co-Operation Procedure for Issuing Common Opinions on "Contractual Clauses" Considered as Compliant with the EC Model Clauses, 14/EN WP 226 (2014), http://ec.europa.eu/justice/data-protection/article-29/documentation/opinion-recommendation/files/2014/wp226_en.pdf.
32. *See* Office of the Australian Information Commissioner, Chapter 8: APP 8 – Cross-border disclosure of personal information (Mar. 2015), https://www.oaic.gov.au/agencies-and-organisations/app-guidelines/chapter-8-app-8-cross-border-disclosure-of-personal-information#taking-reasonable-steps-to-ensure-an-overseas-recipient-does-not-breach-the-apps.
33. European Commission, *Binding Corporate Rules Procedure* (2017), http://ec.europa.eu/justice/data-protection/international-transfers/binding-corporate-rules/procedure/index_en.htm.

localization, but may also be called *data residency, data nationalism*, or *data protectionism*. The purpose of data localization laws is usually one of three of the following: (1) to guarantee access of the government to updated records regarding their residents for any number of reasons, (2) to encourage technology development and economic stimulus within borders, or (3) to reduce potential injury due to lack of legal control and oversight. Data localization will be discussed in more detail in Chapter 10.

§1.09 INFORMATION PRIVACY LAW MODELS, ENFORCEMENT, AND GUIDANCE

Information privacy laws typically fall into two categories: omnibus and sectoral laws. Most countries have *omnibus* privacy laws in place, or laws that provide broadly applicable privacy requirements. The U.S. has taken a *sectoral* law approach to information privacy, or laws specific to industry sector. Many countries that have omnibus privacy laws also have specialized sectoral laws that incorporate privacy requirements, as well.

In terms of oversight and enforcement, countries with omnibus information privacy laws have one regulatory authority that provides guidance and guidelines for interpreting the law, investigates non-compliance and complaints, and issues fines. For regions that have consolidated regulatory frameworks, such as the EU, a common point of escalation also exists to resolve any issues (the European Data Protection Supervisor (EDPS)). For countries with sectoral information privacy laws, multiple regulatory authorities exist, though typically one authority often becomes more involved, such as China's Ministry of Information and Internet Technology (MIIT), or the United States' Federal Trade Commission (FTC).

Some regulatory authorities operate an audit framework, such as Russia's Roscommandzor, which conducts an annual audit for its data localization law, France's CNIL, which has performed cookie compliance audits in the past, or the United States' Office for Civil Rights (OCR), which conducts periodic audits for HIPAA compliance. Most regulatory authorities perform investigations, involving audits, after receiving complaints from data subjects. In Europe, the DPA, a regulatory authority, conducts the primary investigation in collaboration with other affected country DPAs.

For example, the DPA for each country in the EU has accountability for reviewing organizational compliance, leading investigations, influencing guidelines and opinions regarding the law, reviewing proposed contractual clauses, and assisting organizations through a BCRs process. EU DPAs perform a more involved role overall than most regulatory authorities in the world.

In many other countries, where a primary regulatory authority is specified and authority finalized, the regulatory authority conducts investigations, enforces compliance, issue fines, and may issue guidelines.[34] In countries where one primary regulatory authority does not exist, such as the Japanese ministry systems, each ministry conducts investigations and enforces compliance for its sector.

34. Some countries have full data protection laws as stringent as or more stringent than the EU, but nevertheless do not have the authority to enforce such laws, such as Chile and Mexico.

CHAPTER 2

European Region, European Economic Area, and Canada

European privacy law has captured the attention of organizations and countries around the world for its individual's rights approach to information privacy as an extension of human civil rights. The EU has led much of this development, creating a powerful framework to protect data subjects and advancing global privacy developments. Indeed, most worldwide omnibus laws have followed both in time and in content the EU Data Protection Directive, including Canada.

§2.01 EUROPEAN PRIVACY LAW

European information privacy law has characteristically operated with three layers of the law. At its most foundational layer, *fundamental rights* reflect what individual countries have established constitutionally for protection of residents or citizens, similar to guarantees in Latin American (LATAM) countries. The European Convention on Human Rights and the Charter of Fundamental Rights guaranteed fundamental rights. *Statutory rights* reflect both regional data protection laws (such as directives and regulations, which are applicable only to EU Member States) and individual country laws, which reflect the regional law passed within the country or country laws for non-member states.

Country-specific laws, especially those reflecting a deviation (*derogation*) from regional laws, often are called *local laws*. Finally, *representatives* from individual countries align to determine appropriate guidelines and issue opinions interpreting the law for EU Member States, previously called the Article 29 Working Party (WP), now the European Data Protection Board (EDPB). The Article 29 WP drafted the General Data Protection Regulation (GDPR), which regulates EU member countries and organizations providing sales or services to EU residents when processing personal information.

The EDPB includes Data Protection Authority (DPA) representatives, each of whom is accountable for member state-specific leadership, guidance, and enforcement of EU information privacy laws. Organizations providing service to multiple Member States designate a primary country for operations and have a primary relationship with a Lead DPA.

A *Lead DPA* serves as the primary DPA for multi-national organizations providing service to multiple member states. The Lead DPA is usually the DPA from an organization's principle place of business or designated headquarters location. Organizations without a principle place of business within the EU will usually select the country with greatest concentration of customers or business activity and designate the DPA in that location. Lead DPAs then coordinate activities across countries on behalf of the organization, when needed, such as review of Binding Corporate Rules (BCRs) and during investigations. In addition to DPA engagement for privacy activities, individual European countries may have decision-making bodies for reviewing organization practices with respect to employment, Works Councils (described later in this chapter).[35] Many countries delegate DPA responsibility within a country to specific states; for example, each state in Germany has a DPA.

Together, four areas for law-making illustrate the complexity of European information privacy law compliance. An organization must not only comply with constitutional guarantees, but also regional requirements, specific country laws, local laws, and representational opinions and guidance. *See* Table 2.1 for a short summary of legal decision-making in the EU. Please note: many countries in additional regions, such as the Asia-Pacific Region (APAC) and LATAM, also have levels 1–3 outside of the EU.

Table 2.1 European Information Privacy Law

Level	*Name*	*Description*	*Example*
Level 4 (Guidance and Opinions)	Representative Decisions	EDPB opinions and guidelines, Works Council decisions	Opinion 2/2017: Data Processing in a Work Environment (Article 29 WP)
Level 3 (Regional Law)	Local Laws	Country laws, as passed; state and municipality	French Labor Code
Level 2 (Country Law)	Statutory Rights	Country laws (non-EU), GDPR, E-Privacy Directive	Federal Act on Data Protection (FADP, Switzerland), DPAs

35. Countries in the EU have also developed specific councils and government agencies, which may require additional collaboration or clearance procedures for specific sectors. For example, the ASIP Santé in France (a country that has established robust cybersecurity requirements in addition to EU-level privacy laws) requires submission of substantial security and privacy evidence for the health sector.

Level	*Name*	*Description*	*Example*
Level 1 (Foundational)	Individual Rights	Constitutional guarantees, treaties	European Convention on Human Rights, ECHR, European Court of Justice (ECJ)

Under EU law, directives and regulations enjoy different legal models. Because the EU is a regional agreement, countries within the EU must pass any law, directive or regulation within that country, in line with international law commitment to a convention or treaty. However, countries passing *directives* have considerably more latitude in passing deviations from the EU language, *derogations*.[36] When passing a directive, countries may reduce or increase compliance obligations, strengthening or weakening certain provisions and reducing harmonization encouraged by regional collaboration. Although directives appear to provide regional consistency, organizations complying with requirements in multiple countries must still analyze individual legal requirements.

A *regulation* does not require individual country passage, which eliminates some derogation. However, if a regulation permits derogations on particular subjects, a country may do so through local laws. Within the GDPR, for example, derogations include Article 23, related to collection, handling, and protection of Sensitive Personal Information (SPI), and Articles 85–91 list these derogations.

Article 23

(1) Union or Member State law to which the data controller or processor is subject may restrict by way of a legislative measure the scope of the obligations and rights provided for in Articles 12 to 22 and Article 34, as well as Article 5 in so far as its provisions correspond to the rights and obligations provided for in Articles 12 to 22, when such a restriction respects the essence of the fundamental rights and freedoms and is a necessary and proportionate measure in a democratic society to safeguard:
   (a) national security;
   (b) defence;
   (c) public security;
   (d) the prevention, investigation, detection or prosecution of criminal offences or the execution of criminal penalties, including the safeguarding against and the prevention of threats to public security;
   (e) other important objectives of general public interest of the Union or of a Member State, in particular an important economic or financial

36. The term "derogation" is used in various legal contexts, but within the regulatory context it often means discouraged but limited deviation, or approved non-passage or addition of certain provisions.

interest of the Union or of a Member State, including monetary, budgetary and taxation a matters, public health and social security;
(f) the protection of judicial independence and judicial proceedings;
(g) the prevention, investigation, detection and prosecution of breaches of ethics for regulated professions;
(h) a monitoring, inspection or regulatory function connected, even occasionally, to the exercise of official authority in the cases referred to in points (a) to (e) and (g);
(i) the protection of the data subject or the rights and freedoms of others;
(j) the enforcement of civil law claims.

The derogations are specifically important for Human Resources (HR) or employment information privacy law purposes, as derogations often involve details regarding background checks,[37] surveillànce, and ethical expectations (such as fiduciary duties or other confidentiality expectations).

For multi-national organizations, the most applicable derogations involve those for data transfer. Data transfer rules usually permit transfer based on European Commission (EC) adequacy decisions (Article 44), BCRs (inter-organizational transfer, Article 47), and Model Contractual Clauses (MCCs, Article 46). Under some limited circumstances, additional transfer derogations may apply:

Article 49

1. the data subject has explicitly consented to the proposed transfer, after having been informed of the possible risks of such transfers for the data subject due to the absence of an adequacy decision and appropriate safeguards;
2. the transfer is necessary for the performance of a contract between the data subject and the controller or the implementation of pre-contractual measures taken at the data subject's request;
3. the transfer is necessary for the conclusion or performance of a contract concluded in the interest of the data subject between the controller and another natural or legal person;
4. the transfer is necessary for important reasons of public interest;
5. the transfer is necessary for the establishment, exercise or defence of legal claims;
6. the transfer is necessary in order to protect the vital interests of the data subject or of other persons, where the data subject is physically or legally incapable of giving consent;
7. the transfer is made from a register which according to Union or Member State law is intended to provide information to the public and which is open to consultation

37. http://whoswholegal.com/news/features/article/29116/background-checks-europe/.

either by the public in general or by any person who can demonstrate a legitimate interest, but only to the extent that the conditions laid down by Union or Member State law for consultation are fulfilled in the particular case.

Derogations, according to the GDPR, may be used when preferred transfer mechanisms do not apply. For derogations like data subject consent-based transfer, transfers should be singular, for limited data subjects, and necessary for compelling legitimate interests. Organizations must inform both the DPA and the data subject prior to transfer.

§2.02 INTRODUCTION TO THE GDPR

The European Economic Area (EEA) includes both members of the EU and European Free Trade Association members, and exists to extend trade to countries that are not part of the EC: Iceland, Liechtenstein, and Norway. EU Member States must comply with the GDPR (passed in 2016), with enforcement beginning May 2018.[38] Prior to GDPR passage, the Data Protection Directive 95/46/EC applied, as also providing a comprehensive model for global data protection law. Many non-EU countries in the EU also have passed data protection laws, such as Switzerland and Norway.

[A] The Data Protection Directive

Although the GDPR has effectively superseded the Data Protection Directive, the Directive established many of the same commitments the GDPR has incorporated, including:

- Availability of a clear, easy to read, distinct notice provided before gathering consent:
  - Controller identity and contact details
  - Articulation of purposes of use, and rights of access and correction[39]
  - Categories of data processed and third parties
  - Information regarding data transfer and storage locations
  - Information regarding administrative and technical security measures
- Explicit, prior consent for personal information processing (IP) in most cases.
- Processing proportionate and not excessive, specific to disclosed purposes.

38. The GDPR Regulation (Regulation (EU) 2016/679). A well-organized and clean version is available online: GENERAL DATA PROTECTION REGULATION (GDPR), https://gdpr-info.eu/ (last accessed Jul. 10, 2017).
39. Although the Data Protection Directive required notice of rights of access and correction, the GDPR requires information about additional data subject rights, including rights of objection to automatic processing, data portability, and erasure.

- General prohibition on SPI processing (overcome by highly specific, detailed disclosure, and consent).
- Administrative and technical security measures proportionate to data processed to prevent risk of misuse or data loss, to maintain data accuracy and availability.
- Inclusion of retention requirements and secure technical processes to remove data when no longer required.
- Controller rights with respect to data processors, including explicit approval of processing activities; processors should act only within specified direction of the controller.[40]
- Transfer restricted to EU member states, except: to another country that has an established law approved as adequate by the EC, intraoffice transfer within a multi-national organization after BCRs reviewed and approved, or via MCCs drafted by the Article 29 Working Group.

[B] EU Regulatory Authorities and Courts

The Data Protection Direction established the concept of DPAs for each member state, which has continued under the GDPR. DPAs have specific internal country names. Some of the most active DPAs are listed below:

- Commission Nationale de l'Informatique et des Libertés (CNIL—France)
- Information Commissioner's Office (ICO—United Kingdom)
- Garante per la Protezione dei Dati Personali (GPDP—Italy)
- Autoriteit Persoonsgegevens (AP—Netherlands)
- *Bundesbeauftragter für den Datenschutz und die Informationsfreiheit (BfDI—Germany)*[41]
- Agencia Española de Protección de Datos (AEPD—Spain).

The DPA establishes, monitors, and enforces the GDPR within its country. Although the DPAs may individually fine an organization for non-compliance, data subjects may also institute a civil suit under the GDPR against an organization. In most cases, this suit is resolved under that country's laws. When one or both of the parties appeal, eventually the European Court of Human Rights (ECHR) may elect to decide the case. The ECHR also has the ability to accept and provide advisory opinions on questions of legal interest with respect to a variety of human rights topics, including information privacy. The ECJ, the highest court for the EU region will, from time to

40. Under the Data Protection Directive, activity outside the bounds of controller instruction (e.g., for data aggregation purposes) likely will transform a processor into a controller, triggering additional responsibilities for notice, consent, access requests, correction requests, retention requirements.
41. Although Germany has a federal commissioner, most DPA activities occur at the state level. *See* North Rhine-Westphalia Commissioner for Data Protection and Freedom of Information, *Data Protection Authorities in Germany*, https://www.ldi.nrw.de/LDI_EnglishCorner/mainmenu_DataProtection/Inhalt2/authorities/authorities.php (last accessed 8 Jul. 2017).

time, decide an information privacy-related case and incorporate ECHR opinions, although the ECHR provides more regular judgments.[42]

[C] GDPR Roles

The European Parliament passed the GDPR, (EU) 2016/679, in 2016 to replace the Data Protection Directive, (EU) 95/46/EC. The GDPR provides consistency within the EU, codifies European Court of Justice (ECJ) decisions, increases extra-territorial application of the law, increases the fine structure, and establishes timely data breach notification. The GDPR is organized into ninety-nine articles, but this chapter will provide sample sections and describe application within an organization's potential environment, including key considerations and challenges.

The following definitions in Article 4 have critical importance throughout the articles and are fundamental to understanding the meaning of provisions in the GDPR. The *data subject* is the individual to whom duties of privacy are owed. Data subject is used because it connotes a status with regard to the data: the *natural person* about whom data is collected. Data subjects may be residents living in the EU or citizens who are from the EU. The organization that collects and uses data from data subjects for its business purposes is the *controller*.

Controllers determine the purpose and nature of processing and must fulfill data subject rights enumerated under the GDPR. In most circumstances, the controller has a direct relationship with the data subject, such as a bank with its customers, or a hospital with its patients. However, some controllers outsource their responsibilities to a processor, which either wholly or partially fulfills these obligations on the controller's behalf. The *processor* is any downstream receiver that accesses, edits, transfers, stores, or otherwise acts on the data it receives from a controller. Most processors are vendors of some kind (providing products or services to data controllers) and act at the direction of the controller via a contract between the controller and the processor.

Although not explicitly stated within the GDPR, determining "controller" status usually includes the following factors: (1) whether the entity directs activities regarding data collection for itself or third parties, (2) degree of direct relationship or direct data collection from a data subject, and (3) purposes of data collection and use, within or beyond explicit direction.

The primary determinant for determining whether an organization is controller or processor is explicitly defined under the GDPR: which organization directs activities of other parties and determines purposes of use. Although this concept might appear relatively simple initially, controller organizations frequently contract with third parties to introduce technical innovation or alternative business models. Within these relationships, the controller may not actually "direct" activity or truly understand purposes of data collection and use. In these cases, would-be processors should take

42. For a complete summary of EU court decisions (to 2015) regarding data protection between 2000 and 2015, *see* Laraine Laudati, *Summaries of EU Court Decisions Relating to Data Protection 2000–2015* (28 Jan. 2016), https://ec.europa.eu/anti-fraud/sites/antifraud/files/caselaw_2001_2015_en.pdf.

the time to inform and train controllers on services provided, including working with the controller organization to ensure privacy notices reflect controller, rather than processor activities, whenever possible. This model reinforces the role of the controller and minimizes confusion for data subjects (and potential surprises for processor organizations).

Some data processors have a direct relationship or collect data directly from a data subject, such as mobile apps branded with the controller's name and information, or provided by the controller to its customers or employees.[43] However, most often processors receive and process data downstream in a sub-contracting capacity (e.g., accounting services) or in provision of technology resources, such as IT consulting services, SaaS solutions, or cloud storage provisioning (to be discussed in more detail in Chapter 16).

Controllers must fulfill substantial legal obligations with respect to data subjects; therefore, organizations do not usually seek to define themselves as controllers when they are working on behalf of an entity that has a direct relationship with the data subject. Typically, a contract will establish these roles with respect to the data. When both parties expect to use data subject data for each of their respective purposes, the parties may execute additional agreements, such as data exchange agreements or data transfer agreements. When both parties plan to use data subjects' personal information for their respective purposes, processors may become *co-controllers* or *joint controllers*.[44]

Although parties typically define controller and processor status by contract, in some cases a processor can become a controller through its actions with respect to a data subject or in agreement with the controller. A processor will likely be considered a controller when their use of the data goes beyond the bounds of the controller's direction, or *secondary use*. For example, if a processor receives information about a patient from the controller and by contract is limited to store information, yet the processor instead uses this data to create a predictive health-tracking tool for commercial distribution, the processor has exceeded the controller's direction. When a processor exceeds the controller's direction, the processor will generally be deemed a controller under the GDPR and must adhere to enhanced obligations related to these additional activities, such as notice, consent, data subject rights, deletion, and data breach notification. Because many processor organization leaders do not expect government authorities to categorize the organization as a controller, processors do not

43. Organizations should take note of "branded" third party apps, as many apps will include standard privacy notice and consent language. However, organizations branding such apps will need to ensure their own notice language and commitments regarding data collection and processing (e.g., third-party use, contact information) are included in such notices, rather than boilerplate language.
44. Often, organizations may perceive personal data collection as giving rights to an organization with respect to the data, i.e., "we own the data." This concept forms an expectation that any organization collecting personal information from data subjects have rights to it. However, data subjects alone have the power to determine how information will be used or to revoke consent for using it. Therefore, practitioners should think of controller status (whether co-controller or controller) as *license* to use personal information. Co-controllers then share license to data collected whereas a processor has no license to any data collected.

fulfill controller regulatory requirements, triggering enforcement actions and fines. Processors, therefore, must clearly define business processes with respect to data subject personal information and communicate these uses to controllers when negotiating service agreements.[45]

An organization as a whole may hold more than one designation: although generally most processors provide services for many controllers (and often do not involve themselves in controller activities), in limited cases a large organization with many different functions may be a controller or processor with respect to different activities and different customers. For example, a bank may have individual relationships with customers and effectively "control" purpose and use of data collected. However, the bank may also process payments for a local retailer, where they receive financial credit information about that retailer's customers and act at the retailer's direction. In the former, the bank is likely considered a controller, in the latter, the bank is likely considered a processor. Although the bank can only hold one designation at a time for a business process, the bank has both controller and processor roles with respect to different processes and different data.

Two or more controllers with common obligations with respect to the same data processed will be considered *co-controllers* or *joint controllers*. A processor may or may not become a co-controller as a result of secondary use. *Secondary use* results when a processor uses data processed for its own purposes. Secondary use outside the boundaries of what the controller has designated for data processing. Co-controllers have identified that secondary use will occur and have negotiated their respective rights for data processed. Usually, secondary uses will be communicated to a data subject to adequately inform the data subject prior to processing when co-controller status exists. However, in some situations, processors may not notify the controller or the data subject, triggering legal issues both with the controller contractually and with DPAs when data subjects are not adequately informed as to these secondary uses.

Usually a contract between two organizational entities will establish co-controller status. Organizations that have not executed such terms with other organizations should not assume any particular status. Despite private contracting determinations, the DPAs may not agree with the role distinction (private agreements are not dispositive). For this reason, parties should take great care in understanding their respective roles and ensure these roles are consistent with GDPR definitions. *See* Table 2.2 for the formal GDPR definitions of data subject, controller, and processor.

45. When controllers do not understand processor activities, these organizations may not effectively communicate downstream personal information use (by the processor) to the data subject. Therefore, data use beyond the privacy notice scope may appear to be "secondary use" triggering controller obligations when in reality a controller has not effectively notified the data subject.

Table 2.2 GDPR Definitions

Term	*GDPR Definition*
Data Subject	An identified or identifiable natural person who can be identified, directly or indirectly, in particular by reference to an identifier such as a name, an identification number, location data, an online identifier or to one or more factors specific to the physical, physiological, genetic, mental, economic, cultural or social identity of that natural person.
Controller	The natural or legal person, public authority, agency or other body which, alone or jointly with others, determines the purposes and means of the processing of personal data; where the purposes and means of such processing are determined by Union or Member State law, the controller or the specific criteria for its nomination may be provided for by Union or Member State law.
Processor	A natural or legal person, public authority, agency or other body which processes personal data on behalf of the controller. A processor may become designated as a controller if acting beyond the instructions of the controller with respect to a data subject (e.g., broader data use).

As previously mentioned, in addition to the roles of controller, co-controller, and processor, some processors may become controllers with respect to data processed for the processor's own use and benefit. A critical factor in determining controller status involves the purposes of data collection, and whether the controller has continued to direct collection and use. Processors, especially those storing data subject data, may desire to use data collected for purposes other than what the controller has disclosed to the data subject or may collect different or additional data than what the controller specifies.

Scenario: Financial Investment App

A financial services company made available a financial management app, FinanceUP, to its customers to assist customers in their investments. The company that created the app and maintains its database wants to use app usage data and other customer details to improve its service to all app users, such as predicting investment risk balance. The app company also wants to use statistics on usage and results for marketing claims, such as "50 % of users have increased their long-term investments within two months of using this app."

In this example, an attorney will have to determine initially if these uses are reasonably connected to the primary purposes of use. Although in some circumstances, product improvement and usage statistics, including data aggregation, could be reasonably connected to the primary purpose of use, attorneys will need to interpret whether data subjects would reasonably expect this kind of data use in giving their consent. Here, it is more likely that data usage has eclipsed the original purpose of providing the app to financial services customers to support financial investments.

Under most circumstances, the processor would be barred from collecting data for these purposes. However, processors have a few options for collecting data: (1) contractually obligating the controller to include these uses within its privacy notice provided to its customers; (2) contractually obligating the controller to execute another privacy notice on behalf of the processor; (3) providing a privacy notice within the app that gives the data subject an opportunity to consent (or refuse consent) to secondary use.

Entities might choose the first option if the controller has a continuous, direct relationship with the data subject that might enable timely and efficient communication or when co-controller status exists. Having the controller execute language describing these additional purposes gives the impression that the controller is still directing downstream activities of the process. However, in this circumstance, unless co-controller status exists, controllers may also accept some regulatory risk. A DPA may ask to what extent collection for these additional purposes meets the "minimum necessary" and "proportionate" requirements for data collection, especially when handling SPI.

Entities would likely choose the second option when both parties understand that data processed will benefit both parties separately. Providing different privacy notices to a data subject communicates individual relationships between the controllers and the data subject. However, relying on another controller to execute a privacy notice can become onerous when privacy notices change, and serious questions remain regarding execution of notices and retention of consent by another party.

Controllers, including processors engaged in secondary use, may prefer to execute privacy notices and retain consent independently through technology or other means when a direct relationship with the data subject exists. However, processors that do not communicate to their controllers regarding secondary use or additional data collection may find the agreement unfavorable to these activities, resulting in breach of contract.

The concept of a co-controller can be complex and heavily situation-specific. Usually, co-controllers are defined by rights with respect to the *same data set*. For example, if the financial services provider collects financial investment details, which are captured in the FinanceUP app, and the app company will use these same details for different purposes, it is likely that the organizations will be co-controllers. If the app company collects data not viewed or used by the financial services provider for any purpose, such as location or activity data, the app company is likely just a different controller with respect to the same data subject.

[D] Personal Information

As referenced in the definition for data subject, the GDPR requires protection and grants privacy rights for two classifications of information: *sensitive personal information* and *personal information*. SPI is defined as specially enumerated data elements defined by the EU as most likely to infringe on a data subject's inherent privacy rights if misused, or *special categories* of personal data. Under the GDPR, SPI collection is prohibited, although organizations may process SPI when a data subject provides explicit consent to processing and the organization protects SPI with a higher threshold of data protection requirements (e.g., additional cybersecurity requirements may apply). Individual EU Member States may establish additional requirements or prohibitions on SPI use.

Personal information, in contrast, can include *any* information about a data subject that is *identifiable* (as in, able to be tied to a natural person, *directly* or *indirectly*). For information not to be regulated under the GDPR, an *impossibility* of re-identification standard exists.[46] As in statutes reviewed later in this book, this purposefully broad definition seeks to develop a flexible definition that can evolve with changing technology and data collection. Personal information requires fewer protection requirements, yet the GDPR does provide a minimum threshold of rights and protections for all personal information. *See* Table 2.3 for a definition and list of SPI data elements.

Table 2.3 Personal Information and SPI

Term	*GDPR Definition*	*Examples*
Personal Information	Any information relating to an identified or identifiable natural person ("data subject")	Web browsing history, name and address, e-mail address, photographs
SPI	Personal data which are, by their nature, particularly sensitive in relation to fundamental rights and freedoms merit specific protection as the context of their processing could create significant risks to the fundamental rights and freedoms	Racial or ethnic origin, biometric data, genetic data, political opinion, religion or beliefs, trade union membership, genetic or health status or sexual orientation, criminal convictions or offenses

§2.03 APPLYING THE GDPR

Applying the GDPR can prove challenging for some organizations, due to the complexity, length, and anticipated enforcement of this law. Concepts that usually present the most challenges include determining when the GDPR applies to an organization, the role of an organization within the GDPR, questions of data transfer, and the role of the new EDPB in relation to ongoing GDPR interpretation and compliance.

46. The impossibility standard requires organizations to protect all information about a natural person, even if it is de-identified under another procedure to meet a different international law, as it if it identifiable. The EDPB has not yet issued or approved specific procedures or methods for meeting the impossibility standard.

[A] Applicability

The GDPR applies when controllers or processors *process* personal information or SPI. For this reason, the definition of processing is particularly important. Unlike some laws that limit applicability to certain activities, the GDPR defines processing as:

> Any operation or set of operations which is performed on personal data or on sets of personal data, whether or not by automated means, such as collection, recording, organisation, structuring, storage, adaptation or alteration, retrieval, consultation, use, disclosure by transmission, dissemination or otherwise making available, alignment or combination, restriction, erasure or destruction.

In this definition, processing does not mean transfer or storage only. Simply retrieving data for some reason, such as updating a record or accessing a file for support purposes, will require an organization using EU data subjects' personal information to comply with GDPR. The GDPR requires all organizations processing personal information of EU data subjects (residents of the EU) to comply with the GDPR.[47]

This definition has a tremendous impact on how organizations plan to manage concepts of transparency, choice, and appropriately manage data transfer. The GDPR squarely includes organizations handling EU data subject data, regardless of their physical location or country of incorporation. Although the Data Protection Direction applied to fewer organizations with a business presence in the EU, government authorities will require organizations with any customers or employees in the EU (even via e-commerce services like signing up for free software or mobile apps) to follow the GDPR.[48]

Further impact involves third parties of an organization. As these an organization now must follow the GDPR as a controller, third parties processing data collected by the GDPR must also comply with the GDPR via contract, or the data controller will be in violation of the GDPR and could face sanctions of up to 4% of annual global revenue.

47. It is unclear, at the date of writing, whether such obligations travel with EU citizens outside EEA borders. Usually the receiving country's legal guarantees apply when any individual travels within its borders. However, a more conservative view might advocate, for example, that U.S. educational institutions fulfill GDPR obligations for EU citizens studying at the institution. Transferability of laws do create multiple challenges, both in operational management and in optics: organizations do not want to encourage "disparate treatment" for data subjects based on country of origin.

48. For example, many U.S. companies have expected that Privacy Shield compliance (described in Chapter 3) sufficiently meets GDPR obligations. In reality, Privacy Shield permits data transfer outside of the EU for adequacy purposes, *not* for business conducted with EU data subjects. The GDPR is designed to be extra-territorial in application.

[B] Data Processing and Lawful Basis

Data processing under the GDPR applies to a wide variety of activities. *Data processing* involves not only transferring, using, or sharing data, it also includes accessing, editing, changing, or storing data. Almost all controllers or processors handling personal information in any way will be *processing* personal information under GDPR. For this reason, organizations should identify business processes and operational circumstances where EU resident data will be handled and document these processes, systems used, and physical location of processing activities (including support activities) in a data inventory. A data inventory should provide a starting point for understanding potential compliance obligations with respect to GDPR overall.
Before an organization may collect any personal information, the organization must have a *lawful basis* for data collection, sometimes called the *conditions for processing*. The lawful basis is formed by one of three conditions:

- **Necessity – Contract:** information must be collected pursuant to an enforceable contract, for example an employment agreement
- **Necessity – Vital Interests:** information must be collected to protect an individual, for example in a medical emergency where consent is not practical
- **Legal Obligation:** information must be collected to fulfill a legal interest owed (other than a contractual agreement)
- **Administration of Justice:** Pursuant to a government disclosure obligation, such as a subpoena or warrant, or other lawful government demand
- **Consent:** the data subject consents to data collection (most common)
- **Legitimate Interests:** There may be other legitimate interests not specifically allocated by other lawful bases

Consent is the most common lawful basis for personal information processing, followed by contractual processing. When the legal basis for collection involves consent, organizations must collect and retain data subject consent records in order to illustrate that the organization has met legal requirements and to fulfill data subject rights requests. In order for consent to be legally valid, it must be *informed* consent, meaning that a data subjects rights to transparency must be fulfilled prior to consenting by providing the data subject with a legally sufficient privacy notice communicating the processing details. When organizations do not execute a legally sufficient notice, data subjects have not had *prior notice* and do not have accurate information to have executed informed consent. Furthermore, processing data in a manner not communicated in the privacy notice also will not have resulted in informed consent. For these reasons, privacy notice and consent procedures must be contemplated together, as they form the foundational basis for lawful processing under the GDPR.

Contractual processing provides a substitute for consent in that a data subject has consent via contract to processing connected with the fulfillment of the contract. However, lawful basis reliant on a contract has its restrictions. Similar to a privacy notice, the bases for personal information processing must be communicated within the contract, and downstream processing must be reasonably consistent with fulfillment of the contract and bases for processing. Some organizations expect that simply having a contract, such as an employment agreement, permits the organization to process personal information without additional consent. However, processing outside declared processing bases in a manner not reasonably consistent with a contract, will not fulfill prior notice obligations, either. Organizations should consider logging the lawful basis for processing in the data inventory where possible.

Once an organization has fulfilled its lawful basis obligation for processing personal information, it must also ensure such processing is necessary and proportionate in relation to purposes for processing. *Necessity* relates to business need, and requires that strict justification exists for processing to benefit the data subject. *Proportionality* refers to reasonable processing compared to services provided, which is often raised in relation to complementary services that collect personal information. For example, processing personal information via a free children's mobile app might be necessary and proportionate if personal information is collected ensures children under a particular age receive special privacy considerations, such as a "what is your age" question.[49]

The same mobile app's data processing might not be necessary and proportionate if it also collects location data or GPS, IP address or unique mobile identifiers from the device, a child's contacts or images from the mobile device despite no service or features requiring location information. Proportionality balances benefits gained and information disclosures required; necessity ensures that despite proportionality, personal information collected is required for the business to provide service.

To comply with the GDPR, organizations collecting information should document all justifications for data collection, by data element. The reasons for collection, including data aggregation and service improvement, should be clearly articulated within the privacy notice text. Further, organizations collecting information for systems providing relatively low benefit to users, such as games or entertainment apps, should strictly review data elements collected and reduce to a minimum necessary. Necessity and proportionality together fulfill data minimization required by GDPR.

[C] Data Subject Rights

In addition to informed consent, data subject rights include rights to revoke consent, access and correct personal information, objection to automated processing, data portability, and erasure. Under the GDPR, data subjects have the right to informed consent, which includes both adequate, prior notice of purposes of processing that are necessary and proportionate. Organizations must also collect expressed consent, rather than implicit consent, which requires the user to consent prior to processing, rather than objecting to processing after it has commenced. When organizations may collect SPI, explicit consent is required: organizations must specifically describe how SPI will

49. GDPR mandates enhanced scrutiny regarding the collection of children's information, especially SPI, and requires parental notice and consent to process this data. Although the GDPR does not specify an age limit for requiring parental consent, local country laws will applicable age.

be processed in a highly specific manner, including enhancements for protecting SPI during transfer, if applicable. The basic requirements for notice have been described earlier in this chapter in relation to the Data Protection Directive. Organizations building on previous notices will need to include additional data subject rights of objection to automated processing, data portability, and erasure.

In addition to informed consent, organizations must fulfill data subject requests under the GDPR, which require specific procedures for all organizational functions processing personal information:

- **Consent revocation:** Data subjects may revoke consent at any time and in any reasonable manner. This includes by phone, e-mail, web form, or postal service. Organizations must have procedures to receive and process these requests and triggers within systems to no longer process information on these individuals (e.g., database flags or blocking technologies).
- **Access requests:** Access requests require an organization to provide a copy of the data subject's personal information within 30 days at no cost to the data subject. An additional two months may be granted for organizations receiving multiple requests, but these organizations must provide a reply advising of this additional timeframe within 30 days and justification for delay.
- **Correction requests (rectification):** Correction requests must also be completed within 30 days. Often correction requests follow access requests. Organizations should determine which types of personal information may be available for correction: financial, investment, and health records may not be corrected in some circumstances.
- **Data portability request:** Data subjects may request data be transferred to a new provider. Organizations must transfer these data to the new provider in a reasonably usable format within 30 days.
- **Objection to automated processing:** Data subjects may object to automated processing, or personal information processing often associated with mechanical decision-making. This often applies to industries such as loan and mortgage application or in employment scenarios. Objecting to automated processing requires organizations to remove an individual from automated processing, if routine, and provide a human (rather than computerized) review of information where applicable within 30 days.
- **Data erasure request:** Data subjects may request personal information contained in the organization's systems be erased. Organizations will need to maintain a comprehensive data inventory to effectively identify and erase copies of data processed and have adequate practices for removal of temporary and backup copies, as well. Organizations requiring compliance with other laws for maintenance of public records (e.g., investment or financial organizations) should develop clear procedures for maintaining required data and removing other personal information.

Some organizations may find that specific types of data subject rights do not apply to a particular functional area. For example, correction requests may not apply to readings from an Electrocardiogram at a clinician's office.

[D] Data Transfer and Adequacy

One of the more complicated EU requirements involves conditions for data transfer. From the European perspective, information privacy obligations safeguard individual civil rights. Transferring data to another country then begs a question: will another country protect civil rights as if the EU protected these rights?

IT and consumer service globalization necessitated development of legal data transfer models that: (1) ensure personal information is processed with consistently stringent legal protection within a geographic boundary or (2) approve certain inter-organizational commitments to follow EU law, regardless of personal information location. In the EU, countries must be deemed *adequate* to receive EU resident personal information transferred without additional protection, and adequacy is determined through a relatively lengthy process. As a result of this lengthy process, the EU has permitted individual organizations to guarantee safeguards through Binding Corporate Rules (BCR) and use of Model Contractual Clauses (MCCs).

Adequacy is central to European Member State constitutional guarantees because these constitutions form the basis for subsequent data protection laws passed. Adequacy fulfills these guarantees by ensuring personal information transferred from one country to the other will receive comparable protection. Adequacy requirements apply to controllers, processors, sub-processers, and so forth, so long as they process EU resident personal information. Of existing adequacy determinations, the EC facilitated these determinations prior to GDPR passage, prompting questions regarding current adequacy. Although currently unknown, countries with current adequacy status will likely consider moving to GDPR-acceptable model in coming years.

Countries without status must propose adequacy to the EC and receive sponsorship by the EC. Next, member states' DPAs and the European Data Protection Supervisor (EDPS, the EU supervisor reviewing DPA activities) review the country's laws and draft a report. Then, the Article 31 WP (including representatives from each member state) recommends a course of action, and finally the European College of Commissioners ("EC") makes the decision. *See* Figure 2.1 for a process flow illustrating adequacy decision-making in the EU.

Figure 2.1 Adequacy Determination[50]

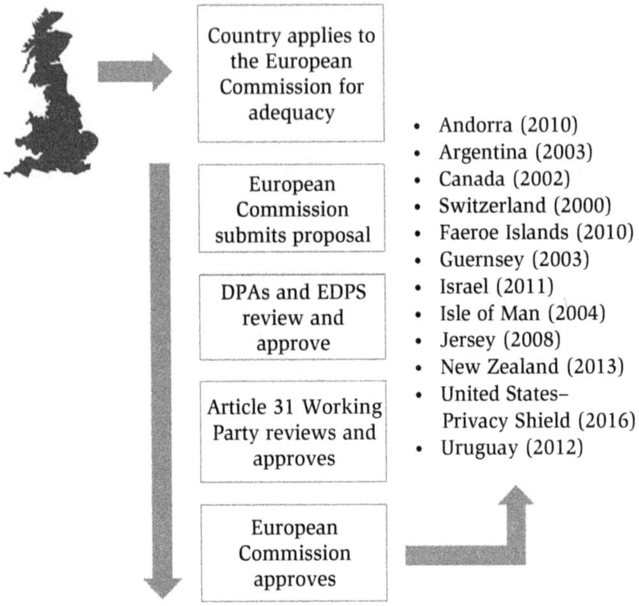

When adequacy is not possible, another option involves establishing BCRs within an organization, which requires working with a Lead DPA. BCRs acknowledge that although a multi-national organization may operate in many countries, most organizations with common control (even with different legal entities under the common organization) can create a consolidated set of policies, procedures, training, and other information. The BCR approval process, then, includes a review of these documents and verification that internal controls adequately reflect applicable EU law, so that transfer within the organization is acceptable.

The process for approving BCRs is a lengthy, dedicated organizational effort, including developing or changing documentation and processes, conducting training, and demonstrating implementation before submission for review. After the materials have been submitted, the Lead DPA reviews may provide recommendations for changes. Figure 2.2 illustrates the process for BCR review and approval.

50. Please note: this figure includes reference to U.S. adequacy, however, as described in Chapter 3, the U.S. Privacy Shield process requires self-registration by U.S. companies. This means that the U.S. overall does not meet adequacy requirements. *See* EUROPEAN COMMISSION, *Commission Decisions on the Adequacy of the Protection of Personal Data in Third Countries* (2017), http://ec.europa.eu/justice/data-protection/international-transfers/adequacy/index_en.htm.

Figure 2.2 BCR Review and Approval[51]

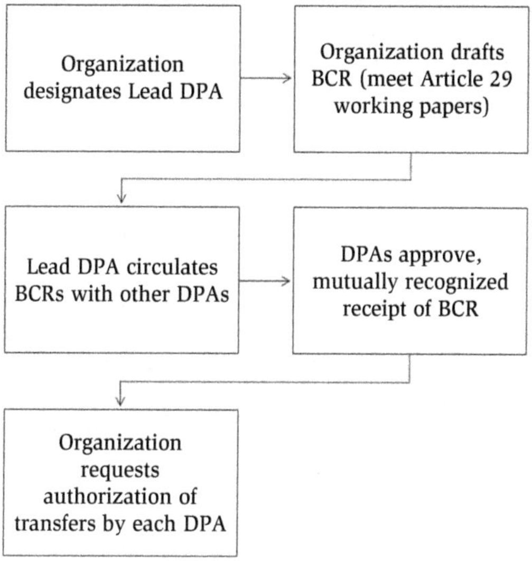

At the time of writing, only eighty-eight organizations had achieved BCR registration, evidencing the time investment required to receive approval.[52] Organizations seeking similar treatment in the APAC region may apply for both BCR and Cross-Border Privacy Regulation (CBPR) approvals, described further in Chapter 5.

Adopting BCRs and meeting adequacy requirements can prove tremendously difficult for organizations, and the speed of business often does not match lengthy approval processes. Organizations increasingly use distributed technology and computing or work with third parties in other geographic locations for operational and financial efficiencies. Often this includes transferring personal information to third parties in locations without the stringency of EU legal requirements, necessitating a third option. The EU accomplished this through MCCs, sometimes called standard contractual clauses.

Drafted by the former Article 29 WP, MCCs convert the former EU Data Protection Directive into contractual terms. The MCCs, to effectuate facilitation of legal personal information transfer, must be attached to contracts without any changes, and organizations must select the appropriate version that matches status as a controller or

51. European Commission, *BCR Procedure* (2017), http://ec.europa.eu/justice/data-protection/international-transfers/binding-corporate-rules/procedure/index_en.htm; European Commission, *Available Tools* (2017), http://ec.europa.eu/justice/data-protection/international-transfers/binding-corporate-rules/tools/index_en.htm.
52. European Commission, *List of Companies for Which the EU BCR Cooperation Procedure is Closed* (2017), http://ec.europa.eu/justice/data-protection/international-transfers/binding-corporate-rules/bcr_cooperation/index_en.htm.

processor. The MCCs currently available today reflect requirements of the Data Protection Directive, not the GDPR.[53]

Standard or MCCs provide the easiest route to establish adequacy requirements at an organization not residing in a country that requires commensurate protections, although it is not yet known whether contractual clauses will change based on the GDPR. There are also challenges using existing MCCs. Third parties may not accept MCCs or cannot in good faith fulfill MCC requirements, complicating the negotiation process.[54] Further, organizations may find that the MCCs do not fit business purposes. In this case, alternative contractual clauses may be submitted to the Lead DPA for review and approval.[55] Alternative language should avoid deviating substantially from the MCCs.

Many organizations have previously appended MCCs reflecting Data Protection Directive requirements to contracts with third parties and processors, yet whether the EDPB will accept previously executed MCCs that do not include additional GDPR guarantees (and for how long) is unknown. If the EDPB does not accept previously executed MCCs, organizations should plan to develop a streamlined plan to execute new addendums with processors and third parties.

[E] Data Protection Program Implementation

In addition to managing compliance obligations for third parties and ensuring adequacy of receiving jurisdictions, controllers and processors must also establish a data protection program, including designation of a Data Protection Officer (DPO) when: (1) activities involve "regular and systematic monitoring of data subjects on a large scale", and (2) with processing of sensitive personal information. The DPO can be a shared resource across multiple organizations, but must have "expert knowledge of data protection law" and be aware of organizational risks for the controller or processor, necessitating programmatic and organizational integration (rather than consultation).

Controllers and processors must develop internal policy to ensure internal obligations with GDPR and conduct an annual enterprise risk assessment to assess the effectiveness of the organizational privacy program. The organization must also establish a data inventory of data processing activities and associated systems, conduct Data Protection Impact Assessments (DPIA) for high risk processing activities, and implement Privacy by Design (PbD) or Privacy by Default as part of organizational

53. European Commission, *Model Contracts for the Transfer of Personal Data to Third Countries*, http://ec.europa.eu/justice/data-protection/international-transfers/transfer/index_en.htm (last accessed 4 Jun., 2017).
54. Some vendors are so large that bargaining power wins out over legal obligations; other small vendors do not have the financial ability to establish all that the MCCs require. For these reasons, private contracting often falls to doing business within the EU, simply to avoid these challenges.
55. It should be mentioned that achieving approval for altered MCCs takes a substantial period of time, incompatible with a typical contract negotiation timeframe. Usually, organizations engage Lead DPAs to review MCC templates where the organizational purposes and function cannot fit within the standard MCCs, not for issues negotiating with third parties.

processes.[56] The data inventory, DPIA, and PbD processes will be discussed further in Chapter 7. DPIA findings that could have high risk to the rights and freedoms of data subjects must be disclosed to the Lead DPA using required documents for the particular authority.

[F] Data Breach Notification

One of the most substantial changes from the EU Data Protection Directive is the data breach notification requirement. The GDPR establishes different data breach obligations depending on whether the organization is a processor or controller. Controllers are responsible for timely data breach notification activities including individual data subject notification and Lead DPA notification.[57] Controllers may contractually outsource notification obligations to processors; however, controllers are responsible for any failure to meet time or notification content objectives.

Under the GDPR, controllers must notify their Lead DPA of any data breach as soon as reasonably possible and in any event within 72 hours. Organizations may have a difficult time: (1) ascertaining that a data breach has occurred, and (2) determining who has been affected, and at the time of writing, it is not clear when the 72-hour maximum begins. Organizations that cannot meet the 72-hour requirement must provide a "reasoned justification" for the delay.

Circumstances that are unlikely to result in a risk to the "rights and freedoms of natural persons" do not require notification. These circumstances likely include situations where organizations have validated that no personal information has been compromised, or when personal information has been accessed, it was unreadable (e.g., encrypted, masked, pseudonymized, obfuscated). However, circumstances that are likely to result in high risk to the rights and freedoms of individuals will require notification to data subjects in addition to the DPA. When data subject notification efforts are considered "disproportionate," organizations may use alternative communication means, such as media announcements.

One can expect that a reasonable organization would notify as soon as it can reasonably ascertain data subjects affected by the data breach. Organizations complying with GDPR will therefore need to reinvest in incident response processes to ensure timely and efficient data breach identification and notification procedures (described in Chapter 13). Notification contents include:

- Nature of the data breach (number of records affected, categories of data subjects)
- Data protection officer's contact information
- Likely consequences of the data breach

56. For more information on contents for a DPIA, *see* Data Protection Working Party, Guidelines on Data Protection Impact Assessments, 17/EN, WP 248 (4 Apr. 2017), http://ec.europa.eu/newsroom/document.cfm?doc_id=44137.

57. It is strongly advised for co-controllers to determine contractually which organization is responsible for data breach notification and under which circumstances to reduce confusion and clearly establish accountability.

- Description of how the controller will respond to the breach and mitigate damages

Organizations should provide the information as soon as possible, and the information may be provided in phases to ensure timely notification. Organizations that do not notify without undue delay may be subject to fines or penalties under the GDPR, although at the time of writing, no specific guidelines have been provided for determining to what actions will be considered "undue delay."

§2.04 EUROPEAN DATA PROTECTION BOARD

The Article 29 WP, created by the EU Data Protection Directive (95/46/EC), has shown tremendous leadership in shepherding the GDPR through passage and drafting Guidelines to ensure understanding of EU concepts. The Article 29 WP has played an important role in recommending legislative changes, leading data protection agreements, such as the United States (U.S.) Privacy Shield, and issuing opinions that interpret data protection law.

Under the GDPR, the Article 29 Working Party is now the EDPB:

> Article 68
>
> 1. The European Data Protection Board (the "Board") is hereby established as a body of the Union and shall have legal personality.
> 2. The Board shall be represented by its Chair.
> 3. The Board shall be composed of the head of one supervisory authority of each Member State and of the EDPS, or their respective representatives.

Although it is unknown to what extent the EDPB will adopt previously passed opinions, it is likely that previous interpretations of legal concepts under the Data Protection Directive will meet the same concepts under the GDPR. The most recent opinions (Guidelines are adopted as official opinions in these versions) are as follows:

- 2016 Guidelines on the right to "data portability"[58]
- 2017 Guidelines on the right to "data portability"[59]
- 2017 Data Processing in a Work Environment.[60]

The Article 29 WP also adopted guidelines (recommended but not an official opinion) in cooperation with DPAs representing each member country:

---

58. Opinion 04/2016: Guidelines on the right to "data portability", http://ec.europa.eu/newsroom/document.cfm?doc_id=40820.
59. Opinion 01/2017: Guidelines on the right to "data portability", http://ec.europa.eu/newsroom/document.cfm?doc_id=44103.
60. Opinion 2/2017: Data Processing in a Work Environment, http://ec.europa.eu/newsroom/document.cfm?doc_id=45631.

- Guidelines on Data Protection Impact Assessment (DPIA) and determining whether processing is "likely to result in a high risk" for the purposes of Regulation 2016/679[61]
- Guidelines on the right to "data portability."[62]

Opinions and guidelines usually provide additional, practical information and interpretations necessary for organizations when implementing information privacy programs concerning EU data subjects.

§2.05 THE ePRIVACY DIRECTIVE

The EC passed the Directive on Privacy and Electronic Communications, "ePrivacy Directive" in 2002. When passed, the ePrivacy Directive aimed to provide additional information and "complement and particularise" similar but uncovered topics in the Data Protection Directive.[63] Most of the ePrivacy Directive applies to Internet Service Providers (ISPs) or Web application developers that provide communications or other services, although commentary on cookies applies to Website providers. Article 13 applies to any organization involved in unsolicited phone calls using auto-dialing activities and distribution of unsolicited e-mails. In line with the GDPR, service providers must securely protect communications within systems and notify subscribers of data breaches.

Under Article 6, providers must anonymize traffic data related to subscribers, but may market to subscribers with subscriber consent. Providers may process location data other than traffic data, but only with subscriber consent. Under Article 13, organizations may contact individuals via automated dialing for direct marketing purposes when they have given prior consent and via e-mail when the recipient can clearly identify the sender and can easily opt out of future mailings.

The ePrivacy Directive also references cookies, although it does not specify procedures with regard to notice and consent, resulting in various cookie standards established through country law. *Cookies* are small text files stored on an individual's computer, allowing for the individual's identity or activities to be recorded (explained further in Chapter 8). Many organizations include information about cookies in the standard privacy notice because it appropriately reinforces any other cookie notification techniques used, such as banners or "pop-up" windows.

Cookie notice requires consent of some type, and each country interprets the consent requirement for its residents. Some countries have permitted banner display

---

61. ARTICLE 29 WORKING PARTY, *Guidelines on Data Protection Impact Assessment (DPIA) and determining whether processing is "likely to result in a high risk" for the purposes of Regulation 2016/679*, http://ec.europa.eu/newsroom/document.cfm?doc_id=44137.
62. ARTICLE 29 WORKING PARTY, *Guidelines on the right to "data portability"*, http://ec.europa.eu/newsroom/document.cfm?doc_id=44099.
63. EUROPEAN Commission, Directive 2002/58/EC of the European Parliament and of the Council of July 12, 2002 concerning the processing of personal data and the protection of privacy in the electronic communications sector (2002), http://eur-lex.europa.eu/legal-content/EN/ALL/?uri=CELEX:32002L0058.

with a requirement for an individual to click "I agree" within the banner as explicit consent. Other countries require visible cookie notice without interaction or implied consent. Although countries have not agreed on the appropriate method, individuals can refuse to have a cookie placed on their machine. Further, the cookie notice used must appear when an individual first accesses the Website, from any link.

Although the ePrivacy Directive may have limited use to date, the GDPR has co-established a marketing consent requirement, and the EU has begun drafting an ePrivacy regulation to complement the GDPR and resolve inconsistencies in current ePrivacy Directive implementation.

[A] Passages of Note: ePrivacy Directive

Article 13

Unsolicited communications

1. The use of automated calling systems without human intervention (automatic calling machines), facsimile machines (fax) or electronic mail for the purposes of direct marketing may only be allowed in respect of subscribers who have given their prior consent.
2. Notwithstanding paragraph 1, where a natural or legal person obtains from its customers their electronic contact details for electronic mail, in the context of the sale of a product or a service, in accordance with Directive 95/46/EC, the same natural or legal person may use these electronic contact details for direct marketing of its own similar products or services provided that customers clearly and distinctly are given the opportunity to object, free of charge and in an easy manner, to such use of electronic contact details when they are collected and on the occasion of each message in case the customer has not initially refused such use.
3. Member States shall take appropriate measures to ensure that, free of charge, unsolicited communications for purposes of direct marketing, in cases other than those referred to in paragraphs 1 and 2, are not allowed either without the consent of the subscribers concerned or in respect of subscribers who do not wish to receive these communications, the choice between these options to be determined by national legislation.
4. In any event, the practice of sending electronic mail for purposes of direct marketing disguising or concealing the identity of the sender on whose behalf the communication is made, or without a valid address to which the recipient may send a request that such communications cease, shall be prohibited.
5. Paragraphs 1 and 3 shall apply to subscribers who are natural persons. Member States shall also ensure, in the framework of Community law and applicable national legislation, that the legitimate interests of subscribers other than natural persons with regard to unsolicited communications are sufficiently protected.

Article 4

Security

1. The provider of a publicly available electronic communications service must take appropriate technical and organisational measures to safeguard security of its services, if necessary in conjunction with the provider of the public communications network with respect to network security. Having regard to

the state of the art and the cost of their implementation, these measures shall ensure a level of security appropriate to the risk presented.

2. In case of a particular risk of a breach of the security of the network, the provider of a publicly available electronic communications service must inform the subscribers concerning such risk and, where the risk lies outside the scope of the measures to be taken by the service provider, of any possible remedies, including an indication of the likely costs involved.

Article 5

Confidentiality of the communications

1. Member States shall ensure the confidentiality of communications and the related traffic data by means of a public communications network and publicly available electronic communications services, through national legislation. In particular, they shall prohibit listening, tapping, storage or other kinds of interception or surveillance of communications and the related traffic data by persons other than users, without the consent of the users concerned, except when legally authorised to do so in accordance with Article 15(1). This paragraph shall not prevent technical storage which is necessary for the conveyance of a communication without prejudice to the principle of confidentiality.

(25) However, such devices, for instance so-called "cookies", can be a legitimate and useful tool, for example, in analysing the effectiveness of website design and advertising, and in verifying the identity of users engaged in on-line transactions. Where such devices, for instance cookies, are intended for a legitimate purpose, such as to facilitate the provision of information society services, their use should be allowed on condition that users are provided with clear and precise information in accordance with Directive 95/46/EC about the purposes of cookies or similar devices so as to ensure that users are made aware of information being placed on the terminal equipment they are using. Users should have the opportunity to refuse to have a cookie or similar device stored on their terminal equipment. This is particularly important where users other than the original user have access to the terminal equipment and thereby to any data containing privacy-sensitive information stored on such equipment. Information and the right to refuse may be offered once for the use of various devices to be installed on the user's terminal equipment during the same connection and also covering any further use that may be made of those devices during subsequent connections. The methods for giving information, offering a right to refuse or requesting consent should be made as user-friendly as possible.

§2.06 WORKPLACE PRIVACY

In Europe, privacy considerations combine regional and country laws and council decisions. For EU Member States, collection and processing of personal information extends to personnel within an employment relationship in an organization. However, personnel privacy considerations in Europe also depend heavily on local employment law within each European country.[64] In addition to laws on appropriate background check procedures and surveillance protocol, organizations with employees located in European countries will likely work closely with Works Councils for a variety of privacy and cybersecurity-related activities.[65]

Although many multi-national organizations manage employee data differently than customer data, under the GDPR both enjoy similar protection. Employee personal information (including information considered public in other countries) such as name, organization, business address, or e-mail, likely will be considered personal information under the GDPR. Individuals, in a business capacity, can request information removal if collected, consistent with consent revocation or informed consent procedures, as well as rights of access, correction, and erasure.

Under the GDPR, data subjects (such as prospective or current personnel) must explicitly consent to sharing SPI with a prospective or current employer, which organizations may or may not specify in employment contracts. Organizations should clearly understand where the employer requires SPI to support explicit employment requirements, such as a national identifier to validate work status, as well as voluntary information used for participation in other programs, e.g., health screening provided as a service to employees or club membership.

The legal basis for processing personal information in an employment situation usually involves a contractual relationship. The employment agreement provides this contractual basis for processing; therefore, organizations should consider potential employment-related uses for personal information when drawing up standard employment language. Some examples of other contents recommended for inclusion in contracts follow:

- Required information for employment verification
- A description of standard employment personal information processed and for what purposes
- Communication of the data subject's rights with respect to information processed (access, transfer, correction, revocation, deletion)
- An incidental employment "benefits" description involving personal information considered part of the employment offer (e.g., information required to provide a company car)
- Internal surveillance policies for equipment or physical premises
- Obligations to follow internal policies and potential impacts for not following such policies (e.g., reprimand or termination)
- Data transfer processes (e.g., multi-national organizations may transfer data to another country for storage).

64. Organizations with operations in other regions should clearly understand both: (1) applicable employee surveillance laws and (2) validate whether the omnibus or sectoral privacy laws apply to employee personal information, which may additionally restrict information collected during surveillance. For example, organizations operating in countries that include pictures or sounds in the description of personal information and extend the law to employment activities may require consent to capture any surveillance information, as well.

65. European Trade Union Association, *European Works Councils* (2016), http://www.worker-participation.eu/European-Works-Councils.

For processing activities outside reasonably expected employment activities, organizations should consider executing a separate consent document. Specifically, organizations should provide notice and collect consent for SPI collected outside basic employment verification and for personal information collection outside the foundational employment relationship, such as additional services like insurance, well-being initiatives, family information, or conflict of interest activities.

Organizations collecting personal information within an employment relationship must implement procedures consistent with other types of data processing: understand data location via a data inventory, appropriately manage notice versions and consent records, provide access and correction opportunities for data subjects, and delete records upon request and when no longer necessary (affording appropriate retention time according to applicable employment law).

[A] Surveillance

Many countries limit SPI collection to prevent employment discrimination. Often, a five-year limit of inquiry applies, including credit checks. Although these laws protect employees, they can also cause due diligence challenges regarding data subject privacy and cybersecurity for an organization. Most organizations, for example, do not prefer to hire individuals who have committed financial, fraud, or identity theft crimes for positions directly handling data subject or other highly confidential organizational data. Further, many controllers working with a data processor also expect processors to exhibit due diligence when hiring personnel and sub-contractors. From a cybersecurity perspective, often individuals engaged in complex plans to compromise organizations seek employment at the target organization or at a provider for the organization in lower-level roles with access to data (e.g., social engineering described in Chapter 13). Organizations should clearly understand employment data collection restrictions in each country prior to collecting this information.

Some countries do not permit criminal background checks, and when they do limit information collected. In the United Kingdom (U.K.), for example, criminal records checks are permitted only if they are relevant for the role, for an individual the organization intends to hire (after narrowing the field of applicants), and for unspent convictions (spent convictions reflect past convictions without re-offending). Prior to engaging in a search for prospective employees, organizations should determine which crimes directly affect employment fitness for a particular role.

In the EU, organizations should provide notice and collect consent for background checks, including specific references to SPI collected through this process and intention to conduct public checks (e.g., Internet searches). Organizations should share the results of these background checks with the individual and allow for an opportunity to object and provide a correction. Organizations should then conduct a recheck and retain any formal contestation. After hiring, internal policies should reiterate the presence of physical surveillance, and entry/exit areas should make individuals aware of surveillance activities.

Physical surveillance not only protects human and property assets, but also surveillance provides critical information to detect information exposure and loss (personal information loss and proprietary or trade secret information). As is evident under the GDPR, notice and consent form the cornerstone of surveillance in the workplace, and several privacy concepts apply to surveillance, as well.

Surveillance creates challenges largely due to the intersection of personal and professional lives, including personal activities within a facility, use of personal devices, and personal conversations. For this reason, organizations should not install surveillance equipment in personal spaces, such as bathrooms, locker rooms, offices, or cubicles. Instead, organizations should install closed-circuit television (CCTV) only in public areas, such as entrances/exits of floors or buildings, elevators, hallways, or areas where visitors sign in and out or personnel must use a keycard, key, or biometric information to enter the premises. Further, CCTV should only record images, not sound, clearly and visibly provide notice as to camera presence and image recording. Recording and should meet a reasonable, documented purpose.[66] Personnel verbally share detailed personal information or other protected information within the work day (political opinions, health information), including on mobile or cellular phones brought into the workplace; sound recordings pose more potential harm to employees than images taken from shared and public spaces, although all recordings pose some risk.

CCTV video footage retention may also challenge organizations. Video retention can require substantial and expensive digital storage resources and may require additional justification for retention, video retention often aids investigations and may provide evidence. Both in cybersecurity investigations which involve insiders or outsiders gaining access to a facility and in non-cybersecurity investigations, CCTV recordings can provide a critical piece of information in a chain of events. However, even where organizations choose to retain recordings for a longer period of time, local laws may restrict duration. Organizations should work with internal records retention personnel to ensure CCTV retention timeframes match applicable laws.

[B] Remote Monitoring of Computer Systems

Organizations also routinely surveil computer use through *remote monitoring*. Remote monitoring may include reviewing Websites visited, e-mails sent and received from organizational addresses, files downloaded or uploaded, and resource use by date and time. Organizations conduct remote monitoring to ensure personnel use organization-owned resources primarily for business use, to avoid data loss, and also to prevent cyberattacks. Organizations typically manage privacy expectations with remote monitoring by: (1) notifying personnel of acceptable use practices before hire, (2) providing an acceptable use policy, (3) disclosing computer monitoring before computer log-in, and (4) providing alternative connectivity or devices for personal use.

66. Organizations often include placards where individuals enter the premises or in outside areas, such as parking lots, stating "This facility is monitored for security purposes. Cameras will record images in all public areas of this building" or similar.

In the EU, although organizations may surveil personnel, limits apply.[67] The EU has established a foundational understanding that phone calls and e-mail used from work phone numbers or accounts may constitute personal correspondence and enjoy reasonable privacy considerations. Most recently, *Bărbulescu v. Romania*, decided by the ECHR in early 2016, established that although organizations may surveil personnel and terminate based on surveillance, organizations must adequately notify personnel prior to surveillance activities commencing.

The ECHR stated in *Bărbulescu* that although organizations permitting resource use for personal matters must afford personnel a reasonable expectation of privacy, organizations barring resource use for personal matters may have reasonable rights to surveil activities. The employer's interference should still be limited in scope, proportionate, and fulfill a legal purpose, rather than indeterminant and broad.

After *Bărbulescu*, organizations may have comparably more latitude in surveillance when limited, but organizations must still notify personnel of the surveillance. Usually prior surveillance notification will be accomplished through employment contract provisions, the acceptable use policy, and a specific disclosure upon log-in of the employer's intention to monitor communications:

> All Organization A resources are monitored to protect organizational resources from misuse and misappropriation. By logging onto this machine, you understand that any communications may be monitored for these purposes.

Many EU member countries have Works Councils that will approve monitoring activities. Organizations working in these should expect to provide information about monitoring or other security activities, such as personal Webmail blocking or other activities affecting employee rights and privacy, to Works Councils at least a year or more before implementing these processes. Works Councils represent European workers, and organizations with European employees should consider Works Council's approval for any major changes in work processes and activities. When the Works Council ha not approved process changes (including standard work processes, not just those affecting cybersecurity or privacy), they will not permit the organization to release process changes in that country.

In line with the Works Councils' determination related to reasonable affordances for EU workers, several organizations have implemented a "separation" approach. For example, following *Bărbulescu*, employers have begun more rigorously blocking personal Webmail and messaging Websites, communicating monitoring activities, but have also provided alternative resources for personal activities. These organizations usually have dedicated space and resources for personal use, such as a room where personnel may conduct personal activities, such as placing a phone call or using a

67. European Court of Human Rights, Bărbulescu v. Romania, 61496/08 (12 Jan. 2016), http://www.clujust.ro/wp-content/uploads/2016/01/CASE-OF-BARBULESCU-v.-ROMANIA.pdf.

mobile device, as well as public terminal computers or a "guest" wireless network for this purpose.

Although very restrictive, organizations employing a separation approach have also improved their cybersecurity posture. For example, organizations prohibiting personal mobile or other peripheral use (e.g., USB sticks, external hard drives, or CD-ROMs) within the workspace generally experience less information loss. Further, organizations blocking Webmail, online messaging, and file download sites often reduce the occurrence of viruses or malware, improving organizational cybersecurity.

[C] Passages of Note: GDPR

[1] Definitions

Article 6

Processing shall be lawful only if and to the extent that at least one of the following applies:

(a) the data subject has given consent to the processing of his or her personal data for one or more specific purposes;
(b) processing is necessary for the performance of a contract to which the data subject is party or in order to take steps at the request of the data subject prior to entering into a contract;
(c) processing is necessary for compliance with a legal obligation to which the controller is subject;
(d) processing is necessary in order to protect the vital interests of the data subject or of another natural person;
(e) processing is necessary for the performance of a task carried out in the public interest or in the exercise of official authority vested in the controller;
(f) processing is necessary for the purposes of the legitimate interests pursued by the controller or by a third party, except where such interests are overridden by the interests or fundamental rights and freedoms of the data subject which require protection of personal data, in particular where the data subject is a child.

[2] Internal Code of Conduct

Article 40

1. The Member States, the supervisory authorities, the Board and the Commission shall encourage the drawing up of codes of conduct intended to contribute to the proper application of this Regulation, taking account of the specific features of the various processing sectors and the specific needs of micro, small and medium-sized enterprises.
2. Associations and other bodies representing categories of controllers or processors may prepare codes of conduct, or amend or extend such codes, for the purpose of specifying the application of this Regulation, such as with regard to:
   (a) fair and transparent processing;

(b) the legitimate interests pursued by controllers in specific contexts;
(c) the collection of personal data;
(d) the pseudonymisation of personal data;
(e) the information provided to the public and to data subjects;
(f) the exercise of the rights of data subjects;
(g) the information provided to, and the protection of, children, and the manner in which the consent of the holders of parental responsibility over children is to be obtained;
(h) the measures and procedures referred to in Articles 24 and 25 and the measures to ensure security of processing referred to in Article 32;
(i) the notification of personal data breaches to supervisory authorities and the communication of such personal data breaches to data subjects;
(j) the transfer of personal data to third countries or international organisations; or
(k) out-of-court proceedings and other dispute resolution procedures for resolving disputes between controllers and data subjects with regard to processing, without prejudice to the rights of data subjects pursuant to Articles 77 and 79.

3. In addition to adherence by controllers or processors subject to this Regulation, codes of conduct approved pursuant to paragraph 5 of this Article and having general validity pursuant to paragraph 9 of this Article may also be adhered to by controllers or processors that are not subject to this Regulation pursuant to Article 3 in order to provide appropriate safeguards within the framework of personal data transfers to third countries or international organisations under the terms referred to in point (e) of Article 46(2). Such controllers or processors shall make binding and enforceable commitments, via contractual or other legally binding instruments, to apply those appropriate safeguards including with regard to the rights of data subjects.
4. A code of conduct referred to in paragraph 2 of this Article shall contain mechanisms which enable the body referred to in Article 41(1) to carry out the mandatory monitoring of compliance with its provisions by the controllers or processors which undertake to apply it, without prejudice to the tasks and powers of supervisory authorities competent pursuant to Article 55 or 56.

[3] Controller and Processor

Article 27

1. Where Article 3(2) applies [controller or processor not in the EU], the controller or the processor shall designate in writing a representative in the Union . . .
3. The representative shall be established in one of the Member States where the data subjects, whose personal data are processed in relation to the offering of goods or services to them, or whose behaviour is monitored, are.
4. The representative shall be mandated by the controller or processor to be addressed in addition to or instead of the controller or the processor by, in particular, supervisory authorities and data subjects, on all issues related to processing, for the purposes of ensuring compliance with this Regulation.

Article 4

7. "Controller" means the natural or legal person, public authority, agency or other body which, alone or jointly with others, determines the purposes and

means of the processing of personal data; where the purposes and means of such processing are determined by Union or Member State law, the controller or the specific criteria for its nomination may be provided for by Union or Member State law.

Article 26

1. Where two or more controllers jointly determine the purposes and means of processing, they shall be joint controllers. They shall in a transparent manner determine their respective responsibilities for compliance with the obligations under this Regulation, in particular as regards the exercising of the rights of the data subject and their respective duties to provide the information referred to in Articles 13 and 14, by means of an arrangement between them unless, and in so far as, the respective responsibilities of the controllers are determined by Union or Member State law to which the controllers are subject. The arrangement may designate a contact point for data subjects.

Article 28

1. Where processing is to be carried out on behalf of a controller, the controller shall use only processors providing sufficient guarantees to implement appropriate technical and organisational measures in such a manner that processing will meet the requirements of this Regulation and ensure the protection of the rights of the data subject.

Article 30

1. Each controller and, where applicable, the controller's representative, shall maintain a record of processing activities under its responsibility. That record shall contain all of the following information:
   (a) the name and contact details of the controller and, where applicable, the joint controller, the controller's representative and the data protection officer;
   (b) the purposes of the processing;
   (c) a description of the categories of data subjects and of the categories of personal data;
   (d) the categories of recipients to whom the personal data have been or will be disclosed including recipients in third countries or international organisations;
   (e) where applicable, transfers of personal data to a third country or an international organisation, including the identification of that third country or international organisation and, in the case of transfers referred to in the second subparagraph of Article 49(1), the documentation of suitable safeguards;
   (f) where possible, the envisaged time limits for erasure of the different categories of data;
   (g) where possible, a general description of the technical and organisational security measures referred to in Article 32(1).

Article 40

1. The controller or the processor and, where applicable, the controller's or the processor's representative, shall make the record available to the supervisory authority on request.

Article 28

3. Processing by a processor shall be governed by a contract or other legal act under Union or Member State law, that is binding on the processor with regard to the controller and that sets out the subject-matter and duration of the processing, the nature and purpose of the processing, the type of personal data and categories of data subjects and the obligations and rights of the controller. That contract or other legal act shall stipulate, in particular, that the processor:
   (a) processes the personal data only on documented instructions from the controller, including with regard to transfers of personal data to a third country or an international organisation, unless required to do so by Union or Member State law to which the processor is subject; in such a case, the processor shall inform the controller of that legal requirement before processing, unless that law prohibits such information on important grounds of public interest;
   (b) ensures that persons authorised to process the personal data have committed themselves to confidentiality or are under an appropriate statutory obligation of confidentiality;
   (c) takes all measures required pursuant to Article 32;
   (d) respects the conditions referred to in paragraphs 2 and 4 for engaging another processor;
   (e) taking into account the nature of the processing, assists the controller by appropriate technical and organisational measures, insofar as this is possible, for the fulfilment of the controller's obligation to respond to requests for exercising the data subject's rights laid down in Chapter III;
   (f) assists the controller in ensuring compliance with the obligations pursuant to Articles 32 to 36 taking into account the nature of processing and the information available to the processor;
   (g) at the choice of the controller, deletes or returns all the personal data to the controller after the end of the provision of services relating to processing, and deletes existing copies unless Union or Member State law requires storage of the personal data;
   (h) makes available to the controller all information necessary to demonstrate compliance with the obligations laid down in this Article and allow for and contribute to audits, including inspections, conducted by the controller or another auditor mandated by the controller.
   (i) With regard to point (h) of the first subparagraph, the processor shall immediately inform the controller if, in its opinion, an instruction infringes this Regulation or other Union or Member State data protection provisions.

Article 4

8. "processor" means a natural or legal person, public authority, agency or other body which processes personal data on behalf of the controller;

Article 28

2. The processor shall not engage another processor without prior specific or general written authorisation of the controller. In the case of general written authorisation, the processor shall inform the controller of any intended changes concerning the addition or replacement of other processors, thereby giving the controller the opportunity to object to such changes.

4. Where a processor engages another processor for carrying out specific processing activities on behalf of the controller, the same data protection obligations as set out in the contract or other legal act between the controller and the processor as referred to in paragraph 3 shall be imposed on that other processor by way of a contract or other legal act under Union or Member State law, in particular providing sufficient guarantees to implement appropriate technical and organisational measures in such a manner that the processing will meet the requirements of this Regulation. Where that other processor fails to fulfil its data protection obligations, the initial processor shall remain fully liable to the controller for the performance of that other processor's obligations.

Article 40

2. Each processor and, where applicable, the processor's representative shall maintain a record of all categories of processing activities carried out on behalf of a controller, containing:
   (a) the name and contact details of the processor or processors and of each controller on behalf of which the processor is acting, and, where applicable, of the controller's or the processor's representative, and the data protection officer;
   (b) the categories of processing carried out on behalf of each controller;
   (c) where applicable, transfers of personal data to a third country or an international organisation, including the identification of that third country or international organisation and, in the case of transfers referred to in the second subparagraph of Article 49(1), the documentation of suitable safeguards;
   (d) where possible, a general description of the technical and organisational security measures referred to in Article 32(1).

[4] Data Protection Officer

Article 37

1. The controller and the processor shall designate a data protection officer in any case where:
   (a) the processing is carried out by a public authority or body, except for courts acting in their judicial capacity;
   (b) the core activities of the controller or the processor consist of processing operations which, by virtue of their nature, their scope and/or their purposes, require regular and systematic monitoring of data subjects on a large scale; or
   (c) the core activities of the controller or the processor consist of processing on a large scale of special categories of data pursuant to Article 9 and personal data relating to criminal convictions and offences referred to in Article 10.
2. A group of undertakings may appoint a single data protection officer provided that a data protection officer is easily accessible from each establishment.
5. The data protection officer shall be designated on the basis of professional qualities and, in particular, expert knowledge of data protection law and practices and the ability to fulfil the tasks referred to in Article 39.
6. The data protection officer may be a staff member of the controller or processor, or fulfil the tasks on the basis of a service contract.

7. The controller or the processor shall publish the contact details of the data protection officer and communicate them to the supervisory authority.

Article 38

1. The data protection officer shall have at least the following tasks:
   (a) to inform and advise the controller or the processor and the employees who carry out processing of their obligations pursuant to this Regulation and to other Union or Member State data protection provisions;
   (b) to monitor compliance with this Regulation, with other Union or Member State data protection provisions and with the policies of the controller or processor in relation to the protection of personal data, including the assignment of responsibilities, awareness-raising and training of staff involved in processing operations, and the related audits;
   (c) to provide advice where requested as regards the data protection impact assessment and monitor its performance pursuant to Article 35;
   (d) to cooperate with the supervisory authority;
   (e) to act as the contact point for the supervisory authority on issues relating to processing, including the prior consultation referred to in Article 36, and to consult, where appropriate, with regard to any other matter.
2. The data protection officer shall in the performance of his or her tasks have due regard to the risk associated with processing operations, taking into account the nature, scope, context and purposes of processing.

[5] Collection Limitations

Article 5

1. Personal data shall be:
   (a) processed lawfully, fairly and in a transparent manner in relation to the data subject ("lawfulness, fairness and transparency");
   (b) collected for specified, explicit and legitimate purposes and not further processed in a manner that is incompatible with those purposes; further processing for archiving purposes in the public interest, scientific or historical research purposes or statistical purposes shall, in accordance with Article 89(1), not be considered to be incompatible with the initial purposes ("purpose limitation");
   (c) adequate, relevant and limited to what is necessary in relation to the purposes for which they are processed ("data minimisation");
   (d) accurate and, where necessary, kept up to date; every reasonable step must be taken to ensure that personal data that are inaccurate, having regard to the purposes for which they are processed, are erased or rectified without delay ("accuracy");
   (e) kept in a form which permits identification of data subjects for no longer than is necessary for the purposes for which the personal data are processed; personal data may be stored for longer periods insofar as the personal data will be processed solely for archiving purposes in the public interest, scientific or historical research purposes or statistical purposes in accordance with Article 89(1) subject to implementation of the appropriate technical and organisational measures required by this Regulation in order to safeguard the rights and freedoms of the data subject ("storage limitation");

(f) processed in a manner that ensures appropriate security of the personal data, including protection against unauthorised or unlawful processing and against accidental loss, destruction or damage, using appropriate technical or organisational measures ("integrity and confidentiality").

2. The controller shall be responsible for, and be able to demonstrate compliance with, paragraph 1 ("accountability").

[6] Notice

Article 13

1. Where personal data relating to a data subject are collected from the data subject, the controller shall, at the time when personal data are obtained, provide the data subject with all of the following information:
   (a) the identity and the contact details of the controller and, where applicable, of the controller's representative;
   (b) the contact details of the data protection officer, where applicable;
   (c) the purposes of the processing for which the personal data are intended as well as the legal basis for the processing;
   (d) where the processing is based on point (f) of Article 6(1), the legitimate interests pursued by the controller or by a third party;
   (e) the recipients or categories of recipients of the personal data, if any;
   (f) where applicable, the fact that the controller intends to transfer personal data to a third country or international organisation and the existence or absence of an adequacy decision by the Commission, or in the case of transfers referred to in Article 46 or 47, or the second subparagraph of Article 49(1), reference to the appropriate or suitable safeguards and the means by which to obtain a copy of them or where they have been made available.
2. In addition to the information referred to in paragraph 1, the controller shall, at the time when personal data are obtained, provide the data subject with the following further information necessary to ensure fair and transparent processing:
   (a) the period for which the personal data will be stored, or if that is not possible, the criteria used to determine that period;
   (b) the existence of the right to request from the controller access to and rectification or erasure of personal data or restriction of processing concerning the data subject or to object to processing as well as the right to data portability;
   (c) where the processing is based on point (a) of Article 6(1) or point (a) of Article 9(2), the existence of the right to withdraw consent at any time, without affecting the lawfulness of processing based on consent before its withdrawal;
   (d) the right to lodge a complaint with a supervisory authority;
   (e) whether the provision of personal data is a statutory or contractual requirement, or a requirement necessary to enter into a contract, as well as whether the data subject is obliged to provide the personal data and of the possible consequences of failure to provide such data;
   (f) the existence of automated decision-making, including profiling, referred to in Article 22(1) and (4) and, at least in those cases, meaningful information about the logic involved, as well as the significance and the envisaged consequences of such processing for the data subject.

3. Where the controller intends to further process the personal data for a purpose other than that for which the personal data were collected, the controller shall provide the data subject prior to that further processing with information on that other purpose and with any relevant further information as referred to in paragraph 2.

Article 7

2. If the data subject's consent is given in the context of a written declaration which also concerns other matters, the request for consent shall be presented in a manner which is clearly distinguishable from the other matters, in an intelligible and easily accessible form, using clear and plain language. Any part of such a declaration which constitutes an infringement of this Regulation shall not be binding.

[7] Consent

Article 4

11. "Consent" of the data subject means any freely given, specific, informed and unambiguous indication of the data subject's wishes by which he or she, by a statement or by a clear affirmative action, signifies agreement to the processing of personal data relating to him or her.

Article 7

4. When assessing whether consent is freely given, utmost account shall be taken of whether, inter alia, the performance of a contract, including the provision of a service, is conditional on consent to the processing of personal data that is not necessary for the performance of that contract.
   (32) Consent should be given by a clear affirmative act establishing a freely given, specific, informed and unambiguous indication of the data subject's agreement to the processing of personal data relating to him or her, such as by a written statement, including by electronic means, or an oral statement. This could include ticking a box when visiting an internet website, choosing technical settings for information society services or another statement or conduct which clearly indicates in this context the data subject's acceptance of the proposed processing of his or her personal data. Silence, pre-ticked boxes or inactivity should not therefore constitute consent. Consent should cover all processing activities carried out for the same purpose or purposes. When the processing has multiple purposes, consent should be given for all of them. If the data subject's consent is to be given following a request by electronic means, the request must be clear, concise and not unnecessarily disruptive to the use of the service for which it is provided.
   (42) Where processing is based on the data subject's consent, the controller should be able to demonstrate that the data subject has given consent to the processing operation. In particular in the context of a written declaration on another matter, safeguards should ensure that the data subject is aware of the fact that and the extent to which consent is given. In accordance with Council Directive 93/13/EEC (1) a declaration of consent pre-formulated by the controller should be provided in an intelligible and easily accessible form, using clear and plain language and

it should not contain unfair terms. For consent to be informed, the data subject should be aware at least of the identity of the controller and the purposes of the processing for which the personal data are intended. Consent should not be regarded as freely given if the data subject has no genuine or free choice or is unable to refuse or withdraw consent without detriment.

(51) Such personal data should not be processed, unless processing is allowed in specific cases set out in this Regulation, taking into account that Member States law may lay down specific provisions on data protection in order to adapt the application of the rules of this Regulation for compliance with a legal obligation or for the performance of a task carried out in the public interest or in the exercise of official authority vested in the controller. In addition to the specific requirements for such processing, the general principles and other rules of this Regulation should apply, in particular as regards the conditions for lawful processing. Derogations from the general prohibition for processing such special categories of personal data should be explicitly provided, inter alia, where the data subject gives his or her explicit consent or in respect of specific needs in particular where the processing is carried out in the course of legitimate activities by certain associations or foundations the purpose of which is to permit the exercise of fundamental freedoms.

Article 9

1. Processing of personal data revealing racial or ethnic origin, political opinions, religious or philosophical beliefs, or trade union membership, and the processing of genetic data, biometric data for the purpose of uniquely identifying a natural person, data concerning health or data concerning a natural person's sex life or sexual orientation shall be prohibited.
2. Paragraph 1 shall not apply if one of the following applies:
   (a) the data subject has given explicit consent to the processing of those personal data for one or more specified purposes, except where Union or Member State law provide that the prohibition referred to in paragraph 1 may not be lifted by the data subject;
   (b) processing is necessary for the purposes of carrying out the obligations and exercising specific rights of the controller or of the data subject in the field of employment and social security and social protection law in so far as it is authorised by Union or Member State law or a collective agreement pursuant to Member State law providing for appropriate safeguards for the fundamental rights and the interests of the data subject.

[8] Choice

Article 6

4. Where the processing for a purpose <u>other than that for which the personal data have been collected</u> is not based on the data subject's consent or on a Union or Member State law which constitutes a necessary and proportionate measure in a democratic society to safeguard the objectives referred to in Article 23(1), the controller shall, in order to ascertain whether processing for another purpose is compatible with the purpose for which the personal data are initially collected, take into account, inter alia:

(a) any link between the purposes for which the personal data have been collected and the purposes of the intended further processing;
(b) the context in which the personal data have been collected, in particular regarding the relationship between data subjects and the controller;
(c) the nature of the personal data, in particular whether special categories of personal data are processed, pursuant to Article 9, or whether personal data related to criminal convictions and offences are processed, pursuant to Article 10;
(d) the possible consequences of the intended further processing for data subjects;
(e) the existence of appropriate safeguards, which may include encryption or pseudonymisation.

[9] Revocation/Objection

Article 7

3. The data subject shall have the right to withdraw his or her consent at any time. The withdrawal of consent shall not affect the lawfulness of processing based on consent before its withdrawal. Prior to giving consent, the data subject shall be informed thereof. It shall be as easy to withdraw as to give consent.

[10] Retention

Article 7

1. Where processing is based on consent, the controller shall be able to demonstrate that the data subject has consented to processing of his or her personal data.

[11] Access

Article 20

1. The data subject shall have the right to receive the personal data concerning him or her, which he or she has provided to a controller, in a structured, commonly used and machine-readable format and have the right to transmit those data to another controller without hindrance from the controller to which the personal data have been provided, where:
   (a) the processing is based on consent pursuant to point (a) of Article 6(1) or point (a) of Article 9(2) or on a contract pursuant to point (b) of Article 6(1); and
   (b) the processing is carried out by automated means.

[12] Correction

(71) In order to ensure fair and transparent processing in respect of the data subject, taking into account the specific circumstances and context in which the personal data are processed, the controller should use appropriate mathematical or statistical procedures for the profiling, implement technical and organisational measures appropriate to ensure, in particular, that factors which result in inaccuracies in personal data are corrected and the risk of errors is minimised.

[13] Interoperability/Portability

(68) Data controllers should be encouraged to develop interoperable formats that enable data portability.

Article 20

1. The data subject shall have the right to receive the personal data concerning him or her, which he or she has provided to a controller, in a structured, commonly used and machine-readable format and have the right to transmit those data to another controller without hindrance from the controller to which the personal data have been provided, where:
   (a) the processing is based on consent pursuant to point (a) of Article 6(1) or point (a) of Article 9(2) or on a contract pursuant to point (b) of Article 6(1); and
   (b) the processing is carried out by automated means.
2. In exercising his or her right to data portability pursuant to paragraph 1, the data subject shall have the right to have the personal data transmitted directly from one controller to another, where technically feasible.

[14] Automated Processing

(68) To further strengthen the control over his or her own data, where the processing of personal data is carried out by automated means, the data subject should also be allowed to receive personal data concerning him or her which he or she has provided to a controller in a structured, commonly used, machine-readable and interoperable format, and to transmit it to another controller.

(71) The data subject should have the right not to be subject to a decision, which may include a measure, evaluating personal aspects relating to him or her which is based solely on automated processing and which produces legal effects concerning him or her or similarly significantly affects him or her, such as automatic refusal of an online credit application or e-recruiting practices without any human intervention. Such processing includes "profiling" that consists of any form of automated processing of personal data evaluating the personal aspects relating to a natural person, in particular to analyse or predict

aspects concerning the data subject's performance at work, economic situation, health, personal preferences or interests, reliability or behaviour, location or movements, where it produces legal effects concerning him or her or similarly significantly affects him or her.

Article 21

1. The data subject shall have the right to object, on grounds relating to his or her particular situation, at any time to processing of personal data concerning him or her which is based on point (e) or (f) of Article 6(1), including profiling based on those provisions. The controller shall no longer process the personal data unless the controller demonstrates compelling legitimate grounds for the processing which override the interests, rights and freedoms of the data subject or for the establishment, exercise or defence of legal claims.
2. Where personal data are processed for direct marketing purposes, the data subject shall have the right to object at any time to processing of personal data concerning him or her for such marketing, which includes profiling to the extent that it is related to such direct marketing.
3. Where the data subject objects to processing for direct marketing purposes, the personal data shall no longer be processed for such purposes.

[15] Erasure

(65) A data subject should have the right to have personal data concerning him or her rectified and a "right to be forgotten" where the retention of such data infringes this Regulation or Union or Member State law to which the controller is subject. In particular, a data subject should have the right to have his or her personal data erased and no longer processed where the personal data are no longer necessary in relation to the purposes for which they are collected or otherwise processed, where a data subject has withdrawn his or her consent or objects to the processing of personal data concerning him or her, or where the processing of his or her personal data does not otherwise comply with this Regulation. That right is relevant in particular where the data subject has given his or her consent as a child and is not fully aware of the risks involved by the processing, and later wants to remove such personal data, especially on the internet. The data subject should be able to exercise that right notwithstanding the fact that he or she is no longer a child.

Article 17

1. The data subject shall have the right to obtain from the controller the erasure of personal data concerning him or her without undue delay and the controller shall have the obligation to erase personal data without undue delay where one of the following grounds applies:
   (a) the personal data are no longer necessary in relation to the purposes for which they were collected or otherwise processed;
   (b) the data subject withdraws consent on which the processing is based according to point (a) of Article 6(1), or point (a) of Article 9(2), and where there is no other legal ground for the processing;
   (c) the data subject objects to the processing pursuant to Article 21(1) and there are no overriding legitimate grounds for the processing, or the data subject objects to the processing pursuant to Article 21(2).

[16] Special Considerations

(38) Children merit specific protection with regard to their personal data, as they may be less aware of the risks, consequences and safeguards concerned and their rights in relation to the processing of personal data. Such specific protection should, in particular, apply to the use of personal data of children for the purposes of marketing or creating personality or user profiles and the collection of personal data with regard to children when using services offered directly to a child. The consent of the holder of parental responsibility should not be necessary in the context of preventive or counselling services offered directly to a child.

Article 8

1. Where point (a) of Article 6(1) applies, in relation to the offer of information society services directly to a child, the processing of the personal data of a child shall be lawful where the child is at least 16 years old. Where the child is below the age of 16 years, such processing shall be lawful only if and to the extent that consent is given or authorised by the holder of parental responsibility over the child.

   Member States may provide by law for a lower age for those purposes provided that such lower age is not below 13 years.
2. The controller shall make reasonable efforts to verify in such cases that consent is given or authorised by the holder of parental responsibility over the child, taking into consideration available technology.

[17] Marketing

(70) Where personal data are processed for the purposes of direct marketing, the data subject should have the right to object to such processing, including profiling to the extent that it is related to such direct marketing, whether with regard to initial or further processing, at any time and free of charge. That right should be explicitly brought to the attention of the data subject and presented clearly and separately from any other information.

[18] Transfer Adequacy

(108) In the absence of an adequacy decision, the controller or processor should take measures to compensate for the lack of data protection in a third country by way of appropriate safeguards for the data subject. Such appropriate safeguards may consist of making use of binding corporate rules, standard data protection clauses adopted by the Commission, standard data protection clauses adopted by a supervisory authority or contractual clauses authorised by a supervisory authority. Those safeguards should ensure compliance with data protection requirements and the rights of the data subjects appropriate to processing within the Union, including the availability of enforceable data subject rights and of effective legal remedies, including to obtain effective administrative or judicial redress and to claim compensation, in the Union or

in a third country. They should relate in particular to compliance with the general principles relating to personal data processing, the principles of data protection by design and by default. Transfers may also be carried out by public authorities or bodies with public authorities or bodies in third countries or with international organisations with corresponding duties or functions, including on the basis of provisions to be inserted into administrative arrangements, such as a memorandum of understanding, providing for enforceable and effective rights for data subjects. Authorisation by the competent supervisory authority should be obtained when the safeguards are provided for in administrative arrangements that are not legally binding.

Article 45

1. A transfer of personal data to a third country or an international organisation may take place where the Commission has decided that the third country, a territory or one or more specified sectors within that third country, or the international organisation in question ensures an adequate level of protection. Such a transfer shall not require any specific authorisation.

Article 49

1. In the absence of an adequacy decision pursuant to Article 45(3), or of appropriate safeguards pursuant to Article 46, including binding corporate rules, a transfer or a set of transfers of personal data to a third country or an international organisation shall take place only on one of the following conditions:
   (a) the data subject has explicitly consented to the proposed transfer, after having been informed of the possible risks of such transfers for the data subject due to the absence of an adequacy decision and appropriate safeguards;
   (b) the transfer is necessary for the performance of a contract between the data subject and the controller or the implementation of pre-contractual measures taken at the data subject's request;
   (d) the transfer is necessary for important reasons of public interest.

Article 28

7. The Commission may lay down standard contractual clauses for the matters referred to in paragraph 3 and 4 of this Article and in accordance with the examination procedure referred to in Article 93(2).
8. A supervisory authority may adopt standard contractual clauses for the matters referred to in paragraph 3 and 4 of this Article and in accordance with the consistency mechanism referred to in Article 63.

[19] DPIA

Article 35

1. Where a type of processing in particular using new technologies, and taking into account the nature, scope, context and purposes of the processing, is likely to result in a high risk to the rights and freedoms of natural persons, the controller shall, prior to the processing, carry out an assessment of the impact of the envisaged processing operations on the protection of personal data. A

single assessment may address a set of similar processing operations that present similar high risks.

Article 35

2. The controller shall seek the advice of the data protection officer, where designated, when carrying out a data protection impact assessment.
3. A data protection impact assessment referred to in paragraph 1 shall in particular be required in the case of:
   (a) a systematic and extensive evaluation of personal aspects relating to natural persons which is based on automated processing, including profiling, and on which decisions are based that produce legal effects concerning the natural person or similarly significantly affect the natural person;
   (b) processing on a large scale of special categories of data referred to in Article 9(1), or of personal data relating to criminal convictions and offences referred to in Article 10; or
   (c) a systematic monitoring of a publicly accessible area on a large scale.

3. Article 35-7. The assessment shall contain at least:

(a) a systematic description of the envisaged processing operations and the purposes of the processing, including, where applicable, the legitimate interest pursued by the controller;
(b) an assessment of the necessity and proportionality of the processing operations in relation to the purposes;
(c) an assessment of the risks to the rights and freedoms of data subjects referred to in paragraph 1; and
(d) the measures envisaged to address the risks, including safeguards, security measures and mechanisms to ensure the protection of personal data and to demonstrate compliance with this Regulation taking into account the rights and legitimate interests of data subjects and other persons concerned.

Article 36

1. The controller shall consult the supervisory authority prior to processing where a data protection impact assessment under Article 35 indicates that the processing would result in a high risk in the absence of measures taken by the controller to mitigate the risk.

Article 36

3. When consulting the supervisory authority pursuant to paragraph 1, the controller shall provide the supervisory authority with:
   (a) where applicable, the respective responsibilities of the controller, joint controllers and processors involved in the processing, in particular for processing within a group of undertakings;
   (b) the purposes and means of the intended processing;
   (c) the measures and safeguards provided to protect the rights and freedoms of data subjects pursuant to this Regulation;
   (d) where applicable, the contact details of the data protection officer;
   (e) the data protection impact assessment provided for in Article 35; and
   (f) any other information requested by the supervisory authority.

[20] Privacy by Design/Default

Article 25

1. Taking into account the state of the art, the cost of implementation and the nature, scope, context and purposes of processing as well as the risks of varying likelihood and severity for rights and freedoms of natural persons posed by the processing, the controller shall, both at the time of the determination of the means for processing and at the time of the processing itself, implement appropriate technical and organisational measures, such as pseudonymisation, which are designed to implement data-protection principles, such as data minimisation, in an effective manner and to integrate the necessary safeguards into the processing in order to meet the requirements of this Regulation and protect the rights of data subjects.
2. The controller shall implement appropriate technical and organisational measures for ensuring that, by default, only personal data which are necessary for each specific purpose of the processing are processed. That obligation applies to the amount of personal data collected, the extent of their processing, the period of their storage and their accessibility. In particular, such measures shall ensure that by default personal data are not made accessible without the individual's intervention to an indefinite number of natural persons.
3. An approved certification mechanism pursuant to Article 42 may be used as an element to demonstrate compliance with the requirements set out in paragraphs 1 and 2 of this Article.

[21] Security

(49) The processing of personal data to the extent strictly necessary and proportionate for the purposes of ensuring network and information security, i.e. the ability of a network or an information system to resist, at a given level of confidence, accidental events or unlawful or malicious actions that compromise the availability, authenticity, integrity and confidentiality of stored or transmitted personal data, and the security of the related services offered by, or accessible via, those networks and systems, by public authorities, by computer emergency response teams (CERTs), computer security incident response teams (CSIRTs), by providers of electronic communications networks and services and by providers of security technologies and services, constitutes a legitimate interest of the data controller concerned.

Article 32

1. Taking into account the state of the art, the costs of implementation and the nature, scope, context and purposes of processing as well as the risk of varying likelihood and severity for the rights and freedoms of natural persons, the controller and the processor shall implement appropriate technical and organisational measures to ensure a level of security appropriate to the risk, including inter alia as appropriate:

(a) the pseudonymisation and encryption of personal data;
(b) the ability to ensure the ongoing confidentiality, integrity, availability and resilience of processing systems and services;
(c) the ability to restore the availability and access to personal data in a timely manner in the event of a physical or technical incident;
(d) a process for regularly testing, assessing and evaluating the effectiveness of technical and organisational measures for ensuring the security of the processing.

2. In assessing the appropriate level of security account shall be taken in particular of the risks that are presented by processing, in particular from accidental or unlawful destruction, loss, alteration, unauthorised disclosure of, or access to personal data transmitted, stored or otherwise processed.

[22] Data Breach

Article 4

(12) "personal data breach" means a breach of security leading to the accidental or unlawful destruction, loss, alteration, unauthorised disclosure of, or access to, personal data transmitted, stored or otherwise processed.

Article 33

1. In the case of a personal data breach, the controller shall without undue delay and, where feasible, not later than 72 hours after having become aware of it, notify the personal data breach to the supervisory authority competent in accordance with Article 55, unless the personal data breach is unlikely to result in a risk to the rights and freedoms of natural persons. Where the notification to the supervisory authority is not made within 72 hours, it shall be accompanied by reasons for the delay.
2. The processor shall notify the controller without undue delay after becoming aware of a personal data breach.
3. The notification referred to in paragraph 1 shall at least:
   (a) describe the nature of the personal data breach including where possible, the categories and approximate number of data subjects concerned and the categories and approximate number of personal data records concerned;
   (b) communicate the name and contact details of the data protection officer or other contact point where more information can be obtained;
   (c) describe the likely consequences of the personal data breach;
   (d) describe the measures taken or proposed to be taken by the controller to address the personal data breach, including, where appropriate, measures to mitigate its possible adverse effects.
4. Where, and in so far as, it is not possible to provide the information at the same time, the information may be provided in phases without undue further delay.
5. The controller shall document any personal data breaches, comprising the facts relating to the personal data breach, its effects and the remedial action taken. That documentation shall enable the supervisory authority to verify compliance with this Article.

Article 33

1. In the case of a personal data breach, the controller shall without undue delay and, where feasible, not later than 72 hours after having become aware of it, notify the personal data breach to the supervisory authority competent in accordance with Article 55, unless the personal data breach is unlikely to result in a risk to the rights and freedoms of natural persons. Where the notification to the supervisory authority is not made within 72 hours, it shall be accompanied by reasons for the delay.
2. The processor shall notify the controller without undue delay after becoming aware of a personal data breach.
3. The notification referred to in paragraph 1 shall at least:
   (a) describe the nature of the personal data breach including where possible, the categories and approximate number of data subjects concerned and the categories and approximate number of personal data records concerned;
   (b) communicate the name and contact details of the data protection officer or other contact point where more information can be obtained;
   (c) describe the likely consequences of the personal data breach;
   (d) describe the measures taken or proposed to be taken by the controller to address the personal data breach, including, where appropriate, measures to mitigate its possible adverse effects.
4. Where, and in so far as, it is not possible to provide the information at the same time, the information may be provided in phases without undue further delay.
5. The controller shall document any personal data breaches, comprising the facts relating to the personal data breach, its effects and the remedial action taken. That documentation shall enable the supervisory authority to verify compliance with this Article.

Article 34

1. When the personal data breach is likely to result in a high risk to the rights and freedoms of natural persons, the controller shall communicate the personal data breach to the data subject without undue delay.
2. The communication to the data subject referred to in paragraph 1 of this Article shall describe in clear and plain language the nature of the personal data breach and contain at least the information and measures referred to in points (b), (c) and (d) of Article 33(3).
3. The communication to the data subject referred to in paragraph 1 shall not be required if any of the following conditions are met:
   (a) the controller has implemented appropriate technical and organisational protection measures, and those measures were applied to the personal data affected by the personal data breach, in particular those that render the personal data unintelligible to any person who is not authorised to access it, such as encryption;
   (b) the controller has taken subsequent measures which ensure that the high risk to the rights and freedoms of data subjects referred to in paragraph 1 is no longer likely to materialise;
   (c) it would involve disproportionate effort. In such a case, there shall instead be a public communication or similar measure whereby the data subjects are informed in an equally effective manner.
4. If the controller has not already communicated the personal data breach to the data subject, the supervisory authority, having considered the likelihood of

the personal data breach resulting in a high risk, may require it to do so or may decide that any of the conditions referred to in paragraph 3 are met.

[23] Disputes & Enforcement

Article 65

1. In order to ensure the correct and consistent application of this Regulation in individual cases, the Board shall adopt a binding decision in the following cases:
   (a) where, in a case referred to in Article 60(4), a supervisory authority concerned has raised a relevant and reasoned objection to a draft decision of the lead authority or the lead authority has rejected such an objection as being not relevant or reasoned. The binding decision shall concern all the matters which are the subject of the relevant and reasoned objection, in particular whether there is an infringement of this Regulation;
   (b) where there are conflicting views on which of the supervisory authorities concerned is competent for the main establishment.

[24] Cause of Action

Article 77

1. Without prejudice to any other administrative or judicial remedy, every data subject shall have the right to lodge a complaint with a supervisory authority, in particular in the Member State of his or her habitual residence, place of work or place of the alleged infringement if the data subject considers that the processing of personal data relating to him or her infringes this Regulation.

Article 82

1. Any person who has suffered material or non-material damage as a result of an infringement of this Regulation shall have the right to receive compensation from the controller or processor for the damage suffered.
2. Any controller involved in processing shall be liable for the damage caused by processing which infringes this Regulation. A processor shall be liable for the damage caused by processing only where it has not complied with obligations of this Regulation specifically directed to processors or where it has acted outside or contrary to lawful instructions of the controller.
3. A controller or processor shall be exempt from liability under paragraph 2 if it proves that it is not in any way responsible for the event giving rise to the damage.
4. Where more than one controller or processor, or both a controller and a processor, are involved in the same processing and where they are, under paragraphs 2 and 3, responsible for any damage caused by processing, each controller or processor shall be held liable for the entire damage in order to ensure effective compensation of the data subject.
5. Where a controller or processor has, in accordance with paragraph 4, paid full compensation for the damage suffered, that controller or processor shall be

entitled to claim back from the other controllers or processors involved in the same processing that part of the compensation corresponding to their part of responsibility for the damage, in accordance with the conditions set out in paragraph 2.

[25] Derogations[68]

1. In the absence of an adequacy decision pursuant to Article 45(3), or of appropriate safeguards pursuant to Article 46, including binding corporate rules, a transfer or a set of transfers of personal data to a third country or an international organisation shall take place only on one of the following conditions:
   (a) the data subject has explicitly consented to the proposed transfer, after having been informed of the possible risks of such transfers for the data subject due to the absence of an adequacy decision and appropriate safeguards;[69]
   (b) the transfer is necessary for the performance of a contract between the data subject and the controller or the implementation of pre-contractual measures taken at the data subject's request;[70]
   (c) the transfer is necessary for the conclusion or performance of a contract concluded in the interest of the data subject between the controller and another natural or legal person;
   (d) the transfer is necessary for important reasons of public interest.

§2.07 EEA COUNTRIES NOT IN THE EU[71]

[A] Switzerland

Switzerland's FADP was passed in 1992, shortly after Convention 108, and passed the Ordinance to the FADP in 1993.[72] Laws in Switzerland reflect much of the former EU

68. Derogations are non-preferential steps an organization may take when GDPR requirements are not reasonably possible. Organizations should use derogations only when a deviation from process is legitimately needed, and process should not embody routine derogations.
69. Explicit consent provides one option for transfer outside of MCCs, adequacy determination, or BCRs. However, the challenge here involves appropriately apprising the data subject of risks in a manner that adequately enables meaningful choice, and disproportionate bargaining power might make this derogation untenable in practice.
70. Most frequently, this derogation applies to employment contracts. However, controllers should take care to determine when employee personal information is used outside the bounds of such a contract, for example, in relation to insurance, health, or family matters, which generally are not reflected in such a contract.
71. Iceland has passed the Act on the Protection of Privacy as regards the Processing of Personal Data No. 77/2000.
72. Federal Act on Data Protection 235.1 (19 Jun. 1992), available at: https://www.admin.ch/opc/en/classified-compilation/19920153/201401010000/235.1.pdf.

Data Protection Directive, which means that controllers must register data processing activities, in particular out of country data transfers, with the Federal Data Protection and Information Commissioner (FDPIC). Switzerland requires notice and subsequent consent to the following three categories prior to processing: (1) identity of the controller of the data file, (2) the purpose of processing, and (3) categories of data recipients if disclosed.

Although federal law applies, each state of the Swiss Confederation, *cantons*, also have passed data protection-related laws (although the laws are relatively harmonized) and DPAs conduct investigations (as well as the FDPIC).[73] Individual data subjects may also bring civil actions and usually recover for actual damages and lost profits, although in limited cases individuals may recover without economic damages. Organizations and persons intentionally breaking data protection laws may face criminal penalties.

§2.08 CANADIAN PRIVACY

Canada passed its first privacy law applicable to government activities, the Privacy Act, in 1983.[74] The Privacy Act created the role of a Privacy Commissioner for Canada, charged with creating standards, investigating complaints, and managing enforcement of the Privacy Act. The Privacy Act importantly established the concepts of notice and consent for Canadian government data collection, which later formed the basis for commercial privacy. Organizations working in sectors where government provides financial or operational support, such as healthcare, will likely need to comply with Privacy Act requirements and should establish obligations via a government contract. In 2000, the Canadian Parliament passed the Personal Information Protection and Electronic Documents Act (PIPEDA), applicable to private use of personal information. Canada has also passed anti-spam legislation, the Canadian Anti-Spam Legislation (2014), and has established confidentiality in the financial sector via the Bank Secrecy Act (1970).

Across all legislation, PIPEDA is the most comprehensive and restrictive, supporting Canada receiving adequacy status in 2001. PIPEDA does not require exact replication of PIPEDA requirements within each Canadian province. Instead, PIPEDA permits some deviation so long as the province establishes "substantially similar" legislation via a standard determination process.[75] Notably, substantial similarity does permit comparatively more strict requirements, such as health data localization (prohibition on data transfer) in some provinces described in Chapter 10.

---

73. Federal Data Protection and Information Commissioner, *Data Protection – Switzerland* (2017), https://www.edoeb.admin.ch/org/00146/00147/index.html?lang=en.
74. The Privacy Act, R.S.C. 1985, c. P-21, http://laws-lois.justice.gc.ca/eng/acts/P-21/.
75. Industry Canada, *Process for the Determination of "Substantially Similar" Provincial Legislation by the Governor in Council* (2002), http://publications.gc.ca/gazette/archives/p1/2002/2002-08-03/pdf/g1-13631.pdf.

PIPEDA adopts ten principles of personal IP:

(1) Accountability: Organizations must designate an individual accountable for following principles.
(2) Identifying Purposes: Organizations must identify and disclose purposes for use prior to collection.
(3) Consent: Individuals must have knowledge of practices and manifest consent prior to collection, use, or disclosure of personal information.
(4) Limiting Collection: Organizations shall not collect personal information other than what is necessary for disclosed purposes and under fair and lawful means.
(5) Limiting Use, Disclosure, and Retention: Organizations may only use and disclosure data for the purpose collected and may only retain so long as necessary.
(6) Accuracy: Organizations must ensure accuracy, completeness, and timeliness of personal information.
(7) Safeguards: Organizations must protect information by security safeguards according to the data's sensitivity.
(8) Openness: Organizations should disclose information regarding policies and practices to individuals.
(9) Individual Access: Individuals may request access to information stored about them and correct such information as needed.
(10) Challenging Compliance: Individuals may submit a complaint regarding institutional non-compliance.

Conditions for consent both reflect and differ somewhat from EU requirements. Data subjects must provide consent prior to processing and when uses change, which means that organizations whose business practices change require new consent. However, PIPEDA generally accepts implied consent, unless SPI will be processed. Consent can be provided through multiple means including an online form, a phone call, a checkbox, or when using a product or service when contextually it is clear that information is being collected.

[A] Passages of Note: The Privacy Act[76]

[1] Definitions

Personal information means information about an identifiable individual that is recorded in any form including, without restricting the generality of the foregoing,

76. Most organizations will not require knowledge of the Privacy Act. However, organizations handling health information on behalf of health care providers likely will require some knowledge, as health care providers may be government-managed providers.

(a) information relating to the race, national or ethnic origin, colour, religion, age or marital status of the individual,
(b) information relating to the education or the medical, criminal or employment history of the individual or information relating to financial transactions in which the individual has been involved,
(c) any identifying number, symbol or other particular assigned to the individual,
(d) the address, fingerprints or blood type of the individual,
(e) the personal opinions or views of the individual except where they are about another individual or about a proposal for a grant, an award or a prize to be made to another individual by a government institution or a part of a government institution specified in the regulations,
(f) correspondence sent to a government institution by the individual that is implicitly or explicitly of a private or confidential nature, and replies to such correspondence that would reveal the contents of the original correspondence,
(g) the views or opinions of another individual about the individual,
(h) the views or opinions of another individual about a proposal for a grant, an award or a prize to be made to the individual by an institution or a part of an institution referred to in paragraph (e), but excluding the name of the other individual where it appears with the views or opinions of the other individual, and
(i) the name of the individual where it appears with other personal information relating to the individual or where the disclosure of the name itself would reveal information about the individual.

Government institution means

(a) any department or ministry of state of the Government of Canada, or any body or office, listed in the schedule, and
(b) any parent Crown corporation, and any whollyowned subsidiary of such a corporation, within the meaning of section 83 of the Financial Administration Act; (institution fédérale).

[2] Collection Limitations

No personal information shall be collected by a government institution unless it relates directly to an operating program or activity of the institution.

5 (2) A government institution shall inform any individual from whom the institution collects personal information about the individual of the purpose for which the information is being collected.

7 Personal information under the control of a government institution shall not, without the consent of the individual to whom it relates, be used by the institution except

(a) for the purpose for which the information was obtained or compiled by the institution or for a use consistent with that purpose; or
(b) for a purpose for which the information may be disclosed to the institution under subsection 8(2).

8 (1) Personal information under the control of a government institution shall not, without the consent of the individual to whom it relates, be disclosed by the institution except in accordance with this section.

(2) Subject to any other Act of Parliament, personal information under the control of a government institution may be disclosed

(a) for the purpose for which the information was obtained or compiled by the institution or for a use consistent with that purpose;

[3] Access

12 (1) Subject to this Act, every individual who is a Canadian citizen or a permanent resident within the meaning of subsection 2(1) of the Immigration and Refugee Protection Act has a right to and shall, on request, be given access to

(a) any personal information about the individual contained in a personal information bank; and
(b) any other personal information about the individual under the control of a government institution with respect to which the individual is able to provide sufficiently specific information on the location of the information as to render it reasonably retrievable by the government institution.

13 (1) A request for access to personal information under paragraph 12(1)(a) shall be made in writing to the government institution that has control of the personal information bank that contains the information and shall identify the bank.

14 Where access to personal information is requested under subsection 12(1), the head of the government institution to which the request is made shall, subject to section 15, within thirty days after the request is received,

(a) give written notice to the individual who made the request as to whether or not access to the information or a part thereof will be given; and
(b) if access is to be given, give the individual who made the request access to the information or the part thereof.

[4] Accuracy & Correction

6 (2) A government institution shall take all reasonable steps to ensure that personal information that is used for an administrative purpose by the institution is as accurate, up-to-date and complete as possible.

[5] Other Rights Relating to Personal Information

(2) Every individual who is given access under paragraph (1)(a) to personal information that has been used, is being used or is available for use for an administrative purpose is entitled to

(a) request correction of the personal information where the individual believes there is an error or omission therein;
(b) require that a notation be attached to the information reflecting any correction requested but not made; and
(c) require that any person or body to whom that information has been disclosed for use for an administrative purpose within two years prior to the time a correction is requested or a notation is required under this subsection in respect of that information
    (i) be notified of the correction or notation, and
    (ii) where the disclosure is to a government institution, the institution make the correction or notation on any copy of the information under its control.

[6] Retention & Deletion

6 (1) Personal information that has been used by a government institution for an administrative purpose shall be retained by the institution for such period of time after it is so used as may be prescribed by regulation in order to ensure that the individual to whom it relates has a reasonable opportunity to obtain access to the information.

6 (3) A government institution shall dispose of personal information under the control of the institution in accordance with the regulations and in accordance with any directives or guidelines issued by the designated minister in relation to the disposal of that information.

[7] Regulatory Authority and Complaints

53 (1) The Governor in Council shall, by commission under the Great Seal, appoint a Privacy Commissioner after consultation with the leader of every recognized party in the Senate and House of Commons and approval of the appointment by resolution of the Senate and House of Commons.

29 (1) Subject to this Act, the Privacy Commissioner shall receive and investigate complaints

(a) from individuals who allege that personal information about themselves held by a government institution has been used or disclosed otherwise than in accordance with section 7 or 8;
(b) from individuals who have been refused access to personal information requested under subsection 12(1);
(c) from individuals who allege that they are not being accorded the rights to which they are entitled under subsection 12(2) or that corrections of personal information requested under paragraph 12(2)(a) are being refused without justification;

31 Before commencing an investigation of a complaint under this Act, the Privacy Commissioner shall notify the head of the government institution concerned of the intention to carry out the investigation and shall inform the head of the institution of the substance of the complaint.

37 (1) The Privacy Commissioner may, from time to time at the discretion of the Commissioner, carry out investigations in respect of personal information under the control of government institutions to ensure compliance with sections 4 to 8.

CHAPTER 3
United States

The United States (U.S.) legal structure operates under a substantially different model, the *sectoral* model. This sector-specific approach extends from a lack of direct privacy recognition within the U.S. Constitution and a general unwillingness to solidify general privacy safeguards in federal and state laws, both of which require public support and congressional approval.[77]

The sectoral model focuses on specifically addressing sectors or uses that pose risk to an individual, but does not provide a baseline level of protection across all industries.[78] The result of a sectoral model, then, involves increased scrutiny for regulated sectors and less scrutiny for unregulated sectors. For this reason, although the U.S. is often criticized for lacking privacy protection, some sectors apply more stringent requirements and enforcement activities than in the EU. Further, the U.S. has embedded a substantial number of privacy requirements within broader laws.[79]

The U.S. does not have a dominant model for its privacy laws, with the exception of similarities between the Health Insurance Portability and Accountability Act of 1996 (HIPAA), pertaining to specific entities handling Protected Health Information (PHI); the Gramm-Leach-Bliley Act of 1999 (GLBA), pertaining to financial institutions handling *non-public information* or personal financial records; and Regulation S-P (Reg S-P), passed by the Securities Exchange Commission in 2000 (SEC), pertaining to

77. The U.S. Constitution does provide such guarantees, yet such guarantees mostly reflect physical privacy concepts rather than information privacy.
78. The Federal Trade Commission has, in exercising its rights to sanction organizations for unfair or deceptive trade practices under the FTC Act's Section 5, attempted to provide at least enforcement protection, yet no omnibus law establishes specific requirements.
79. The Video Privacy Protection Act of 1988, the Cable Communications Privacy Act of 1984, the Video Voyeurism Prevention Act of 2004 will not be discussed in this chapter. The FERPA, will also not be discussed. However, the Author encourages reviewing provisions if interested in educational privacy. *See* 20 U.S.C. § 1232g; 34 CFR Part 99, https://www.law.cornell.edu/uscode/text/20/1232g. Standard conceptions of prior notice and consent apply for disclosure of educational records.

securities transactions.[80] HIPAA was the first privacy law in the U.S. to include explicit security concepts for protecting information, followed by GLBA and Reg S-P. Subsequent updates, regulatory rule changes, and audit protocols have increased stringency of these requirements.

Information like name, address, phone number, e-mail address, financial account information, corporate financial information, and others specific information types have been embedded into sectoral, industry-specific consumer laws in the health care, banking, and for corporate entities including: HIPAA, GLBA, Reg-SPI, Sarbanes–Oxley (SOX) for publicly traded businesses, and the Dodd–Frank Wall Street Reform and Consumer Protection Act (Dodd–Frank) for investments.[81] Consumers also gain limited fraud compensation from alternate financial regulation. Regulation Z caps out-of-pocket expenses for fraud on payment cards at USD 50, though many banks do not charge any fee in order to incentivize future credit card usage and buying behavior.[82]

All of these federal laws regulate big business in a variety of capacities and restrict collection and use of personal information while requiring security controls on PHI and security for other personal information in specific sectors. Individual regulatory bodies enforce these laws, similar to Japanese Ministries: the Office of the Comptroller of the Currency (OCC) enforces GLBA, the Securities Exchange Commission handles SOX and Dodd–Frank compliance (while promulgating additional rules for publicly traded companies), and the Department of Health & Human Services' (HHS) Office for Civil Rights (OCR) supports the health sector.[83] While self-governance by the payment card industry has, to some extent, protected payment account numbers (PANs), personal identification numbers (PINs), service codes, magnetic stripe data, expiration date, and the cardholder's name, other personal information, such as date of birth, tax ID, or driver's license number, has not always been protected by Payment Card Industry – Data Security Standards (PCI-DSS)-compliant companies (described further in Chapter 11).[84] In short, while protecting limited types of information based on a business sector

80. Reg S-P expressly adopted GLBA for the securities sector.
81. Health Insurance Portability and Accountability Act of 2003, 42 U.S.C. § 1320d–6; Health Insurance Technology for Economic and Clinical Health Act of 2009, §§ 42 U.S.C. 17931-4; Gramm–Leach–Bliley Act of 1999, 15 U.S. C. §§ 6801-6809; Sarbanes–Oxley Act of 2002, Pub. L. No. 107-204, 116 Stat. 745 (codified in scattered sections of 11, 15, 18, 28, and 29 U.S.C.); Dodd–Frank Wall Street Reform and Consumer Protection Act of 2010, Pub. L. 111-203, 124 Stat. 1376-2223.
82. U.S.C. §§ 1643(a)(1)(B) (2006); 12 C.F.R. §§ 226.12(b) (2009). Consumers bear costs for fraud in only two situations: when they purposefully delay reporting or do not review statements in two months.
83. *Guidelines Establishing Standards for Safeguarding Customer Information*, Office of the Comptroller of the Currency (2001), *available at* http://www.occ.gov/news-issuances/bulletins/2001/bulletin-2001-8.html; *Information Security and Section 404 of the Sarbanes-Oxley Act*, SANS (2005), *available at* http://www.sans.org/reading-room/whitepapers/legal/information-security-section-404-sarbanes-oxley-act-1582; Gina Stevens, *Data Security Breach Notification Laws*, Congressional Research Service (Apr. 10, 2012), *available at* https://www.fas.org/sgp/crs/misc/R42475.pdf.
84. *See PCI Data Storage Do's and Don'ts*, PCI Security Standards Council (Oct. 2008), https://www.pcisecuritystandards.org/pdfs/pci_fs_data_storage.pdf.

can provide highly specialized protection, selective protection may create a false sense of SPI not subject to specific requirements.[85]

§3.01 U.S. STATE LAWS

Because the U.S. does not have an omnibus privacy law, increasingly more often parties pursue legal action under the common law. The common law, adopted from England and established in the Middle Ages, evolved in the U.S. to become the largest body of law, most frequently interpreted at the state level and to some extent informed by legal frameworks, such as uniform commercial codes and restatements.

In contrast with civil codes, which codify and frequently update codes, the common law evolves on its own to include new causes of action and duties owed to others through interpretation of limited statutes, or laws. The common law consists of two primary case types: torts or contracts. Torts, or civil wrongs, occur when a party has a reasonable duty, undertakes a duty, or is ascribed duty through contract or law and the party does not perform the duty, which is the proximate cause for another party's reasonably foreseeable, cognizable injury. Consumer protection laws in the U.S. are designed to describe a regulated entity's duties, and what punishment might result from failure to fulfill them, including or not including a private right of action. However, common laws over time have developed to recognize type of duties that attach to a party through circumstance or status, such as fiduciary duty or other special duties.

Some specially recognized torts exist today in the U.S., including appropriation of name and likeness, false light, intrusion upon seclusion, invasion of privacy, and public disclosure of private facts. Appropriation of name and likeness focuses primarily on the commercial aspect of a person's identity, and false light pertains to incorrect information intentionally shared about a person publicly. Intrusion upon seclusion, public disclosure of private facts, and invasion of privacy may be found in various combinations within state laws, as some states recognize some but not all torts. Intrusion upon seclusion is usually defined for a physical setting, rather than informational privacy, whereas public disclosure of private facts and invasion of privacy may apply under some circumstances to private information. However, for both intrusion upon seclusion and invasion of privacy, a plaintiff bringing the legal action must prove intentionality of the privacy violation. For this reason, it is tremendously difficult to successfully bring a common law cause of action based on a recognized privacy tort when an organization negligently did not protect information, as in most data breaches.

85. Suni Munshani, *It's Not Just about Credit Cards any More: 2011 Data Breaches Signal the Need for a Different Strategy*, Protegrity Website (Aug. 2011), http://www.protegrity.com/wp-content/uploads/2011/08/protegrity-Anatomy-of-a-Data-Breach.pdf.

In some cases, state laws are more stringent than federal laws, because some federal laws do not *preempt* state laws.[86] Preemption is an important concept because it instructs when state laws may be enforced and when they may not.

State laws can establish additional duties organizations must perform because some federal laws do not preempt more stringent state laws. Organizations that will provide health services and collect PHI as HIPAA Covered Entities (CEs) within the U.S. often must collect and retain consent to a HIPAA privacy notice in states, even though HIPAA does not require explicit consent, except for specialized requests, called *authorizations*.[87] The Family Educational Rights Privacy Act (FERPA) also does not preempt state laws, and states may further limit record access for state officials.[88] The Telephone Consumer Protection Act (TCPA) and the Children's Online Privacy Protection Act (COPPA) also permit more stringent state laws.[89] However, some laws do prohibit states from including more stringent requirements, at least under some circumstances, such as GLBA and Controlling the Assault of Non-Solicited Pornography and Marketing Act (CAN-SPAM). For these reasons, organizations doing business in the U.S. should evaluate applicable federal laws for preemption language and review applicable state laws where necessary.

State laws also include privacy notice contents and data breach notification.[90] Because the U.S. does not have an omnibus privacy law, privacy notices are not required directly by federal law. The FTC, which prosecutes unfair and deceptive trade practices and previously drafted the Fair Information Practices (FIPs), has established privacy guidance for organizations operating in the U.S. However, federal laws do not require specific notice content. Most organizations providing service to U.S. consumers today use the California state notice law, California Civil Code § 22575, to inform privacy notice contents. Under this law, the following minimum information is required in privacy notices:

- Identify the categories of personally identifiable information that the operator collects ... and the categories of third-party persons or entities with whom the operator may share that personally identifiable information.

86. Federal laws in the U.S. generally fall into one of the three categories: *express preemption*, the law specifically preempts any state laws; *express non-preemption* or when no preemption language is listed, the law specifically does not preempt more restrictive state laws (most federal laws establish a minimum, but do not permit less restrictive laws); *field preemption*, where upon analysis, the law was drafted to occupy a particular industry or sector although preemption is not referenced in the law (e.g., an administrative agency issues rules, actively audits or regulates a space, illustrating that states have less of a role).
87. Several additional health law provisions apply to organizations doing business within particular states.
88. U.S. Dept. of Education, *Legislative History of Major FERPA Provisions* (Feb. 11, 2004), https://www2.ed.gov/policy/gen/guid/fpco/ferpa/leg-history.html.
89. Telephone Consumer Protection Act, 47 U.S.C. § 227. Recent cases regarding COPPA and Federal Trade Commission (FTC) amicus briefs seem to argue that more restrictive state laws are not preempted. This is important for COPPA, because state laws, such as California Civil Code § 3344, which provides rights to revoke consent and delete data collected during age of minority up to age 18.
90. Data breach notification will be discussed thoroughly in Chapter 15.

- If the operator maintains a process for an individual consumer who uses or visits its commercial Website or online service to review and request changes to any of his or her personally identifiable information that is collected through the Website or online service, provide a description of that process.
- Describe the process by which the operator notifies consumers who use or visit its commercial Website or online service of material changes to the operator's privacy policy for that Website or online service.
- Identify its effective date.
- Disclose how the operator responds to Web browser "do not track" signals or other mechanisms that provide consumers the ability to exercise choice regarding the collection of personally identifiable information about an individual consumer's online activities over time ... if the operator engages in that collection. An operator may satisfy ... [this requirement] ... by providing a clear and conspicuous hyperlink in the operator's privacy policy to an online location containing a description.
- Disclose whether other parties may collect personally identifiable information about an individual consumer's online activities over time and across different Websites when a consumer uses the operator's Website or service.
- Describe the process by which the operator notifies consumers who use or visit its commercial Website or online service of material changes to the operator's privacy policy for that Website or online service.
- Identify its effective date.
- Disclose how the operator responds to Web browser "do not track" signals or other mechanisms that provide consumers the ability to exercise choice regarding the collection of personally identifiable information about an individual consumer's online activities over time ... if the operator engages in that collection. An operator may satisfy ... [this requirement] ... by providing a clear and conspicuous hyperlink in the operator's privacy policy to an online location containing a description.
- Disclose whether other parties may collect personally identifiable information about an individual consumer's online activities over time and across different Websites when a consumer uses the operator's Website or service.

Although several state and federal privacy laws exist, the remainder of this chapter will describe the most frequently discussed privacy laws.

§3.02 HEALTH INFORMATION PRIVACY

The HHS OCR actively drives privacy and cybersecurity requirements in the digital health market for entities subject to HIPAA and is the regulatory authority for HIPAA.[91] HIPAA, updated in 2003, and the HITECH Act, which modified HIPAA in 2009, together

---

91. Health Insurance Portability and Accountability Act (HIPAA) of 1996, 45 C.F.R. § 160 et seq (1996).

establish a compliance framework for a limited subset of digital health providers: Covered Entities (CEs and third-party Business Associates (BAs).

CEs usually have a primary business relationship with individuals, such as patients, who disclose PHI to CEs for health services or coverage of health services. Under HIPAA, CEs fall into three categories: health plans, insurance providers or self-insured organizations; health care providers, organizations providing health care to individuals, such as hospitals, clinics, or research institutions; and health care clearinghouses, or organizations that process or facilitate the processing of nonstandard data elements to standard data. BAs, or organizations that perform a support role for CEs, perform activities involving the use or disclosure of PHI on behalf of, or to perform services for, a CE.[92] Statutory interpretation clearly illustrates that the categorization of a BA is dependent upon the primary organization's classification as a CE.[93] If an organization is *not* a CE or BA and a third party is involved, that third party is also not subject to HIPAA with respect to that entity.[94]

For HIPAA to require organizational compliance, organizational activities must involve PHI, which is information that relates to the past, present, or future physical or mental health condition of an individual. PHI can include a wide variety of data elements including name, address, admission date, birth date, medical record numbers, health plan beneficiary numbers, age (when over age 89), IP address, biometric identifiers, and a variety of other elements. From a data perspective, HIPAA is broad in application, though limited to specific entities, the CE and the BA. HIPAA, however, makes clear that PHI potentially includes any health information, although de-identification procedures (removing specific identifiers from a data set) do not require protection under HIPAA.

The HIPAA Privacy Rule enforces the privacy concepts of collection, notice, consent, and authorization to use or disclose PHI. HIPAA restricts collection or subsequent use of PHI to the "minimum necessary."[95] To this end, CEs must implement policies and practices to reasonably limit PHI collected, used, or disclosed to only what is necessary for personnel to perform their job duties. Even though a CE may have access to a significant amount of PHI, it may not disclose unrestricted copies of this information to third parties, except at the direction and authorization of the individual or as previously communicated and authorized.

HIPAA applies to all identifiable health information, although the de-identification procedure in HIPAA names specific health information. By implication, when data element removal enables free transfer of data, introduction of these

92. Similar to the GDPR, CEs map to the role of controller, BAs to the role of processor.
93. 45 C.F.R. § 160.103. The statutory language "on behalf of" a CE illustrates a dependency within HIPAA on CE status. However, BAs must individually and independently comply with HIPAA under the HITECH updates; somewhat severing a compliance responsibility for CEs of their BAs, though CEs must still hold BAs accountable to compliance with HIPAA via monitoring activities. *See* Health Insurance Technology for Economic and Clinical Health Act § 17921 (providing the definition of breach and its exceptions).
94. Health Insurance Technology for Economic and Clinical Health Act § 17921. This distinction is important because many third parties, such as technology suppliers, may provide service to organizations falling under HIPAA in some cases and not in others.
95. 45 C.F.R. § 164.502(b), 164.514(d) (2013).

elements triggers HIPAA applicability. For this reason, CEs and BAs typically apply HIPAA requirements when the following data elements are present:[96]

- Names
- All geographic subdivisions smaller than a state, including street address, city, county, precinct, ZIP code, and their equivalent geocodes, except for the initial three digits of the ZIP code
- All dates (except year) for dates directly related to an individual, including birth date, admission date, discharge date, death date, and all ages over 89 and all elements of dates (including year) indicative of such age, except that such ages and elements may be aggregated into a single category of age 90 or older
- Telephone numbers and fax numbers
- E-mail addresses
- Medical record numbers, Health plan beneficiary numbers, Social Security Numbers (SSNs), account numbers, and license number
- Vehicle identifiers and serial numbers, including license plate numbers
- Device identifiers and serial numbers
- Web Universal Resource Locators (URLs)
- Internet Protocol (IP) addresses
- Biometric identifiers, including finger and voice prints
- Full-face photographs and any comparable images.

Although CEs must adhere to the minimum necessary requirement when handling PHI, CEs may use, transfer, or disclose PHI pursuant to individual authorization. When a CE uses an individual's PHI for purposes beyond the scope of necessity outlined in the privacy notice, written consent (authorization) communicating the details of this use is required from the individual.

HIPAA provides precise requirements of how an individual must receive notice about a CE's privacy practices. Individuals must receive a Notice of Privacy Practices before a CE collects PHI, and the CE must distribute updates to this notice every three years or within sixty days of material changes.[97] The Notice of Privacy Practices includes an effective date; information about use, such as third-party use and data transfer; what type of PHI may be collected; identity of the CE; and information about how to file a complaint. The CE must provide the privacy notice upon request, post the notice in an easily accessible location, written clearly and in an easy to read style, provide the notice on-demand. The notice must be complete with respect to CE and BA practices. The individual then consents to the notice by written consent (electronic or in paper form).[98]

96. The Safe Harbor de-identification procedure includes removal of these elements. However, organizations may also remove elements following an expert determination of acceptable risk by a qualified assessor, such as an actuarial scientist.
97. 45 C.F.R. § 164.520. The three-year distribution depends on material changes not being made. If material changes are made to the notice, the notice must be posted and distributed within sixty days.
98. 45 C.F.R. § 164.506, 164.510, 164.512; STANDARDS FOR PRIVACY OF INDIVIDUALLY IDENTIFIABLE HEALTH INFORMATION, U.S. DEP'T HEALTH & HUM. SERVS. (Jul. 6, 2001), https://aspe.hhs.gov/basic-report

Under HIPAA, specific authorization may be needed for PHI use beyond the scope of the Notice of Privacy Practices, such as transfer to a third party, data sale, or data aggregation and analytics if not previously disclosed. In short, notice and consent are often not a one-time activity and may require future user interaction.

In 2011 and 2012, the OCR developed, pursuant to new HITECH responsibilities, an audit framework transitioning HIPAA specifications into an audit control set and worked with 115 CEs to test the audit process.[99] In 2015, the OCR selected and initiated its first candidate pool for audits, and in 2016, performed its first full-scale audits. The audit protocol matches HIPAA statutory requirements and mirrors HIPAA privacy, security, and data breach notification rules. The Security Rule and Breach Notification Rule will be discussed in more depth in Chapter 10.

§3.03 FINANCIAL AND INVESTMENT SECTORS

The GLBA or GLB Act and Reg S-P require privacy and security measures (less comprehensive than HIPAA) both for prospective and current financial and investment customers' non-public information.[100] The incorporation of security, as well as privacy, requirements for specific consumer information showcases the relationship between legal process (such as collecting informed consent) and technical implementation (such as restricting access to PHI or non-public information).

[A] The Gramm-Leach Bliley Act

Congress passed GLBA in 1999 and most recently updated its text in 2014.[101] The OCC regulates financial institutions under GLBA and conducts periodic audits on institutions doing business in the U.S.. The OCC audits as a matter of course, auditing for some large financial institutions annually. All audits, including non-OCC audits generally require a substantial compilation of documentation and evidence. Financial institutions under a certain financial threshold do not undergo a full OCC audit, instead arranging for an independent audit of these

/standards-privacy-individually-identifiable-health-information. Individuals can also use electronic signatures. Although the use of electronic signatures is not definitely prescribed under HIPAA, the Electronic Signatures in Global and National Commerce (E-SIGN) would apply to the Notice of Privacy Practices; *see* Kathy Bakich & Kaye Pestaina, *Security and Electronic Signature Standards*, EMPLOYER'S GUIDE TO HIPAA PRIVACY REQUIREMENTS ¶ 1030 (Kathryn Bakich & Joanne Hustead eds., 2015), Westlaw (database updated 2016) (explaining that the standard for electronic signatures were never finalized in the security rules).

99. HIPAA PRIVACY, SECURITY, AND BREACH NOTIFICATION AUDIT PROGRAM, U.S. DEP'T OF HEALTH & HUM. SERVS., http://www.hhs.gov/hipaa/for-professionals/compliance-enforcement/audit/ (last visited Oct. 7, 2016).

100. Reg S-P incorporated GLBA obligations by virtue of a SEC rule.

101. THE GRAMM-LEACH-BLILEY ACT OF 1999, Pub. L. No. 106-102, 113 Stat. 1338 (Nov. 12, 1999) (*codified at* 15 U.S.C. §§ 6801, 6809, 6821, and 6827), https://www.gpo.gov/fdsys/pkg/PLAW-106publ102/pdf/PLAW-106publ102.pdf.

practices.[102] The OCC has GLBA examination procedures that enable an organization to better determine specific controls. For example, financial institutions must have implemented a compliance management system that involves board and senior management review, a compliance officer, internal controls, an organizational structure, policies and procedures, training, and an audit function.[103]

The OCC also reviews compliance obligations overall with respect to applicable privacy laws in addition to GLBA, including the COPPA, CAN-SPAM, and the Right to Financial Privacy Act.[104] The FTC has regulatory authority for all financial institutions not under GLBA and has passed a Safeguards Rule for financial institutions under its purview that adds more requirements for non-GLBA financial institutions.[105]

The GLBA applies to financial institutions both in relation to prospective customers and current customers. Financial institutions must protect *nonpublic personal information*, defined as financial information related to an identifiable individual. Under the GLBA, non-public information includes:

(4) Non-public personal information

(A) The term "nonpublic personal information" means personally identifiable financial information—
   (i) provided by a consumer to a financial institution;
   (ii) resulting from any transaction with the consumer or any service performed for the consumer; or
   (iii) otherwise obtained by the financial institution.
(B) Such term does not include publicly available information, as such term is defined by the regulations prescribed under section 6804.
(C) Notwithstanding subparagraph (B), such term
   (i) shall include any list, description, or other grouping of consumers (and publicly available information pertaining to them) that

102. Office of the Comptroller of the Currency, *OCC Bulletin 1999-37, Interagency Policy Statement on External Auditing Programs* (Oct. 7, 1999), https://www.occ.gov/news-issuances/bulletins/1999/bulletin-1999-37.html.
103. Office of the Comptroller of the Currency, *Compliance Management System Comptroller's Handbook* (Aug. 1996), https://www.occ.gov/publications/publications-by-type/comptrollers-handbook/cms.pdf. Organizations involved in audits of any kind, especially with the OCC, should develop strong documentation, as often auditors judge presence or absence of a requirement first by its documentation, second by department awareness, and third by training.
104. Office of the Comptroller of the Currency, *Other Consumer Protection Laws and Regulations*, https://www.occ.gov/publications/publications-by-type/comptrollers-handbook/other.pdf. Children's Online Privacy Protection Act, Right to Financial Privacy Act, 12 U.S.C. § 3401 (1970). COPPA and CAN-SPAM will be discussed later in this chapter.
105. Federal Trade Commission, *Safeguards Rule* (Apr. 2006), https://www.ftc.gov/enforcement/rules/rulemaking-regulatory-reform-proceedings/safeguards-rule.

is derived using any non-public personal information other than publicly available information; but

(ii) shall not include any list, description, or other grouping of consumers (and publicly available information pertaining to them) that is derived without using any non-public personal information.

[B] Privacy Obligations

The GLBA Privacy Rule requires financial institutions to provide notice both to consumers (non-customers) and to customers. A short form privacy notice may be provided to consumers who are not current customers to facilitate non-public personal information transfer for purposes of, for example, providing particular product information or reviewing loan qualifications. Current customers must receive an annual privacy notice that is distributed to the customer. This notice requires information about categories of information collected, how that information is disclosed, and categories of third parties (GLBA does not consider affiliates third parties). Consumers can opt-out of notice, which involves a conspicuous checkbox on a paper form or by electronic means. Financial institutions must distribute the privacy notice to consumers upon material change, which means that organizations changing business processes and updating privacy notices frequently must distribute multiple changes to current customers. GLBA includes a draft model privacy form in Appendix A of the law, making compliance relatively easy.

Although data sharing originally must occur via explicit, prior consent, data sharing with unaffiliated third parties only requires implied consent, if the original privacy notice covers third party sharing:

15 U.S. Code § 6802

(a) Notice Requirements

Except as otherwise provided in this subtitle, a financial institution may not, directly or through any affiliate, disclose to a nonaffiliated third party any non-public personal information, unless such financial institution provides or has provided to the consumer a notice that complies with section 503.

(b) Opt Out

(1) A financial institution may not disclose non-public personal information to a nonaffiliated third party unless—(A) such financial institution clearly and conspicuously discloses to the

> consumer, in writing or in electronic form or other form permitted by the regulations prescribed under section 504, that such information may be disclosed to such third party; (B) the consumer is given the opportunity, before the time that such information is initially disclosed, to direct that such information not be disclosed to such third party; and (C) the consumer is given an explanation of how the consumer can exercise that nondisclosure option.

Despite flexible data sharing with unaffiliated third parties, financial institutions may not distribute any account numbers for marketing purposes.

§3.04 THE FAIR CREDIT REPORTING ACT

The U.S. Congress passed the Fair Credit Reporting Act, 15 U.S.C. § 1681, in 1970.[106] The Fair Credit Reporting Act, for organizations other than credit reporting agencies, involves two steps: (1) Gathering consent to run a consumer report with a credit reporting agency for permissible purposes and (2) Providing a copy of the consumer report to the individual, including details of any adverse action. Permissible purposes include extending a line of credit, for employment purposes, or underwriting insurance.

Organizations doing business in the U.S. often use consumer reporting to determine credit worthiness for purposes of providing a loan or validating credit health or personal reputation when hiring employees for roles involving high-risk assets or money management. Some organizations conduct routine background checks that involve a consumer report that does not include financial health. Consumer reports involve more than just credit worthiness:

> **15 U.S.C. § 1681a**
>
> (d) Consumer Report
>
> (1) In general
>
> The term "consumer report" means any written, oral, or other communication of any information by a consumer reporting agency bearing on a consumer's credit worthiness, credit standing, credit capacity, character, general reputation, personal characteristics, or mode of living which is used or expected to be used or collected in whole or in part for the purpose of serving as a factor in establishing the consumer's eligibility for

106. The Fair Credit Reporting Act 15 U.S.C § 1681 (1970).

(A) credit or insurance to be used primarily for personal, family, or household purposes;
(B) employment purposes; or
(C) any other purpose authorized under section 604 [§ 1681b].

Before submitting a request for a consumer report, an organization, such as a prospective employer, must provide a summary of the consumer's rights, a clear and conspicuous disclosure of the reason for the consumer report, and a formal request to run such a report, in writing. The consumer must also authorize the request in writing. The organization then certifies to a consumer reporting agency preparing the report that disclosed personal information will not be used unlawfully,[107] the request meets a legitimate purpose, and the consumer received a consumer rights document. After receiving the consumer report, an organization must provide a copy of the consumer report to the consumer, a notice of any adverse action resulting from the report's contents, and specifics on the nature of the investigation.

§3.05 MARKETING ACTIVITIES

In the U.S., civil actions relating to marketing activities have increased in frequency, bringing statutes like the TCPA to the forefront of compliance concerns. CAN-SPAM and the Do Not Call (DNC) Registry have provided additional procedural requirements for organizations sending marketing e-mail and engaging in unsolicited cold-calling, respectively.

[A] TCPA

The TCPA was originally passed in 1991 amid increased frequency of unsolicited telephone calls and faxes using auto-dialing technology.[108] Unlike manual dialing, auto-dialing machinery could place thousands of calls at one time, often at unusual times of day or night. In June 2015, the Federal Communications Commission (FCC) established additional rules extending TCPA to cover text messages received on mobile devices.[109]

107. It should be noted that many other laws indirectly affect information privacy for an individual. The FCRA expressly prohibits unlawful activity, which includes statutory discrimination based on information prepared or inferred from a consumer report, such as disability status or country of origin.
108. The Telephone Consumer Protection Act (47 U.S.C. § 227), https://transition.fcc.gov/cgb/policy/TCPA-Rules.pdf.
109. Federal Communications Commission, *FCC Strengthens consumer Protection against Unwanted Calls and Texts* (18 Jun. 2015), https://apps.fcc.gov/edocs_public/attachmatch/DOC-333993A1.pdf.

Overall, the TCPA bars for-profit organizations placing marketing calls to phone numbers and fax machines without explicit, written consent.[110] The basic rules of TCPA involve informed consent and revocation of consent. Prior to the invention of text messaging, providing notice and gathering consent involved paper forms, online Web forms, and phone calls, all of which involved disclosing privacy terms and gathering consent (consent need not be in writing under TCPA). However, text messaging has complicated consent-gathering for organizations, due to the potential for text message abuse and cost to consumers.

To comply with TCPA, organizations should separate consent to marketing communications from consent to another privacy notice or TOU. Marketing communications, such as phone or text, should be presented as a separate checkbox or other consent that is *not* preselected and provides a link to a privacy notice:

> I want an associate to contact me about promotional deals on my favorite products. To read our Privacy Notice click here.

When the entire privacy notice or reason for collecting data relates to promotional materials, an organization may include phone or text messaging disclosures in the privacy notice or TOU if presented in a highly visible manner. In both cases, organizations must collect explicit, informed consent prior to using computerized means to call or text an individual. Under new FCC rules, an individual may revoke this consent at any time, in any convenient manner.

Organizations involved in autodialed text messaging may have additional hurdles under marketing trade associations and potentially under FCC rules. First, under FCC rules, using a mobile app that accesses third-party contacts cannot transfer consent from the individual downloading the app to third-party contacts on the device. Further, organizations sending text messages to a transferred phone number may only send one text before TCPA rules apply, called the "one text rule."

Marketing associations have established standardized methods employing best practices for meeting FCC rules. First, associations suggest using a checkbox with details about text messages, including frequency of messages and content of messages:

> I want to receive text messages on my mobile device on the newest trends, sales, and fashion tips from Organization A (Text messages will be sent to the cellular number provided. Up to three messages per month. Msg & Data rates may apply.).

In addition to the additional disclosure for text messaging, associations also recommend dual consent, or "double consent" to comply with FCC requirements. This involves sending an introductory text requiring the recipient to respond affirmatively to receive marketing text messages:

> Reply YES to confirm you want to receive mobile content from Organization A. Msg & Data rates may apply." After YES: "You are now subscribed to receive mobile content. Text STOP to end and HELP for more information. 3 messages per month.

110. Non-profit organizations enjoy an exemption from the consent requirement. However, non-profit organizations must remove individuals from their contact lists when requested.

The TCPA permits civil actions, often combined as class action lawsuits, with a ceiling fine of USD 1,500 per illegal call or text. One can imagine how much one marketing campaign could cost if not following TCPA. Although the FCC has not yet established whether the FCC rules require explicit text details during consent and extensive text disclosures, organizations with text message campaigns should consider taking a more conservative approach.

[B] The DNC Registry

The FTC manages the DNC Registry, which allows U.S. residents to place their phone numbers on a registry that organizations must use prior to calling individuals for marketing purposes. Any organization placing marketing phone calls, not just telemarketing agencies, must consult the DNC Registry before placing a call. Organizations in and outside the U.S. must lease the registry annually and update their internal lists every thirty days.
It is still unclear whether placement on the DNC Registry would bar an organization from gathering consent under the TCPA and placing an auto-dialed call.

[C] CAN-SPAM

The CAN-SPAM (2003) is co-regulated by the FCC and the FTC. CAN-SPAM bars organizations sending unsolicited e-mail communication and sending previously consented e-mail communication that does not include appropriate identifying information or an ability to easily opt-out of future communications. CAN-SPAM requires organizations to:[111]

- collect explicit, written consent to receive marketing materials (includes pre-selected checkboxes);- use accurate header information, such as To:, From:, and Subject lines (not misleading)
- include your physical address (postal address);
- provide an easy opt-out option, and honor opt-out requests promptly;
- monitor vendors sending e-mail on your behalf to ensure compliance.

CAN-SPAM does not apply to non-marketing e-mails within an existing business relationship (EBR). For example, an organization may have an existing relationship with an individual even if that relationship existed in the past. When an EBR applies, an organization can send e-mails without requiring additional consent from the individual. Under CAN-SPAM, each e-mail in violation of CAN-SPAM may be fined up

111. Federal Trade Commission, *CAN-SPAM Act: A Compliance Guide for Business* (Sept. 2009), https://www.ftc.gov/tips-advice/business-center/guidance/can-spam-act-compliance-guide-business.

to USD 40,654, so organizations should develop a CAN-SPAM-compliant approach for e-mail dissemination.

§3.06 GOVERNMENT AND ISPs

The Federal Wiretapping Act of 1968 first established a prohibition on wiretapping, or telephonic surveillance. In 1986, Congress updated the Federal Wiretapping Act of 1968 to include the Electronic Communications Privacy Act (ECPA) and the Stored Communications Act (SCA). Each act established a prohibition on accessing or monitoring telephonic or digital communications absent subscriber consent upon collection, in transit, or in storage. The U.S. government has included specific legal processes for access to data from U.S. providers according to the act, including subpoenas, warrants, special court orders, and other streamlined processes for the Federal Bureau of Investigation (FBI) when a circumstance is a matter of national security.

Congress passed the ECPA and SCA to update the Federal Wiretapping Act to cover digital technologies. Under the ECPA and SCA, organizations providing digital services are prohibited from eavesdropping on digital messaging. Most organizations, such as Internet Service Providers (ISPs) and digital service providers (e.g., e-mail and other providers) comply with this requirement by disclosing information handling practices via a privacy notice and collecting explicit consent from subscribers.

§3.07 CHILDREN'S ONLINE PRIVACY PROTECTION ACT

The U.S. Congress passed COPPA in 1998 following several failed attempts to censor Internet content, many of which the Supreme Court of the U.S. invalidated as infringing freedom of speech. COPPA regulates websites and online services (and manufacturers of connected toys) where an organization has actual knowledge or strong suspicion that children use the services, and requires appropriate parental consent prior to processing personal information of children under the age of 13. Parental consent is revocable at any time, requiring organizations to be able to stop collecting personal information on a particular child, even if a child continues to use a particular product or service.

Personal information covered under COPPA includes both information about a child and information about the child in their computer interactions. Online interactions generate other types of information which could compromise the safety of the child. Information protected includes:

- A child's first and last name
- Home or physical address and telephone number
- SSN—a national employment identifier
- Image, including avatar or voice recording
- Online screen name and online contact information

- IP address
- Device serial number or device ID
- Geolocation information
- Non-listed identifiers where multiple identifiers together may identify a child (e.g., school, grade, hair color, gender).

Notice provided to parents requires a description of information type collected, a description of how personal information will be used, to whom it will be disclosed, and instructions for refusing future use. Organization must use transparent, obvious, and reasonable means to obtain information. One-time responses to a specific request, such as a child learning more about the service, do not require parental consent.

Under COPPA, parents may terminate data processing when desired, and organizations must timely revoke consent and stop processing children's information. COPPA anticipated circumstances likely to trigger a child disclosing information, so additional provisions focus on limiting children's participation in games receiving prizes or other highly motivating activities. Finally, organizations must protect the confidentiality, security, and integrity of data collected. To comply with these requirements, organizations have pursued de-identification procedures specifically tailored for children's information.

The FTC sponsors a "safe harbor" for organizations handling children's information, which involves a self-disclosure and preapproval process to ensure compliance. However, organizations should also consider models for reducing data collection overall and avoiding collection if possible and practicable. For example, organizations might consider employing age verification techniques or not collecting information for children under age 13.[112] Furthermore, in the privacy notice organizations should make clearly noticeable higher risk data uses that could be concerning to parents to avoid downstream issues.

§3.08 FEDERAL TRADE COMMISSION

The FTC was created by the FTC Act of 1914 and is the primary consumer protection agency in the U.S.. The FTC Act's Section 5 gives the FTC the ability to prosecute "unfair and deceptive trade practices."[113] The FTC has, under Section 5, provided broad coverage for unregulated industries and organizations in the U.S., due to the lack of both omnibus privacy law and enforceable cybersecurity legal requirements. Under the FTC Act, the FTC has prosecuted actions involving data breaches as unfair and

112. The U.S. state of California has extended a right of revocation and data removal to minors under the age of 18. *See* The Online Privacy Protection Act, California Business and Professions Code §§ 22575-22579, S.B. No. 568, https://leginfo.legislature.ca.gov/faces/billNavClient.xhtml?bill_id=201320140SB568.

113. The Federal Trade Commission Act, 15 U.S.C §§ 41-58, as amended (1914).

deceptive trade practices, pursuing fifty-three actions as of August 2014.[114] The FTC has testified before the Senate Committees on Judiciary and Homeland Security and Government Affairs and the Banking Subcommittee, urging heightened FTC enforcement powers and federal data protection legislation, and has brought administrative actions against entities it suspects of unreasonable data protection practices.[115]

The FTC has generally focused most frequently on deceptive trade practices, rather than unfair trade practices, as deceptive trade practices often are easier to prove with respect to privacy and cybersecurity matters because they usually involve some manifestation of information and actions that do not match the claim. For example, a privacy notice could claim certain business uses for collecting personal information, yet the organization sells an individual's information to a third party for profit.

The FTC has full rule making and enforcement authority under COPPA, has created a data breach requirement for health data not under Health Information Portability and Accountability Act (HIPAA), developed the DNC Registry, enforces CAN-SPAM, and co-extensively regulates TCPA. The FTC provides guidelines and studies on a wide variety of emerging topics involving information privacy and cybersecurity topics. For example, the FTC has recently drafted a variety of business-oriented guides on children's privacy, consumer privacy, and data security.[116]
The FTC has also created frameworks for organizations to responsibly manage privacy obligations. Many privacy-conscious organizations in the U.S. leverage the Fair Information Practices (FIPs), inspired by the OECD Guidelines, as an organizational information privacy framework. FIPs safeguard an individual's ability to manage data collected about them (collection limitation), communication of the purpose for collection (purpose verification), use limited to disclosed purposes (use limitation), accountability, security, communication of practices through notice, and choice of whether data will be collected.[117] *See* Table 3.1 for details about the principles.

---

114. 15 U.S. C. §§ 41-58 (2006); Tripp Baltz, *Brill: FTC 'Not Looking for Perfect Security,' Only Small Number of Breach Cases*, Bloomberg BNA (Aug. 22, 2014), *available at* http://www.bna.com/brill-ftc-not-n17179894096/.
115. *See Testifying Before the Senate Judiciary Committee, FTC Reiterates Support for Data Security Legislation*, Federal Trade Commission (Feb. 4, 2014), http://www.ftc.gov/news-events/press-releases/2014/02/testifying-senate-judiciary-committee-ftc-reiterates-its-support; Melissa Maalouf, *FTC Calls Again for Nationwide Data Breach Legislation and Heightened Enforcement Powers*, ZwillGen Blog (Apr. 3, 2014), http://blog.zwillgen.com/2014/04/03/ftc-calls-nationwide-data-breach-legislation-heightened-enforcement-powers/; *FTC Testifies on Data Security before Senate Banking subcommittee*, Federal Trade Commission (Feb. 3, 2014), http://www.ftc.gov/news-events/press-releases/2014/02/ftc-testifies-data-security-senate-banking-subcommittee; LabMD, Inc. v. FTC, 776 F.3d 1275 (11th Cir. 2015); FTC v. Wyndham Worldwide Corp., 10 F.Supp. 3d (D. N.J. 2014); Farschad Farzan & Natasha Saggar Sheth, *Scope of FTC's Authority to Enforce Cybersecurity is Questioned*, NOSSAMAN LLP (Mar. 18, 2015), http://www.nossamanlitigationadvocates.com/2015/03/scope-of-ftcs-authority-to-enforce-cybersecurity-is-questioned/.
116. Federal Trade Commission, *Privacy and Security*, https://www.ftc.gov/tips-advice/business-center/privacy-and-security (last accessed Mar. 20, 2017).
117. FIPs are incorporated in large part into global data protection laws, with the exception of additional privacy principles included in the GDPR. In large part, FIPs were established following the OECD Guidelines Governing the Protection of Privacy and Transborder Flows of Personal Data, as were the first global laws for data protection, such as the EU Data Protection

Table 3.1 FIPs Privacy[118]

Principle	*Description*	*Example*
Transparency	Disclose in readable detail what you are doing with the data.	Privacy notice
Individual Participation	Let the individual choose how their data will be used.	Consent
Purpose Specification	Disclose the purpose of collection	Privacy notice contents
Data Minimization	Minimize data collected	Reduce data elements
Use Limitation	Use data according to disclosure	Limit repurposing
Data Quality and Integrity	Ensure data integrity	File Integrity Monitoring
Security	Protect the data	Access reviews
Accountability and Auditing	Assurance you follow the principles	Privacy program, training

§3.09 THE EU-U.S. PRIVACY SHIELD

Following a successful lawsuit to invalidate the US-EU Safe Harbor program, in 2016 the U.S. Department of Commerce and the EU Article 29 WP launched the EU-U.S. Privacy Shield program, seeking to repair aspects of the Safe Harbor program invalidated by the European Court of Justice.[119] Privacy Shield is not a law or treaty, but rather a contractual agreement between the U.S. and the EU, intended to facilitate cross-border transfer from the EU to a country that otherwise does not meet adequacy requirements.

Privacy Shield is designed for U.S. companies that routinely transfer data of EU data subjects to the U.S. U.S. companies self-regulate under Privacy Shield by submitting a self-assessment and committing to certain privacy obligations within the organization.[120] Example obligations are as follows:

- Comply with notice and choice principles

Directive (95/46/EC), which inspired several other global data protection laws. *See* Bartosz Marcinkowski, *Privacy Paradox(es): In Search of a Transatlantic Data Protection Standard*, 75 OHIO ST. L.J. 1167, 1179 (2013).

118. UNITED STATES FEDERAL TRADE COMMISSION, *Privacy Online: Fair Information Practices in the Electronic Marketplace: A Federal Trade Commission Report to Congress* (May 2000), https://www.ftc.gov/reports/privacy-online-fair-information-practices-electronic-marketplace-federal-trade-commission.

119. *Maximillian Schrems v. Data Protection Commissioner* (ECJ case C-362/14); EUROPEAN COMMISSION, *Restoring trust in transatlantic data flows through strong safeguards: European Commission presents EU-U.S. Privacy Shield* (29 Feb. 2016), http://europa.eu/rapid/press-release_IP-16-433_en.htm.

120. PRIVACY SHIELD NETWORK, *Key New Requirements* (2017), https://www.privacyshield.gov/Key-New-Requirements.

- Transfer data for only limited and specified purposes
- Take reasonable and appropriate steps to stop and remediate unauthorized processing
- Maintain data integrity and purpose limitation
- Respond to complaints within 45 days
- Provide a dispute resolution process at no cost to the individual with binding arbitration

U.S. companies apply for Privacy Shield self-certification by submitting an online form and associated documents on the Privacy Shield Website. Companies then receive confirmation of successful or failed certification. U.S. administrative agencies retain a right to validate compliance and bring administrative actions for incorrect information provided.

Although the Department of Commerce has facilitated the creation of the Privacy Shield program and manages complaints filed with the EC, the Federal Trade Commission (FTC) enforces obligations via consumer complaints.[121] In late 2017, the FTC brought its first two privacy shield cases, alleging two companies had fraudulently claimed Privacy Shield status, despite not receiving approval through the Privacy Shield program.

Despite higher visibility enforcement of Privacy Shield, EU privacy commentators and advocates have criticized the terms of the agreement. The substantially more stringent GDPR has particularly cast doubt on the enforceability of Privacy Shield, which passed under the Data Protection Directive. Critically, the EU-U.S. Privacy Shield does not address new data subject rights, such as the right of erasure and objection to automated processing. It is yet to be determined to what extent Privacy Shield participants will be required to comply with GDPR.

121. Federal Trade Commission, *Submit a Consumer Complaint* (2017), https://www.ftc.gov/faq/consumer-protection/submit-consumer-complaint-ftc.

CHAPTER 4

Latin America Region

Latin America (LATAM) exhibits a wide range of privacy protection within a substantially large geographical location. Twenty countries belong to the LATAM region, and many countries have acknowledged rights to privacy via constitutional protections. Fewer countries have omnibus data protection laws. Today, seven countries have the most comprehensive privacy laws, with two receiving an EU adequacy determination: Argentina, México, Uruguay, Chile, Costa Rica, Nicaragua, and Colombia. In addition, Brazil has developed a law specifically oriented towards Internet Service Providers (ISPs) with limited information privacy restrictions.

Although Chapter 4 does not examine the Caribbean islands in detail, Aruba, the Bahamas, Curaçao, the Dominican Republic, and Trinidad and Tobago (South America) have omnibus privacy laws that roughly model the EU Data Protection Directive, while others, as territories, follow laws from the U.S., France, U.K., and the Netherlands.[122]

§4.01 ARGENTINA

Argentina passed the Personal Data Protection Law (PDPL) No. 25,326 in 2000, which substantially matches the former EU Data Protection Directive's substantive civil rights. Argentina has a national regulatory authority, the Argentine Personal Data Protection Agency, that oversees the PDPL and also includes other laws, such as the Do

122. The Personal Data Protection Ordinance of 2011 (Aruba), The Data Protection (Privacy of Personal Information) Act 2003 (Bahamas) (The Bahamas do not restrict data transfer, require a Data Protection Officer or registration of processing activities); The Personal Data Protection Act 1 Oct. 2013 (PDPA) (Curaçao); The Organic Law 172-13 on the Protection of Personal Data (Dominican Republic); Data Protection Act, 2011 (Trinidad & Tobago).

Not Call DNC Registry.[123] The PDPL applies to "data treatment," rather than processing, defined as "systematic procedures that enable collection, preservation, organization, storage, modification, relation, evaluation, blocking, distraction, or handling of personal information," a very broad definition. The PDPL applies within the Argentinian territory, thus presumably applying to organizations operating within Argentina. In 2015, Argentina also adopted rules on the use of closed-circuit television (CCTV), limiting surveillance of employees without appropriate notice and subsequent consent.[124]

The PDPL requires purpose proportionality, so that data collected by data files, registers, bases, or banks (similar to a controller) is relevant and not excessive in relation to the purposes for collecting. Data about a data owner (data subject) must be maintained as correct and accurate, and organizations cannot collect information for reasons not disclosed in the privacy notice. The privacy notice includes the following information:

- purpose for data collection
- third-party information
- identity or location of the controller
- information about individual rights to access, update, correct, or delete data.

Following an opportunity to review the privacy notice, data subjects must provide explicit consent before organizations process personal information. Explicit consent must be provided in writing. Sensitive information must be protected by advanced security measures.

For organizations examining credit worthiness, the PDPL also describes obligations with respect to credit check processes. The PDPL limits discovered information regarding credit to only economic and financial information over the last five years. However, a data bank is not required to collect prior consent of the data owner, if inquiry is connected to report recipients' "commercial or credit activities.".

[A] Passages of Note: Argentine Constitution

[1] Section 43

> Any person shall file this action to obtain information on the data about himself and their purpose, registered in public records or data bases, or in private ones intended to supply information; and in case of false data or discrimination, this action may be filed to request the suppression, rectification, confidentiality or updating of said data. The secret nature of the sources of journalistic information shall not be impaired.[125]

123. The DNC Registry requires organizations marketing to download a new version of the registry every thirty days prior to marketing. Sanctions Regulation (Disp. 9/2015).
124. CCTV Regulation (Disp. 10/2015).
125. Argentine Federal Constitution, § 43.

[B] Passages of Note: Personal Data Protection Act

[1] Definitions

Chapter I

Section 2

Data owner: Any physical person or legal entity having a legal domicile or local offices or branches in the country, whose data are subject to the treatment referred to in this Act.

Data treatment: Systematic operations and procedures, either electronic or otherwise, that enable the collection, preservation, organization, storage, modification, relation, evaluation, blocking, destruction, and in general, the processing of personal information, as well as its communication to third parties through reports, inquiries, interconnections or transfers.

Data Dissociation: Treatment of personal data in such a way that the information obtained cannot be related to any certain or ascertainable person.

[2] Data

Chapter I

Section 2

Personal data: Information of any kind referred to certain or ascertainable physical persons or legal entities.

Sensitive data: Personal data revealing racial and ethnic origin, political opinions, religious, philosophical or moral beliefs, labor union membership, and information concerning health conditions or sexual habits or behavior.

Chapter II

Section 4

1. - The personal data collected for treatment purposes must be certain, appropriate, pertinent, and not excessive with reference to the scope within and purpose for which such data were secured.
2. - The collection of the data shall not be carried out using disloyal or fraudulent means, or in a manner contrary to the provisions of this Act.
3. - The data subject to treatment shall not be used for any purpose or purposes which are different from or incompatible with those giving rise to their collection.
4. - The data shall be accurate and updated, if necessary.
5. - Any data totally or partially inaccurate, or incomplete, must be suppressed and replaced, or, as the case may be, completed, by the person responsible for the file or data base upon notification of the inaccuracy or incompleteness of the relevant information, without prejudice to the data owner's rights set forth in Section 16 of this Act.
6. - The data must be stored in such a way that enables the data owner to exercise his or her right of access.
7. - The data shall be destroyed once it has ceased to be necessary or relevant to the purposes for which it has been collected

Section 7

1. - No person can be compelled to provide sensitive data.
2. - Sensitive data can be collected and subjected to treatment only in case there exist circumstances of general interest authorized by law, or with statistical or scientific purposes provided data owners cannot be identified.
3. - It is prohibited to create files, banks or registers storing information that directly or indirectly reveals sensitive data. Without prejudice to the foregoing, the Catholic Church, religious associations, and political and labor organizations shall be entitled to keep a register of their members.
4. - Data referring to criminal or other offense-commission records can be treated only by the competent public authorities, within the framework established by the corresponding laws and regulations.

[C] Data Bank

Chapter I

Section 2

Data file, register, base or bank: These terms designate, interchangeably, any organized set of personal data which is subject to treatment or processing, either electronically or otherwise, whatever form its collection, storage, organization or access may take.

Data user: Any person, either public or private, performing in its, his or her discretion the treatment of data contained in files, registers or banks, owned by such persons or to which they may have access through a connection.

Chapter II

Section 8

Public or private health institutions, as well as medical science professionals are entitled to collect and treat such personal data as they relate to the physical or mental condition of patients who make use of their services or who are or may have been in their care, in pursuance of the principles of professional secret.

[D] Notice

Chapter II

Section 6

Whenever personal data are requested, data owners shall be previously notified in an express and clear manner:

a) The purpose for which the data shall be treated, and who their addressees or type of addressees may be;
b) The existence of the relevant data file, register or bank, whether electronic or otherwise, and the identity and domicile of the person responsible therefor;
c) The compulsory or discretionary character of the answers to the questionnaire the person is presented with, particularly, in relation to the data connected with in the following Section;

d) The consequences of providing the data, of refusing to provide such data or of their inaccuracy;
e) The possibility the party concerned has to exercise the right of data access, rectification and suppression.

[E] Consent

Chapter II

Section 5

1. - The treatment of personal data is unlawful when the data owner has not given his or her express consent, which must be given in writing, or through any other similar means, depending on the circumstances.
   The consent above, given with other statements, must appear in a prominent and express manner, together with the warnings set forth in Section 6 hereof.
2. - The consent above shall not be deemed necessary when:
   a. the data are secured from source of unrestricted public-access; b. are collected for the performance of the duties inherent in the powers of the State;
   c. consist of lists limited to name, national identity card number, taxing or social security identification, occupation, date of birth, domicile and telephone number,
   d. arise from a contractual relationship, either scientific or professional of data owner, and are necessary for its development or fulfillment;
   e. refer to the transactions performed by financial entities, and arise from the information received from their customers in accordance with the provisions of Section 39 of Act Number 21.526.

[F] Access

Chapter III

Section 13

Any person may request information from the competent controlling body regarding the existence of data files, registers, bases or banks containing personal data, their purposes and the identity of the PR therefor. The register kept for such purpose can be publicly consulted, free of charge.

Section 14

1. - Data owners, once they have duly evidenced their identity, have the right to request and obtain information on their personal data included in public data registers or banks, or in private registers or banks intended for the provision of reports.
2. - The person responsible or user shall provide the requested information within ten calendar days of being demanded of such request. Upon expiration of the said term without such request being answered, or if the report is deemed insufficient, the proceeding to protect personal data or habeas data herein provided for shall be started.

3. - The right of access dealt with in this Section may only be exercised free of charge within intervals no shorter than six months, unless a legitimate interest to do otherwise is shown.
4. - In the event of death persons, their general heirs shall be entitled to exercise the right mentioned in this Section.

Section 15

1. - The information must be provided clearly, without any codes and, where applicable, enclosing an explanation of the terms used, in a language that is understood by a citizen with an average degree of education.
2. - The information must be extensive and deal with the full record corresponding to the owner, even in case the request submitted refers to only one item of personal data. In no case shall the report disclose information corresponding to third parties, even if such third parties are related to the requesting party.
3. - The information may, at the owner's option, be provided in writing, by electronic, telephonic, visual, or other adequate means for such purpose.

[G] Correction

Chapter III

Section 16

1. - Every person has the right to rectify, update, and when applicable, suppress or keep confidential his or her personal data included in a data bank.
2. - The person responsible for or the user of the data bank, must proceed to rectify, suppress or update the personal data belonging to the affected party, by performing the operations necessary for such purpose within the maximum term of five business days of the complaint being received or the mistake or false information being noticed.
3. - Noncompliance with such obligation within the term established in the preceding paragraph, will enable the interested party to bring, without any further proceedings, the action for the protection of personal data or habeas data contemplated in this Act.
4. - In the event of a data communication or transfer the person responsible for or the user of the data bank must notify the recipient of such rectification or suppression within five business days of the data treatment being effected.
5. - Such suppression must not be effected in the event it could cause harm to the rights or legitimate interests of third parties, or there existed a legal obligation to preserve such data.
6. - During the process for the verification and rectification of the relevant mistake or falsehood in the information, the person responsible for or the user of the data bank must either block the access to the file, or indicate, when providing the information relating thereto, the circumstance that such information is subject to revision.
7. - The personal data must be kept during the terms contemplated in the applicable provisions or, where appropriate, in the contractual relationships between the person responsible for or the user of the data bank and the data owner.

[H] Transfer

Chapter II

Section 12

1. - The transfer of any type of personal information to countries or international or supranational entities which do not provide adequate levels of protection, is prohibited.

Chapter IV

Section 30

1. - The associations or entities representing persons responsible for or users of privately-owned data banks may create professional practice codes of conduct, establishing the rules for the treatment of personal data tending to assure and improve the operational conditions of information systems on the basis of the principles established by this Act.
2. - Such codes shall be registered with the register kept by the controlling body, who may deny registration whenever it considers that the said codes do not conform with the legal and regulatory provisions governing the matter.

[I] Third Party

Chapter III

Section 25

1. - When personal data treatment services are provided for the account of third parties, such data cannot by applied or used with any purpose other than the one appearing on the corresponding contract for the provision of the service, nor can such data be communicated to other parties, even for storage purposes.
2. - Once the corresponding contractual obligations have been performed, the treated personal data must be destroyed, except in case there is an express authorization given by the person for account of whom such services are rendered, by reason of a possibility of the data being used for future services, in which case the data may be stored under due security conditions for a maximum term of up to two years.

[J] Marketing

Chapter III

Section 27

1. - Data suitable to establish certain profiles with promotional, commercial or advertising purposes may be treated in the collection of domiciles, distribution of documents, advertising or direct sales and other similar activities. This shall also include data which permit to determine consumption habits, when such data appear on documents which are accessible to the public or have been provided by the owners themselves or have been obtained with their consent.
2. - In the instances contemplated in this Section, the data owner may exercise the right of access free of any charge.

3. - The owner may at any time request the withdrawal or blocking of his name from any of the data banks referred to in this Section.

§4.02 BRAZIL

Brazil has struggled to pass an information privacy law, and despite multiple efforts, no omnibus law exists today. However, Brazil does recognize constitutional protections for privacy and private life as well as activities impacting personal reputation (similar to defamation laws in the U.S.) that allow for civil recovery. Constitutional protection also extends to secrecy of correspondence or communications, which could protect digital privacy under some circumstances.

Despite not passing omnibus legislation, Brazil has several regulations that could apply to digital communication and exchange of personal information. The Brazilian Civil Rights Framework for the Internet (RFI) regulates collection, use, storage, processing, disclosure, and third-party use of personal information. ISPs and Internet application providers with a presence in Brazil, such as a server or office, must follow the RFI, even if such business activities are multi-national in nature.[126]

The RFI does require express consent, including clear and complete notice of practices (visibly distinct from other contractual language) for processing personal information; it also requires express, informed consent for personal information transfer to third parties. If individuals' rights have not been protected, a natural person may recover for economic or moral damages. The RFI also requires protection of personal information in the form of cookie data and browsing history by ISPs. When the RFI was originally passed, it was designed to accompany a broader omnibus piece of legislation. For this reason, although the RFI does provide some protection to citizens, it is not considered comprehensive from an information privacy perspective.

The Brazilian Consumer Defense Code (CDC) also protects personal information and consumer-related databases. Under the CDC, organizations providing products or services that capture personal information must inform consumers, provide access to records about them, and restricts adverse information collection for more than five years. Although the CDC does not require prior notice and consent, this model avoids increased effort for organizations in the future.

[A] Passages of Note: Brazilian Civil RFI

[1] User Rights

Chapter II

I – inviolability of intimacy and private life, safeguarded the right for protection and compensation for material or moral damages resulting from their breach;

126. Marco Civil da Internet Law No. 12.965 24 Apr 2014, available at: https://www.publicknowledge.org/documents/marco-civil-english-version.

II - inviolability and secrecy of the flow of users' communications through the Internet, except by court order, as provided by law;
III - inviolability and secrecy of user's stored private communications, except upon a court order;
X - the definitive elimination of the personal data provided to a certain internet application, at the request of the users, at the end of the relationship between the parties, except in the cases of mandatory log retention, as set forth in this Law.

Chapter III

Section 2

Art. 10. The retention and the making available of connection logs and access to internet applications logs to which this law refers to, as well as, of personal data and of the content of private communications, must comply with the protection of privacy, of the private life, of the honor and of the image of the parties that are directly or indirectly involved.

§4° The security and confidentiality measures and procedures shall be informed in a clear manner by the responsible for the provision of the services, and meet the standards set in regulation, in compliance with rights of confidentiality of business secrets.

[2] *Notice*

Chapter II

VIII - clear and complete information on the collection, use, storage, processing and protection of users' personal data, which may only be used for the purposes of:

a) justifies its collection;
b) are not prohibited by law; and
c) are specified in the agreements of services or in the terms of use of the internet application

XI - the publicity and clarity of any terms of use of the internet connection providers and internet applications providers.

[3] *Consent*

Chapter II

IX - the expressed consent for the collection, use, storage and processing of personal data, which shall be specified in a separate contractual clause.

[4] *Third Parties*

Chapter II

VII - nondisclosure to third parties of users' personal data, including connection records and records of access to internet applications, unless with express, free and informed consent or in accordance with the cases provided by law.

§4.03 CHILE

Chile led the LATAM region for statutory information privacy developments, passing an omnibus information privacy law, Law No. 19.628, in 1999, on a foundation of privacy guarantees in Article 19 of the Chilean Constitution.[127] Although Chile includes similar provisions to the EU Data Protection Directive, Chile's lack of a dedicated regulatory authority does not currently make Chile eligible for adequacy standing, and some deviations from the Organisation for Economic Co-operation and Development (OECD) framework have prompted recent discussions regarding replacement. The Consumer Protection Law No. 19.496 also regulates commercial and marketing communications.[128]

Law No. 19.628 requires authorization prior to personal information processing, and organizations collecting personal information must provide notice prior to collection, including purposes for collection and third parties processing or receiving data. Data subjects additionally have rights to access, modify, or block information use.[129] Further, the Law restricts sensitive personal information (SPI) use where potentially damaging, such as for financial transactions and credit data, where organizations may only use data to make business decisions (such as mortgage qualifications).

§4.04 COLOMBIA

Colombia protects individual rights to information privacy through its constitution, omnibus Law No. 1581 (2012) and Decree 1377 (2013), which provide broad information, privacy protection, and sectoral laws. Law No. 1581, passed in 2012, follows the EU Data Protection Directive model and complements this with sectoral Law No. 1266/08 for credit, financial, and banking services.[130]

The Colombian Constitution was updated in 1991, and guarantees fundamental rights to privacy in Article 15, including that every individual has the right to personal and family privacy, as well as access, correction, and rectification rights with respect to

127. Ley No. 19.628, Sobre la Proteccion de la Vida Privada (1999).
128. Ley No. 19.496 Sobre Protección de los Derechos de los Consumidores (1997).
129. Chile and Russia have used terminology of "blocking" to communicate a technological change that halts further processing (and implies consent revocation). Chile balances a right to access against business, confidentiality, and national security, including circumstances that could compromise business practices.
130. Law No. 1581/2012.

personal information.[131] Decree 1377 built on this foundation, adding additional obligations for PR (controllers).

Under Decree 1377, data subjects are considered "Titleholders" with respect to personal information, and for this reason must "authorize" processing activities. Children require parental authorization, and collecting children's personal information and adult SPI is banned, except under certain circumstances. Children's personal information may be processed, but only upon authorization from a parent and when processing substantially benefits the child, rather than the Persons Responsible (PR). PR can collect SPI when Titleholders expressly authorize and PR disclaim that provision of SPI is not required to receive service.

Law No. 1581/2012 requires prior, express consent in the form of an authorization. Decree 1377 requires PR to apprise Titleholders of internal policies regarding personal information handling. In the event that this is not possible, PR may provide a Privacy Notice that contains:

- Contact information for PR
- Processing activities and purpose of processing
- Titleholder rights with respect to personal information
- Mechanisms for accessing and reviewing the PR's policies, and information about changes to the Notice of Privacy and process for updates and new authorization
- Express indication of the "optional nature" of responding to questions involving SPI.

Data transmission and transfer have different meanings under Decree 1377. Data transmission includes data transmitted within Colombia to a third party. Legal data transmission requires execution of contractual terms ensuring obligation with the PR policies and legal obligations. Data transfer means extra-Colombian data movement, and requires compliance with requirements in 1581/2012. Under 1581/2012, transfers outside of Colombia, even for inter-company transfer, are prohibited. Receiving countries must exhibit similar or more stringent information privacy protections or either: (1) have been deemed "adequate" by the Superintendent of Industry and Commerce (SIC) or (2) a treaty governs such a transfer.

Decree 1377 requires substantial procedural rigor and documentation to illustrate practices. PR must develop procedures for notice updates, access requests, correction, deletion, maintenance of authorizations and revocation, as well as train personnel on these processes. PR must also develop auditable information privacy policies, as these policies by law should be provided to Titleholders whenever possible and may be reviewed by the SIC.

Adding to this data protection rigor, Act 1273 (updated in 2009) criminalizes unauthorized access, use, purchase, sales, disclosure, or modification for benefit of self or a third party. The penalty involves 48–96 months of jail time and fines.

---

131. Colombian Constitution, Art. 15, available at: http://confinder.richmond.edu/admin/docs/colombia_const2.pdf.

[A] Passages of Note: Decree 1377

[1] Data

Chapter 1

Article 3

3. Sensitive data: It is understood by sensitive data those that affect the intimacy of the Titleholder or whose improper use can generate his discrimination, such as those that disclose the racial or ethnic origin, political orientation, religious or philosophical beliefs, membership to labor unions, social organizations, human rights or that foster interests of any political party or that guarantee the rights and guarantees of opposition political parties, as well as data relative to health, sex life, and biometric data.

[2] Persons Responsible

Chapter II

Article 11

Temporary limitations to personal data Processing. The Processing person Responsible and In Charge shall only be able to collect, store, use or circulate personal data during the time that it is reasonable and necessary, according to the purposes that justified the Processing, applying the provisions applicable to the subject matter that it deals with and the administrative, accounting, fiscal, judicial and historical aspects of the information. Once fulfilled the purpose or purposes of the Processing and notwithstanding legal rules that provide otherwise, the person Responsible and In Charge must proceed to the suppression of the personal data in their possession. Notwithstanding the foregoing, the personal data must be kept when so required for compliance with a legal or contractual obligation.

The Processing person Responsible and In Charge must document the procedures for the Processing, preservation and suppression of personal data pursuant to the provisions applicable to the subject matter that it deals with, as well as the instructions to that regard imparted by the Superintendence of Industry and Trade.

Article 12

Special requirements for the Processing of boys, girls, and teenagers' personal data. The Processing of boys, girls and teenagers' personal data is banned, except when it deals with data of a public nature, pursuant to that stipulated in article 7 of Law 1581/2012 and when said Processing complies with the following parameters and requirements:

1. That it responds and respects the superior interest of boys, girls, and teenagers.
2. That the respect for their fundamental rights is ensured.

Fulfilled the foregoing requirements, the legal representative of the boy, girl or teenager shall grant the authorization prior to the minor's exercise of his right to be heard, opinion that shall be valued taking into account the maturity, autonomy and capacity of understanding the matter.

All persons Responsible and In Charge involved in the Processing of personal data of boys, girls, and teenagers, must watch over their appropriate use. To this end the principles and obligations stipulated in Law 1581/2012 and the present Decree must be applied.

Chapter IV

Article 27

Effective internal policies. In each case, according to the circumstances mentioned in sections 1, 2, 3, and 4 of the foregoing article 26, the effective and appropriate measures implemented by the person Responsible must be consistent with the instructions imparted by the Superintendence of Industry and Trade. Said policies must guarantee:

1. The existence of an administrative structure proportional to the Responsible person's business structure and size for the adoption and implementation of policies consistent with Law 1581/2012 and this Decree.
2. The adoption of internal mechanisms in order to put these policies into practice including implementation tools, training and education programs.
3. The adoption of processes for the attention and response to the Titleholder's inquiries, petitions and claims, with respect to any aspect of the Processing.

[3] Notice

Chapter 1

Article 3

1. Privacy notification: Verbal or written communication generated by the Responsible person, addressed to the Titleholder for the Processing of his personal data, by means of which he is informed about the existence of information Processing policies that shall be applicable to him, the manner of accessing them and the purposes of the Processing that is intended to be given to the personal data.

Chapter II

Article 5

Authorization. The Processing Responsible person must adopt procedures to request, no later than at the time of collecting his data, the Titleholder's authorization for their Processing and inform him of the personal data that shall be collected as well as all the purposes specific to the Processing for which the consent is obtained.

In case of substantial changes occurring in the contents of the Processing policies referred to in Chapter III of this Decree, referring to the identification of the person Responsible and to the purpose of the personal data Processing, which can affect the contents of the authorization, the Processing Responsible person must communicate these changes to the Titleholder before or no later than at the time of implementing the new policies. In addition, he must obtain from the Titleholder a new authorization when the change refers to the purpose of the Processing.

Article 6

On the authorization for the Processing of sensitive personal data. The Processing of sensitive data to which article 5 of Law 1581/2012 refers is banned, except in the cases expressly indicated in article 6 of the cited law.

In sensitive personal data Processing, when said Processing is possible pursuant to that stipulated in article 6 of Law 1581/2012, the following obligations must be complied with:

1. Inform the Titleholder that as it is concerning sensitive data he is not obligated to authorize its Processing.
2. Explicitly and previously inform the Titleholder, in addition to the general requirements of the authorization for the collection of any type of personal data, which of the data that shall be object to Processing are sensitive and the purpose of the Processing, as well as obtain his express consent.

No activity may be conditioned to the Titleholder providing sensitive personal information.

Chapter III

Article 13

Information Processing Policies. The Processing Responsible persons must develop their policies for the Processing of personal data and ensure that the Processing persons In Charge fully comply with them.

The information Processing policies must be on record in physical or electronic means, in a clear and simple language, and made known to the Titleholders. Said polices must include, at least, the following information:

1. The Responsible person's name or company name, domicile, address, electronic mail and telephone.
2. Processing to which the data shall be subject and its purpose when this has not been informed by means of the Notice of Privacy.
3. Rights that assist him as Titleholder.
4. Person or area responsible for attending petitions, inquiries and claims before which the information Titleholder can exercise his rights to know, update, rectify and suppress the data or revoke the authorization.
5. Procedure so that the information Titleholders can exercise the rights to know, update, rectify and suppress information or revoke the authorization.
6. Date the information Processing policy entered into force and period during which the databases remain in force.

Any substantial change in the Processing policies, in the terms described in article 5 of the present decree, must be timely communicated to the Titleholders of the personal data, before implementing the new policies.

Article 14

Notice of Privacy. In cases in which it is not possible to put at the disposal of the Titleholder the Information Processing policies, the person Responsible must inform the Titleholder by means of a Notice of Privacy of the existence of such policies and the manner to access them, in a timely manner and in all cases no later than at the time of the personal data collection.

[4] *Consent*

Chapter II

Article 7

Method of obtaining the authorization. For purposes of complying with that provided in article 9 of Law 1581/2012, the personal data Processing Responsible persons shall establish mechanisms to obtain the authorization of the Titleholders or those legally authorized pursuant to that stipulated in article 20 of the present decree, that guarantee their consultation. These mechanisms can be predetermined through technical means that facilitate their automated manifestation for the Titleholder. It shall be understood that the

Collection/Processing authorization complies with these requirements when it is manifested (i) in writing, (ii) verbally or (iii) by means of unequivocal behaviors of the Titleholder that allow to reasonably conclude that he granted authorization. In no case may silence be assimilated as an unequivocal behavior.

Article 8

Proof of the authorization. The persons Responsible must keep proof of the authorization granted by the personal data Titleholders for their Processing.

Article 9

Revocation of the authorization and/or data suppression. The Titleholders may at any time request the person Responsible or In Charge the suppression of their personal data and/or revoke the authorization granted for their Processing, by means of filing a claim, pursuant to that stipulated in article 15 of Law 1581/2012.

The person Responsible and in Charge must put at the disposal of the Titleholder free and easy access mechanisms to file the request for the suppression of data or the revocation of the granted authorization.

Chapter II

Article 4

Personal data collection. In development of the principles of purpose and freedom, the data collection must be limited to those personal data that are pertinent and adequate to the purpose for which they are collected or required pursuant to the regulation in force. Except in cases expressly provided in the Law, personal data cannot be collected without the authorization of the Titleholder.

[5] Access

Chapter IV

Article 21

On the right to access. The Processing persons Responsible and In Charge must establish simple and agile mechanisms that are found permanently available to the Titleholders with the purpose that these can access the personal data that are under the control of those and exercise their rights on them.

The Titleholder shall be able to consult his personal data for free: (i) at least once each calendar month, and (ii) each time that substantial modifications to the information Processing Policies exist that motivate new consultations.

[6] Transfer/Transmission

Chapter 1

Article 3

4. Transfer: Data transfer occurs when the person Responsible and/or In Charge of personal data Processing, located in Colombia, sends the information or personal data to a recipient, that in turn is the Responsible for Processing and is found within or outside of the country.
5. Transmission: Personal data Processing that implies its communication within or outside the territory of the Republic of Colombia when it has as purpose carrying out Processing by the person In Charge on behalf of the person Responsible.

Chapter V

Article 25

Transmission of personal data contract. The contract that the person Responsible subscribes with the persons In Charge for the Processing of personal data under his control and responsibility shall indicate the Processing scope, the activities that the person In Charge shall conduct on behalf of the person Responsible for the Processing of personal data and the obligation the person In Charge has with the Titleholder and the person Responsible.

By means of said contract the person In Charge shall commit to implementing the Responsible person's obligations under the information Processing policy established by the latter and to conduct the data Processing in accordance with the purpose that the Titleholder has authorized and with the applicable laws.

In addition to the obligations imposed by the applicable rules within the cited contract, the following obligations under the responsibility of the respective person In Charge must be included:

1. Process, on behalf of the person Responsible, the personal data pursuant to the principles that protect them.

2. Safeguard the security of the databases in which personal data is contained.

3. Keep confidentiality with regards to the Processing of personal data.

§4.05 COSTA RICA

Costa Rica has implemented two information privacy laws: Law No. 7975, *Undisclosed Information Law* and Law No. 8968, *Protection in the Handling of the Personal Data of Individuals*. Costa Rica follows the EU Data Protection Directive model, but applies laws only to organizations administering databases.[132]

Costa Rica's Law No. 7975 bars disclosure for both personal information and other confidential or business restricted information, including trade secrets and absent consent. Although it does not explicitly mention personal information, it would restrict unauthorized employee disclosures that often lead to privacy implications (e.g., other employee personal information). Law No. 8968 specifies specific information privacy obligations.

Law No. 8968 follows standard omnibus legislative rights, including informed and explicit consent, purpose disclosure, rights to access and correction, necessity of collection and processing, and reasonable administrative and technical measures.

132. No. 7975 Law on Undisclosed Information (2012), available at: http://www.wipo.int/wipolex/en/text.jsp?file_id=276332.

However, Law No. 8968 only applies to operators of databases within Costa Rica, which likely does not apply to most services provided in the country. The Prodhab regulates this law and publishes guidelines for interpretation.[133]

§4.06 MÉXICO

México's omnibus information privacy law, the Federal Law on the Protection of Personal Data ("Federal Law") of 2010, focuses on collection, use, disclosure, storage, access, transfer, and disposal activities, similar to the EU Data Protection Directive.[134] The executive branch has also passed regulations, the Regulations to the Federal Law, Guidelines for Privacy Notices, and Parameters for Self-Regulation.

The Federal Law Regulations apply to any organization doing business in México, with a Mexican controller, or using technology located in México. Controllers collecting and processing personal information must also direct the activities of processors to adhere to these requirements, though cross-border transfers to out-of-country processors must meet sufficiency requirements.

Data collected under this law must be relevant, necessary, accurate, and updated for purposes collected. Controllers must obtain consent to process data, whether that consent is express or implied, and processors must also adhere to privacy notice disclosures. In addition to retention limitations and security requirements including administrative technical or physical safeguards, México recognizes special recovery not only for economic harm but also for moral rights relating to a data breach. Unlike the EU Data Protection Directive, México requires data breach notification. Data subjects enforce Access, Rectification, Cancellation, and Opposition (ARCO rights) against a controller in a court of law.

§4.07 PERÚ

Perú has enacted a very comprehensive data protection program. Perú's Constitution Article 2, No. 6 guarantees information privacy, "information services, whether computerized whether public or private, will not provide information affecting personal and family privacy." Perú published the PDPL No. 29733 on July 3, 2011, but most of the law was not in effect until 2013, when the Supreme Decree passed.[135] The Ministerio de Justicia y Derechos Humanos is responsible for information privacy within Perú.[136]

---

133. Agencia de Protección de Datos de los Habitantes, PRODHAUB (2017), http://prodhab.go.cr/.
134. Federal Law on the Protection of Personal Data (*Ley Federal de Protección de Datos Personales en Posesión de los Particulares) (5 Jul. 2010), available at: http://inicio.ifai.org.mx/English/1%20Data%20Protection%20Law.pdf.*
135. The Personal Data Protection Law No. 29733 (Ley No. 29733, Ley de Protección de Datos Personales); Supreme Decree 003-2013-JUS (2013). Translation provided via Google Translate with some adaptation by the Author.
136. For copies of Perú's Data Protection laws in Spanish, *see* Ministerio de Justicia y Derechos Humanos, *Dirección General de Protección de Datos Personales – Legislación* (2017), https://www.minjus.gob.pe/legislacion/.

The PDPL follows the EU Data Protection Directive model, and Perú applies the PDPL similar to México: a business within Perúvian territory, business subject to Perúvian law by international or contractual provision, a database holder is established in Perú, or a database located in Perú is used by a controller in a country outside Perú. The PDPL describes obligations for cloud providers, illustrating a modernization of the PDPL. Perú has further strengthened its approach to information privacy by passing the Security Policy on Information Managed by Databanks of Personal Data enacted by Directorial Resolution No. 019-2013-JUS/DGPDP on October 11, 2013, discussed in Chapter 10.[137]

Perú defines personal information to include all forms and versions of personal information, including pictures and acoustic copies, and applies protection to "all modalities" of personal information capture and storage, demonstrating a broad application intended to avoid application gaps. Through the broad and comprehensive PDPL, Perú has demonstrated its strong commitment to individual choice, including high standards for manifesting consent and prior notice, with specific conditions for children's consent. To satisfy notice requirements, the PDPL requires notice communicated in clear, "expressly and undoubtedly," in a "simple language." Perú's PDPL offers an excellent example of a comprehensive data protection law in LATAM.

[1] *Passages of Note: PDPL*

[1] Applicability

Title 1

Article 3

Scope of application. This regulation applies to the processing of personal data contained in a personal database or intended to be contained in personal database. Pursuant to section 6 article 2 of the Political Constitution of Peru and article 3 of Law No. 29733, Personal Data Protection Law, this regulation will apply to any personal data processing modality, be it done by natural persons, public entities or private sector institutions, regardless of the medium on which the data is found.

Article 5

Territorial scope of application. The provisions of the Law and this regulation apply to the processing of personal data when:

1. It is done in an establishment located in Peruvian territory, corresponding to the holder of the database or the data controller.
2. It is done by a data processor, regardless of its location, in the name of a holder of the database established in Peruvian territory, or the data controller.
3. The holder of the database or the data controller is not established in Peruvian territory, but is subject to Peruvian legislation, by contractual or international law provision; and
4. The holder of the database or the controller is not established in Peruvian territory, but uses means located in said territory, except if such means are used only for transit purposes that do not imply processing.

137. Directiva de Seguridad de la Información, No. 019-2013-JUS/DGPDP (2013).

For these purposes, the controller must provide the means necessary for actual performance of the obligations imposed by Law and this regulation and will designate a representative or will implement sufficient mechanisms to be able to comply effectively, in Peruvian territory, with the obligations imposed on it by Peruvian law.

When the holder of the database or the data controller are not established in Peruvian territory, but the data processor is, the latter will be subject to the provisions concerning the security measures contained in this regulation.

In the case of natural persons, the establishment will be understood as the premises where the main place of its business is located, or that used for the performance of its activities or its domicile.

In case of legal persons, it will be understood as the establishment the place where the main administration of the business is located. In case of legal persons residing abroad, it will be understood that it is the premises where the main administration of the business is located in Peruvian territory, or in the absence thereof that designated by them, or any stable installation that allows the actual or real performance of an activity.

If it is not possible to establish the address of the domicile or the establishment, it will be considered that it has an unknown domicile in Peruvian territory.

[2] Data

Title 1

Article 2

4. Personal data: Numerical, alphabetical, graphic, photographic, acoustic or any other time of information concerning natural persons that identifies them or makes them identifiable through means that may be reasonably used.
5. Health-related personal data: Information concerning past, present or predicted physical or mental health of a person, including the degree of disability and his genetic information.
6. Sensitive data: Information concerning personal data referring to physical, moral or emotional characteristics, facts or circumstances of the affective or family life, personal habits, information concerning the physical or mental health and others similar, that affect a person's privacy.

[3] Controller/Processor/Receiver

Title 1

Article 2

14. Data controller: Party deciding on the processing of personal data, even when they are not in a database.
10. Data processor: Party processing the personal data, which may be the holder of the database or the processor of the database or another person by the order of the holder of the database, pursuant to a legal relationship that binds him to it, and delimits the scope of his action. Includes the party processing personal data by order of the processor of the database, when it is done in the absence of a database.
11. Receiver or importer of personal data: Any private natural or legal person, including the branches, affiliates, related or similar companies, or public entities, who receive the data in the event of international transfer, be it as holder or processor of the personal database, or as third party

[4] Database Registration

Chapter V

Chapter 1

Article 76

Registration. The National Register of Personal Data Protection is the storage unit intended to contain mainly the information on databases publicly or privately owned, and its purpose is to give advertising to the registration of said bases, so that it would be possible to exercise the rights of access to the information, rectification, cancellation, opposition and others regulated by the Law and this regulation.

Article 77

Acts and documents that may be recorded in the Register. The following will be registered in the National Register of Personal Data Protection, pursuant to the Law and this Title:

1. Publicly administered databases, with the exceptions provided in the Law and this regulation.
2. Privately administered databases, with the exceptions provided in section 1) article 3 of the Law.
3. The codes of conduct referred to in article 31 of the Law.
4. The sanctions, provisional or corrective measures imposed by the General Department of Personal Data Protection pursuant to the Law and this regulation.
5. The communications referring to the trans-border flow of personal data.

Any person may consult the information referred to in article 34 of the Law and any other contained in the Register.

Title V

Chapter III

Article 89

Scope of application of code of conducts.

1. The code of conducts will be voluntary.
2. Industry code of conducts may refer to all or part of the processing carried out by the sector, being formulated by representative organizations.
3. The code of conducts promoted by a company or corporate group must refer to all processing done by them.

Article 90

Content.

1. The code of conducts must be drafted in clear and accessible terms.
2. The code of conducts must be suitable to the provisions of the law and include as a minimum the following aspects:
   - 2.1. Clear and precise delimitation of their scope of application, the activities to which the code refers and the processing subject to it.
   - 2.2. The specific provisions for the application of the principles of data protection.
   - 2.3. Establishment of homogenous standards for compliance by those adhering to the code with the obligations established in the Law.

2.4. Establishment of procedures facilitating the exercise by the appropriate parties of their rights of information, access, update, inclusion, rectification, suppression and opposition.
2.5. The determination of the national and international transfers of personal data which, if applicable, are provided with indication of the guarantees to be adopted.
2.6. The actions of support and spreading in matter of protection of data intended for the parties processing them, especially concerning their relationship with the parties affected.
2.7. The inspection mechanisms which guarantee compliance by the adhering parties of the provisions of the code of conduct.
3. In particular, the code must contain:
3.1. Clauses to obtain consent of the data subjects for the processing or transfer of their data.
3.2. Clauses to inform the data subjects about the processing when the data are not obtained from them.
3.3. Models for the exercise by the affected parties of their rights of information, access, updating, inclusion, rectification, suppression and opposition.
3.4. If applicable, models of clauses for compliance with the formal requisites to contract a data processor.

[5] Choice

Title II

Article 13

Privacy policies. The publication of privacy policies, as provided in the second paragraph of article 18 of the Law, must be understood as a form of complying with the duty of information, which does not exempt it from the requisite of obtaining the consent of the data subject.

[6] Consent

Title II

Article 7

Principle of consent. Given the principle of consent, personal data processing is legal when the data subject gave his free, prior, express, informed and unequivocal consent. Formulas of consent are not permitted in which the consent is not expressed directly, as such in which it is necessary to presume or assume the existence of a will that was not expressed. Even the consent given with other declarations must be declared expressly and clearly.

Article 12

In addition to the provisions of article 18 of the Law and the previous article of this regulation, obtaining consent must be:

1. Free: Without error, bad faith, violence or fraud that may affect the declaration of will of the data subject.

   The delivery of gifts or the granting of benefits to the data subject in connection with his consent do not affect the condition of freedom he has to grant it, except in the case of minors, in the events that their consent is admitted, since the consent granted against gifts or benefits will not be considered free.

The conditioning of the performance of a service, or the notice or warning of threat of denying access to benefits or services that normally have unrestricted access, if it affects the freedom of the person consenting to the processing of his data.

2. Prior: Before recompiling the data or if applicable prior to the processing other than that for which they were already recompiled.
3. Express or Unequivocal: When the consent has been declared under conditions that do not admit doubts about its granting.

It is considered that the express consent was verbally given when the subject expresses it orally, while being present, or by the use of any technology that allows oral questioning.

It is considered written consent that granted by the subject in a document with his autograph signature, fingerprint or any other mechanism authorized by the legal system, which remains or may be printed on a surface of paper or similar.

The express condition is not limited to the verbal or written declaration.

Restrictively, and always in agreement with article 7 of this regulation, express consent is considered that indicated by the conduct of the subject who shows that he has consented unequivocally, since otherwise his conduct would have necessarily been different.

In case of digital environment, it is also considered express the declaration consisting of "clicking," or "tapping," or "touch" or "pad."

In this context, written consent may be granted by electronic signature, by printed written document, so that it may be read and a printout made, or by any other mechanism or procedure established that may identify the subject and receive his consent, by a written text. It may also be granted by pre-established text, easily visible, legible and in simple language, which the subject may adopt or not, by a written or graphic answer or by click or tap.

The only conduct of expressing the will in any of the forms regulated by this section does not eliminate or considers complied with the other requisites of consent referring to freedom, opportunity and information.

4. Informed: When the data subject is communicated clearly, expressly and undoubtedly, in a simple language, at least the following:
   a. The identity and domicile or address of the holder of the database or data controller which he may address to evoke the consent or exercise his rights.
   b. The purpose or purposes of the processing to which his data will be subject.
   c. The identity of those who are or may be his addressees, if applicable.
   d. The existence of databases in which they will be stored, when such is the case.
   e. The mandatory or optional character of his answers to the questionnaire offered to him, when applicable.
   f. The consequences of providing his personal data and his refusal to do so.
   g. If applicable, national and international transfer of data made.

Article 14

Consent and sensitive data. In the case of sensitive data, the consent must be granted in writing, by handwritten signature, digital signature or any other mechanism of authentication guaranteeing the unequivocal will of the subject.

Chapter IV

Title III

Chapter IV

Article 27

Processing of personal data of minors. For the processing of personal data of a minor, the consent of the holders of parental authority or guardians will be required, as the case may be.

Article 28

Exceptional consent. The personal data of children over fourteen years of age and less than eighteen years of age may be done with their consent, provided that the information supplied is expressed in a language that is understandable for them, except if the law requires the assistance of the holders of parental authority or guardianship to be granted.

In no case may the consent to process personal data of minors be granted in order to have them access activities or related to goods or services that are reserved for persons of legal age.

[7] Access

Chapter II

Article 62

Means to comply with the right of access. The information corresponding to the right of access, at the choice of the data subject, may be provided in writing, by electronic means, by telephone, image or other appropriate means for this purpose.

The data subject may choose through one or several of the following forms:

1. Visualization on site.
2. Writing, copy, photocopy or fax.
3. Electronic transmission of the answer, provided that the identity of the interested party is guaranteed, the same as the confidentiality, integrity and receipt of the information.
4. Any other form or means that are adequate to the configuration or material implementation of the database or the nature of the processing, established by the holder of the database or data controller.

Regardless of the form used, the access must be in clear, legible and intelligible format, without using keys or codes that require mechanical devices for proper understanding and, if applicable, accompanied by an explanation. Furthermore, the access must be in accessible language to the average knowledge of the population, of the terms used. Notwithstanding, in order to use the most ecological communication means available in each case, the data controller may agree with the subject on the use of reproduction means of the information other than those established in this regulation.

[8] Transfer

Article 19

Conditions for transfer. Any transfer of personal data requires the consent of its subject, except for the exceptions provided in article 14 of the Law, and must be limited to the purpose that justifies it.

[10] Third Party

Title I

Article 2

15. Third party: Any natural person, private or public legal person other than the subject of personal data, the holder or processor of the personal database, and of the data controller, including those who process data under their direct authority.

Title IV

Article 37

Processing by subcontracting. Personal data processing may be done by a third party other than the data processor, through an agreement or contract between these two.

In this event, it will be required to have a prior authorization from the holder of the database or data controller. Said authorization will also be understood granted if it was provided in the legal instrument formalizing the relationship between the data controller and the data processor. The processing done by the subcontractor is done in the name and on behalf of the data controller, but the burden of proving the authorization lies with the data processor.

Article 38

Responsibility of the third party subcontracted. The natural or legal persons subcontracted assumes the same obligations established for the data processor under the Law, this regulation and other applicable provisions. However, he will assume the obligations of the holder of the database or data controller, when:

1. It intends or uses the personal data for a different purpose than that authorized by the holder of the database or data controller; or
2. It makes a transfer, violating the instructions of the holder of the database, even when it is for the conservation of the data.

[11] Data Transfer

Chapter III

Article 19

Conditions for transfer. Any transfer of personal data requires the consent of its subject, except for the exceptions provided in article 14 of the Law, and must be limited to the purpose that justifies it.

Article 21

Transfer within a sector or corporate group and code of conduct. In the event of transfers of personal data within corporate groups, subsidiaries, affiliated or related companies under common control of the same group of the holder of the database or data controller, or the affiliates or companies related to a parent company or to any company of the same group of the holder of the database or data controller, the personal data processing will be guaranteed if there is a code of conduct that establishes the internal rules for the protection of personal data with the content provided in article 31 of the Law, and recorded according to articles 89 to 97 of this regulation.

Article 22

Receiver of personal data. The receiver of the personal data assumes the condition of holder of the database or data controller in the aspects referred to by the Law and this regulation, and must process the personal data complying with the provisions of the information given by the issuer prior to the consent obtained from the data subject.

Article 24

Trans-border flow of personal data. Trans-border flows of personal data will be possible when the receiver or importer of the personal data assumes the same obligations of the holder of the database or the data controller who transferred the personal data as issuer or exporter.

[12] Contractual Clauses

Chapter III

Article 25

Formalization of the trans-border data flow. For the purposes of the previous article, the issuer or exporter must use contractual clauses or other legal instruments, establishing at least the same obligations as to those to which it is subject, as well as the conditions under which the subject consented to the processing of his personal data.

§4.08 URUGUAY

Uruguay, with Argentina and Perú, has led the evolution of information privacy in LATAM, passing the Data Protection Act Law No. 18.331 in 2008 and by decree in 2009. Uruguay was the second LATAM country granted adequacy under the EU standard in 2012, and Uruguay also manages a list of countries deemed adequate according to its standards. Much of Uruguay's law matches that of Perú and Argentina in content (previously discussed and referenced in passages of note). *The Unidad Reguladora y de Control de Datos Personales* (URCDP) enforces the Data Protection Act.

Uruguay follows the EU Data Protection Directive requirements with respect to personal data. First, PR must securely delete personal data when no longer in use, and data owners must provide advance, informed, written consent for SPI use, and express consent for personal information transfer. Certain data types enjoy different protection under Uruguay law, such as banking and health data when used for executing transactions and providing medical care, respectively, where laws establish other legal responsibilities. Unlike the EU Data Protection Directive, however, Uruguay only makes passing mention of contractual clauses accomplishing adequacy, so it is unclear to what degree EU MCCs might fulfill adequacy requirements.

[A] Passages of Note: Data Protection Law No. 18.331

[1] Access

Article 14

The information must be provided within five business days of being requested. Once the deadline has expired without the order being satisfied or if it has been denied for reasons not justified under this law, the habeas data action shall be authorized.

The information must be supplied in a clear way, free of codifications and, if applicable, accompanied by an explanation, in a language accessible to the average knowledge of the population, of the terms used.

The information must be comprehensive and cover the whole of the registry belonging to the owner, even if the request only includes one aspect of the personal data. In no case may the report disclose data belonging to third parties, even if they are linked to the interested party.

The information, at the option of the owner, may be provided in writing, by electronic means, telephone, image, or other suitable for this purpose.

[2] Correction

Article 15

Right of rectification, updating, inclusion or deletion.- Every natural or legal person shall have the right to request the rectification, updating, inclusion or deletion of the personal data that correspond to him / her included in a database, upon finding an error or falsehood Or exclusion in the information it holds.

The person responsible for the database or the processing must proceed to make the correction, updating, inclusion or deletion, through the operations necessary for this purpose within a maximum period of five working days of receipt of the request by the holder of the data or, in Your case, inform the reasons why you think does not correspond.

Failure to comply with this obligation by the database manager or the processing or expiration of the term, will entitle the data owner to promote the action of habeas data provided in this law.

[3] Data Transfer

Chapter V

Article 23

Data transferred internationally - The transfer of personal data of any kind with international countries or organizations that do not provide adequate levels of protection according to the standards of International or Regional Law in the matter is prohibited.

The prohibition shall not apply in the case of:

It will also be possible to carry out the international transfer of data in the following cases:

1) International judicial cooperation, according to the respective international instrument, either Treaty or Convention, given the circumstances of the case.

2) Exchange of medical data, when required by the treatment of the affected person for reasons of public health or hygiene.
3) Bank or stock exchanges, in relation to the respective transactions and according to the legislation that is applicable to them.
4) Agreements within the framework of international treaties in which the Eastern Republic of Uruguay is a party.

[4] Marketing

Chapter IV

Article 21

Data relating to databases for the purpose of publicity.- In the collection of domiciles, distribution of documents, publicity, sale or other similar activities, data may be processed that are capable of establishing profiles determined for promotional, commercial or Advertising; Or permit to establish habits of consumption, when these appear in documents accessible to the public or have been provided by the owners themselves or obtained with their consent.

In the cases contemplated in this article, the data subject may exercise the right of access without charge.

The holder may at any time request the withdrawal or blocking of his data from the databases referred to in this article.

[5] Security

Chapter IV

Article 20

Likewise, they must adopt the appropriate technical and management measures to preserve security in the operation of their network or in the provision of their services, in order to guarantee their levels of protection of the personal data that are required by the development regulations of this law in this matter. In the event of a particular risk of a breach of the security of the public electronic communications network, the operator operating the said network or providing the electronic communications service shall inform the subscribers of the said risk and of the measures to be taken.

The regulation contained in this law is understood without prejudice to the provisions of the specific regulations on telecommunications related to public security and national defense.

CHAPTER 5

Asia-Pacific Region

The Asia-Pacific Region (APAC) began its movement towards protecting data subject rights first in 1988 and 1993, with Australia and New Zealand, respectively, and continuing until the Asia-Pacific Economic Council (APEC) created the APEC Privacy Framework, loosely based on the Organisation for Economic Co-operation and Development (OECD) Guidelines, in 2004.[138] Despite establishing several similar principles, the APEC Privacy Framework relaxed data transfer requirements by permitting data subject consent as a valid transfer mechanism. This relaxation of transfer requirements contrasted sharply with trade-restrictive EU cross-border transfer rules.[139]

Despite an uptick in information privacy law passage following the OECD Guidelines, the APAC region still varies tremendously in information privacy recognition, as many countries have not yet passed information privacy laws.[140] The Association of Southeast Asian Nations (ASEAN) member states, however, have substantially increased regional information privacy law passage over the past five years.

Most APAC countries with information privacy laws have incorporated considerably more flexibility in data transfer than their European counterparts, permitting data receipt in substantially similar jurisdictions, rather than formal adequacy proceedings. In some countries, consent-based transfer has also provided a useful vehicle for cross-border transfer for individual data subjects.

Created by APEC, the Cross-Border Privacy Regulation (CBPR) process also provides regional and global approval for cross-border transfer within multi-national companies, similar to the existing EU BCR process. The CBPR differs slightly from the

---

138. ASIA-PACIFIC ECONOMIC COUNCIL, *APEC Privacy Framework* (2005), available at: https://www.apec.org/Groups/Committee-on-Trade-and-Investment/~/media/Files/Groups/ECSG/05_ecsg_privacyframewk.ashx.
139. AUSTRALIAN LAW REFORM COMMISSION, *31. Cross-border Data Flows*, http://www.alrc.gov.au/publications/31.%20Cross-border%20Data%20Flows%20/international-privacy-protection (last accessed: Aug. 1, 2017).
140. For a highly complete and detailed review of the APAC building on Professor Greenleaf's considerable expertise and direct experience, *see* GRAHAM GREENLEAF, DATA PRIVACY LAWS IN ASIA–CONTEXT AND HISTORY (Oxford: 2014).

BCR process, in that APEC does not have direct regional legal accountability and rather relies on an application process and Cross-border Privacy Enforcement Arrangement (CPEA) signatories. The CBPR process does not supplant any independent obligation to meet individual country laws, but does permit internal company data transfer outside signatories. CPEA countries that will enforce the CBPR process within their own countries include: The United States (U.S.), México, Canada, Hong Kong, Australia, New Zealand, Korea, Japan, and Singapore. Third-party organizations, such as audit firms or assessment companies, can apply for CBPR approval to become an Accountability Agent. Accountability Agents determine CBPR process satisfaction, including policy review, self-assessment, compliance assessment, and review of complaint statistics.[141]

In 2015, APEC began working with the European Council to determine a more efficient methodology for combining CBPR and BCR processes, and since 2016, organizations have begun using a "Cross-Referential" document to fulfill both BCR and CBPR qualifications.[142] The Cross-Referential enables multi-national companies to dually satisfy requirements for internal company transfer across geographic borders from APEC and EU countries to each other, and to countries outside these regions.

§5.01 AUSTRALIA AND NEW ZEALAND

Australia led implementation of information privacy rights in the APAC region, passing the Privacy Act in 1988.[143] New Zealand followed Australia with the similarly structured Privacy Act in 1993.[144] Although New Zealand has received adequacy determination from the EU, Australia's Privacy Act exempts small business and employment activities from Privacy Act requirements, which may have limited Australian adequacy status.[145]

Australia has passed an omnibus information privacy law and sectoral laws, including the Privacy Act and the Personally Controlled Electronic Health Records Act (described in Chapter 10 on localization).[146] The Privacy Act includes thirteen Australian Privacy Principles (APPs). The APPs require:[147]

141. Asia-Pacific Economic Council, *APEC Cross-Border Privacy Rules System*, available at: https://www.apec.org/Groups/Committee-on-Trade-and-Investment/~/media/Files/Groups/ECSG/CBPR/CBPR-PoliciesRulesGuidelines.ashx (last accessed Aug. 2, 2017).

142. Asia-Pacific Economic Cooperation, Referential on Requirements for Binding corporate Rules Submitted to National Data Protection Authorities in the EU and Cross Border Privacy Rules Submitted to APEC CBPR Recognized Accountability Agents (3 Jul. 2014), available at: https://www.apec.org/~/media/Files/Groups/ECSG/20140307_Referential-BCR-CBPR-reqs.pdf.

143. The Privacy Act No. 119, 1988.

144. The Privacy Act No. 28, 1993.

145. *See supra* note 139.

146. New Zealand has passed a similar act.

147. Please note: these have been truncated and rephrased. For specific language of the APPs, *see* Office of the Australian Information Commissioner, *Privacy fact sheet 17: Australian Privacy Principles* (Feb. 2013), https://www.oaic.gov.au/individuals/privacy-fact-sheets/general/privacy-fact-sheet-17-australian-privacy-principles#australian-privacy-principle-2-anonymity-and-pseudonymity.

(1) APP 1: Manage personal information openly and transparently.
(2) APP 2: Provide an opportunity to participate in an anonymous or pseudonymous manner, except where prohibited by other laws.
(3) APP 3: Limit collection to personal information reasonably necessary or directly connected to an entity's functions or activities.
(4) APP 4: Treat unsolicited personal information.
(5) APP 5: Collect information by lawful and fair means, provide notice at or before the time of collection or soon thereafter.
(6) APP 6: Do not use or disclose data for a secondary purpose unless an individual has consented.
(7) APP 7: Use personal information for marketing purposes only when the organization has collected the information, the individuals expects it, and opt-out is reasonable/available.
(8) APP 8: Ensure any overseas recipient of data transferred does not breach the APPs, except where laws are substantially similar or subject to binding scheme.
(9) APP 9: Do not use government identifiers for internal identifiers unless required.
(10) APP 10: Ensure data to ensure personal information is accurate, updated, and complete.
(11) APP 11: Protect information from misuse, interference, loss, unauthorized access, modification, and disclosure.
(12) APP 12: Provide individuals access to information about them.
(13) APP 13: Provide individuals with right of correction.

The privacy notice implied in APP 1 includes the purpose for collection storage and disclosure, how an individual can access information about themselves, information about overseas transfers, and how to report breach complaints. As with many other schemes, collection should be reasonably necessary according to the business purpose, although the EU standard articulates a high stringency as "strictly necessary," organizations operating in Australia may collect when reasonably necessary for business purposes disclosed in the privacy notice.

Under the Privacy Act, organizations can transfer personal information beyond Australian borders under the Privacy Act, but there are conditions, and often it is restricted by sector. Australia accepts substantially similar legal schemes for a receiving country, BCRs, CBPRs, or contractual clauses to transfer data.

New Zealand has implemented twelve similar privacy principles within its own Privacy Act and applies the law to all organizations, public or private, under all circumstances involving personal information. Under both Australian and New Zealand laws, the Information Commissioner reserves the right to change or pass new *codes of practice*, which can include the APPs or New Zealand privacy principles, or other codes specific to a particular use, such as handling credit information. Each Information Commissioner can respond to a changing information handling landscape by adapting laws without revising the Privacy Acts.

§5.02 THE PEOPLE'S REPUBLIC OF CHINA

At the time of writing, China has not passed an omnibus federal law that applies to information privacy. However, China has promulgated several laws that indirectly promote information privacy and similarly created a dedicated regulatory authority. Laws include the People's Republic of China (PRC) Constitution, the National People's Congress (NPC) Decision on Strengthening Network Information Protection ("NPC Decision"), and various consumer rights laws mostly issued by the Ministry of Information and Internet Technology (MIIT).

The PRC Constitution fulfills a similar purpose to an omnibus privacy law and limits what organizations may do with personal information. First, organizations must comply with principles of legitimacy and necessity and collection. This means an organization should not collect more information than necessary based on the business need and expected uses for the personal information with respect to the data subject. Organizations must post a privacy notice, comply with that notice, and obtain consent from an individual before collection, although the PRC Constitution does not require a specific form of consent.

The NPC Decision includes information privacy considerations:[148]

- Requires necessity and legitimacy for data collection
- Provide public notice of personal electronic data use and collection mechanisms
- Requires consent prior to processing
- Protect data confidentiality and integrity
- Bars data sales
- Ensures information security
- Requires Internet Service Providers (ISPs) to delete data if gathered illegally
- Bars commercial advertisements over phone lines and e-mail.

MIIT regulates online information privacy, and has written orders involving limitations on medical records and population health information, online transaction administration, and communication security, and the Provisions on Personal Information of Telecoms and Internet Users established formal definitions of personal information in China, although these Provisions apply only to ISPs and telecommunications service providers.[149] Personal data is defined broadly as identifiable information about an individual, but specific examples include name, address, birth date, ID numbers,

148. Laney Zhang, *China: NPC Decision on Network Information Protection*, LIBRARY OF CONGRESS (Jan. 4, 2013), http://www.loc.gov/law/foreign-news/article/china-npc-decision-on-network-information-protection/.

149. Provisions on Regulating the Internet Information Service Market Order (15 Mar. 2012); Provisions on Protecting the Personal Information of Telecoms and Internet Users (Sept. 1, 2013). China's Standardization Administration has also issued non-binding Guidelines for Personal Information Protection within Information Systems for Public and Commercial Services on Information Security Technology in 2013.

and account information (e.g., user ID, password).[150] Many conditions for ISPs and telecom providers match the decision, including obligations of confidentiality, prior notice and subsequent consent, necessity limitations, and implementation of security protection.

The State Administration for Industry and Commerce (SAIC) issued Measures for Penalties for Infringing upon the Rights and Interests of Consumers ("SAIC Measures") in 2015, governing consumer rights with respect to products and services.[151] The SAIC Measures' Article requires organizations providing products and services to consumers communicate purpose, manner, and scope of information collection; collect consent, and overall follow principles of necessity when collecting personal information. Personal information includes: "name, gender, occupation, date of birth, identification document number, residential address, contact information, status of income and assets, health status, consumption habits," and other information attendant to service and product provision.[152]

[A] Decision on Strengthening Network Information Protection[153]

In order to protect network information security, protect the lawful interests of citizens, legal persons and other organizations, safeguard national security and social order, the following decision is hereby made:

(I) The State protects electronic information by which the individual identity of citizens can be distinguished as well as involving citizens' individual privacy. No organization or individual may steal or obtain in other illegal manners obtain citizens' individual electronic information, sell or illegally provide citizens' individual electronic information to other persons.

(II) Network service providers and other enterprise and undertaking work units that collect or use citizens' individual electronic information during their business activities, shall abide by the principles of legality, legitimacy and necessity, clearly indicate the objective, methods and scope for

150. The Guidelines for Personal Information Protection (non-binding) also include a definition of SPI that includes an intrinsic personal harm: "identity card numbers, mobile telephone numbers, ethnicity, political viewpoints, religious beliefs, genes, fingerprints." Dr. Rogier Creemers, *Information Security Technology Guidelines for Personal Information Protection on Public and Commercial Service Information Systems*, China Copyright and Media Blog, (Jan. 21, 2013), https://chinacopyrightandmedia.wordpress.com/2013/01/21/information-security-technology-guidelines-for-personal-information-protection-on-public-and-commercial-service-information-systems/.

151. Measures for Penalties for Infringing Upon the Rights and Interests of Consumers, SAIC Order No. 73 (Jan. 5, 2015).

152. Covington & Burling, LLC, *Measures for Penalties for Infringing Upon the Rights and Interests of Consumers* (unofficial translation), https://www.cov.com/files/Publication/ce6cb750-a926-4bb3-aa11-031d05f60cb4/Presentation/PublicationAttachment/6b6af7b2-4942-4063-a781-063d706d56c5/Measures_for_Penalties_for_Infringing_Upon_the_Rights_and_Interest_of_Consumers_2015-01_CN_EN.pdf.

153. Dr. Rogier Creemers, of the University of Oxford and Leiden University has graciously provided a translated copy of this Decision. Decision on Strengthening Network Information Protection, Dec. 28, 2012, translated by Dr. Rogier Creemers.

collection and use of information, and obtain agreement from the person whose data is collected, they may not violate the provisions of laws and regulations, and the agreement between both sides, in collecting or using information. Network service providers and other enterprise and undertaking work units collecting or using citizens' individual electronic information shall make public their collection and use rules.

(III) Network service providers, other enterprise and undertaking work unit and their staff must strictly preserve the secrecy of citizens' individual electronic information they collect in their business activities, they may not divulge, distort, or damage it, and may not sell or illegally provide it to other persons.

(IV) Network service providers and other enterprise and undertaking work units shall adopt technological measures and other necessary measures to ensure information security and prevent that citizens' individual electronic information collected during business activities is divulged, damaged or lost. When divulging, damage to or loss of information occurs or may occur, remedial measures shall be adopted immediately.

(V) Network service providers shall strengthen management of information disseminated by users, where it occurs that information violated by laws or regulations is published or disseminated, handling measures such as ceasing the dissemination of the said information, deleting it, etc., relevant records are to be preserved, and the relevant controlling departments informed.

(VI) Network service providers that handle website access services for users, handle fixed telephone, mobile telephone and other surfing formalities, or provide information publication services to users, shall, when concluding agreements with users or affirming the provision of service, require users to provide real identity information.

(VII) No organization or individual may, without having obtained agreement of or a request from the electronic information receiver, or where the electronic information receiver has clearly indicated refusal, send commercial electronic information to fixed telephones, mobile telephones and individual e-mail boxes.

(VIII) Where citizens discover that their individual identity has been divulged, individual privacy has been disseminated or other network information infringes their lawful rights and interests, or are harassed by commercial electronic information, they have the power to require the network service provider to delete the relevant information or adopt other necessary measures to cease this.

(IX) Any work unit or individual has the power to report or file accusations with the relevant controlling departments against unlawful or criminal acts of stealing citizens' individual electronic information or gaining it by other illegal means, selling it or providing it illegally to other persons, as well as other unlawful and criminal acts concerning network information; departments receiving reports and accusations shall timely deal with them according to the law. The infringed person may file a lawsuit according to the law.

(X) Relevant controlling department shall, within the scope of duties and responsibilities of each, carry out their duties according to the law, adopt technological measures and other necessary measures to guard against, prevent, investigate and prosecute unlawful or criminal acts of stealing citizens' individual electronic information or gaining it by other illegal means, selling it or providing it illegally to other persons, as well as other unlawful and criminal acts concerning network information. When relevant controlling departments carry out their duties according to the law, network service providers shall grant cooperation and provide technological support. State organs and their staff shall protect the secrecy of citizens' individual electronic information that they learn when carrying out their duties, may not divulge, distort or damage it, and may not sell or illegally provide it to other persons.

(XI) Acts violating this Decision, are subject to warnings, fines, confiscation of unlawful income, cancellation of permits or cancellation of fines, closure of websites, prohibition of relevant responsible personnel to engage in network service business and other punishments, they are entered into social credit files and published; where acts constitute violations of public order management, public order management punishments are imposed according to the law. Where they constitute a crime, criminal liability is prosecuted according to the law. Where other persons' civil rights are infringed, civil liability is borne according to the law.

(12) This Decision takes effect on the date of promulgation.

§5.03 MALAYSIA

In 2010, Malaysia passed the omnibus Personal Data Protection Act (PDPA). The PDPA has a similar framework to Australia's Privacy Act and the EU Data Protection Directive, and codifies seven "PDPA Principles": General, Notice and Choice, Disclosure, Security, Retention, Data Integrity, and Access.[154] Malaysia does not categorize organizations collecting personal information as controllers; rather, organizations collecting data and using such data are *data users*, and an organization receiving personal information from a data user and performing an activity on behalf of the data user would be classified as a *processor*. *Third parties*, then, are any users that are not data users, processors, or data subjects.

The *General Principle* requires consent prior to processing data subject personal information and prohibits SPI processing, except when that data subject explicitly

154. Security, Retention, and Data Integrity Principles will be discussed in Chapter 10.

consents. A data user and processor may only process data subject personal information under other circumstances when fulfilling a contractual obligation, out of necessity, and other standard purposes. The processing must also fulfill a previously disclosed, lawful purpose, and data transfer is subject to data subject consent.

The *Notice and Choice Principle* requires data users to provide a notice disclosure to the data subject, including:

- Personal data processed
- Purposes for collection/processing
- Information regarding rights to access and correction
- Contact information for the data user
- Classification of third parties receiving personal data
- Choices and means for limiting processing, including for other individuals who could be identified.
- Whether obligatory or voluntary to provide personal data and consequences of not supplying personal data.

The data user must provide the notice "as soon as practicable," usually when the data subject first is asked to provide data, less preferentially when the data user collects data, but at the least, before processing for a purpose other than original collection purposes or third-party disclose. The *Disclosure Principle* further reiterates that a data user and processor cannot disclose personal data for purposes other than disclosed at the time of collection or for a purpose directly related to the disclosed purpose. Under the *Access Principle*, data subjects may request information about data collected and processed by a processor. Upon receipt, data subjects may submit corrections to such data if inaccurate.

Data transfer may be facilitated outside of Malaysia when the Minister publishes a notification and the location has a substantially similar information privacy law ensuring an adequate level of protection. However, a data user may also facilitate transfer by collecting a data subject's consent or when necessary for performance of a contract.

A unique aspect of the PDPA involves punishment for organizational personnel who commit an offense. When personnel of a business commit an offense or the business commits an offense, officers of the business including directors, CEOs, COOs, managers, or secretaries can be charged for the offense. Because Malaysia extends its law to organizations located outside Malaysia when equipment (e.g., servers or other devices) resides in Malaysia, regulatory authorities could serve traveling business leaders while traveling in Malaysia and potentially receive civil or criminal sanctions.

[A] Passages of Note – PDPA

[1] Data

Part I

Section 4

"personal data" means any information in respect of commercial transactions, which—

(a) is being processed wholly or partly by means of equipment operating automatically in response to instructions given for that purpose;
(b) is recorded with the intention that it should wholly or partly be processed by means of such equipment; or
(c) is recorded as part of a relevant filing system or with the intention that it should form part of a relevant filing system,

that relates directly or indirectly to a data subject, who is identified or identifiable from that information or from that and other information in the possession of a data user, including any sensitive personal data and expression of opinion about the data subject; but does not include any information that is processed for the purpose of a credit reporting business carried on by a credit reporting agency under the Credit Reporting Agencies Act 2010;

"sensitive personal data" means any personal data consisting of information as to the physical or mental health or condition of a data subject, his political opinions, his religious beliefs or other beliefs of a similar nature, the commission or alleged commission by him of any offence or any other personal data as the Minister may determine by order published in the Gazette.

[2] Data User and Processor

Part I

Section 4

"data user" means a person who either alone or jointly or in common with other persons processes any personal data or has control over or authorizes the processing of any personal data, but does not include a data processor;

"data processor", in relation to personal data, means any person, other than an employee of the data user, who processes the personal data solely on behalf of the data user, and does not process the personal data for any of his own purposes;

"processing", in relation to personal data, means collecting, recording, holding or storing the personal data or carrying out any operation or set of operations on the personal data, including—

(a) the organization, adaptation or alteration of personal data;
(b) the retrieval, consultation or use of personal data;
(c) the disclosure of personal data by transmission, transfer, dissemination or otherwise making;
(d) the alignment, combination, correction, erasure or destruction of personal data.

Part I

Section 2

(2) Subject to subsection (1), this Act applies to a person in respect of personal data if—
  (a) the person is established in Malaysia and the personal data is processed, whether or not in the context of that establishment, by that person or any other person employed or engaged by that establishment; or
  (b) the person is not established in Malaysia, but uses equipment in Malaysia for processing the personal data otherwise than for the purposes of transit through Malaysia.

(3) A person falling within paragraph (2)(b) shall nominate for the purposes of this Act a representative established in Malaysia.

(4) For the purposes of subsections (2) and (3), each of the following is to be treated as established in Malaysia:
  (a) an individual whose physical presence in Malaysia shall not be less than one hundred and eighty days in one calendar year;
  (b) a body incorporated under the Companies Act 1965 [Act 125];
  (c) a partnership or other unincorporated association formed under any written laws in Malaysia; and
  (d) any person who does not fall within paragraph (a), (b) or (c) but maintains in Malaysia—
    (i) an office, branch or agency through which he carries on any activity; or
    (ii) a regular practice.

[3] *Data Subject*

Part I

Section 4

"relevant person", in relation to a data subject, howsoever described, means—

(a) in the case of a data subject who is below the age of eighteen years, the parent, guardian or person who has parental responsibility for the data subject;

(b) in the case of a data subject who is incapable of managing his own affairs, a person who is appointed by a court to manage those affairs, or a person authorized in writing by the data subject to act on behalf of the data subject; or

(c) in any other case, a person authorized in writing by the data subject to make a data access request, data correction request, or both such requests, on behalf of the data subject.

[4] *Transfer*

Part I

Section 4

"code of practice" means the personal data protection code of practice in respect of a specific class of data users registered by the Commissioner pursuant to section 23 or issued by the Commissioner under section 24.

Part X

Section 129

(1) A data user shall not transfer any personal data of a data subject to a place outside Malaysia unless to such place as specified by the Minister, upon the recommendation of the Commissioner, by notification published in the Gazette.
(2) For the purposes of subsection (1), the Minister may specify any place outside Malaysia if—
    (a) there is in that place in force any law which is substantially similar to this Act, or that serves the same purposes as this Act; or
    (b) that place ensures an adequate level of protection in relation to the processing of personal data which is at least equivalent to the level of protection afforded by this Act.
(3) Notwithstanding subsection (1), a data user may transfer any personal data to a place outside Malaysia if—
    (a) the data subject has given his consent to the transfer;
    (b) the transfer is necessary for the performance of a contract between the data subject and the data user;
    (c) the transfer is necessary for the conclusion or performance of a contract between the data user and a third party which—
        (i) is entered into at the request of the data subject; or
        (ii) is in the interests of the data subject.

[5] Third Party

Part I

Section 4

"third party", in relation to personal data, means any person other than—

(a) a data subject;
(b) a relevant person in relation to a data subject;
(c) a data user;
(d) a data processor; or
(e) a person authorized in writing by the data user to process the personal data under the direct control of the data user.

[6] Regulatory Authority

(1) If a body corporate commits an offence under this Act, any person who at the time of the commission of the offence was a director, chief executive officer, chief operating officer, manager, secretary or other similar officer of the body corporate or was purporting to act in any such capacity or was in any manner or to any extent responsible for the management of any of the affairs of the body corporate or was assisting in such management—
    (a) may be charged severally or jointly in the same proceedings with the body corporate; and

(b) if the body corporate is found to have committed the offence, shall be deemed to have committed that offence unless, having regard to the nature of his functions in that capacity and to all circumstances, he proves—
   (i) that the offence was committed without his knowledge, consent or connivance; and
   (ii) that he had taken all reasonable precautions and exercised due diligence to prevent the commission of the offence.

(2) If any person would be liable under this Act to any punishment or penalty for his act, omission, neglect or default, he shall be liable to the same punishment or penalty for every such act, omission, neglect or default of any employee or agent of his, or of the employee of the agent, if the act, omission, neglect or default was committed—
   (a) by that person's employee in the course of his employment;
   (b) by the agent when acting on behalf of that person; or
   (c) by the employee of the agent in the course of his employment by the agent or otherwise on behalf of then agent acting on behalf of that person.

§5.04 INDONESIA

To date, Indonesia does not have an omnibus data protection law, yet Indonesia has passed several laws related to the treatment of data. The Information and Electronics Transactions (IET) Act, however, does require consent prior to information use, as does the Regulation No. 82 of 2012 Concerning Electronic System and Transaction Operation.[155] Privacy is referenced in sectoral laws, including banking law and capital markets, though requirements are not robust in comparison to omnibus information privacy laws. General law principles require basic privacy protection: organizations must establish a legitimate reason for processing personal information and data subjects must consent prior to processing.

§5.05 JAPAN

Japan updated the Act on Protection of Personal Information (APPI), enforced by the Consumer Affairs Agency, in May 2017. However, multiple ministries in Japan, such as banking and health care ministries, provide guidelines in addition to the APPI and enforce the law for their respective industries. Industrial associations, such as securities dealers, also provide requirements. Japan has passed several guidelines for specific industries, for example, robust security requirements in the health sector under the Kōsei Rōdō Daijin.[156]

The APPI applies to data controllers with a presence in Japan. Controllers in Japan must communicate the purpose of use, respond to requests, and individuals

155. LAW OF THE REPUBLIC OF INDONESIA NUMBER 11 OF 2008 CONCERNING ELECTRONIC INFORMATION AND TRANSACTIONS.

156. MINISTRY OF HEALTH, LABOUR, AND WELFARE, *Homepage* (2017), http://www.mhlw.go.jp/english/index.html

must consent for third-party transfer. Furthermore, the privacy notice must be presented and describe opportunities for correction, information regarding disclosure, whether that means to a third-party or to another location, and procedures for deletion of data. Consent only applies to a disclosed scope of use, and any change in scope regarding information collection requires new, prior consent from the data subject. The type of consent required depends on the ministry establishing guidelines, although organizations might benefit from simply ensuring informed, prior, explicit consent.

§5.06 THE RUSSIAN FEDERATION

The Russian Federal Law of July 27, 2006 N 152-FZ on Personal Data was passed in 2006 and focuses on data operator (controller) obligations. The Federal Law on Personal Data defines an operator as a "state agency, municipal authority, legal entity or individual who independently or in cooperation with other entities organizes and/or processes personal data as well as determines the purposes and scope of personal data processing."[157] The Federal Law on Personal Data applies broadly to organizations operating in Russia and to organizations handling Russian personal information extraterritorially. The Federal Law on Personal Data defines data processing broadly, as well:

> any action (operation) or a combination of actions (operations) performed both automatically and manually with personal data, including collection, recording, arrangement, accumulation, storage, specification (updating, changing), extraction, use, distribution (including transfer), anonymizing, blocking and destruction of personal data.

This definition of processing appears to include access to personal information.

Operators processing data in Russia must register with the Roskomnadzor; the data protection enforcement department of the Federal Service for Supervision of Communications, Information Technology, and Mass Media if a complaint is filed or for investigatory purposes. Processing requires consent from the data subject. While personal information processing requires explicit consent, SPI requires explicit written consent, although electronic signatures fulfill the written consent requirement, which specifies several pieces of information to include in the written consent. Transferring data to a third party also requires consent. Similar to other laws, the data subject can correct information and choose, with a separate consent, whether to receive marketing materials.

Importantly, a data subject may file a complaint with the Roskomnadzor, which if successful, results in recovery for injuries, including moral damage.[158] The Russian privacy notice requires:

---

157. Федеральный закон от 26.07.2006 № 152-ФЗ "О персональных данных" (Federal Law of July 27, 2006 N 152-FZ On Personal Data), available at: http://pd.rkn.gov.ru/authority/p146/p164/.

158. Although the U.S. does not recognize purely moral damages except in limited statutory circumstances, several countries, with omnibus information privacy laws, including the EU region, do recognize recovery for moral damages.

- the name and address of the operator,
- the purposes for processing,
- expected volume of data collected,
- categories of personal data pertaining to the data subject, especially SPI,
- a description of IT systems and specific security protection for these systems,
- the name and contact details of the data protection officer,
- when the processing will begin and the duration for processing,
- cross-border transfer information, and
- the location of an operator's database.

The Russian Labor Code specifically addresses employee data protection.[159] Under Chapter 14 of the Russian Labor Code, an employer and representatives must guarantee personal information protection, including consent to gathering information about an employee (e.g., background check information). Employers also must not process SPI, such as political information, criminal convictions, and political or employment affiliations (e.g., labor unions, industry memberships). As in the Federal Law on Personal Data, the Russian Labor Code also requires the protection of personal information using appropriate cybersecurity measures.

[A] Passages of Note: Federal Law on Personal Data

[1] Data

Chapter 1

Article 3

1) personal data – any information referring directly or indirectly to a particular or identified individual (hereinafter referred to as "personal data subject");
3) personal data processing – any action (operation) or a combination of actions (operations) performed both automatically and manually with personal data, including collection, recording, arrangement, accumulation, storage, specification (updating, changing), extraction, use, distribution (including transfer), anonymizing, blocking and destruction of personal data;
9) anonymization of personal data – actions performed on personal data that do not permit the identity of the individual concerned to be verified solely from such anonymized data;
10) personal data information system – a database that contains personal data as well as information technologies and hardware used for data processing;

Chapter 2

Article 10

1. The processing of special categories of personal data concerning racial or ethnic origin, political opinions, religious or philosophical beliefs, health or

159. The Russian Labor Code, Federal Law No. 197-FZ of 2001.

sexual life shall not be permitted except in the instances envisaged by part 2 of this Article.

2. The processing of the special categories of personal data referred to in part 1 of this Article shall be permitted in instances where:
   1) the subject of the personal data has given his written consent to the processing of his personal data;
   2) the personal data have been made public by the personal data subject;
      2.1) the processing of personal data is necessary in connection with the implementation of international agreements of the Russian Federation on readmission;
      2.2) the processing of personal data is carried out in accordance with Federal Law No. 8-FZ of 25 January 2002 "Concerning the Russian Census";
      2.3) the processing of personal data is carried out in accordance with the legislation concerning state social assistance, labour legislation or the legislation of the Russian Federation concerning state-provided pensions and retirement pensions;
   3) the processing of personal data is necessary to protect the life, health or other vital interests of the personal data subject or the life, health or other vital interests of other persons and it is impossible to obtain the consent of the personal data subject;
   4) the processing of personal data is carried out for the purposes of preventative medicine, medical diagnosis or the provision of medical and social care services, provided that the processing of personal data is carried out by a person who is professionally involved in medical activities and has a duty in accordance with the legislation of the Russian Federation to maintain medical confidentiality;
   5) the processing of personal data of members (participants) of a social association or a religious organization is carried out by the social association or religious organization in question acting in accordance with the legislation of the Russian Federation for the purpose of the achievement of legitimate goals which are provided for by their foundation documents, provided that the personal data are not disseminated without the written consent of the personal data subjects;
   6) the processing of personal data is necessary in order to enable the rights of the personal data subject or of third parties to be established or exercised, and in connection with the administration of justice;
   7) the processing of personal data is carried out in accordance with the legislation of the Russian Federation concerning defence, security, counter-terrorism, transport safety, anti-corruption measures, investigative activities and enforcement proceedings and the penal legislation of the Russian Federation;
   8) the processing of personal data is carried out in accordance with legislation concerning compulsory types of insurance and insurance legislation;
   9) the processing of personal data is carried out in cases provided for in the legislation of the Russian Federation by state bodies, municipal bodies or organizations for the purpose of placing children deprived of parental care in the care of families of citizens.
3. The processing of personal data concerning criminal convictions may be carried out by state bodies or municipal bodies within the limits of the powers conferred on them in accordance with the legislation of the Russian Federation, and by other persons in instances and according to procedures to be determined in accordance with federal laws.

Chapter 2

Article 11

1. Information concerning a person's physiological and biological characteristics from which he/she may be identified (biometric personal data) and which is used by an operator to establish the identity of a personal data subject may be processed only subject to the written consent of the personal data subject, except in the cases provided for in part 2 of this Article.
2. The processing of biometric personal data may be carried out without the consent of the personal data subject in connection with the implementation of international agreements of the Russian Federation on readmission, in connection with the administration of justice and the enforcement of judicial acts and in cases provided for in the legislation of the Russian Federation concerning defence, security, counter-terrorism, transport safety, anti- corruption measures, investigative activities and state service, the penal legislation of the Russian Federation and the legislation of the Russian Federation concerning the procedure for exit from the Russian Federation and entry into the Russian Federation.

[2] Applicability

Chapter 2

Article 5

1. Personal data shall be processed on a legal and equitable basis.
2. Personal data processing shall be restricted by achieving specific predetermined and legal purposes. It is not allowed to process personal data for the purpose incompatible with that one of personal data collection.
3. It is not allowed to combine the data bases containing personal data to be processed for incompatible purposes.
4. There shall be processed only personal data that comply with the purposes of their processing.
5. The scope and character of personal data to be processed shall comply with the intended purposes of such data processing. The personal data to be processed shall not be irrelevant to the declared purposes of their processing.
6. In the course of personal data processing it shall be necessary to ensure the personal data accuracy, their sufficiency and in case of need their adequacy for processing purposes. Operators shall take the required measures or ensure their adoption to delete or specify incomplete or inaccurate data.
7. Personal data shall be stored in a form that allows verification of the identity of personal data subjects only to the extent necessary for processing purposes unless the personal data storage time is not established by federal laws, agreements concluded with personal data subjects as a beneficiary or guarantor party. Personal data shall be destroyed or depersonalized upon achieving the set goals as well as when such goals cease to be relevant unless otherwise stipulated by federal laws.

[3] Collection Limitations

Chapter 2

Article 6

1. Personal data processing shall be subject to compliance with the principles and rules stipulated by the Federal law. Personal data processing shall be allowed in the following cases:
   1) processing of personal data is carried out with the consent of the data subject to the processing of his personal data;
   5) personal data processing is required for performance of an agreement to which a personal data subject is a party or under which the data subject is a beneficiary or surety, or for conclusion of an agreement on the initiative of a personal data subject or an agreement under which a personal data subject shall be a beneficiary or surety;
   6) personal data processing is required for protection of life, health or other vital interests of the personal data subject in case it is not possible to obtain his/her consent;
   7) processing of personal data is required for realization of the rights and legitimate interests of an operator or third parties or for the attainment of socially significant objectives, provided that this not cause the rights and freedoms of the personal data subject to be violated.

[4] Notice/Consent

Chapter 4

Article 18

1. When collecting personal data, an operator shall be obliged to provide to the personal data subject, upon his request, the information which is provided for in part 7 of Article 14 of this Federal Law.
2. Where the provision of personal data is compulsory in accordance with federal laws, the operator shall be obliged to explain to the personal data subject the legal consequences of refusing to provide his personal data.
3. Where personal data have been obtained other than from the personal data subject, the operator shall be obliged, except in cases provided for in part 4 of this Article, to provide the following information to the personal data subject before beginning to process the personal data:
   1) name or surname, first name and patronymic and the address of the operator or its representative;
   2) the purpose and legal basis of the processing of the personal data;
   3) the expected users of the personal data;
   4) the rights of the personal data subject as established by this Federal Law;
   5) the source from which the personal data were obtained.

Chapter 2

Article 9

1. A personal data subject shall decide whether or not to provide his personal data and shall give consent to the processing thereof freely, of his own will and

in his own interest. Consent to the processing of personal data shall be specific, informed and conscious. Consent to the processing of personal data may be given by the personal data subject or his representative in any form which provides evidence of its receipt, except as otherwise established by federal laws. Where consent to the processing of personal data is received from a representative of the personal data subject, the authority of that representative to give consent on behalf of the personal data subject shall be verified by the operator.

2. Consent to the processing of personal data may be withdrawn by the personal data subject. In the event that a personal data subject withdraws his consent to the processing of personal data, the operator shall have the right to continue the processing of personal data without the consent of the personal data subject if any of the grounds set out in clauses 2 to 11 of part 1 of Article 6, part 2 of Article 10 and part 2 of Article 11 of this Federal Law exist.
3. The obligation to provide a proof of the receipt of the consent of a personal data subject to the processing of his personal data or a proof of the existence of grounds specified in clauses 2 to 11 of part 1 of Article 6, part 2 of Article 10 and part 2 of Article 11 of this Federal Law shall be assigned to the operator.
4. In cases provided for in federal laws, the processing of personal data shall be carried out only with the written consent of the personal data subject. A consent in the form of an electronic document signed with an electronic signature in accordance with a federal law shall be deemed equivalent to a written consent on paper containing the handwritten signature of the personal data subject. The written consent of a personal data subject to the processing of his personal data shall contain, in particular:
   1) surname, first name and patronymic and the address of the personal data subject, the number of his principal identification document and information as to the date of issue of that document and the body which issued it;
   2) surname, first name and patronymic and the address of the representative of the personal data subject, the number of his principal identification document, information as to the date of issue of that document and the body which issued it and details of the power of attorney or other document confirming the representative's authority (where consent is received from a representative of a data subject);
   3) name or surname, first name and patronymic and the address of the operator which is receiving the consent of the personal data subject;
   4) the purpose of personal data processing;
   5) a list of personal data to the processing of which the consent of the personal data subject is given;
   6) name or surname, first name and patronymic and the address of the person who is to carry out the processing of the personal data on the instruction of the operator, if the processing is to be assigned to such a person;
   7) a list of actions involving personal data to the performance of which consent is given, and a general description of the methods of personal data processing which are to be used by the operator;
   8) the period for which the consent of a personal data subject is given, and the procedure for withdrawal of that consent, except as otherwise established by federal laws;
   9) the signature of the personal data subject.
5. The procedure for the receipt in the form of an electronic document of the consent of a personal data subject to the processing of his personal data for the purpose of the provision of state and municipal services and services which

are necessary and essential for the provision of state and municipal services shall be determined by the Government of the Russian Federation.

6. Where a personal data subject is legally incapable, the consent to the processing of his personal data shall be given by a legal representative of the personal data subject.
7. Where a personal data subject has died, the consent to the processing of his personal data shall be given by the heirs of the personal data subject, unless the personal data subject gave such consent while he was alive.
8. The personal data may be obtained by an operator from a person who is not the personal data subject on condition of the provision to the operator of a confirmation of the existence of grounds specified in clauses 2 to 11 of part 1 of Article 6, part 2 of Article 10 and part 2 of Article 11 of this Federal Law.

[5] Access

Chapter 3

Article 14

1. A personal data subject shall have the right to receive information referred to in part 7 of this Article except in cases provided for in part 8 of this Article. A personal data subject shall have the right to request an operator to rectify, block or destroy his personal data in the event that the personal data are incomplete, out-of-date, inaccurate or unlawfully obtained or are not needed for the stated purpose of the processing, and shall have the right to take measures provided for by law to protect his rights.
2. The information referred to in part 7 of this Article shall be provided to a personal data subject by an operator in an accessible form, and shall not contain personal data relating to other data subjects, except where there are lawful grounds for the disclosure of such personal data.
7. A personal data subject shall have the right to receive information concerning the processing of his personal data, including information containing:
   1) confirmation of the processing of personal data by the operator;
   2) the legal grounds for and purposes of the processing of the personal data;
   3) the purposes and methods used by the operator for the processing of personal data;
   4) the name and location of the operator and information on persons (other than employees of the operator) who have access to personal data or to whom personal data may be disclosed on the basis of a contract with the operator or on the basis of a federal law;
   5) the processed personal data relating to the personal data subject in question and the source from which they were obtained, unless a different procedure for the presentation of such data is prescribed by a federal law;
   6) the period of the processing of the personal data, including the period for which they are kept;
   7) the procedure for the exercise by the personal data subject of the rights provided for in this Federal Law;
   8) information on any actual or planned cross-border transfer of personal data;
   9) name or surname, first name and patronymic and the address of the person carrying out the processing of personal data on the instruction of the

operator, if the processing has been or is intended to be assigned to such a person;

10) other information provided for in this Federal Law or other federal laws.

[6] Automated Processing

Chapter 3

Article 16

1. It shall be prohibited for making decisions which give rise to legal consequences for a personal data subject or otherwise affect his rights and legitimate interests to be taken solely on the basis of the automated processing of personal data, except in the instances envisaged by part 2 of this Article.
2. A decision which gives rise to legal consequences for a personal data subject or otherwise affects his rights and legitimate interests may be taken solely on the basis of the automated processing of his personal data only if the subject of the personal data has given his written consent or in instances envisaged by federal laws which also establish measures to safeguard the rights and legitimate interests of the subject of the personal data.
3. An operator shall be obliged to make clear to a personal data subject the procedure whereby a decision is taken solely on the basis of the automated processing of his personal data and the possible legal consequences of such a decision, to allow him the opportunity to present an objection against such a decision, and to explain the means by which the personal data subject may protect his rights and legitimate interests.
4. An operator shall be obliged to consider an objection such as is referred to in part 3 of this Article within thirty days from the day of receiving it, and to notify the personal data subject of the results of the consideration of that objection.

[7] Marketing

Chapter 3

Article 15

1. The processing of personal data for the purpose of the market promotion of goods, work and services by means of making direct contact with a potential consumer with the aid of communications facilities, and for purposes of political campaigning, shall be permitted only on condition of the prior consent of the subject of the personal data. Such processing of personal data shall be deemed to be carried out without the prior consent of the personal data subject unless the operator is able to prove that such consent was obtained.
2. An operator shall be obliged, upon the request of a data subject, immediately to terminate the processing of his personal data which is referred to in part 1 of this Article.

[8] Transfer

Chapter 2

Article 12

1. The cross-border transfer of personal data into the territories of foreign states which are the parties to the Council of Europe Convention on the Protection of Individuals with Regard to Automatic Processing of Personal Data, as well as other foreign states providing adequate protection of the data subjects' rights shall be carried out in accordance with this Federal Law and may be prohibited or restricted for the purposes of protecting the foundations of the constitutional order of the Russian Federation, public morality and health, rights and legitimate interests of citizens and providing for national defence and state security.
2. The authorized body for the protection of the personal data subjects' rights shall approve a list of foreign states which are not the parties to the Council of Europe Convention on the Protection of Individuals with Regard to Automatic Processing of Personal Data and ensure adequate protection of the data subjects' rights. A state which is not a party to the Council of Europe Convention on the Protection of Individuals with Regard to Automatic Processing of Personal Data may be included in the list of foreign states which provide adequate protection of the personal data subjects' rights if the current legal rules of the relevant state and measures taken for the security of personal data conform to the provisions of the above-mentioned Convention.
3. An operator shall be obliged to satisfy itself that the foreign state into whose territory personal data are to be transferred provides adequate protection of the personal data subjects' rights before commencing the cross-border transfer of personal data.
4. The cross-border transfer of personal data into the territories of foreign states which do not provide an adequate protection of the personal data subjects' rights may be carried out in the following cases:
   1) where the personal data subject has given his/her consent to the cross-border transfer of his/her personal data;
   2) in cases provided for in agreements of the Russian Federation;
   3) in cases provided for in federal laws where this is necessary to protect the foundations of the constitutional order of the Russian Federation, to provide for national defence and state security, to secure the stable and safe operation of the transport complex and to protect the interests of the individual, society and the state in the transport sphere against acts of unlawful interference;
   4) for the purpose of the performance of a contract to which the personal data subject is a party;
   5) for the purpose of protecting life, health and other vital interests of a personal data subject or of other persons where it is impossible to obtain the written consent of the personal data subject.

[9] Third Party

Chapter 2

Article 6

3. An operator shall have the right to assign the processing of personal data to another person with the consent of a personal data subject, except as otherwise provided by federal laws, on the basis of a contract concluded with that person, including a state or municipal contract, or by means of adoption of an appropriate act by a state or municipal body (hereinafter referred to as "instruction of an operator"). A person carrying out the processing of personal data on the instruction of an operator shall be obliged to comply with the principles and rules for the processing of personal data which are stipulated by this Federal Law. The operator's instruction shall set out a list of actions (operations) to be performed with personal data by the person carrying out the processing of personal data and the purposes of the processing, shall establish the obligation of that person to observe the confidentiality of personal data and to ensure that the personal data remain secure while being processed, and shall specify the requirements relating to protection of processed personal data in accordance with Article 19 of this Federal Law.
4. A person carrying out the processing of personal data on the instruction of an operator shall not be obliged to obtain the consent of the data subject to the processing of his personal data.
5. Where an operator assigns the processing of personal data to another person, liability to the personal data subject for the actions of that person shall be borne by the operator. A person carrying out the processing of personal data on the instruction of an operator shall be liable to the operator.

Article 3

2) operator – state agency, municipal authority, legal entity or individual who independently or in cooperation with other entities organizes and/or processes personal data as well as determines the purposes and scope of personal data processing;

[B] Passages of Note: Russian Labor Code

Part III

Section III

Chapter 14

Article 85

Personal information of an employee is an information required by an employer because of labor relationship and that refers to a specific employee.

Processing of personal information of an employee is reception, storing, combining, sharing or any other usage of personal information of an employee.

Article 86

To guarantee human rights and freedoms of a citizen, employer and his representatives must follow the general requirements listed below during processing of personal information of an employee:

1. processing of personal information of an employee can be performed only to assure compliance to laws and other legislative standard acts, aiding employees in employment, education and promotion, assuring personal safety of employees, control of quality and quantity of performed work and guaranteeing safety of organization's property;
2. an employer must follow regulations of the Constitution of the Russian Federation, this Code and other federal laws for determination of volume and content of processed personal information of an employee;
3. all personal information of an employee can be received only directly from employee. If personal information of an employee can be only received from a third party, then employee must be notified of it in advance and written permission of employee is required. Employer must inform employee about purpose, possible sources and means of receiving personal information and about type of necessary personal information and consequences of refusal of employee to provide a written permission on receiving of necessary personal information;
4. an employer has no right to receive and process personal information about political, religious and other convictions of an employee and personal information about private life of an employee. According to Article 24 of the Constitution of the Russian Federation, an employer has right to receive and process personal information about private life of an employee only with written permission of an employee and only in cases when this information is relevant to job relationship;
5. an employer has no right to receive and process personal information of an employee about membership of an employee in professional organizations, public organizations and about activities of an employee in trade unions, except cases specified by a federal law;
6. an employer has no right to base on personal information of an employee that was received electronically or as a result of automated processing in making decisions concerning this employee;
7. protection of personal information of an employee from improper usage, damage or loss must be guaranteed by an employer on expenses of an employer. The order of this protection is specified in federal law;
8. employees and their representatives must be acquainted with documents of an organization that regulate order of processing of personal information of employees and with rights and obligations of employees in this area. Confirmation of employees is required after this acquaintance;
9. employees must not renounce their rights on keeping and protection of their secrets;
10. employers, employees and their representative must together work on the development of measures for protection of personal information of employees.

Article 88

An employer must follow the below regulations in all cases of sharing personal information of an employee:

- an employer must not share personal information of an employee with a third party without written permission of an employee, except cases when this is

necessary to prevent a threat to health and life of an employee and except cases, specified by federal law;
- an employer must not share personal information of an employee for commercial purposes without written permission of an employee;
- an employer must warn entities who are receiving personal information of employee that this personal information can be used only for purposes it was provided for and request a confirmation of following this regulation from these entities. Entities that receive personal information of an employee must keep secrecy (confidentiality) of this personal information. This statement doesn't govern cases when personal information of an employee is shared according to federal laws;
- an employer must perform transition of personal information of employee within one organization according to local standard acts of this organization. Confirmation of an employee about acquaintance with this act is required;
- an employer must allow access to personal information of an employee only to authorized entities and these entities have right to receive only personal information of an employee that is required for their specific functions;
- an employer must not demand information about state of health of an employee, except information that is relevant to question of capability of performing job functions by an employee;
- an employer must share personal information of an employee with representatives of employees in order, specified by this Code, and limit this information with personal information that is required by functions of these representatives.

Article 89

To guarantee protection of their personal information that is stored by employer, employees have the following rights:

- right to receive complete information about their personal information and processing of their personal information.;
- right of free access to their personal information, including right of receiving copies of any record where their personal information is contained, except cases specified by federal law;
- right to choose representatives for protection of their personal information;
- right to access medical information relevant to their personal information with aid of a medical specialist of their choice;
- right to demand exclusion or correction of incorrect or incomplete personal information and information that was processed with violation of requirements of this Code. If an employer refuses to exclude or correct personal information of an employee, then an employee has right to inform employer in written form about disagreement and provide correspondent reasons for this disagreement. A notice by an employee, expressing point of view of the employee can be added to personal information of estimative type;
- right to demand from employer informing of all entities who were previously given incorrect or incomplete personal information of an employee about all exclusions, additions and corrections in personal information of an employee;
- right to appeal to court about any non-legitimate actions or inactions of an employer relevant to processing and protection of personal information of an employee.

§5.07 PHILIPPINES

The Philippines passed the Data Privacy Act in 2012, which created a national DPA. Unusually, the Philippines Data Privacy Act does not restrict cross-border transfer: no additional assurances are needed but the controller remains responsible for any illegal personal information handling. Following transfer, if a processor does not protect personal information according to the Data Privacy Act, the authority will hold the controller accountable.

Notably, the Data Privacy Act bars SPI transfer, meaning that information about health or finance or other SPI cannot leave the Philippines' geographic boundaries. Furthermore, organizations must notify the national DPA in the event of a data breach and to any affected data subjects. Otherwise, the Data Privacy Act reflects several other data privacy laws. For example, notice must be provided and the data subject must consent before processing commences. The data subject must explicitly consent to SPI processing. In order to process personal information, collection must be necessary, specifically disclosed, legitimate for the purposes of processing, and reasonable in relation to the purpose for collection. Controllers must maintain data accuracy.

§5.08 HONG KONG

Hong Kong passed the Personal Data (Privacy) Ordinance (PDPO) in 1996 and amended most recently in 2013.[160] The PDPO requires compliance with six Data Protection Principles (DPPs):

(1) DPP 1: Personal data must be collected lawfully and fairly, for a purpose directly connected to the user's activities (necessary and not excessive).
(2) DPP 2: Personal data should be accurate and not retained longer than needed for the purpose collected.
(3) DPP 3: Data must be used for the purpose collected or a directly related purpose, unless voluntary and explicit consent is obtained.
(4) DPP 4: A data user (controller) must take practicable steps to safeguard personal data.
(5) DPP 5: A data user (controller) must take practicable steps to make data policies known to the public (data types collected and how it is used).
(6) DPP 6: A data subject must be given access to his/her personal data and be able to make corrections if inaccurate.

The PDPO also includes restrictions for marketing activities. A data user who intends to engage a data subject in direct marketing must inform the data subject of the intent to use personal data and that the data user may not use the data without consent.

160. The Personal Data (Privacy Ordinance), E.R. 1 of 2013, http://www.blis.gov.hk/blis_pdf.nsf/CurAllEngDoc/B4DF8B4125C4214D482575EF000EC5FF/$FILE/CAP_486_e_b5.pdf.

The data user must also disclose the type of data used and classes of marketing subjects, and provide a channel where a data subject may consent.

§5.09 REPUBLIC OF KOREA

The Republic of Korea passed the Personal Information Protection Act (PIPA) in 2011.[161] PIPA follows the APEC Privacy Framework, but many of the rules do reflect more stringent privacy laws, including restrictions on transfer and special handling of SPI. PIPA requires personal information processing be explicit and specific to the purposes disclosed in notice provided to the data subject.

§5.10 SINGAPORE

Singapore's PDPA generally prohibits transfer of personal information outside Singapore geographic boundaries, unless there are some assurances of compliance. Similar to Australia, Singapore requires legally binding commitments for transfer that are comparable to Privacy Act protections: for example, contract language, BCRs, or adequate legal frameworks, would qualify. Transfer is necessary for fulfillment of a contract are permitted, however, the PDPA does not apply to employees or non-business circumstances. This means that typical contracts contemplated by the GDPR do not apply in Singapore. Before processing, consent is required and organizations may only collect in a reasonable manner for purposes disclosed before a data subject consents.

Singapore routinely issues advisory guidelines for interpreting or meeting PDPA requirements:[162]

- Advisory Guidelines on Key Concepts in the PDPA
- Advisory Guidelines on the PDPA for Selected Topics
- Advisory Guidelines on the DNC Provisions
- Advisory Guidelines on Requiring Consent for Marketing Purposes
- Advisory Guidelines on Enforcement of Data Protection Provisions.

§5.11 TAIWAN

Taiwan originally passed the Personal Data Protection Law (PDPL) in 2010 and recently updated the law in 2016. Similar to Japan, multiple ministries enforce the PDPL for their sectors. In Taiwan, a data subject must either consent or have formed a contract with the data controller, as well as some additional limited conditions for collection (e.g., necessity, legal stipulation, publicly available sources). When a data

161. Personal Information Protection Act, Mar. 29, 2011.
162. Personal Data Protection Commission Singapore, *Main Advisory Guidelines* (27 Jul. 2017), https://www.pdpc.gov.sg/legislation-and-guidelines/advisory-guidelines/main-advisory-guidelines.

controller transfers personal information to a recipient, the data must only transfer to jurisdictions with proper regulations that will not harm the rights and interests of the data subject.

The data controller should additionally protect personal information with appropriate technical and administrative measures, and must notify the data subject when a data breach occurs. Taiwan also utilizes a Trustmark product, which enables self-regulatory auditing for data controllers.[163]

163. Third party organizations provide Trustmark products for a fee, and increasingly APAC countries have expressed interest in developing these marks. Singapore, for example, also uses a Trustmark product.

CHAPTER 6
The Middle East and Africa

The Middle East and Africa together cover a substantially large breadth of geographic space, yet few Data Protection laws currently exist. In the Middle East, the most substantial data protection law is Israel's Protection of Privacy Law, 5741-1981 (PPL), although Dubai has increasingly developed regulations to attract business interests.[186]

On the African continent, some countries, such as the Republic of Angola, Cote d'Ivoire, Gabon, Ghana, South Africa, and Zimbabwe have passed information privacy laws. However, recent developments of the African Union (AU) to create a privacy framework may influence standardization and broader passage in the region.

§6.01 ISRAEL

Israel does not require substantial information privacy activities with the current version of the PPL. The PPL bars infringement of privacy, except with consent.[187] Organizations soliciting personal information must provide details about a data subject's legal duties to provide any information, the purpose for information requested, and recipients of information and reasons for receipt. Individuals may inspect their own information in a database in Hebrew, Arabic, or English, and may request a correction. Database owners must employ reasonable security protect the information. The PPL includes limited marketing considerations, as well. Direct mailing for marketing purposes requires special registration in addition to standard database registration.

164. Protection of Privacy Law, 5741-1981, http://www.justice.gov.il/En/Units/ILITA/Documents/ProtectionofPrivacyLaw57411981unofficialtranslatio.pdf (unofficial translation).
165. Listed privacy infringements also include common law privacy allegations under U.S. law, such as appropriation of likeness, intrusion upon seclusion, public disclosure of privacy facts, and surveillance.

§6.02 UNITED ARAB EMIRATES: DUBAI (DIFC)

The DIFC passed the DIFC Law No. 5 in 2012, following an earlier version in 2007, as well as the Data Protection Regulation (DPR).[188] The DIFC created the role of the Commission of Data Protection (CDP), which initially passed the DPR under the responsibility created in the DIFC Law. The DIFC has also created Dubai Healthcare City, which includes its own law, similar to the DIFC Law and DPR.[189]

The DIFC Law requires registration of processing activities, controller identity, and data type processing. For sensitive personal information (SPI), data controllers must disclose specific security measures implemented to protect SPI from loss, alteration, and unauthorized disclosure or access. Data controllers may select appropriate controls based on attendant risks. If a data breach occurs, the data controller must notify the CDP "as soon as practically possible."

Under the DIFC, collection of SPI requires written consent, and personal information requires explicit consent, as well, absent necessity and other standard legitimate justifications found under most data protection laws. Data controllers must provide notice appropriately informing data subjects of personal information uses and processing activities, including plans to use such data for marketing purposes. Controllers may transfer data outside of the DIFC when the receiving country is deemed *adequate*, judged from CDP approval.[190] Data may also transfer with data subject consent or pursuant to a contract.

§6.03 THE AFRICAN CONTINENT

The countries of the Republic of Angola, Cote d'Ivoire, Gabon, Ghana, South Africa, and Zimbabwe have currently passed Data Protection laws, in large part modeling the Organisation for Economic Co-operation and Development (OECD) principles.[191] However, many other African countries, including Egypt, have not. For this reason, the AU Convention on Cyber Security and Personal Data Protection was held in 2014, modeled after OECD principles.[192]

In Chapter II, the Personal Data Protection Convention establishes a common understanding for signatories that they will establish a legal framework for the

166. DIFC Law No. 1 of 2007 (amended by DIFC Law No. 5 of 2012) and by the Data Protection Regulations (Consolidated Version No. 2 in force on 23 Dec. 2012).
167. Dubai Healthcare City Regulation No. 7 of 2008.
168. Dubai International Financial Centre, *Adequate Data Protection Regimes* (2017), https://www.difc.ae/laws-regulations/data-protection/adequate-data-protection-regimes.
169. Republic of Angola: Data Protection Law No. 22/11, 17 June; Electronic Communications and Information Society Services Law (Law No. 23/11, 20 June); Cote D'Ivoire: Law No. 2013-450 on Protection of Personal Data. Gabon: Law No. 001/2011 on the Protection of Personal Data. Ghana: Data Protection Act, 2012 (Act 843). South Africa: Protection of Personal Information Act (19 Nov. 2013). Zimbabwe: Access to Information and Protection of Privacy Act (Chapter 10:247).
170. The African Union Convention on Cyber Security and Personal Data Protection, EX.CL/846(XXV), Malabo, 27 Jun. 2014, available at: https://ccdcoe.org/sites/default/files/documents/AU-270614-CSConvention.pdf.

protection of personal information, including appointment of a national DPA, and ensure data processing respects fundamental rights, with appropriate punishment and enforcement for violations. Organizations may not engage in processing genetic information and health research information, collection of biometric data, or processing of criminal offenses without prior authorization of the national protection authority.

The Convention listed six principles for personal data processing:

(1) Consent and legitimacy of data processing (consent required except under limited conditions, explicit consent required to process SPI).
(2) Lawfulness and fairness of data processing.
(3) Purpose, relevance, and storage (collection specific, explicit, legitimate, adequate and not excessive in light of purpose).
(4) Accuracy of personal data.
(5) Transparency of personal data processing (notice).[193]
(6) Confidentiality and security of processing.[194]

The Convention also established a variety of common understandings regarding data protection, including questions of consent. Using personal information for marketing activities, for example, requires separate consent.

It is unclear to what extent other regional affiliations, such as the Economic Community of West African States (ECOWAS), the Southern African Development Community (SADC), and the East African Community (EAC) might join this effort. ECOWAS, for example, drafted a Supplementary Act A/SA.1/01/10 on Personal Data Protection within ECOWAS in 2010.[195] The SADC, followed, drafting a model law on Data Protection and a model law on Cybercrime, both in 2012.[196]

171. Notice requires: data controller identity, purposes of processing, categories of data, recipient of data, capacity to request removal, right of access and correction, data storage timeframe, and proposed third country transfers.
172. The Convention also include details for a co-extensive National cybersecurity framework, including legislation against cybercrime, a focus on critical infrastructure, national cybersecurity systems, public-private partnerships, education and training, monitoring structures, and institutional frameworks.
173. Economic Community of West African States, Supplementary Act A/SA.1/01/10 on Personal Data Protection (2010), available at: http://www.statewatch.org/news/2013/mar/ecowas-dp-act.pdf.
174. Harmonization of ICT Policies in Sub-Saharan Africa, *Data Protection: Southern Africa Development Community (SADC) Model Law* (2012), http://www.itu.int/en/ITU-D/Projects/ITU-EC-ACP/HIPSSA/Documents/FINAL%20DOCUMENTS/FINAL%20DOCS%20ENGLISH/sadc_model_law_data_protection.pdf.

CHAPTER 7

Privacy Programs and Practical Strategies

In addition to understanding applicable laws and having a sense for where laws might diverge or fit a particular model, attorneys and practitioners must learn to apply legal knowledge to practical management circumstances to protect organizational legal interests. Chapter 7 describes the fundamental, foundational considerations for building an effective information privacy program.

§7.01 THE PRIVACY CHARTER AND PRIVACY POLICIES

When organizations begin creating a privacy program, often leaders do not know where to begin. However, in line with new business functions, privacy programs should begin by drafting a charter that will shape future goals, build privacy activity awareness, and assess growth and program development. Although an organization's privacy officer or another leader with overall privacy accountability should draft the charter or declaration of purpose, upper management and senior leaders should review and approve for the organization. Without support for a common privacy vision, organizations will struggle receiving appropriate financing and governance.

A privacy charter should clearly describe the position of an organization serving as both a compass and an aspirational tool for shaping future discussions. Some organizations embracing a multi-functional team approach may include both privacy and cybersecurity in a common charter. Organizations may choose to write the charter for only internal use, or include the charter within privacy notices presented to customers or consumers on Websites. The following illustrates a privacy charter reviewed and approved by organizational leadership:

> Organization A is committed to responsible collection and protection of the personal information of our employees, affiliates, customers, and direct product consumers. Responsible use of personal information requires Organization A

personnel to respect individual privacy and ensure integrity, availability, confidentiality, and overall safety of employees and customers. Organization A commits to the belief that privacy is not only a protected civil right, but also Organization A differentiates itself from competitors by addressing employee, customer, and consumer needs.
Our Principles:
- Our internal policies clearly articulate acceptable and unacceptable behavior with respect to personal information.
- Organization A's approach to privacy and cybersecurity involves preventative, proactive measures, built into design the first time.
- We remain committed to continuous improvement through transparency, choice, and data protection.

As referenced in the privacy and cybersecurity charter, internal policies also help an organization manage internal expectations and clearly articulate expectations to personnel. When organizations formally approve policies, execute employment contracts requiring compliance with internal policies, and routinely communicate privacy policy updates to their personnel; organizations have given personnel fair warning of their obligations. Therefore, if an employee does not fulfill policy expectations, organizations may caution or reprimand the employee, include details of the incident on the employee's employment record, or terminate employment (pursuant to local employment laws).

The *privacy policy* is an internal document notifying personnel about organizational expectations, and therefore must communicate these expectations in as clear and easy to understand language as possible for a wide range of personnel. Privacy policies may also be included in a *code of conduct*.[175] Privacy policies incorporate legal requirements as well as organizational expectations, such as requiring notice of privacy practices for employees, even where local laws do not require. For this reason, multi-national organizations may prefer to create multiple privacy notices for different regions of the world, as privacy expectations can differ substantially, e.g., the European Union to China. The privacy policy supports policy reviews, such as PIAs, by establishing baseline requirements. However, organizations should consider the difficulties of managing multiple versions of multiple regional privacy policies and associated approvals before committing to this model. Privacy policies usually include:

- Effective date
- An applicability statement
- Definitions
- Specific obligations of each employee or contractor
- A minimum set of privacy requirements for every system or business process

175. For jurisdictions requiring a code of conduct for registration purposes, Cross-Border Privacy Regulation (CBPR), or Binding Corporate Rules (BCRs), the code of conduct and applicable privacy policy should be provided to the regulatory authority.

- Approvals and dates of approval.

A primary challenge for multi-national organizations involves determining a strategic approach for compliance management and internal policy. At the root of this discussion is a question of whether organizations should strive for minimum legal compliance or whether protecting privacy more broadly makes sense for an organization. Organizations often experience challenges with a "compliance-minimum" approach: the vast number of information privacy laws applicable in a multi-national setting can dramatically reduce efficiency. At its extreme, organizations might draft individual privacy notices for each country and determine privacy requirements for each individual combination of countries applicable to a given project. This approach requires individual updates as soon as laws change and heavy legal involvement in all parts of the process to determine how individual laws apply to a project. Although automated tools mapping laws to requirements may improve efficiency, multi-national organizations may find this approach difficult to maintain over time. The benefit of a compliance-only approach includes maximum data availability and freedom of data use for countries without information privacy laws or less restrictive laws.

Organizations that view information privacy as a market differentiator and fully global companies often adopt a "compliance-plus" approach to privacy. Compliance-plus incorporates legal requirements into internal policy and associated processes to ensure compliance, but adopts a regional or global approach to managing privacy. Naturally, a regional or global approach results in more restrictive privacy measures than the law requires for some countries, and some organizations find this approach too restrictive for business operations and potential value proposition, especially when an organization's value depends in large part on using data in dynamic ways (e.g., Facebook or Google). However, this approach also results in fewer privacy policy updates, streamlines privacy reviews and assessments, and improves personnel understanding of internal obligations.

§7.02 PRIVACY NOTICES, DISCLOSURES, AND CONSENT MANAGEMENT

The privacy policy also reflects, to some extent, practices shared in the privacy notice. A *privacy notice* provides details of privacy practices to external parties, including customers and consumers.[176] Organizations use privacy notices in a wide variety of ways: on Websites, for Web applications prior to a customer using the service, on mobile applications, and in paper form (i.e., in a physician's office). Each notice's requirements differ depending on the region, but most notices require:

- the identity of the organization's controller, including instructions for contacting the controller in any reasonable method (e-mail, post, phone);

176. Of note: some organizations call a privacy notice a privacy policy or privacy statement. The author recommends calling externally facing documents something different from internally facing documents to improve internal communication and clarity.

- the identity of the Data Protection Officer, although this is usually included in the registration process with regulatory authorities instead;
- a description of data collected; if sensitive data collected, a specific description of data elements and why these data are required for the service;
- a description of explicit, specific business uses for the data and description of how these uses enable service or product functionality;[177]
- a specific description of third parties or third-party groups receiving personal information;
- an articulation of data subject rights, including access, correction, revocation of consent, and erasure (in some jurisdictions), and how to execute these rights;
- where data will be stored, if not within the jurisdiction collected;
- information about cookies used on the Web application or Website.

Although many Websites may provide a privacy notice, organizations should not be tempted to re-use identical privacy notices for other uses, such as a Web application, mobile app, or for other affiliates. Business uses, data collected, third parties, and data storage often will change, depending on the specific project or process implementation. Externally facing privacy notices, incorrectly executed, pose substantial regulatory risk to an organization because regulatory authorities can easily view and review externally posted notices on Websites or other applications.

Privacy notices also can prove challenging for usability and readability requirements. In many jurisdictions, organizations must not bury privacy notice language in TOU language and may be required to provide a separate privacy notice. Privacy notices have previously included legal language, sometimes in the form of boilerplate; however, privacy notices drafted today require specific information and details communicated at an elementary grade reading level. Further, in order to adequately describe information handling practices, organizations must provide substantial details, lengthening the privacy notice. Organizations also struggle to manage various privacy notice versions, especially across jurisdictions.

Organizations have developed different models for drafting and managing privacy notices. First, organizations should develop standard, dedicated, privacy-only notice templates, based on the country or region, for organizations to paste in appropriate details, depending on the implementation type (website, web application, mobile app, paper copy). Departments using the template(s) must provide final copies of completed templates to a common management function, such as a legal team or privacy team, for recording of date, version, link, and storage.

In the internal privacy policy, organizations should require teams that own privacy notices to review and update notices periodically, annually or every two years at a minimum. Additionally, organizations should update notices quickly after technical or business process changes that would render the privacy notice inaccurate

177. Organizations must distinguish between *primary uses*, or uses intertwined with the service itself, e.g., where an individual cannot receive service without providing personal information, and *secondary uses*, or uses separate from but potentially benefitting the controller, a third party, or otherwise products overall.

("material changes" or "substantial changes").[178] Of course, when organizations change notice contents, in most jurisdictions new consent is required. When data subjects have not consented to the new privacy notice contents, data subjects have *not* consented. Therefore, organizations must: (1) manage data use with respect to multiple notices, which is complex and prone to mistake, (2) treat previously (but not currently) consented data subjects as if they had revoked consent, or (3) execute a new privacy notice and collect consent.

In most jurisdictions, privacy notices must be: (1) separated from other language, usually as a dedicated "Privacy Notice" document, (2) for Websites, easy to locate, such as via a link in the Website footer, but no more than two clicks deep from the main Website, and (3) provided contextually prior to data subject consent. To achieve contextual (or *prior* and *informed*) consent, organizations must choose an appropriate display model. For example, organizations may provide the privacy notice as a whole and require the data subject to review the entire notice prior to consenting (e.g., logic on the Website can determine when a data subject has scrolled through the screen) or provide the privacy notice via a link opening a new Window when clicked.

Privacy notices may embody a variety of communication models, depending on their use. A popular model for privacy notices today is the *layered privacy notice*, often used for Web-based or mobile app privacy notices. A layered privacy notice enables an organization to minimize information overload for customers and consumers by providing high-level information with the opportunity to click into specific topics with more detailed information. For example, organizations may specify high-level information use with a list of products. Clicking on the product links, then, provides details of information use within those products.

In some jurisdictions, organizations must also disclose additional information in a manner distinct from a standard privacy notice. Certain services or business processes may require secondary use disclosures, cookie notices, and marketing disclosures. Secondary use involves disclosing to a data subject when information collection exceeds necessary and proportionate information gathering requirements. Usually this disclosure involves a separate check box with detail next to it, such as "I agree to share my personal information to improve overall service to Organization A customers."

Cookie notices in the EU must appear when an individual clicks on a link to a Website and the Website loads, regardless of which page loads. Different countries require different levels of consent, but a pop-up or banner-type disclosure usually suffices, such as:

> Organization A Website uses cookies, which are small text files stored on your computer, to improve site performance, personalize your experience, and collect information about Website use. Click Cookie Policy to find out more about the type of cookies we use. By clicking "yes," you agree to share this information with Organization A.

178. Organizations must also retain versions of privacy notices according to internal retention schedules for legal purposes, including regulatory investigation or litigation.

Although for some EU countries, continuing to use the Website after viewing the cookie pop-up constitutes legally implied consent, some EU countries require user interaction. The most prudent option involves requiring user interaction, such as explicit clicking of an "I agree" link or button.[179]

When organizations provide marketing disclosures, which inform a data subject about options for receiving marketing communications, often a separate check-box or other selection should display. Some jurisdictions require more specific disclosures, such as the Federal Communications Commission (FCC) in the United States (U.S.), for Telephone Consumer Protection Act (TCPA) and Controlling the Assault of Non-Solicited Pornography and Marketing Act (CAN-SPAM), but most jurisdictions only require that marketing activities receive individual consent, separated from standard service. Usually this disclosure also involves a separate check box with details next to it, such as "I would be interested in receiving information about Organization A's products and services." Organizations should clearly define the organization providing marketing communications; data subjects would not expect to receive marketing communications from an apparently different organization, such as another division of the same multi-national company, if not identified as such in the marketing disclosure.

As previously referenced in relation to privacy notices and disclosures, an individual data subject may provide various consents at various points in time that an organization must manage. For this reason, consent management creates record-keeping challenges for organizations. The following examples illustrate typical consent collected with respect to a data subject (depending on the jurisdiction):

- Privacy notice consent: business use, third party use, and data handling practices described in each version of the privacy notice.
- Processing of SPI: often disclosed in the privacy notice, but may require separate consent in some jurisdictions.
- Data transfer: for some jurisdictions, data transfer is only possible with explicit consent or international treaty.
- Secondary uses: internal to organization or third-party use, may require specific authorization in some jurisdictions.
- Marketing: consent to send marketing communications via e-mail, text message, and phone.
- Cookies: consent to store information about someone who visited the site.

Managing a myriad of consent types can pose challenges for organizations both in the type of consent required and in the manner of executing consent. Some laws permit implied consent for personal information but require informed, explicit consent for SPI, while others require informed explicit consent for all personal information collection and processing.[180] In Russia (Personal Data Protection Act (PDPA)) and

179. When the EU eventually updates the E-Privacy Directive or passes an E-Privacy Regulation, the law likely will resolve this question.
180. Explicit consent includes displaying a privacy notice, then requiring an individual to overtly agree by checking a box, clicking a button, or otherwise positively manifesting agreement to a privacy notice. Implicit consent is derived most often from continued use following notice.

Argentina (Personal Data Protection Law No. 25.326), data subjects evidence informed, explicit consent by signing in writing. For children's Web-enabled products, parents provide consent on a Website rather than on a tiny, limited screen of a child's toy (due to space restrictions).

Data transfer may also require explicit consent. South Korea requires additional consent beyond the standard privacy notice to transfer personal information outside of the country (Personal Information Protection Act (PIPA)), while Japan requires additional consent prior to third party transfer (Act on Protection of Personal Information (APPI)). Transfer limitations overall are a hallmark of most data protection laws. In both cases, organizations should collect and retain a separate consent record or notation. To meet all applicable consent requirements, organizations should develop a notice and consent grid that clearly maps jurisdictions where organizations have customers and employees.

For each individual data subject, organizations must maintain accurate information and facilitate updates to consent in a timely manner, such as revocation of a particular consent (e.g., receipt of marketing materials) or revocation of all data processing. Appropriately managing consent within a large, multi-national, or diverse organization requires strong Customer Records Management (CRM) capabilities and Records Information Management (RIM) practices. Essentially, without a primary data subject record that feeds downstream systems, such as a marketing tool, updating data subject preferences across an organization is nearly impossible efficiently execute.

For organizations with multiple sources of truth, organizations should consider developing a common, secure repository for data subject record identifiers and pseudonyms. The pseudonym, then, can be used across individual systems instead of the data subject name or other unique identifier. This model accomplishes two goals: (1) data set identifiability is reduced, minimizing risk to the data subject and (2) a common mapping of system data to individual data subject can enable procedural processes for consent management, consent revocation, access requests, correction requests, and erasure requests across systems. This activity, however, requires a common inventory of systems containing personal information.

§7.03 PIAs, DPIAs, AND PRIVACY BY DESIGN (DEFAULT)

Effective privacy programs require clear operational privacy processes and clear roles and responsibilities within a privacy organization. Privacy programs must develop seven key processes:

(1) Privacy Impact Assessment (PIA) or EU Data Protection Impact Assessment (DPIA)
(2) Privacy by Design or Privacy by Default
(3) Data Inventory
(4) Access and correction procedures
(5) Data erasure and deletion procedures
(6) Complaint handling

(7) Training and awareness activities

PIAs and DPIAs provide an important check to evaluate privacy compliance activities.[181] Although the privacy policy and associated procedures should provide organizational teams with enough information to comply, PIAs and DPIAs validate that teams are following policy. DPIAs provide compliance verification and are required by law, such as under the General Data Protection Regulation (GDPR) for high risk data processing activities. For purposes of this section, we will use PIA rather than DPIA.

PIAs (P-I-A or pee-ah) evaluate a particular system, project, business process, or data use for compliance with internal privacy policy. PIAs should include: a repeatable, documented assessment process, a common questionnaire or set of questionnaires, and a common methodology for documenting data flows. The assessment process adopts privacy policy contents and translates the policy into measurable controls, or "yes" or "no" questions enabling privacy analyst to determine privacy risks. A *privacy risk* is known non-compliance with the privacy policy, which will require *remediation*, or closing an open privacy risk.

A practitioner conducts PIAs on existing processes, projects about to be released, and future initiatives. The first step for conducting a PIA involves identifying key contacts and business sponsors for the project or process under review. These contacts and sponsors provide answers to questions during the PIA process and to make decisions regarding remediation after the PIA is completed.

Next, the practitioner gathers information about the data type and geographic origin, processing location, and storage location to determine the inherent risk of a particular project. *Inherent risk* includes reviewing what a project intends to do, the data type collected, data subject residency, and planned data transfers, without measuring compliance. Inherent risk determines how risky a project *could be*. Organizations usually conduct some type of inherent risk assessment prior to completing a PIA to prioritize reviews.

Organizations should consider different aspects of data managed within their respective industries to determine what will be considered negligible risk, average risk, and high risk (or low, medium, and high). This delineation between risk levels, then, informs downstream activities. For example, inputs for inherent risk calculation include:

- The organization's role with respect to the project (controller/operator/responsible party, processor, or third party)
- The number of records or data volume
- Data classification, sensitivity, and special data categories
- Geographic location of data subjects
- High-risk activities, such as automated processing
- Nature of data processing, especially secondary uses
- How and where data will be stored or retained

181. PIA is the generic term for most assessments evaluating privacy compliance; DPIA is the name for a similar assessment in the EU with various legal requirements under the GDPR.

- Applicable laws and expected regulatory authority involvement

Prioritization given relatively limited resources (which often is the case for privacy programs), encourages organizations to focus first on inherently high-risk projects. For example, organizations exclusively processing SPI could impact data subject rights more seriously and require more internal scrutiny than organizations routinely processing e-mail contacts. Organizations with substantial volumes of personal information, even if the information is not sensitive, could also pose serious risks to data subjects because a large volume could invite fraud or cyberattack. Under the GDPR, inherent risk should focus more heavily on potential data subject rights impacted.

After initial prioritization is completed, a practitioner begins interviewing the project team. This includes understanding systems involved in the project, what data types reside in certain locations within the system, and how data will transfer within a system (data storage and transfer will be discussed in Chapter 8). The practitioner then records the data flows into a data flow diagram. Data flow diagrams do not have a specific format but may be complex (as in an architecture diagram) or simple boxes representing systems. *See* Figure 7.1 for example of a simple data flow diagram.

Figure 7.1 Data Flow Diagram

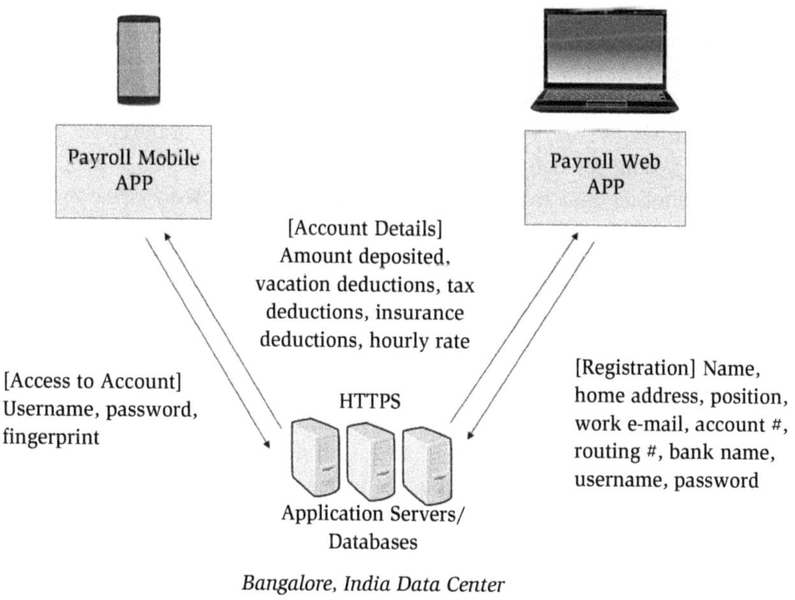

After the practitioner completes a data flow diagram, the questionnaire works directly with the project team to fill out the questionnaire. Practitioners pay special attention to collecting accurate information, as this information drives applicable privacy requirements:

- Countries of current, near future, and future data subject residence.
- Business uses for data collected, including primary and secondary uses (such as marketing, data aggregation, data sales, and third party transfer).
- Nature of processing and role of organization, including vendor support functions.
- Countries of processing activities (including access, support, editing, and backup).
- Data elements processed.

Once the practitioner or organizational contact completes a questionnaire, the practitioner reviews results and determines where non-compliance with the privacy policy exists. For each incident of non-compliance, a *finding*, the practitioner assigns a risk rating, which represents the probability of harm and impact of harm to the organization or to a data subject. The risk rating then drives further action according to internal governance processes.

A residual risk rating process provides an important tool for prioritizing remediation activities. For example, an organization that retains information slightly longer than is required but has a valid retention schedule likely will merit a lower risk rating then an organization that does not provide notice before collecting personal information. For GDPR compliance purposes, an organization will need to analyze risk specifically based on risk to data subject rights and include this consideration in the calculation. When an organization does not plan on remediating high-risk findings, organizations must report these findings to the Lead DPA. For this reason, organizations may prefer to develop a reference sheet for risk findings describing the degree of impact both to an organization and to a data subject.

After identifying a risk rating, the practitioner formalizes a draft report, and sends it to the project team for a full review and approval of the report's accuracy. The practitioner or another team member then monitors finding remediation activities until completion. Organizations may choose to drive certain governance behaviors based on residual risk of findings, such as barring projects from going live with average or higher risks, or requiring specific time periods for remediation (e.g., high risk requires a sixty-day remediation timeframe). Organizations should work internally to determine the appropriate organizational triggers for PIA findings.[182]

Functional privacy programs include remediation tracking as part of a strong risk management practice. When organizations do not track remediation activities, often project teams will not remediate findings, introducing non-compliance unknown to the organization. Practitioners should encourage teams to set specific dates for remediation and routinely check on progress to the date. When privacy teams manage remediation progress, they stress the importance of becoming and staying compliant.

Organizations should consider dedicating privacy program-managed budgets to fund important remediation activities crossing business functions that pose substantial

182. Organizations often have very different thresholds for different activities, including the degree to which a compliance organization has influence to halt projects. In other organizations, lack of specific accountability to halt projects results in an ineffective organizational capability.

risk to the organization overall. However, organizations should also encourage departments to fund remediation for their own products or services, creating a common sense of ownership in compliance activities. Organizations can avoid routine funding requests if privacy by design or privacy by default activities precede system design and development activities.

Privacy by Design or Privacy by Default (PbD), both referenced frequently in Canada and more recently within the GDPR, offer a proactive option for privacy compliance.[183] Rather than assessing a project after completion, a practitioner engages with the project team to design solutions through the development process (described in Chapter 11) that meet compliance obligations. PbD activities typically reduce time spent on remediation by ensuring systems built meet requirements prior to release. However, PbD activities can also be time-consuming for privacy teams, usually requiring more interaction on a regular basis between a practitioner or attorney and a project team.

This high interaction cost usually results from project changes: when the project changes, compliance obligations may also change. Organizations can avoid efficiency traps by developing a library of design requirements, which map to the internal privacy policy. Drafting PbD requirements can prove challenging, as requirements may differ based on data elements, applicable regions, and systems used. However, when organizations invest in developing a requirements library, practitioners may enjoy a comparatively easier effort selecting appropriate requirements, rather than creating new requirements within each engagement.

Ann Cavoukian, Information and Privacy Commissioner of Ontario, Canada, has described PbD through seven principles of a successful program:[184]

(1) Proactive, not Reactive; Preventative, not Remedial
(2) Privacy as the Default
(3) Privacy Embedded into Design
(4) Full Functionality—Positive Sum, not Zero-Sum
(5) End-to-End Security—Life cycle Protection
(6) Visibility and Transparency
(7) Respect for User Privacy.

In developing a PbD program, organizations will likely encounter fewer surprises from projects that have not followed internal policy (and often are not compliant with legal requirements). However, successful programs have both capabilities: PbD for all projects with accompanying requirements, and PIAs, which enable an organization to review higher risk data handling practices to ensure PbD effectiveness.

183. Vendors also provide "Privacy by Design" certification to ensure organizations have implemented PbD appropriately.

184. Ann Cavoukian, *Privacy by Design the 7 Foundational Principles* (Mar. 2011), https://iab.org/wp-content/IAB-uploads/2011/03/fred_carter.pdf.

§7.04 OPERATIONAL PRIVACY PROCESSES AND THE PRIVACY ORGANIZATION

Organizations must also manage operational privacy processes and develop appropriate procedures to support these processes. One foundational process involves the creation of a data inventory. A *data inventory* logs all systems, including third party systems, which contain personal information and maintains a list of data elements collected within each system. Although the concept may appear simple, internal and external data transfer for legitimate information technology (IT) purposes complicates the process of locating data and accurate record-keeping. Organizations that integrate data inventory activities into asset management activities (described in Chapter 8) often see greater success, as do organizations that ensure appropriate IT documentation for architecture diagrams, engineering design documents, and integration documents. These documents can enhance understanding of data storage and potential implications therein, both for cybersecurity and for privacy.

Under most information provide laws, organizations must fulfill access and correction requests on a timely basis. Without appropriate documentation and a data inventory, organizations likely cannot fulfill such requests reliably and accurately. Once organizations understand where data is located, personnel fulfilling data subject rights requests can fulfill these requests in a timely manner.

Data subject rights requests require upfront planning and standardization. Privacy teams should develop standard procedure templates that adapt to different systems, yet create standardization for handling an access or correction request. The first step in fulfilling a rights request is validating a data subject's identity. Organizations must establish identity first to ensure a data breach or unauthorized disclosure does not result from an access or correction request. However, organizations should balance the need for validation with the risk of capturing and retaining sensitive data.

Where possible, organizations should rely on specific knowledge rather than sensitive identifiers. For example, an order number or service account number that organizations must retain can provide one piece of information for validation purposes. Alternatively, an organization may request a data subject respond to their own pre-selected questions. Some organizations may choose to assign a unique image or phrase to an individual for verification. Once verified, contact center personnel must validate the appropriate access to information permitted. In some cases, family members or designated individuals (such as a caretaker) may have access to personal information stored, but perhaps a fraction of the data may be shared, per internal policy or data subject instructions. Local laws will inform these procedures, but organizations should take care not to distribute personal information without sufficient verification.

Contact center personnel should initiate access requests and correction requests immediately, depending on applicable information privacy and consumer protection laws (e.g., credit or financial account corrections). These requests will likely require activity from IT teams via a service request or other prioritized work request. For this reason, the privacy team should work with IT teams in advance to establish appropriate service-level agreements (SLAs), so that access and correction requests meet legal requirements. In some jurisdictions, a data transfer request may accompany a data access request. In these cases, organizations in a particular industry will benefit from collaborative efforts to establish acceptable transfer languages (e.g., HIPAA requires HL7 code to transfer health data). The *Data erasure* requests (currently only in the EU, except where illegal collection has occurred) should follow a similar model to access and correction requests. However, data erasure and deletion requests should also incorporate secure deletion procedures developed or established by cybersecurity standards.

Although organizations can avoid complaints through accurate prior notice, compliance consent management practices, and standard data subject right procedures, organizations should also develop data subject complaint handling processes. Organizations must develop efficient complaint handling processes to ensure ongoing compliance, prevent complaint escalation to regulatory authorities, informatively respond to regulatory authority investigations, and to support alternative dispute resolution proceedings. *Complaint handling* is the process of receiving information about claimed non-compliance regarding organizational activities (or failed commitments) and responding to these complaints. Organizations should provide clear and informative information Websites and within Privacy Notices, as often data subject contact the organization through these channels. When an organization receives a complaint directly from a data subject, the receiver should immediately transfer details to the privacy team, where an individual will begin investigating the complaint.

The privacy team should develop an internal procedure for investigating complaints, including appropriate information to gather, engagement of legal support in the process to establish attorney-client privilege, and to appropriately respond to a data subject with information in a timely, informative manner meeting time constraints within the applicable law. Organizations that respond quickly and take remedial action to correct issues usually do not encounter additional investigation and escalation to regulatory authorities. However, organizations with poor complaint handling procedures often receive formal letters or warnings from regulatory authorities.[185]

Organizations should work closely with legal support to ensure responses to both data subjects and the regulatory authority meet disclosure standards yet do not provide information that: (1) constitutes an admission of known legal non-compliance or (2) is unsubstantiated by investigation discovery. Organizations should provide timely, appropriate, and factual statements only and should similarly provide timely, appropriate, and factual statements to regulatory authority queries. Broader and more substantial complaints (or multiple complaints) may require outside counsel to advise options for regulatory response.

Data inventory development and updates, access, correction, transfer, and erasure requests will not be effectively implemented without effective training activities. Under some laws and industry standards, organizations must train personnel at

185. Please note: regulatory authorities typically send hard copy letters to the physical address and individual listed as the data protection or privacy officer for the organization. Organizations that have changed this role or inaccurately provided a name, will likely have more trouble, should a complain arise, as no one will respond to the letter, causing higher escalation, sometimes up to and including the president or CEO of an organization.

least annually. However, training in an organization should complement other compliance requirements. The most effective training is varied, frequent, short, and contextual. Although organizations typically purchase bulk training to streamline annual training requirements, personnel benefit from training integrated into everyday work. Organizations should consider, wherever possible, training (whether in-person or online) connected to common tasks and communicating critical or important processes and procedures specific to that role.

Organizations should also consider opportunities to share information about privacy with personnel more regularly, such as monthly or quarterly feature stories, internal blog posts, flyers or branded items, or talks from leadership that reiterate the important role personnel play to ensure privacy and data protection. Personnel should know that privacy is everyone's responsibility within an organization, including engineers, contact center operators, and marketing personnel.

§7.05 PRIVACY ORGANIZATION

Organizations, depending on size, may implement different types of privacy organizations. The *privacy officer* is the primary leader for the privacy organization, leading privacy strategy, managing the privacy team, and reporting to upper management, on occasion to the Board of Directors. Under most laws, an organization must name a privacy officer, even if that officer fulfills multiple roles at an organization. Under the GDPR, this privacy officer must report to the highest level of leadership, must be keenly aware of information privacy practices and risks at an organization, must be registered with the Lead DPA for the organization's jurisdiction.

When a privacy officer has a team, personnel often are divided by business area, region, or function. For organizations with diverse business areas, personnel may benefit from direct and continuous relationship with the same teams, enabling the individual to better anticipate long-term needs and changes. For organizations with highly diverse geographic presence (but somewhat similar offerings), an individual may be most effective residing near a geographic region and working directly with the region. Finally, teams can divide activities by function, such as PIA/DPIA review, program development, Privacy by Design, ongoing consultation, and process support, which drives operational ownership for larger teams.

Privacy officers in larger organizations may reside within a legal function or through another function in the company, such as risk management, assurance, or information technology. When privacy officers are separate from the legal team, a specialty privacy counsel role may exist for one or more laws, countries, or regions. When counsel participates in privacy activities with a privacy compliance team, some confusion may result regarding roles and responsibilities. For this reason, counsel and compliance teams should determine appropriate processes and roles with respect to privacy reviews, consultation, and advice.

Overall, the most successful privacy programs build privacy into various parts of the organization, whether formally as a decentralized privacy team or as a method of including various teams in privacy decisions. Organizations accomplish this in a variety of ways, such as including departmental leaders on governance committees, identifying privacy champions within departments, or training privacy practitioners to provide consultation and conduct PIAs. Regional representation can also assist larger multi-national organizations when many laws apply. In regional representation models, usually legal experts fulfill this role for a particular region given their unique perspectives and responsibilities.

PART II Cybersecurity Law and Practice

CHAPTER 8

Introduction to Cybersecurity and Information Technology

Part I discussed international privacy laws and practical compliance approaches to build an effective privacy program. Part II introduces Information Technology (IT) and cybersecurity technology, international cybersecurity laws and cybersecurity impact of privacy laws, substantial discussion on cybersecurity technical concepts and supporting technology capabilities, cybersecurity program necessities, and legal strategies for reducing the potential for liability following security incidents and data breaches.

Indeed, the global impact of cybercrime for Internet-generated revenue is staggering. Stealing personal information has become big business, and data breach frequency is increasing rapidly. Organized crime, formerly involved in illegal drug importation and money laundering, has now turned to a more reliable and lucrative substitute: computer hacking.[186] Additional consumer convenience technologies such as social media, expanded e-commerce offerings, reliance on virtual and digital payments, digital health record-keeping, and predictive marketing has only increased the variety and value of personal information.

Selling personal information has emerged as a lucrative business model with few legal risks, whether a business legally sells personal information like e-mail addresses and information gathered about a consumer or a hacker steals and sells financial or health information. Selling payment card numbers nets from 50 cents to 48 dollars per card, depending on the credit line and location of the cardholder.[187] Often, hackers sell

186. *See generally, Masters of the cyber-universe*, THE ECONOMIST (Apr. 6, 2013), *available at* http://www.economist.com/news/special-report/21574636-chinas-state-sponsored-hackers-are-ubiquitousand-totally-unabashed-masters; *China's cyberhacking: Getting Ugly*, THE ECONOMIST (Feb. 23, 2013), *available at* http://www.economist.com/news/leaders/21572200-if-china-wants-respect-abroad-it-must-rein-its-hackers-getting-ugly; Kenneth Rapoza, *Russia's Million Dollar Hackers*, FORBES (Apr. 24, 2012), *available at* http://www.forbes.com/sites/kenrapoza/2012/04/24/russias-millionaire-dollar-hackers/.

187. Timothy Peacock & Allan Friedman, *Automation and Disruption in Stolen Payment Card Markets* (2014), http://weis2014.econinfosec.org/papers/PeacockFriedman-WEIS2014.pdf, at

to black market, bulk-card purchasers who use the cards to buy merchandise and subsequently sell it at discounted prices through sites like eBay. These activities are highly untraceable, occurring globally where perpetrators cannot be identified and prosecuted.[188] Despite the success of financial fraud, nearly 44% of all breaches now involve health information, and fraudsters can sell health information for ten times the price of an individual payment card to falsify expensive insurance claims.[189]

Information privacy presents both consumer privacy and economic concerns. Data breaches do not only affect corporations and consumers: downstream banks, credit-card-issuing businesses, and health insurance providers also pay for the fallout. Payment cards, for example, process nearly USD 3.5 trillion dollars per year and 3,900 transactions each second for 78% of American households. Recent individual data breaches have cost banking and credit card issuing businesses hundreds of millions per large breach, due to proactive card reissuing and fraud coverage on credit and debit cards.[190]

Cybersecurity focuses on protecting a broad information base including consumer personal information and employee information protected under data protection and privacy laws; proprietary organizational information, such as trade secrets; highly proprietary information or operational data; and critical systems (sometimes called "critical infrastructure"), such as banking, medical, and utilities technology systems. Cybersecurity as a discipline expands on the importance of safeguarding data subject rights to include data critical to organizational operations and financial value. Cybersecurity reduces safety, confidentiality, integrity, availability, and privacy risks through use of process and technology.

Chapter 8 discusses information technologies from cabling and networks to mobile devices and applications to introduce the concepts of cybersecurity and provide enough detail to understand the role of "reasonableness" in technology choice and investment. Readers should not expect to remember all details in this chapter; rather,

---

5-7. Most loss occurs quickly after the breach occurs, so slow breach notification can significantly increase fraud success, increasing reimbursement costs.

188. Raghavendra Patidar & Lokesh Sharma, *Credit Card Fraud Detection Using Neural Network*, 1 (NCAI2011) INTERN. J. SOFT COMP. & ENG. 32 (Jun. 2011), *available at* http://www.ijsce.org/attachments/File/NCAI2011/IJSCE_NCAI2011_025.pdf.

189. *See* Darren Boyle, *Forget your credit card details, hackers make 10 times more money from stealing your medical records – and they're easier to get as hospitals' cyber security is so poor*, DAILYMAIL ONLINE (Sept. 25, 2014), *available at* http://www.dailymail.co.uk/news/article-2769109/Forget-credit-card-details-hackers-make-money-stealing-medical-records.html; Jessica Meyers, *Hackers threaten health care industry's patient records*, THE BOSTON GLOBE (Sept. 6, 2014), *available at* http://www.bostonglobe.com/news/nation/2014/09/05/health-care-industry-ill-prepared-for-vicious-cyberthreats/ZdvDGaipJi7VSN0TogezkL/story.html. Health information per se is not the most valuable, but enough personal information coupled with insurance numbers can assist hackers in perpetuating health care fraud, or impersonating a health care facility to get reimbursed by insurers. Insurance policy numbers are not only captured by insurers (covered entities) and hospitals, but may also be stored by other businesses, such as a person's employer.

190. American Bankers Association, *The Business of Banking, What Every Policy Maker Needs to Know*, ABA.com (Dec. 2013), http://www.aba.com/Tools/Economic/Documents/Businessofbanking.pdf, at 18, 27.

focus on developing an analytical framework for discussing technology in an organizational setting and pay special attention to "Key Takeaways" at the end of each section.

§8.01 WHAT IS CYBERSECURITY?

Cybersecurity is defined as "the activity or process, ability or capability, or state whereby information and communications systems and the information contained therein are protected from and/or defended against damage, unauthorized use or modification, or exploitation."[191] The term "cybersecurity" today focuses on protecting organizational data, be it government, business, or non-profit, from unauthorized access, change, or exposure. Cybersecurity practitioners often use the term "cybersecurity" to describe approaches for managing Internet threats.

The breadth of this definition is critical to understanding cybersecurity: not only do strong cybersecurity practices require technical solutions but also require strong organizational processes. In the cybersecurity field, both administrative controls, controls such as processes and procedures regulating human behavior, and technical controls, or controls managed via computerized mechanisms, must be implemented in a complete cybersecurity program. Controls will be discussed in more detail in Chapters 11 and 12.

Information security, or administrative and technical security measures (or measures) in data protection, as introduced in Part I, focuses on protecting business, customer, or personal information, including verbal, written, or encompassed in a computer system.[192] *See* the Venn diagram in Figure 8.1 illustrating the relationship between privacy, cybersecurity, and data protection.

191. Cybersecurity: A Beginner's Vocabulary, CYBERSECURITYU, http://www.cyber securityu.org /cybersecurity-a-beginners-vocabulary/ (last visited Nov. 16, 2016).

192. Note: although data protection typically refers to security protections for personal information as described in Part I, data protection activities can also apply to other data types that might provide value to an organization, such as operational data, restricted or confidential business data, or customer organizational data.

Figure 8.1 Privacy, Security, and Data Protection

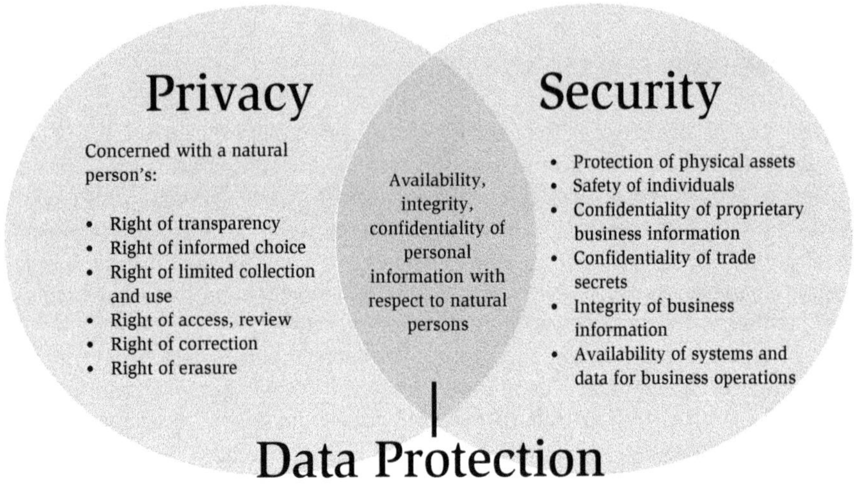

Information security validates a variety of measures used for data protection purposes. For example, an information security practitioner would assess whether organizations use key-card access, maintain an identification-verified visitor log, or employ closed-circuit television to identify and surveil individuals inside a facility. Although these activities focus on process rather than technology, improper controls, including process controls, greatly increase the probability of a data breach. In contrast, cybersecurity includes all information security activities that protect an organization from Internet threats, while physical security protects buildings, physical computer systems, and people from harm. Each of these functional areas reinforces the others, so while it is important to understand these distinctions, cybersecurity benefits from successful execution of all three disciplines. For purposes of Part II, this book focuses on information security functions broadly and uses the term "security" to describe these activities. *See* Table 8.1 illustrating the relationship between physical security, information security, and cybersecurity.

Table 8.1 Security Fields

Name	*Description*	*Goal*
Physical Security	Focuses on businesses, personal property, and individuals	Protect assets and ensure individual safety; prevent tampering or physical manipulation of computer resources

Name	*Description*	*Goal*
Information Security	Focuses on information assets, including digital and physical information assets; encompasses cybersecurity; includes some physical security controls	Protect integrity, availability, and confidentiality of information assets
Cybersecurity	Focuses on networked computer systems, including data stored within systems and data transferred between systems	Protect integrity, availability, confidentiality, and safety of networked computer assets and associated data

Security fulfills three information functions for an organization: Confidentiality, Integrity, and Availability (CIA). *Confidentiality* focuses on permitting authorized access and preventing unauthorized access. When most individuals think of security, confidentiality is of primary concern: can our organization prevent individuals from accessing certain types of data? Confidentiality easily pairs with privacy considerations: the very foundation of privacy world-wide reflects a freedom from prying eyes. Confidentiality observes the need to protect information within organizations to protect not only natural persons, but also organizations and their customers.

Integrity focuses on safeguarding the accuracy of data. Data accuracy dramatically influences the reliability of an organization's services and confidence in organizational performance. Data protection laws reflect this concept in rights of access and correction: individuals may be adversely impacted by incorrect data about them, for example in qualifying for a loan or receiving medical treatment. Automated processing can intensify this risk by calculating decisions based on incorrect data. Further, organizations also need accurate data to run effectively. Organizations with low confidence of data accuracy often face substantial operational issues and efficiency concerns, risking customer and investor confidence.

Availability represents the ability to provide information when needed. When data are unavailable, such as after a ransomware attack, organizations cannot function, preventing their ability to conduct basic operational tasks. This becomes a substantial issue when providing critical services, such as healthcare, utilities, transportation, or investment trading functions. Availability issues can dramatically damage organizations without effective backup plans.

Confidentiality, Integrity, and Availability form the basis for traditional security inquiry, and measures used to protect one function often protect others. For example, restricting access (often called least user access—LUA) reduces the risk of users intentionally or accidentally exposing confidential data, interrupting operations, or making unauthorized changes. CIA assists practitioners in considering, holistically, the potential impact of a situation and reasonable measures to reduce risk to an organization or individuals.

In addition to the CIA model, the increasing concern over physical safety relating to physical computer systems means organizations should also consider potential impact on human life. For example, medical devices increasingly connect to the Internet, potentially exposing devices to additional security issues. Public infrastructure, such as nuclear energy plants, electrical grids, or dams, which are computerized and increasingly exposed to the Internet, have the potential to cause substantial physical injury and property damage. For this reason, *safety* should also be considered when analyzing potential risks to property and individuals.

Practitioners should also consider privacy laws and internal practices, as described in Part I, as part of analyzing potential risk. Although security does not often consider individual rights as denoted in data protection and privacy laws and internal organizational policies, adequate security measures will often reinforce privacy rights. For example, a right to access implies that an organization can timely access and collate data to provide a readable copy to the data subject. If measures do not protect data availability, organizations may encounter difficulties fulfilling data access requests. For this reason, organizations should also consider privacy obligations when determining appropriate security measures. It should be noted that while security practitioners refer to the CIA model, information assurance professionals also adopt a five-pillar model of confidentiality, integrity, availability, as well as authentication and non-repudiation. Authentication and non-repudiation will be discussed later in this chapter. *See* Figure 8.2 for a picture of SCIAP, or Safety, Confidentiality, Integrity, Availability, Privacy.

Figure 8.2 SCIAP Considerations

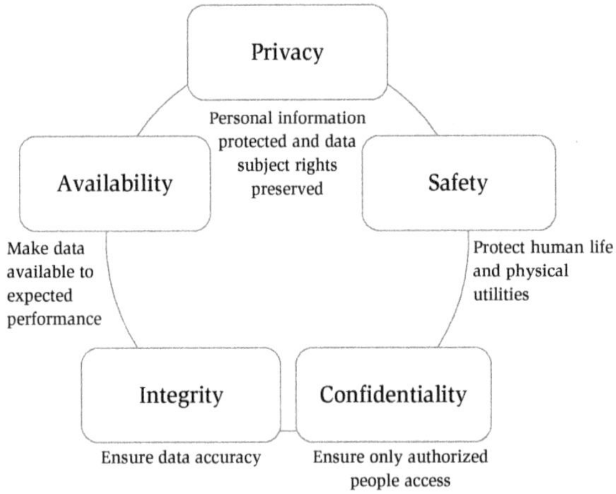

Increasingly, organizations consider both privacy and security together with respect to information management more broadly. Some organizations include these capabilities under an *information governance* function (described further in Chapter 11). Privacy and security teams may or may not report through a common leadership team yet often share similar goals. *See* Table 8.2 for a comparison of privacy and security within an organization.

Table 8.2 Privacy Versus Security

Function/Team	*Security*	*Privacy*	*Similarity*	*Difference*
Data Overall	Security classifies and protects all data	Privacy focuses on personal information or personal data	Both include personal information	Security considers more data
Business Processes Overall	Security uses business process to determine system scope	Privacy reviews business process for legitimate use	Both review business process first, where possible[193]	Privacy needs review to determine use
Technical Systems Overall	Security focuses controls at the system level	Privacy wants systems to enforce rights	Both require system review	Security conducts more detailed review
Integrity	Data must be accurate and reliable	Data must be accurate and reliable	Both need accurate data	N/A
Availability/ Access/ Correction/ Erasure/ Deletion	Data must be available for operations, deletion must be secure	Data must be available to support access/ correction requests, right to be forgotten	Both want to ensure data availability and minimize data	Security requires broader availability for non-PI systems
Confidentiality	Data must be protected from outside exposure	PI must be protected	Both want to avoid exposure	Security requires broader confidentiality
Limited Collection/Use	Less data = less risk	Data collection limited to disclosed, legitimate use	Both prefer less data be collected	Privacy limits data collection based on law, security to reduce risk

Privacy and security focus on many of the same concepts for collecting, managing, and protecting data. Security takes the next step by developing specific approaches to employ measures for ensuring confidentiality, integrity, availability, and safety of systems and data. These measures may be organized differently, depending on the framework an organization uses. ISO 27001, described in Chapter 11, organizes a security program into fourteen domains, which apply across technologies and industries.

193. Security teams may review third parties, such as software or cloud vendors separately, as these tools may support a variety of different business purposes. Once reviewed, third parties may be "qualified" for specific use, such as for transferring sensitive personal information between IT systems.

Underlying fundamental security principles for SCIAP include trust, authenticity, and authorization. All technologies include some variation of these principles in their security features. *Trust* references the computing concept of "trusted computing device," or a device that has been effectively vetted to do some activity further, or *verification*, such as storing organizational data or connecting to organizational resources. These two concepts have led to the audit phrase "trust but verify," which illustrates the practice, both in technology and in risk management, of ensuring the accuracy of information provided and representations made.

Trust also extends to people: standard security practices require that organizations conduct background checks consistent with local law prior to hiring an individual, and some jurisdictions also permit credit checks. Background checks and credit checks do not just identify undesirable attributes for purposes of selecting personnel, they also identify what points of vulnerability an individual might have, making them more likely to behave outside organizational interests, such as providing administrative credentials to an unauthorized user hoping to profit from selling organizational data.

The concept of *authenticity* examines whether data are verifiably accurate when data transferred is received and loosely ties to the SCIAP concept of integrity. Authenticity pertains to data transferred and whether the data received matches data sent. Authenticity includes the concepts of *authorization*, or that an individual or computer has rights to perform a particular function, and *identification*, which ensures individuals (or computers) accurately reflect their identities. These three concepts are foundational for security, privacy, and data protection. If an individual provides unverified, inaccurate identification or security measures do not prohibit an individual from accessing data beyond the scope of their permissions, the individual will likely access personal information in an unauthorized manner. Unauthorized access under most statutes triggers data breach reporting and subsequent notification. If no authentication mechanisms exist, hackers may delete, change, or provide additional misleading data in transit, impacting the integrity of data received, or interrupting technical operations (e.g., causing an outage for critical systems). The concepts of authenticity, authorization, and identification, as well as SCIAP, should be reflected in every IT system. Associated security concepts, such as authentication, non-repudiation, and cryptography will be discussed in Chapter 9.

Key Takeaways:

- Organizations should be concerned about SCIAP: Safety, Confidentiality, Integrity, Availability, and Privacy.
- Privacy and Security require available, accurate, and confidential personal information.
- Security also requires protection of business information.
- Privacy focuses not only on confidentiality, but also on data subject rights. .Authenticity, authorization, and identification provide a foundation for effective security, privacy, and data protection programs.

§8.02 ADMINISTRATIVE MEASURES

Administrative and technical measures, specifically referenced in most information privacy laws, perform two roles: first, they ensure organizations meet legal obligations with respect to laws requiring "reasonable" measures (the law itself). However, administrative and technical measures also protect an organization's reputation, assets, and customer confidential data. Cybersecurity does not only apply to personal information. Without cybersecurity, other legal issues could arise, such as incorrect or falsified record-keeping, safety issues for consumers, and a variety of other business impacts. Attorneys must understand "reasonable" administrative and technical measures with some familiarity, as lack of some measures or insufficiently strong measures can cause substantial damage to an organization.[194]

Administrative measures typically involve processes and procedures, rather than technical solutions or physical measures, to enhance security. Administrative measures include access and identity management (AIM), incident response, and vulnerability management processes. These processes, managed by personnel, substantially increase the effectiveness of a security program.

Effective security risk management processes should implement AIM processes. Part technical, part procedural, AIM ensures identification of a particular user and legitimacy of system access. The "Access" in AIM focuses on how access is requested, approved, granted, denied, escalated, reviewed, or terminated. Management should plan the access lifecycle, including granting access with management approval and timely access revocation when an individual changes roles, voluntarily leaves, or terminates employment. The "Identity" in AIM focuses on developing unique identifiers for an individual, such as tokens or multiple factors to verify identity (and authenticate).

AIM measures protect against malicious and non-malicious (intentional and non-intentional) actions of personnel, such as mistakenly accessing, changing, deleting, or exposing personal information. By limiting access and restricting permissions, organizations can reduce the probability of employees accessing data in an unauthorized manner or using data for unapproved purposes. External malicious actors, such as hackers, also take advantage of lax AIM processes and procedures to access internal resources and data. Additional examples of AIM measures include appropriate approvals for standard access to systems, higher-level approvals for access to more sensitive data, and general prohibitions on administrative or root access to certain systems (e.g., administrative access to a laptop can permit a user to download application that can infect an entire network). AIM measures also include quarterly access reviews (QAR) to ensure departments have removed unnecessary access on a timely basis, especially for systems containing sensitive information.

Incident response processes often begin with an incident response plan, or a formal document specifying who will be involved in the event of an incident. An

194. Measures, safeguards, and controls can be used interchangeably. The term "measures" is used most frequently in data protection laws, while audit and risk management teams use "controls" within a risk assessment context.

incident is best described as an unconfirmed, potential data breach or unauthorized access potentially causing harm to an organization or data subject. In an information security context, *incidents* are situations where protected information within an organization may have been compromised. Organizations handling an "incident" rather than a data breach have not yet confirmed whether the situation has resulted in compromise to data or systems. For this reason, incident response personnel, such as forensic investigators, must conduct an investigation and an incident response manager must manage the incident from detection to closure. This requires developing a clear plan that articulates who may make decisions (the Incident Response Team), who should be involved (roles and responsibilities), and which steps must be taken when an incident is detected. Often incident response processes include detailed procedures for saving system images for forensic investigation purposes and other steps to determine the incident's cause. Incident response will be discussed in more detail in Chapter 13.

Security Development Lifecycle (SecDLC) and Vulnerability management processes focus on development and management of information technology systems. SecDLC focuses on integrating security review steps into the information technology build lifecycle, including security requirements and security testing. Vulnerability management provides a framework and process for identifying known vulnerabilities and making changes to systems to avoid compromise. This often involves patching systems, such as Microsoft servers, on a predetermined schedule based on the attendant risk. These processes will be described more fully in Chapter 12.

§8.03 UNDERSTANDING INFORMATION TECHNOLOGY

Attorneys must understand technology to some extent to effectively work with business, IT, and security partners, analyze internal and external compliance activities, understand organizational risk posture, offer informed opinions on financial investments, and advise during data breaches. Technology is more easily understood using an analytical framework, which assists in understanding details of: collection, transfer (or transmission/transit/in motion), processing, storage, access, and change (editing), as these functions have a very specific technical meaning. A model can describe these concepts for easier understanding: Change, Access, Transfer, Store (CATS) in Figure 8.3.[195]

195. Please note: the CATS model has been developed by the Author to facilitate conceptual understanding of technologies presented in this book.

Figure 8.3 CATS Model

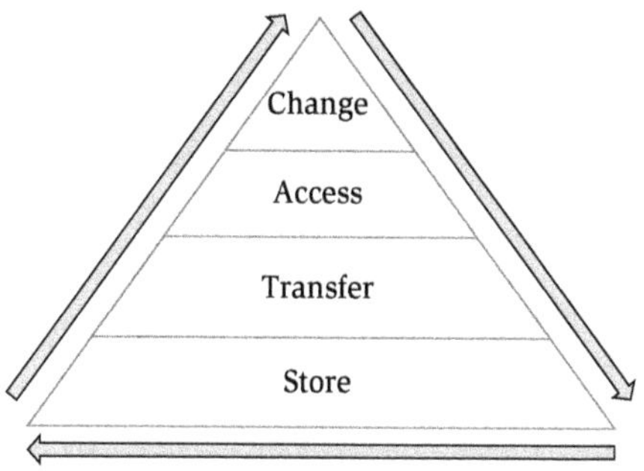

In the CATS model, technology and respective security measures will fall into one of these functions. By following the arrows, it is possible to see that data moving up the pyramid will also move down the pyramid in each cycle. *See* Figure 8.4 for a completed model with a computer system input.

Figure 8.4 Example CATS Model

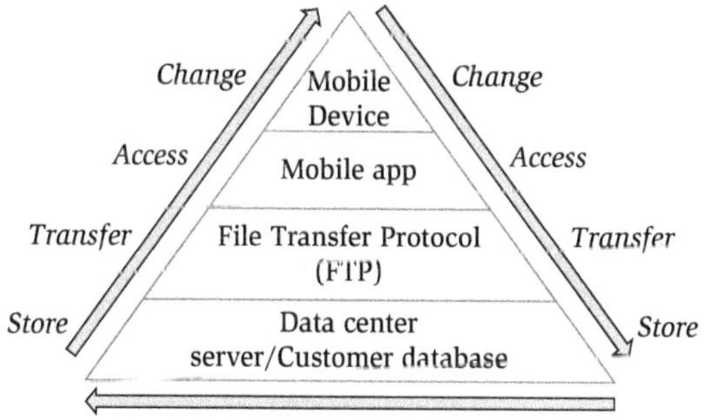

Although technology inputs may change functional components of an analytical model should not. When displaying this information as a *data flow diagram*, described in Chapter 7, storage is often represented by servers or database pictures, data transfer by arrows, and applications or other user interfaces by boxes. *See* Figure 8.5 for an example data flow diagram integrating the analytical model.

Figure 8.5 Data Flow Diagram w/Analytical Model

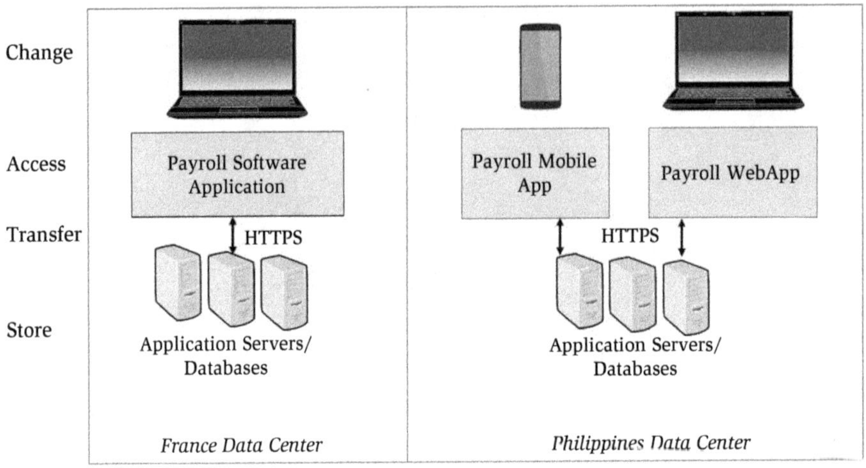

In contrast to the data flow diagram, technical architecture diagrams usually include many more technical details than a data flow diagram. Architecture diagrams visually define the system as a whole, including information about how the system connects to the Internet, for example. Security and privacy practitioners use a data flow diagram for three separate purposes: (1) document technical implementation for posterity and auditability, (2) aid in understanding technical implementation to determine security compliance, and (3) ascertain recipients of data transfers and location of data storage for privacy compliance purposes. For these reasons, practitioners should first create a data flow diagram and technical architecture diagrams to understand the systems involved before engaging in deeper analysis.

More advanced practitioners may benefit from mapping technologies to the Open Systems Interconnection model (OSI Model), a model developed for security practitioners. Although most attorneys will not need to understand this level of detail, it can help to develop common understanding with security practitioners. The OSI Model includes layers 1–7, from most physical to most abstract, with the highest layer closest to a system user (what a user experiences). The OSI Model illustrates one communication from hardware to an application and, rather than completely mapping system relationships, demonstrates how data moves through one communication. Each layer has a specific job, then passes data to the next layer. The process by which systems send data between underlying systems and the user is *transmission*, and the process by which a user sends a response back to underlying systems is *reception*. Data transfer, discussed in relation to privacy laws, includes repeat transmissions and receptions within a system. Understanding each transmission or reception can assist in validating appropriate security measures apply to each and also enable examination of transfer mechanisms, such as cross-border transfer or third-party transfer. *See* Figure 8.6 to see the seven OSI layers and explanations of each layer.

Figure 8.6 OSI Model

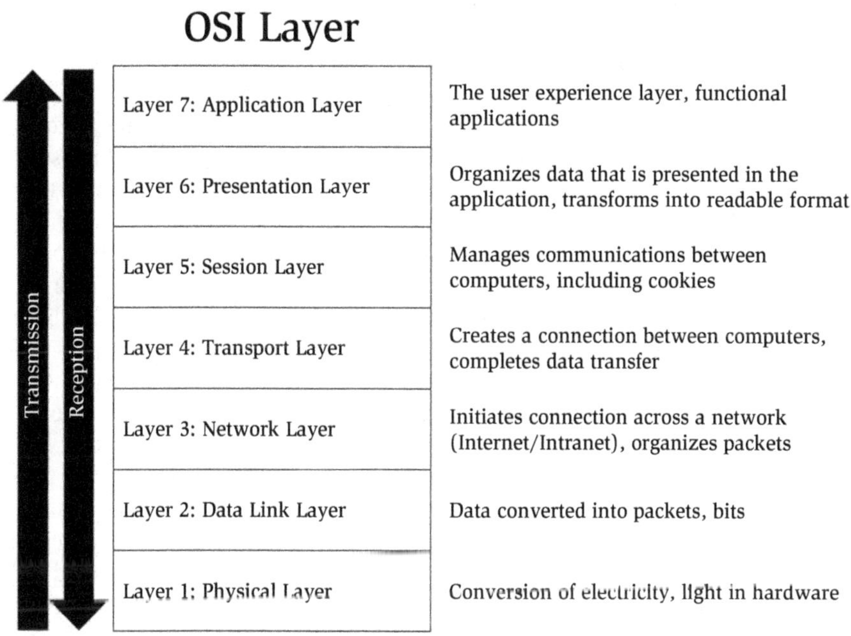

Both the CATS Model and OSI Model illustrate a primary concept in security practice: *defense in depth*. Defense in depth encourages practitioners to think about technology in layers and protect systems and data at each layer. For example, if a system encrypts data when it is stored but does not encrypt the data when transmitted, an individual could view, access, or change data during transmission. Considering security and privacy requirements within the context of a CATS or OSI Model ensures that attorneys and practitioners understand how data flow, data storage location, and data protection measures.

§8.04 IT NETWORKING AND INFRASTRUCTURE

Information Technology (IT) provides a foundation for nearly all modern organizational functions. However, many attorneys do not have a deep understanding of how most technologies operate. Without this understanding, advising on security and privacy issues involving technology proves difficult. Using the CATS model, this section will introduce technologies at a high level.

Networking provides a means of connectivity between systems and machines, CATS-Transfer. A network provides the means for transfer without actually transferring data, similar to the pipes connecting a water source to a spigot. Networks that may be internal to an organization and inaccessible from outside an organization are known as *intranet*. Organizations should tightly control access to the intranet as it connects internal resources, often with highly sensitive data. External networks include the Internet. The Internet is not one connection; it is a series of connections between many individual computers. Each individual computer or device on a network is called a *node*. One node connects to another via a *data link* using *cabling* like fiber-optic cable, which transfers data as light pulses (transferring data at the speed of light), or standard coaxial cable, which transfers data as electrical pulses (comparatively slower). When individuals connect to the Internet, they connect through their ISP, which provides connectivity through the ISP's cabling network. Individuals using a Digital Subscriber Line (DSL) connect to the Internet through a provider's telephone lines, rather than a cable network.

All computers function on a combination of 1s and 0s, represented by *code*. 1s and 0s can be transformed into any communication mechanism: light, sound, or radio waves (analog) or groupings of electronic pulses (digital). The first computers relied on inputs of the numerical 1 (on, yes, or true) and 0 (off, no, or false) to power decisions on a computer, rather than computer codes. Since that time, computers have evolved to function based on complex code representing the original 1s and 0s in unique computer languages. Computers communicate using this short-hand language.

At the physical layer of data transmission, data are still transferred using 1s and 0s. Computer systems reduce data into *bits* and *bytes*; each byte consists of eight bits. Bytes are commonly used to describe connection speed, how quickly data can be transferred or downloaded; storage capacity, how much data can be stored on a device's hard drive providing dedicated space to retain data; and Random Access Memory (RAM), how much data can stored in "short term" memory to improve computing speed. Kilobytes (KB), or one thousand bytes, are referenced in slower data transfer speeds, such as uploading or downloading documents, pictures, or music. Megabytes (MB), or one million bytes, are the most commonly used measurement for personal computing storage capacity and faster data transfer speeds. Personal storage capacity is also measured in MBs, and terabytes (TB), or one trillion bytes, is most commonly used as storage capacity measurement for organizational computing.

Data can also be stored on hardware or within software in temporary memory, called *cache*. Cached data are data stored for easy retrieval based on recent activities for a user or across users. The concept of cached data is that when repeat requests are made, data are easily retrieved from a cached copy. Technology typically does not allocate a large percentage of computing power to the memory cache, as storage capacity is expensive and purchasers often prefer more long-term storage capacity. However, cached data can cause challenges for privacy and security: data can escape deletion or security protection when organizations do not plan for handling cached data.

Data transfer over a network mimics everyday human communication, including a sender, a receiver, the message, and message form and protocol structuring the communication. As in human communication, sender and receiver must communicate using the same language and predetermined protocol. When humans desire not to share communications with third parties, they may communicate somewhere they cannot be seen or heard by eavesdroppers, send a text message, or pass a note. Just like computer systems, if distributing sensitive documents, humans want some guarantee that their message will not be read before it reaches the recipient, so they choose a trusted carrier, like a post office using certified mail. This metaphor for human communication directly reflects the digital world, only imagine that millions of messages are exchanged at any one time, with eavesdroppers and interlopers continuously attempting to intercept, change, or view messages.

Many security technologies protect data over an open network, as data transferred over unsecured networks provide an easy conquest for inexperienced hackers. However, basic computer security does not require substantial effort. For example, when a computer attempts to connect to an external Internet site from an organization's intranet (internal network), it must first pass one or more *firewalls*, or rule-based gatekeepers for Internet connections.

Firewalls, when properly configured, block users from accessing *blacklist* (unauthorized) Websites. Firewalls also include *whitelisted* (expressly reviewed and authorized) Websites, such as connections to resources where personnel need access, either for work or personal approved purposes, as might be mandated by country Works Councils. From a security perspective, Websites may introduce damaging code to the internal network, such as malware. Firewalls also prevent outside entities from connecting to internal systems by blocking external connections to internal resources. Organizations use Demilitarized Zones (DMZ) when organizations require a "middle ground" for external and internal access, such as personal mobile devices connecting to internal applications. DMZs are network segments that provide additional network security, positioned between the local area network (LAN), the intranet, and the Internet.

Unlike the intranet within an organization, the Internet consists of an ever-growing, substantial volume of nodes, and many nodes are not generally discoverable through *Web crawlers* like Google, Yahoo, Bing, or DuckDuck Go. Web crawlers function by logging Websites discovered and serving them up through a search engine. Many computers, however, are not registered through a common search engine and are not readily discoverable by Web crawlers. By design, organizations may not prefer computers be discovered by a Web crawler, for example when making a financial transfer. Organizations conduct millions of transactions per day over undiscoverable computer-to-computer connections, also called the *Deep Web*.

Other individuals may also not prefer their Websites or computers be discovered, such as those involved in covert operations or illegal activities on the *Dark Web*. Because neither the Deep Web or Dark Web have links registered on the major search engines and Web crawlers do not discover them, an individual must know the actual computer address to connect. Websites on the Dark Web use protection mechanisms for communications, for example the Tor encryption tool or I2P, to hide or obscure the actual location of the computer providing Website contents. This makes identification of individuals operating sites dealing in illegal goods and services tremendously difficult.

The process of connecting to the Internet is relatively straightforward. In step one, an individual computer initiates a Web browser. When launching the Web browser, the computer transmits a request to connect through a wireless Internet connection to a *router* at a home or office, also known as a Wide Area Network (WAN), which sends data through cabling to an ISP. The ISP then transmits the request to the receiving computer hosting the Website. An individual computer is usually wired, such as a cable ethernet connection, or wireless through a Wireless Access Point (WAP).

WAPs provide a means for wireless devices to connect to a wired connection. WAPs transmit signals over radio wave, then converted into electric impulses to be sent through the router and cabling. Public WAPs and many home WAPs offer few security protections: even when users of a WAP must use a password, other users on the same wireless network may view traffic. Private organizational WAPs often use higher levels of encryption, so that individuals on the same network cannot view individual transmissions. *See* Figure 8.7 for a sample network diagram including these network capabilities.

Figure 8.7 Network Diagram

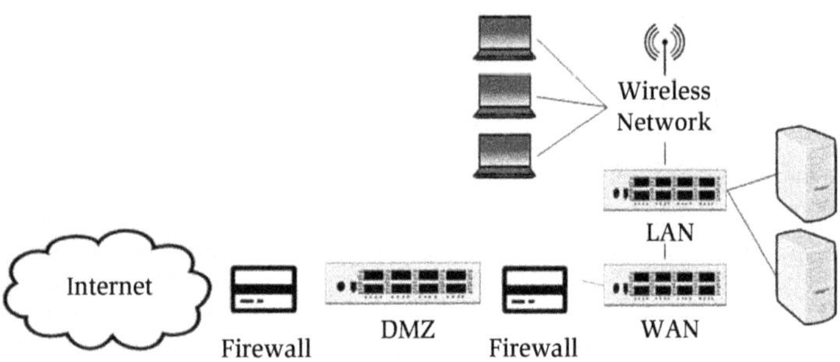

When a server transmits data for a user to access, it moves through a variety of steps as referenced in the OSI. However, servers cannot usually transfer all data needed at one time. Instead, data are transmitted in *packets* containing a segment of data and other information needed for reassembling data in the appropriate order: where the data started, its destination, size, type, and order of assembly. Data transmission uses specialized servers, such as File Transfer Protocol (FTP), Managed File Transfer (MFT), and Hyper Text Transfer Protocol (HTTP) Servers. HTTP servers transfer data for purposes of rendering Websites and provide faster transmission, and MFT promises higher security for file transfers, whereas FTP often is used for basic uploading/downloading and moving files from one location to another. Both FTP and HTTP do not, by default, secure data while in transfer. Instead, SFTP and Hyper Text Transfer Protocol Secure (HTTPS) secure data using encryption technologies (described later in this chapter).

Most individuals and organizations host resources, such as Websites, applications, and software at *data centers* providing a CATS-Store function. *Websites* differ from *applications* (sometimes called *Web applications*) in that Websites display information and may collect limited information through a *form* (*Web form*) while *applications* support workflow and provide information interactively. To support resources like these, organizations may own, lease space, or contract for collocated space within a third party (vendor-owned) data center while individuals typically lease space through a small monthly fee.[196] Organizations that own data centers have more control over security measures applied and location of data storage for privacy purposes, which may provide an advantage when the organization has substantial security maturity. Organizations with fewer resources for managing security may benefit from a reputable third party managing data in their data center. Organizations leasing space in a third-party data center can require dedicated, locked physical space within a data center, which houses organization-owned computers, called a *collocated data center*. Dedicated space minimizes security issues by ensuring organizations can manage their own computers.

Organizations may also house data in the "cloud." *Cloud computing* represents any kind of system where CATS functions are managed by a third party. Cloud implementations include central functions like Infrastructure as a Service (IaaS); where servers, middleware, databases, or other common technology are managed by a third party; Platform as a Service (PaaS), where a specific technology pack of functionality such as a customer-facing application; or Software as a Service (SaaS), or a software implementation an organization uses for operations allowing connectivity over the Internet. Cloud computing will be discussed in more detail in Chapter 14.

Data centers, whether owned, leased, or cloud, provide the hub for all organizational computerized operations. Data centers consist of *servers* and *mainframe* computers, which store data for computer programs to run and facilitate data transfer. Mainframe computers are often remembered as "green screen" IBM computers, with a very large size. Although Mainframe computers have existed for a long time, organizations still use Mainframe computers for operations requiring substantial uptime and have continued to evolve technically, while shrinking in size and increasing computational capacity.[197]

Organizations require substantial computing power, so many servers exist in a data center and are "stacked" on racks.[198] Large cloud computing facilities employ *server farms*, or incredibly large physical spaces full of servers. The largest cloud computing providers employ multiple server farms around the world to satisfy geographical needs (e.g., adequacy determinations) and support business continuity operations that ensure uptime and reduce outages.

196. Individuals on the Dark Web, however, often connect their own servers at home rather than using a data center. All users, however, must have Internet access to an Internet Service Provider (ISP), which makes information ISPs collect regarding criminal or other behavior very valuable.
197. Although mainframe computers will not be discussed in great detail, mainframes still support key operations for organizations handling very sensitive data, such as the banking industry. The mainframe used most today is IBM's Z mainframe, which is typically leased based on resources used. Although many practitioners do not have a strong understanding of the mainframe, mainframes do accommodate some security features. ACF2, for example, provides access management features that can control what users can and cannot access. RACF can manage access to resources as well as logging activities on the mainframe. Newer conceptions of mainframe have introduced pervasive encryption technologies, as well.
198. The term "stack," however, usually references *a technology stack*, or a set of technology selections designed to work together. These technology selections may be used in the servers stacked on racks.

Servers store and run utilities, middleware, databases, and all non-third-party software, and applications/apps and facilitate all connectivity with other nodes, called *clients*. Clients like laptops, personal computers, mobile devices, medical devices, wearable computers, or Internet of Things devices have limited computing power in contrast with servers. Clients connect to servers in a data center by initiating a transmission between the client and the server via the client's connection. The server-client infrastructure allows for clients to access the same resources, such as software hosted in the data center.

Server-client infrastructure supports distribution of consistent updates and software across an enterprise to individual clients, such as a special software that a user requests, and can deliver *security policies*, or computerized restrictions specific to individual clients like laptops or mobile devices. Security policies can, for example, require laptops to require an enterprise username and password be entered before log-on, prevent remote access until a secure connection exists, or require a personal identification number (PIN) for a mobile device before connecting to organizational resources. Security policies, encryption, and other security measures applied to clients are also known as *endpoint security management*.

See Figure 8.8 for a network diagram illustrating a server-client infrastructure.

Figure 8.8 Server-Client Infrastructure

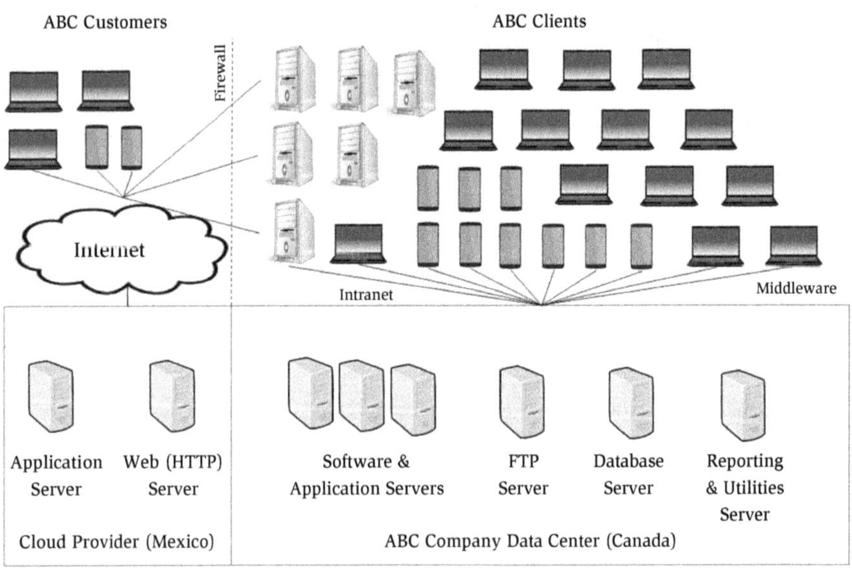

The Server-Client infrastructure, often captured in an architecture diagram, can quickly help an attorney or practitioner ask questions to reveal potential areas of concern, which could implicate geographic restrictions. For example, data origin upon access (in a data center on servers therein) determines the applicable law for data generated and restrictions for downstream transfer, storage, and changes.

The term "infrastructure" is used to describe common resources across an organization. Infrastructure includes physical and virtual resources such as servers, mainframes, utilities, databases, operations systems, and middleware. Organizations install *utilities* or utility software on infrastructure technology to assist the infrastructure in its operations. Operating systems (OS) include basic rules and instructions for all computers to run, including servers, mainframe computers, and clients. Without the OS, computers individually could not function. Popular OS include Linux, Unix, Microsoft Windows, and various Apple OS. *Middleware* is located between software or applications and OS, ensuring a seamless interaction between the client and software or applications on the server. *See* Figure 8.9 for a visual depiction of this relationship using Microsoft products.

Figure 8.9 OS-Middleware Relationship

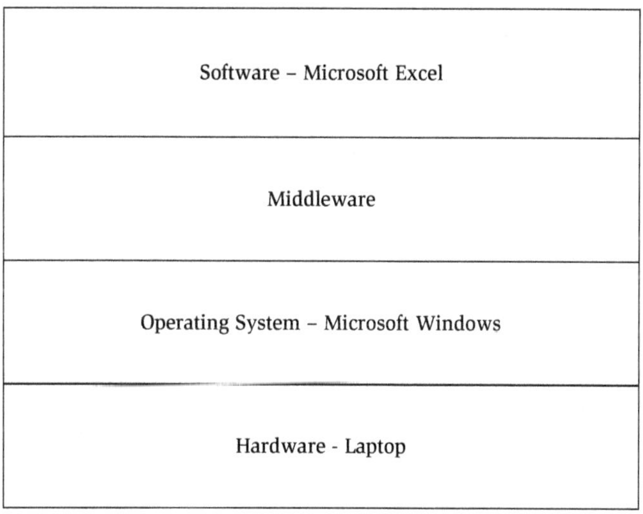

Some servers fulfill a specific purpose. A *proxy server* filters Web traffic between an internal organization's client and an external Website. A *Web server* displays Websites, an *application server* displays Web applications, and *file servers* are responsible for file exchange, such as FTP, described later in this chapter. *Database servers* handle database storage and communications to and from the database, for example a Structured Query Language (SQL) server, a very popular database server type. Other servers manage the connection between a server and multiple clients, called a *session*. Session management is extremely important for security purposes.[199]

Databases store and organize data in a usable format and provide a back end to software, applications, and apps. Data stored in databases are classified as *structured*

199. Session management involves beginning and ending connections. When a connection ends, a user must log-in again. Session management ensures that a user cannot stay logged on indefinitely, reducing the probability of unauthorized access.

and *unstructured* data. Structured data includes data organized by rules (e.g., horizontal rows and vertical columns) stored for specific software, applications, and apps. This structure makes identifying data sources and location relatively easy to inventory, in order to apply security measures or include in a privacy data inventory. Database Administrators (DBA) are responsible for developing these rules and maintaining order within the databases, some of which carry highly specific rules, such as a SQL database.

Databases may store *unstructured data*, such as data found in documents or file shares, in broad repositories with few rules, making discovery difficult. Because organizations do not often document the location of unstructured data, practitioners may experience some difficulty applying appropriate security and privacy measures, requiring additional search tools and substantial manual review. Organizations should consider better structured sources for managing sensitive information, rather than unstructured data repositories, wherever possible.

Big Data references the increased generation and commingling of data for increasingly high-powered operations. Big data usually involves large and complex data sets that challenge traditional database management capabilities. To navigate big data, data science as a field has exploded, focusing on data order and organization and specific rules with respect to data, such as data privacy. Big data has also propelled artificial intelligence forward, especially machine learning. Big data and artificial intelligence and associated security and privacy challenges will be discussed in greater detail in Chapter 16.

Key Takeaways:

- The server-client infrastructure provides a foundational map for understanding networking and system relationships.Servers fulfill a wide variety of functions, housing applications, databases, and other specialized purposes.
- Cloud computing involves remote data storage with various methods.
- Databases usually store and organize data in a usable format, while unstructured data may be stored but not organized.

§8.05 APPLICATIONS, COMMUNICATIONS, AND CLIENTS

Software is organized computer code installed on servers or other computers, accessible only through access to those computers. Applications, as previously described, support workflow and essentially have the same properties as software, except that users can access applications from a Uniform Resource Locator (URL) on the Internet. Software provided via an Internet connection and hosted by a third party is often called *Software-as-a-Service* or SaaS. SaaS does not dramatically differ from Web applications, except that organizations require special credentials to connect to SaaS software while applications are readily discoverable on the Internet and a SaaS stores an organization's data in its own data centers.

Apps are truncated or reformatted versions of applications designed for mobile device access as either *native*, or designed using that mobile device's code, or *hybrid*, or an application available on the Internet, designed to fit the size and shape of different mobile devices (sometimes called *responsive User Interface* [UI]). Mobile device applications have the ability to store data on devices: apps using *thin clients* store little data and are often hybrid, while apps using *thick clients* store a lot of data offline and usually are native. Hybrid apps function on a variety of different mobile devices, such as Android or Apple devices, while app developers design native apps specifically to be used with a particular OS (such as an Apple OS). A large amount of stored data can potentially risk exposure if a mobile device is lost or stolen, especially SPI, so security and privacy practitioners should scrutinize the use of thick clients. Software, applications, and apps both provide CATS-Access and permit CATS-Change with the right permissions.

Software, Applications, and Apps usually are described with relation to their UI or GUI (pronounced GOO-EE) and Software Interface (SI). The GUI represents the part of a computer system with which a user interacts. The GUI is reflected in functional requirements for software development (described in Chapter 12), which often includes privacy requirements such as explicit notice and consent workflow. The SI includes the unseen functional components of software, applications, and apps function. The SI would decide when data should be displayed or not, rules regarding how information is displayed in what order, and where to connect to display data. In software development, developers or engineers determine non-functional requirements for the SI and infrastructure.

Software often poses identification challenges. Users cannot easily memorize individual usernames and passwords without writing them down or using the same credentials, and when each system requires entry of a username and password, a compromise of one system may compromise multiple systems. For this reason and for organizational efficiency, organizations have pursued Single Sign-On (SSO) functions, which enable a user to log-on once and pass credentials onto subsequent systems accessed. SSO usually ties to enterprise access, such as log-on credentials when, for example, personnel log onto PCs and laptops.

For effective SSO to dually provide cross-system authorized access and protect the security of these systems, organizations often implement Multi-Factor Authentication (MFA), usually Two-Factor Authentication (2FA). MFA requires two or more pieces of information about a user: (1) a physical object the user has, (2) something the user knows, or (3) something about the user (i.e., biometric data). For a physical object the user has, organizational personnel used to carry a token or key fob producing randomized passcodes. Today, given the ubiquity of mobile computing, many organizations and online consumer systems use a one-time code sent to a mobile device or to a personal e-mail address. The user then provides what she knows, a username/password combination, and the one-time passcode to verify the user's identity. More advanced organizations may alternatively request the user provide biometric information, such as a finger print scanning, retina or iris scanning, voice recognition, facial biometrics, or palm vein scanning. Organizations may prefer to implement this method for authentication where personnel routinely need access to

SPI, justifying any biometric technology investment. Organizations may also use biometric technologies for hourly employee time management, especially in contact centers.

Call centers, or *contact centers*, provide service to a wide variety of potential callers, from internal technical support to consumer telemedicine. Contact centers leverage specialized technologies to support operations, yet privacy and security considerations still apply. Most contact centers use a blend of a Private Branch Exchange (PBX), which is a dedicated telephone branch line, and an Interactive Voice Response (IVR) utility. The PBX provides the connection by which calls can be directed, and the IVR interacts with the user to determine where to send the call. The IVR is the GUI-equivalent for a phone line. Unlike a dedicated PBX line, Voice-over IP (VoIP) provides phone line services via Internet connection, and chat clients and call recording software are downloaded onto agent laptops. Chat clients and call recording software may capture information about callers, including potentially sensitive information. Therefore, practitioners must plan for security and privacy considerations.

Call center personnel, like most personnel at an organization use PCs, laptops, and tablets to support their operations. These devices function similarly: an OS manages activities on the device, and software enables the user to complete tasks on the device. At an organization, the server-client relationship ensures that PCs, laptops, and tablets have appropriate configurations, such as the ability to receive deployed security policies, updates, and patches (described further in Chapter 12).

One method for managing organization-owned devices is called *desktop virtualization*. Organizations create "virtual workstations" by using PCs, laptops, and tablets as vehicles for accessing workstations stored on servers in a data center, *virtual machines*. Desktop virtualization provides substantial improvements for managing these devices: (1) reduces cost by improving the ease of workstation deployment, (2) increases security policy compliance by managing security policies directly on the server, and (3) enables easier remote access to organizational resources. *Remote access* is the process by which individuals can access resources located within the intranet at organizational data centers from an external, Internet connection.

Organizational workstation devices, or clients, include a wide variety of other unique considerations. As a primary means to access organizational resources, clients pose a substantial amount of risk to the organization as a whole. Some organizations, for example, may permit multiple users to access a client using the same credentials or download applications onto their devices. These practices dramatically increase the likelihood of a client causing downstream security issues. In the server-client model, a client can transmit data back to a server, including viruses or malware that can then distribute to all clients connected to the server.

Mobility of devices, including laptops and mobile devices, also requires an effective Virtual Private Network (VPN) strategy. VPNs allow for remote access, such as a laptop at an employee's home, to connect to the organization's internal, intranet-connected resources without compromising confidential information or internal security measures. By its very nature, opening an organization's internal resources to an external connection poses substantial security and privacy concerns. *See* Figure 8.10 for a diagram of a VPN.

Figure 8.10 Virtual Private Network

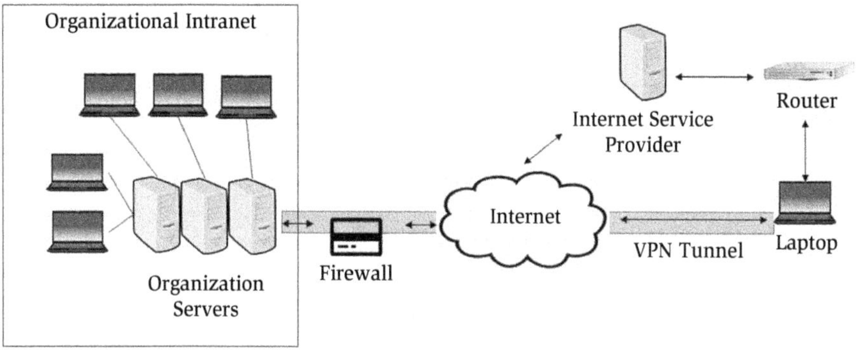

VPNs may also connect offices across geographic areas, enabling resource sharing and data sharing between offices. Although this can cause some challenges with regard to cross-border transfer absent, for example, adequacy/sufficiency status or Binding Corporate Rules (BCR), data transfer and sharing is highly desirable for global offices.[200] VPNs can also offer anonymity for users, depending on the solution implementation, which makes them also desirable for individual users. When an Internet Protocol Address (IP Address) is assigned from a server in another geographic location, Websites, Web applications, and Apps cannot determine the actual location of the VPN user, making tracking across applications almost impossible.

Organizations use VPN substantially around the world, often for very sensitive data transfer activities, such as Business to Business (B2B) data transfers. B2B transfers may include sensitive medical record transfer between health care centers, financial information transfer between branches and a home bank, or highly confidential product development information. Because most global organizations use VPNs routinely for this kind of data transfer, VPNs require robust security authentication and encryption measures to sufficiently secure connections. VPN ensures confidentiality and integrity via *hashing*, *message integrity authentication*, and *encryption*. The concept of double authentication makes sense when considering how unauthorized users might attempt to access highly sensitive data through a VPN. An individual might use their own unauthorized credentials on an authorized laptop connection, or an individual with previous authorization might use an unauthorized device, either to take data for nefarious purposes or exposing the Internal network to an "untrusted" device that could contain malware.

200. VPNs, provide a window into a virtualized version of a laptop. A virtual desktop appears on the screen as if it *is* the screen, yet the user only sees a display of a desktop actually stored and running from a remote data center and interacts with it. For this reason, organizations could argue that no data has transferred, as the user is viewing data located in the original data center and no data has exited geographic boundaries. Remote support personnel might also consider VPN connectivity to minimize data transfer challenges.

Hashing, or a *digital fingerprint*, is the process of taking a small sample of data from a whole document and using that small sample as a fingerprint to identify that an entire message is accurate. However, because a fingerprint in some circumstances can be simulated, hash values should be *salted*. Salting requires that the hash adds a randomly generated, additional large input value beyond the message value included in the hash. This means that data transfer involves two values: the hash value and the salt value. Having two values means that even if hackers determine one value, they likely cannot determine the second. When organizations do not randomly generate salt or set short and guessable values, hackers can easily discover and compromise the connection via a *dictionary attack* or *rainbow attack*. Commonly used hash algorithms today are Message Digest 5 (MD5) and Secure Hash Algorithm 1 (SHA-1), with SHA-1 the better option for a VPN deployment. Message authentication is facilitated via a cryptographic *checksum*, validating data and identifying errors introduced during transmission.

Encryption measures message confidentiality, both in storage and in transmission. For VPN, encryption in transmission includes both encryption of the data before it is sent across the Internet and tunnels the data within the transmission, called *tunneling*. The tunnel connects the origin of the transmission with the receiver of the transmission, encrypts the data, then passes the encrypted data through the tunnel. Two popular protocols for tunneling are Internet Protocol Security (IPSec) and OpenVPN.

In addition to the potential for downloading viruses or malware, Internet connectivity poses additional privacy challenges for individuals and organizations. All clients come pre-loaded with software called a *Web browser*, where the user can enter a URL or navigate to a Search engine and type in search criteria. Additional Web browser software can be downloaded. This browsing functionality poses several privacy issues, specifically what information a Website collects, stores, and aggregates about an individual.

Cookies are small text files deposited on an individual client (or computer), which report information back to a Website about an individual user and are read by a Web browser. Cookies collect a variety of data elements with respect to a user, including information about the browser used, whether an individual is "logged in" to that browser, IP Address specifying physical location, pages visited on the site, and pages visited prior to and following a site visit. Some cookies also gather information stored on a device, such as *MAC address* or unique mobile device identifiers. These identifiers are *pervasive* or permanent identifiers, which do not change, in contrast with *variable* identifiers like an IP address or Global Positioning System (GPS) data built into a mobile device, which changes based on physical address of connectivity and cell phone tower locations for mobile devices.

When organizations must disclose information about cookies in some jurisdictions, implied or explicit consent must be provided by the user, because information that is unique to an individual's physical position or individual device could infringe the rights and freedoms of individuals with respect to their physical safety and privacy (*see* Chapter 2). When data are stored over time, information about a physical position becomes increasingly more sensitive and indicative of an individual's activities, such as routine visits to a health care facility with free, wireless Internet available. Storage of highly sensitive information over time also poses security issues. Although one data point captured by a cookie may not pose much risk for fraud or misuse, multiple data points captured over a period of time likely require a higher degree of security protection. Many Websites storing data do not protect data collected from Websites with similar stringency to, for example, health data. However, data collected about health-related Web searches coupled with location data indicating regular visits to a health care provider over time might actually pose more risk to an individual than information about one office visit. For this reason, organizations should review to what extent cookies are used, the degree to which data collection is necessary, and how data collection could be minimized. Additionally, organizations should consider adding data collected through cookies, such as IP address and browsing history, to sensitive data classifications.

Cookies are classified as either *persistent cookies* or *session cookies.* Persistent cookies collect information and retain it until an individual removes them, such as "remember me" functionality for username and password. Session cookies collect information until a second event occurs, such as closing the browser window or time period elapsing as might occur with an online shopping cart. In geographic locations where consumers do not execute implicit or explicit consent for cookies (in contrast with EU laws), consumers may control cookies via a cookie blocker, Web browser settings, or remove accumulated cookies periodically by clearing cookies in Internet options or settings. AdChoices, created by the non-profit Data & Marketing Association in the United States, tags some advertising with a sideways arrow and "x." Most cookie blocking technologies block nearly all cookies, including those that make a Website function properly. *See* Table 8.3 for a listing of each cookie type and its function.

Table 8.3 Cookie Type and Function

Cookie Name	*Cookie Type*	*Function*
Process	Persistent	Supports Website function, such as page orientation or document display
Preference	Persistent	Retain preferred language, browser size, colors, font size, or other personalization
HTTP (Security)	Persistent	An HTTP cookie is used to enable secure Website transmissions
Third Party, or Cookie Profiling	Persistent	Placed on a site by third parties, not the organization with the hosting site. Examples include Beacon technologies that take data and use it to personalize your Facebook experience or tracking technologies that identify the previous Website visited and downstream Website visits. Third Party cookies can be persistent.
Flash	Highly Persistent	Maintained on your computer after cookies cleared

Cookie Name	*Cookie Type*	*Function*
Zombie	Highly Persistent	Cookie that recreates itself after deletion
Analytics	Persistent	Collects data over time and across users to improve services and advertising
Ordering	Session	Retains information about selections or items in a shopping cart. Without these cookies, e-Commerce would not be possible, as items would disappear from the shopping cart as an individual navigated the site.

Although organizations may target mobile device information for cookies, mobile devices pose a more substantial privacy and security risk than PCs and laptops because of their mobility. Mobility of computerized devices stimulated additional technological development, such as connectivity to a Global Positioning System (GPS), which can pinpoint an individual device's location by satellite; and location pinpointed by cell tower connectivity, which can often be accessed by law enforcement.

Key Takeaways:

- Software-as-a-Services (SaaS) is software access on the cloud.
- Hashing with salt effectively ensures authenticity of communications.
- Two-factor authentication (2FA) requires two of the following to ensure identification and authentication of a user: what you know, what you have, or what you are.
- Cookies are small text files of varying kinds and longevity.

§8.06 MOBILE DEVICES AND THE INTERNET OF THINGS

Mobile devices pack substantial computing power into a convenient, hand-held size, making data access "on demand" very desirable. *Apps*, or applications built for a mobile computing environment, leverage Internet connectivity to view, change, or store personal and organizational information. App developers can build apps using *thin client* or *thick client* functionality. As the name suggests, thick clients require substantially more resources on a mobile device, like memory and storage capacity, because they support heavy app usage. Heavy app usage includes pervasive data storage and robust functionality, even when a mobile device is not connected to the Internet. Many organizations use thick client functionality when supporting critical business operations on mobile devices, such as inventory management, patient check-in, or on-demand payment. Thin clients use substantially less data, usually relying on a live Internet connection to view or change data hosted on a server.

App developers may write the apps in the same code as the device (such as Objective-C for Apple devices and Java for Android devices), also called *native* coding, or *hybrid*, which is written for multiple devices. Some apps function as a smaller version of a Web application. These apps, *responsive UI apps*, are thin clients by default, because they do not pervasively store data on a device. When individuals connect to an app, they actually view the same applications accessible from a Website, only reformatted for mobile viewing.

Unsurprisingly, the dramatic increase in mobile device usage for organizations and consumers opens mobile devices to cybersecurity threats. App developers who design thick client apps that will process sensitive personal information, for example, need to ensure that appropriate cybersecurity measures are implemented for the app and for the device (recall the OSI levels described earlier in this chapter). Because consumer mobile devices and some organizational devices do not employ standard cybersecurity controls, thick client design can unwittingly expose a consumer to privacy risks, if a mobile device is compromised by a hacker or stolen and accessed later. Where an app developer cannot verify mobile device security, a thin client design, or responsive UI might prove a more prudent option.

Mobile devices also include the potential for short distance communications, such as Bluetooth, an industry standard radio communication protocol, Near-field Communications (NFC), or infrared. Bluetooth uses radio frequencies, which makes transfer possible through walls and other surfaces, over tens of feet, and allows multi-dimensional connectivity, which explains its use in home devices, such as baby monitors and CCTV cameras. NFC uses just one wave that can be transferred four centimeters, speeding connectivity time and facilitating faster transfers over a shorter physical space. Android Pay and Apple Pay, applications that facilitate touch-transfer of payment, use NFC. Remote-enabled technologies use wireless infrared communication, or light energy with a slightly longer wavelength than natural light, to transfer information. Each of these communication mechanisms allow for wireless connectivity without the hassle of full wireless networking. Of course, such technologies, especially Bluetooth and other radio communication, pose challenges for communications privacy.

Organizations also use mobile devices for business operations, including organization-managed devices or employee-managed devices. Organization-managed devices connect to organizational servers as clients. Employee-managed devices generally do not connect directly to organizational servers, but may be managed as part of a Bring Your Own Device (BYOD) policy. BYOD can help organizations reduce the devices they manage, reducing cost. However, effective BYOD policies also allow for organization-managed device requirements, such as password protection, encryption, authentication requirements, and segregation of organizational data and apps from personal data and apps.

Appropriate management of mobile devices and data segregation requires use of Mobile Application Management (MAM) or Mobile Device Management (MDM) solutions, which enable an organization to remotely manage a device, such as wiping data from a device, or requiring a passcode to protect any organizational data accessible through the device.[201] MAM solutions tend to allow the most flexibility,

201. Remote wiping is the process by which data are deleted from a device, ensuring that an individual cannot access organizational resources after a specific event, such as termination,

managing access to organizational data only, which means that a terminated employee using her device to connect to organizational resources will not lose her family photos on her personal device when she leaves the organization. MAM solutions do this by "sandboxing" organizational apps from other personal mobile device features and personal mobile apps; MAM for this reason works well for organizations that provide apps for their employees. When a remote wipe is initiated, only data within the sandbox will be deleted. Sandboxes may also prevent malware or viruses downloaded in the personal side of a mobile device from compromising organizational applications or other resources, such as an employee's work e-mail.

MAM solutions may also manage mobile app deployment, and mobile device management teams often provide a great resource for mobile app reviews and governance functions. These teams may develop policies that reduce the likelihood of device and, following, organizational data compromise, such as limits on app data storage within a device or determining acceptable device models and operating system versions.[202] Mobile Content Management (MCM) is a version of MAM that delivers secure document management. MDM solutions focus on managing the device holistically, for example logging the device and permitting remote wiping, but work well for organizations connecting mobile devices without substantial access to organizational apps. Enterprise Mobility Management (EMM) is a more advanced version of MDM.

If organizations permit individuals to connect to organizational resources without effective mobile device management technologies and processes, organizations will substantially increase data misuse risk. A disgruntled employee, for example, may use customer data, trade secret, or other organizational data, or email records for nefarious purposes. If an employee misuses the data, the organization may face fines or other legal action for failing to implement reasonable technical and administrative security controls. It is incredibly important for organizations to calculate the cost of implementing and managing effective MAM or MDM solutions in BYOD cost analyses.

Other devices that may or may not connect with mobile devices also pose unique challenges for security and privacy. Health technology today includes mobile health ("mHealth") and health information technology (IT), wearable devices, telehealth, telemedicine, and personalized medicine. Implanted devices may be network-aware or not, such as an implanted device controlled remotely or continuously transmitting health data to another system in contrast to a device that is designed and calibrated prior to implantation.[203] Implanted devices can also include manufacturer-operated applications (such as a mobile app or a Web-based app) and data storage (such as a database).

---

leaving a job, or after losing a device. Remote wipe capabilities typically require a device to be connected to the Internet, so the percentage of successful "wipes" depends on the status of individual devices when the wipe is initiated.

202. When devices store data within an individual's device, if a device is lost or stolen, a risk of data breach increases. When devices do not incorporate expected security controls and when employees do not update a device to the newest version, it is more likely that organizational data on a device could be compromised.

203. *Cybersecurity for Medical Devices and Hospital Networks: FDA Safety Communication*, U.S. Food & Drug Admin., http://www.fda.gov/MedicalDevices/Safety/AlertsandNotices/ucm356423.htm (last updated Oct. 9, 2014).

Non-implanted devices, by contrast, may aid in performing a medical procedure or diagnostics, but do not pervasively interact with the body. Non-implanted devices may include only the device used to perform a procedure, or devices may connect to an information system. Network-aware devices can transfer data to a hospital data center or to a manufacturer's data center or cloud provider.

Wearables collect information from an individual and display information to a recipient, such as a caregiver or healthcare provider. Wearables do not physiological change the body (e.g., cause cardiac muscle to contract). Wearables include devices like the Fitbit, which measures heartrate, exercise, and sleep data, combining information an individual enters and information gathered simply by being worn. Wearables usually connect to an external mobile device via a wireless network or other communication protocol like Bluetooth to transmit data to a mobile application. Mobile apps can receive data from an implanted device, non-implanted device, or wearable, and can store data either on the device (thick client) or immediately send data to another location (thin client).[204] *See* Table 8.4 for examples of medical device groupings.

Table 8.4 Medical Device Types

Device Type	*Device Example*
Implanted Devices (not network-aware, network-aware, application compatible, data storage); includes monitoring devices	Pacemaker
Non-Implanted Bio Devices (device only, data storage, network-aware)	X-ray Machine
Wearables (device only, network-aware, data storage)	Heart Rate Monitor

Although all devices could pose some risk to patients or consumers, devices with the highest inherent risk of harm include implanted or affixed devices. These devices may directly deliver medication or other stimulus to the human body or gather biological health information directly. When combined with wearables, mobile apps, or Web applications exposed to the open Internet, potential risks of physical injury or substantial data loss increase.

External storage devices, such as USB memory sticks or external hard drives, pose unique challenges for organizations. These devices may contain malware or viruses that directly transmit onto a client through a USB port. A *port* is any physical or virtual place that allows a device to transfer data back and forth. For example, ports also exist to create a connection with a monitor, a mouse, or a keyboard. However, USB ports also permit data transfer, for example from a USB device, a CD-ROM disc drive, or a mobile device. Individuals can connect a device to a home computer, then use it at a work computer, transferring malware from the home computer into the work

204. *See* Vangie Beal, *The Differences Between Thick, Thin & Smart Clients*, WEBOPEDIA (July 14, 2006), http://www.webopedia.com/DidYouKnow/Hardware_Software/thin_client_applications.asp (distinguishing between thick and thin client applications and users).

internal environment. In fact, a common scam involves hackers dropping USB sticks filled with malware in a parking lot outside an organization they hope to hack. Often, at least one person picks up the USB stick considering it a lucky gift and inserts the USB stick into a work computer, compromising the organization's system. Alternatively, disgruntled employees may download internal organization data, such as patient records, salacious emails, or trade secrets to a USB device and later sell data on the Dark Web.

Organizations manage these risks via two methods: block/approval and encrypted use. Block and approval includes blocking USB ports completely, preventing users from using USB sticks and other USB-connected media on any client. Then, business areas require executive approval for removal of USB blocking, for example marketing teams that require USB access for cameras, individual printers, CD-ROMs or external hard drives. Alternatively, encrypted use normalizes use of encrypted USB sticks by giving employees encrypted USB sticks for work use only. Although this method does address initial security risks, it does not necessarily stop insiders from misusing data.

Key Takeaways:

- MAM and MDM solution enable mobile device security within an organization.
- Apps can be thick or thin clients, depending on the amount of data stored on a mobile device.
- Medical devices include implantable devices, sensing devices, and wearables.
- USB devices and other peripherals can introduce malware directly onto a computer.

§8.07 INDUSTRIAL CONTROL SYSTEMS

Industrial Control Systems (ICS) manage the operations of industrial applications, such as nuclear reactors, wind turbines, electrical grids, water and waste treatment, and gas as part of a larger system. ICS have existed for an incredibly long period of time, for much of this time as systems disconnected from the Internet. Breaching ICS systems, then, required substantially more effort, including gaining access through substantial physical security measures and rigorous background checks.

Increasingly more often today, governments and organizations have considered Internet-connected systems for their efficiency and ease of use: operators can manage systems from anywhere, reducing costs. This direction has created new challenges, too, because of the emerging role of nation-states in hacking activities. Many countries now consider both privately and publicly owned ICS a primary focus for cybersecurity protection and a matter of national security. For this reason, most countries now group traditional ICS industries with securities, banking, and health care sectors, as *critical infrastructure* to emphasize the need for prioritizing cybersecurity protection. If ICS do not implement sufficient cybersecurity and physical security measures, a substantial safety issue will result, potentially taking human life or destroying real property.

ICS use a combination of instrumentation and controllers that direct the activity of ICS systems. *Instrumentation* is the primary and ancillary machinery that physically performs work, such as the gates for a dam. *Operators* control operation of the instrumentation using *controllers*. Some controllers physically connect to equipment in a discrete *control system*. Human operators make decisions regarding equipment operation via a *control center*, which combines inputs from various controllers so that operators can manage a system(s) together.

The most popular operational implementations today for an ICS include the Supervisory Control and Data Acquisition (SCADA) and Distributed Control System (DCS) implementations. SCADA systems provide event-based, decentralized, data driven management, and often span large geographic areas. In contrast, DCS systems simplify system implementation, support process-driven operations, and cleanly support continuous local operations. The modern ICS contains elements of both, with some SCADA implementations including DCS systems.

Organizations have used SCADA systems, in their original form, for over sixty years as a means for controlling instrumentation, such as large manufacturing production plants. These first systems, while less sophisticated than modern implementations, are still used by organizations and governments today. Modern SCADA systems include control units that can be configured as Programmable Logic Controllers (PLC), Remote Terminal (or Telemetry) Units (RTU), and Digital Communication Units (DCU). These control units interface on one end with equipment instrumentation and the other with the control center, which operates like a server and can be accessed by the Human Machine Interface (HMI), as individual client computers (such as laptops or mobile devices).

SCADA PLCs provide automated operations for a DCS. Within a DCS, many activities and limits must be automatically managed to ensure a DCS can function without human intervention. Like a standard PC or server, PLCs manage operation of various instrumentation, except they are designed for industrial temperature variation and vibration. PLCs come in various sizes but usually fit on a power-enabled rack and can be various sizes with input/output section and a Central Processing Unit (CPU). The CPU controls the activities of connected instrumentation, based on pre-programmed operations and limits.

SCADA RTUs connect to physical instrumentation and equipment on one side and the PLC on the other, to report telemetry data to the control center and are designed to monitor physical instrumentation in the absence of human equipment operators. *Telemetry data* aggregated data from physical equipment instrumentation referenced against internal rules to determine whether the RTU will send an *alarm(s)* to the control center. *See* Figure 8.11 for an example of a SCADA system.

Figure 8.11 SCADA Architectural Diagram

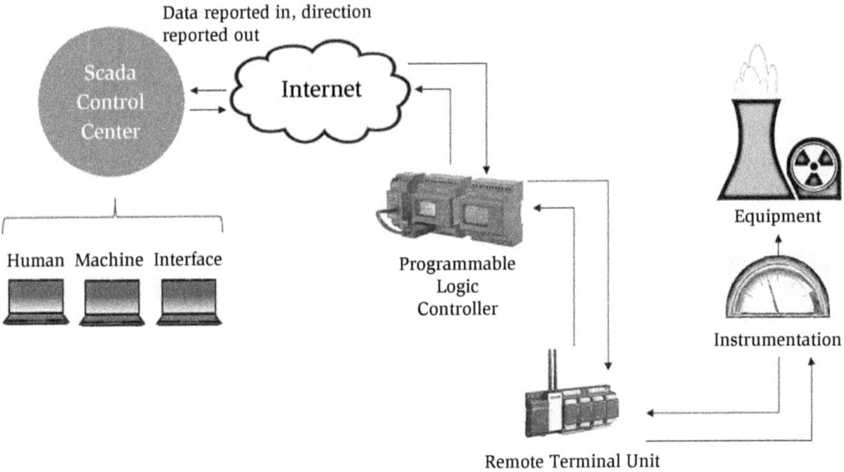

In contrast, DCS uses multiple controllers for different types of equipment, which localizes control near individual system processes. For this reason, DCS control centers usually exist on-premises for a large localized implementation, in comparison to a geographically distributed set of different locations requiring central control. DCS follows a hierarchical model involving direct controllers connected to instrumentation and equipment, supervisory controllers monitoring direct controllers, and coordinating computers managing activities and reporting to a control center. This model enables portions of a location to continue functioning, as it only affects one section managed by an individual controller.

Over time, DCS and SCADA have begun to overlap in many respects, especially as remote access has emerged as a desirable option for many ICS implementations. This has resulted in adding WiFi compatibility and remote transmission with Internet-based functionality, including mobile and Web interfaces. In the past, organizations managed cybersecurity risk by controlling systems on-premises using clients that did not enable Internet connectivity, *air-gapped* computers. The move towards remote management has changed the threat landscape for ICS, introducing new cybersecurity threats.

The most famous recent attack on ICS involved Stuxnet in 2009.[205] Stuxnet was created through a joint Israeli-United States project ("project") to document nuclear facility blueprints and cause substantial damage to Iranian nuclear facilities by causing centrifuges enriching uranium to fail using a virus. In a unique attack, the project designed Stuxnet to infect computers that third parties (businesses manufacturing, assembling, or installing products) would later connect to the nuclear plant's ICS using

205. Kim Zetter, *An Unprecedented Look at Stuxnet, the World's First Digital Weapon*, WIRED (Nov. 3, 2014), available at: https://www.wired.com/2014/11/countdown-to-zero-day-stuxnet/.

an infected USB stick. The project wrote Stuxnet to compromise specific manufacturers' PLCs, in this case a Siemens brand.

On July 2017, the U.S. Federal Bureau of Investigations (FBI) and Department of Homeland Security (NHS) issued a joint warning about potential attacks on nuclear facilities, nuclear power stations, and energy facilities using an attack designed to leverage remote client access and ICS Internet connectivity, an advanced persistent threat attack described later in this chapter.[206] Although ICS requires some specific security considerations, security technologies applicable to other organizations and technologies also apply to ICS.

Key Takeaways:

- Industrial Control Systems support basic community services, such as electrical grids, water, power, and nuclear facilities, often called critical infrastructure.
- ICS runs on SCADA or DCS.
- Increasingly, ICS require remote access over an Internet connection.

206. Nicole Perlroth, *Hackers Are Targeting Nuclear Facilities, Homeland Security Dept. and F.B.I. Say*, The New York Times (July 6, 2017), available at: https://www.nytimes.com/2017/07/06/technology/nuclear-plant-hack-report.html.

CHAPTER 9

Security Technologies

Security technologies build on IT knowledge by focusing on the concepts of Identification, Authorization, Authentication, and Encryption. Security technologies support these goals to ensure SCIAP for organizations and their customers.

§9.01 UNDERSTANDING THE TECHNOLOGY AND SECURITY ECOSYSTEM

Across IT environments, practitioners must understand the types of privacy and security issues resulting from specific technology choices. Attorneys working in this field will also be confronted with questions about technology implementations, such as "should we move this data to the cloud?" or "can we store this data locally on a client device?" Although IT experts usually can assist in understanding how specific technology functions, practitioners and attorneys must have working knowledge of inherent security risks, security technologies and tactics, and common attacks. Table 9.1 describes the most typical devices, interfaces, and storage locations discussed in this chapter.

Table 9.1 Device, Interface, and Storage Types

Device	*Interface/System*	*Storage Description*	*Storage Location*
Mainframe/Server	Command Line, Installed Software, OS	Substantial data volume, servers can store and process data	In-Device, On-prem, Private cloud, Public cloud, PaaS, IaaS, Backup/Archival

Device	*Interface/System*	*Storage Description*	*Storage Location*
Laptop, PC	Website, Web application, Installed Software, SaaS, OS	Less storage data volume than server, connect to storage on intranet and through applications, SaaS	In-Device, On-prem, Private cloud, Public cloud, SaaS, Backup/Archival
Mobile Device	Native App, Hybrid App, Website, Web application, SaaS, OS	Less storage data volume than laptop/PC, store primarily on cloud and through apps	In-Device, On-prem, Private cloud, Public cloud, SaaS, Backup/Archival
IoT	Installed Software, Native App, SaaS, OS	Very little data storage volume available, transfers most data to data center and most likely public cloud	In-Device, On-prem, Private cloud, Public cloud, Backup/Archival
Medical Device	Installed Software, Native app, SaaS, Hybrid App, OS	Limited data storage volume available, transfers data to data centers and cloud	In-Device, On-prem, Private cloud, Public cloud, Backup/Archival

For specific devices, inherent security and data protection concerns with respect to personal information shape risk-based discussions around technology selection. Table 9.2 describes devices with respect to these two focus areas.

Table 9.2 Device Data Protection and Security Concerns

Device	*Data Protection Concerns*	*Security Concerns*
Mainframe	Plain-text personal info is stored in the system	Few native security features, primary model is "security by obscurity," or security because few individuals know how to work on the mainframe
Server	Large volumes of data are processed and stored on servers, including Personal Information collected and processed	Many servers, especially those providing cloud infrastructure or hosting applications that process data, are connected to the Internet to function
PC/Laptop	Personal Information stored on device for some professionals, e.g., HR, health care support, can be lost if Laptop stolen or PC compromised	Encryption of data, appropriate authorization, VPN connectivity, enterprise access to internal resources

Device	*Data Protection Concerns*	*Security Concerns*
Mobile Device	Location, GPS, unique mobile identifiers, connectivity to apps with personal info	Portable nature, inconsistent security features, persistent log-on, on-device data storage
IoT	Lifestyle information, few opportunities to exercise choice, substantial data storage	Focus on cost not robust security, manufacturers not experienced in security, connect to consumer systems w/poor security
Medical Device	Substantial data transfer, highly sensitive data	Significant potential safety issues, outage could cause physical impact

Similar to devices, interfaces can pose inherent risk to an organization from a security and data protection perspective. Table 9.3 describes interfaces with respect to these two focus areas.

Table 9.3 Interface/System Data Protection and Security Concerns

Interface	*Data Protection Concerns*	*Security Concerns*
Website	Collect potential personal information like IP Address, browsing history, Web form data entry	Malware can be stored in Websites that are not protected (HTTP v. HTTPS) affecting consumers or Websites can be defaced.
Web Application/SaaS	Collect any kind of personal information depending on the Web Application	Backend controlled by third parties, could reside in the cloud, data transferred to backend systems could not be encrypted.
Installed Software	Malware downloaded by users can capture personal details like username/password, then log into systems containing personal info.	Reputable software could have Internet connectivity and if security not in place could expose intranet to malware.
Native App -Mobile App	Connects to in-device capabilities, including contacts list, photos, calendar, e-mail, other. Could access data without user notification. Also could store application data on device.	Native applications require periodic device updates, and users may not apply updates as soon as they are released. Lack of encryption on device may expose data stored on device, which may be substantial.
Hybrid App – Mobile App	Connects to Web applications, but can input/upload personal information such as contacts, photos, calendar, e-mail.	Hybrid App functions like a Web app but carries with it potential security challenges of both a mobile device and a Web app.

As with devices and interfaces, storage location can also influence the information security and data protection. Table 9.4 describes storage arrangements and associated data protection and security concerns.

Table 9.4 Storage Data Protection and Security Concerns

Storage Location	*Data Protection Concerns*	*Security Concerns*
In-Device	Devices can change hands, employees can leave companies without returning devices, can expose personal info of self or others.	Substantial data can be stored with limited/variable security protection.
On-premises (On-prem)	It is more likely that caches of personal information reside in the same physical location, making more susceptible to insiders stealing data. Also poses data localization/data transfer/adequacy challenges.	If organizations do not understand data center security or have secure access designed to resources, data could be more exposed than at third party providers.
Private cloud	Private cloud may not be able to accommodate data localization/data transfer/adequacy (geographic) requirements	Private cloud may be at least partially supported by third parties, potentially exposing data. Cloud providers may be more susceptible to large-scale data breaches due to the possibility of large data volume.
Public cloud	Public cloud does not physically segregate data, making the possibility of data exposure higher. Geographic requirements also pose challenges.	Public cloud is fully supported by third parties, potentially exposing data. Cloud providers may be more susceptible to large-scale data breaches due to the possibility of large data volume.
Software as a Service (SaaS)	Many SaaS applications capture personal information and transfer to third party data center or cloud provider. Geographic requirements pose challenges.	SaaS applications are fully supported by third parties and are fully reliant on strong security practices by the third party.
Backup/ Archival Storage	Data erasure requirements include backups and archives, which may be difficult to erase; often geographic limitations are implicated, especially for cloud backup sites.	Backup/archival sites tend to have less rigorous security controls because the systems may not be pervasively connected to the Internet.

In order to protect data and mitigate potential risks within these technologies, security disciplines focus on the key concepts of Trust, Accuracy, and Secrecy, or data integrity and confidentiality of the SCIAP framework. *See* Figure 9.1 for a list of security disciplines focused on these concepts.

Figure 9.1 Security Disciplines

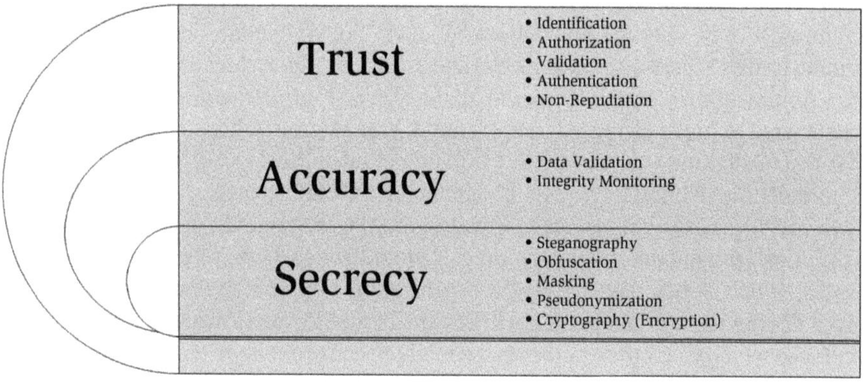

As described at the beginning of Chapter 9, trust is a foundational part of managing security obligations, and security technologies ensure appropriate identification, validation, authorization, authentication, and non-repudiation. Identification involves a user and machine disclosing their respective identities. For users, this might include the user entering a user ID, a Website connecting to a cookie deposited on the user's device, or an IP address. A machine will likely share a Media Access Control, or MAC address, which is considered the *physical address* or identity of an individual computer (in contrast the network address the IP address provides).

Validation and, similarly, authorization, ensures an individual has rights to access a resource or perform an action. *Data validation* or *input validation* requires a system to operate under pre-defined rules to ensure data conform to a specific length or format. Data validation prevents hackers from entering actual code into a Web form that could compromise a system, while also creating greater organization and repeatability in backend databases. Security activities supporting validation and authorization typically include access control management mechanisms.

Access control is the process by which validation and authorization occurs within a computer system. In addition to industry standards, cybersecurity laws often include access control management activities. Systems manage Access Control List (ACL), which contains appropriate users and qualified devices that may connect to the system. If an *unauthorized user* or *unauthorized device* attempts to access the target system, access will be denied. For example, if an individual who has a log-in and password for Windows software that permits the individual to use Microsoft Word, but the device does not have a license to use Microsoft Project, the system will deny access. ACLs for this reason serve dual purposes: ensure only trusted users access the system and ensure the user has rights to access certain resources (an incredibly important goal of legal software license management, as well).

User name may be individual and specific to a particular system, or enterprise in nature. As discussed previously, single sign-on (SSO) technologies or enterprise access can simplify and streamline log-on for personnel. However, implementing SSO can prove challenging: systems do not always integrate onto one platform easily. Further, third party software or SaaS sometimes cannot integrate with SSO technologies. As a result, users often use the same User ID and password for all systems, so when hackers compromise one User ID and password, they can potentially access all systems. Administrative access also introduces substantial risks to organizations.

Administrative access applies to all devices and infrastructure: users who legitimately need to make changes only permitted with administrative access cannot fulfill their responsibilities, but often users who do not need this level of access still receive it. Administrative access proves problematic for PCs and laptops because a user can download files, executables, and software onto the machine directly. Unfortunately, many Internet-available free software comes embedded with damaging malware or viruses, which is then passed over the organization's intranet to the server, where the server distributes it to many more clients, infecting the enterprise. In other cases, an employee who has administrative access might become unhappy with an organization and choose to inflict harm, or another employee could be tricked into clicking on the wrong link in an e-mail. Because these almost unlimited circumstances can result in an unauthorized user or machine accessing relatively sensitive assets, organizations *must* tightly control administrative access.

A few risk mitigation techniques may reduce risk for an organization. First, organizations can purchase a utility, which provides temporary access to administrative IDs on a check-out basis. This utility, then, can also notate which user has checked out an ID, the identity of the device connecting, and a time and date for the check-out (collectively, a *system log* or *audit trail*). Having a system log of this information can improve investigation if needed. Organizations should not be tempted to use a shared user ID/password, however, for administrative access. Specific utilities that manage passwords also use more complex passwords and rotate IDs to protect against unauthorized use.

Further, more frequent reviews of users with administrative access can ensure the *least user access* (LUA) principle is followed. During an *administrative access review*, a manager and often someone familiar with the system and in a management position reviews individuals *access rights*, or the individual permissions an individual within the system. More frequent access review, such as a Quarterly Access Review (QAR), allows for access termination or removal. Last, organizations should reduce the total number of users with administrative access overall. Whether during *access provisioning*, when managers approve access or during administrative access reviews, tightly controlling the number of administrative users dramatically reduces risk to an organization. Organizations also should develop a routine access review management process (described further in Chapter 12) for all other access.

Access management technologies that manage access reviews and SSO may also facilitate appropriate mechanisms for managing passwords, forgotten passwords, and special questions. Under best practices, users must adhere to a specified password complexity (usually consisting of a minimum length and inclusion of capitalized and lower-case letters, numbers, and/or special characters) and rotation frequency (usually ninety days).

Password reset processes should be designed with workforce support in mind. Organizations with strong access management processes require direct LAN connectivity for password resets, which means personnel must connect to the intranet on-premises. However, some organizations with a large decentralized workforce (non-local clients) may consider supporting remote password reset, for example using MFA or another method.

Password management rules also limit the potential for an unauthorized user to guess a password. Organizations usually set a specific number of missed password attempts before lock-out and specify a period of time (if any) that elapses before a user attempts to log-in again. It may be desirable to trigger a call to an IT Service desk to unlock a device rather than permit log-in retries after thirty minutes, but practitioners will need to balance business needs and associated cost of call center traffic before making this type of recommendation.

Forgotten passwords may also benefit from a standard tool and process for permitting password reset. Security best practices today require MFA to reset a forgotten password: for example, sending an email to a secondary email address with notification of a reset attempt and a reset code or sending a text message/phone call to the individual's mobile device with a code included. Some organizations use *special questions*, or questions only the user should know, to reset a password. Special or secret questions often do not provide as useful a defense as one might expect because many special questions include references to publicly available information that a hacker might discover on a public site or social media, such as a dog's name, favorite book, or mother's maiden name. If organizations prefer to use special questions, they should select questions that are more difficult to discover or require users to answer multiple questions successfully.

Authentication is the holistic process of identification, validation, and authorization to confirm the truthfulness of an assertion. In the security space, the authentication means that users have truthfully identified themselves and the user has legitimate access to resources from the machine used. Hackers or internal unauthorized users may spoof credentials and pretend to be an authorized user from an authorized device. For this reason, when a user entering a username and password to authenticate, clients also authenticate to servers using a digital certificate model, Certificate-Based Authentication (CBA).

Digital certificates are a means of authenticating users, clients (including mobile devices with MDM technologies), and servers by exchanging proof of authenticity. Certification Authorities (CA) issue these digital certificates, and digital certificates often are very difficult to forge. IT teams install certificates onto various servers and clients, usually directly, which prevents certificate forging. Digital certificates support encryption, so certificate-based models provide an alternative to VPN technology. *See* Figure 9.2 for a picture of CBA.

Figure 9.2 Certificate-Based Authentication

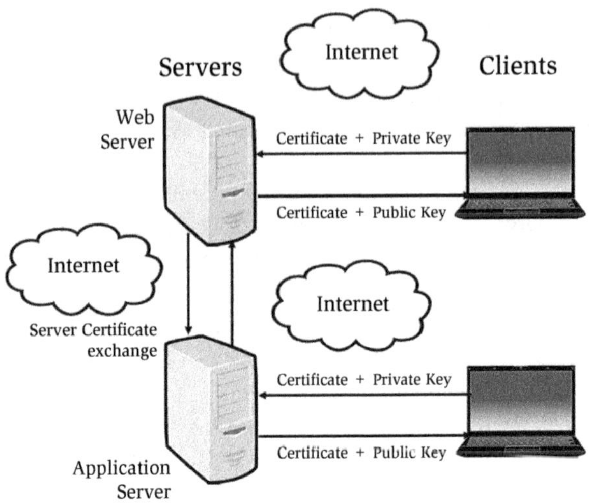

Certificate exchange usually includes exchange of private and public keys. Servers hold public keys, which are issued by a CA and are available to anyone with a valid certificate of their own connecting to the site. Certificates with public keys demonstrate that the server is a trusted (rather than untrusted) machine and ensures that a client connects to a trusted server. A client, then, connects to the server and transfers a certificate(s) with a private key. The exchange of keys permits a secret channel to be created between the server and client. One key is used to encrypt the data, the other is used to decrypt the data. Together, these are called *asymmetric encryption* or *public key encryption* because different keys are exchanged, one public and one private.

Authentication is but one of four necessary requirements to fulfill effective AIM processes. Table 9.5 lays out each requirement at a high level.

Table 9.5 Identification, Validation, Authorization, and Authentication

Security Theme	*Description*	*Answers What Question?*
Identification	Enables users, clients, and servers to provide some indication of who they/are.	Who or what are you?
Validation	Data validation, rights validation related to a provided input or requested resource.	Does my request or input make sense?
Authorization	Determines if the identified resource can access the requested resource.	Do I have permission to access this?

Security Theme	*Description*	*Answers What Question?*
Authentication	Ensures technically and with additional assurance that users, clients, servers are who they say they are, that they can access what is requested, that it is an accurate request.	Have we technically ensured that the above questions are correct?

The concept of accuracy includes the security concepts of non-repudiation and integrity monitoring. *Non-repudiation* is an assurance of authorship, or the ability to ensure a user or machine cannot deny the authenticity of an operation or event having taken place, or that the user or machine signed (authenticated) something. In common terms, non-repudiation takes away deniability. Organizations often solve non-repudiation problems with a salted hash because the hash value and the salt together are nearly impossible to replicate, evidencing authenticity of authorship. *See* Figure 9.3 for a question flow demonstrating how servers and clients determine authentication and non-repudiation.

Figure 9.3 Trust and Accuracy Server Check

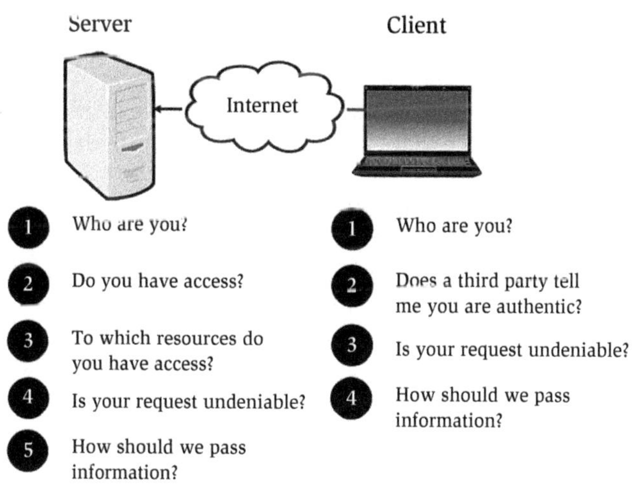

While authentication and non-repudiation focus on the trust between two parties, such as a client and a server, integrity monitoring focuses on ensuring data accuracy between sender and receiver. Data is transmitted using a variety of different data grouping methods based on the length of a particular message and the expected speed of data transfer. If you consider that each letter requires eight 0s or 1s (e.g., H is 01001000), a simple message like "Hello" requires transfer of forty bits (five bytes). A typical email data transfer of a three MB (three million bytes) requires more time, and complex file transfers can be even larger. Data transfer speed is affected by file size, network connectivity speed, and network congestion. For example, some organization's networks slow down around lunchtime because more employees access the Internet during that time. A home cable connection generally uploads and downloads faster than a DSL connection over telephone wire, except when someone in the household streams HD movies. For these reasons, systems break down data sets and files into manageable chunks, which is obvious when watching a Website load over a slow connection: some elements of the Website appear first, such as the text without any style or formatting applied.

A large data volume requires a system to break the data set into *packets*, or smaller groupings of data with information about both the contents and order of packets sent, included, called the *header*. Header information assists in reassembling the message once all packets have been sent. Specific technologies provide data transfer. File Transfer Protocol (FTP) is one of the oldest protocol for sending files, created in the 1970s; Hyper-text Transfer Protocol (HTTP) provides transfer within a Web environment; Real Time Streaming Protocol (RTSP) streams Windows media content; Server Message Block (SMB) provides shared file access, Network File System (NFS) provides service to access and change files on a remote computer, and UDP-based Data Transfer Protocol (UDT) provides fast, high performance transfer for large data sets. Although many file transfer protocols are used beyond those notated above, the primary concerns for data transfer are message integrity and message secrecy.

Message integrity measures usually include File Integrity Monitoring (FIM). FIM uses checksums from the current file and previous file and compares the difference. While understanding every detail of FIM is not necessary for an attorney or practitioner, it is critical to understand that FIM should be used where data integrity is very important for safety or privacy issues.

Although organizations should use FIM to manage organizational risk for high-risk processes (e.g., asset transfers or payment systems), FIM must be used for data transfer involving sensitive personal information used to provide medical care or data transfer for purposes of credit or background check determinations, where decisions could infringe on personal rights. Many laws require integrity checks and processes to ensure data accuracy Data integrity also requires strong foundational trust mechanisms to ensure that only identified and valid users or machines with appropriate, authorized access who have been authenticated can edit or delete data.

§9.02 MAINTAINING DATA SECRECY

In common vernacular, *secrecy* is another word for confidentiality, but secrecy mechanisms in a security mean technical assurance of data or message secrecy with respect to unauthorized users or machines. The goal of secrecy is to dramatically reduce, not eliminate, the probability of ascertaining data contents, unless an authorized user or machine accesses the contents. Organizations apply different technologies based on the type of unauthorized user or machine ("unauthorized parties") that might attempt to access the data and the potential impact if access is successful. Like most technology choices, secrecy security choices may impact system performance or create challenges for operators and impact organizational efficiencies. For this reason, organizations should adopt a "risk-based" approach when selecting appropriate technologies, unless law or some other requirement mandates a specific approach (e.g., certification as described in Chapter 11).

One of the ways to protect information includes rendering information unreadable. When unauthorized parties access unreadable data, the data ceases in many cases to be accessible and the attack is foiled. As a concrete legal matter, HIPAA and several U.S. state data breach notification statutes provide a "safe harbor" for certain kinds secrecy measures, for example encrypted data under HIPAA does not require notification to patients. Some U.S. state data breach notification statutes eliminate the need to notify other measures, such as obfuscation or masking, as well.

Most technologies providing some assurance of secrecy include: steganography, obfuscation, masking, pseudonymization, and cryptography. De-identification and anonymization, which are similar to obfuscation, masking, or pseudonymization, have specific definitions under various laws but also reduce risk of discovery, this time by completely removing data elements from the data set rather than making them unreadable or undiscoverable.

Steganography is the technology of hiding information within other information. In Ancient Greece, messages were sent by etching messages on tablets later covered in wax, which bore a different message. Those who have read the highly popular Dan Brown novel, *The Da Vinci Code*, may recall the importance of clues left in famous works of art or using invisible ink. Today, steganography requires specific software to embed information in an image, video, message, or data, but is used less frequently than other secrecy technologies.

Obfuscation renders readable code difficult to decipher, unreadable machine code, which is not readily ascertained by humans, or use *security by obscurity* methods to conceal values. Security by obscurity relies on the secrecy of a specific coding system or other attributes of a technology, not generally known, to protect information without additional process or technology. Technologists, such as computer engineers, can create obfuscation or automate obfuscation. Obfuscation may be used to conceal trade secret or other highly proprietary data as a defense to reverse engineering concerns.

Masking makes data unreadable by obscuring all or part of information on a user interface or within a database. Organizations mask all or part of SPI to reduce the probability of misuse, yet enable data updates or access to other data in the file. Masking is often used in scenarios where frequent support calls or assistance is needed, but exposing highly sensitive data to a large number of people, such as a contact center, is undesirable. Development teams often need large data sets using accurate information to appropriately test a system before it goes live, and masking may provide adequate security within an *internal* organizational test environment.

Organizations may also leverage masking technologies when a portion of a data set enables an individual to be verified, such as providing a portion of an identifying number to prove identity when inquiring about a financial account. Masking can visually obscure viewing by an operator, enabling validation without unnecessary data exposure. *Blocking* technologies can also prevent transfer of sensitive data by identifying the data element and masking it in transit (or otherwise blocking a file from transfer, such as an email communication). For blocking technologies to work properly, sensitive data must fit a predefined set of formats, such as a credit card number or date of birth.

Pseudonymization is the activity of removing some identifiers for personal information and replacing them with alternative, non-personal identifiers and storing some identifiers in another location, segregated from the original *data set*, or combination of data elements in a database. Although pseudonymization is most often described in relation to personal information, using pseudonyms may also be useful in handling other highly sensitive information, such as names of companies considered for a merger or acquisition, or a highly sensitive trade secret.

Organizations find pseudonymization relatively simple to implement, but implementing *well* can take more effort. For example, pseudonymization requires creation of a pseudonym for an individual that can replace a pervasive identifier, such as a medical record number, but the pseudonym cannot be easily guessable or tied to another identifier, like ZIP code, address, or national identification number. Further, the identifier needs to have enough digits to continue easily into the future and accommodate new data subjects.

Pseudonymization also requires reasonable security protection for two databases: the database containing the pseudonym and identifier being replaced the "key," and the database with the rest of the data and the pseudonym. This includes all of the standard protections discussed so far, such as appropriate considerations for trust and accuracy. In addition to pseudonymization, organizations should also consider encryption, discussed later in this chapter.

Organizations should routinely use pseudonymization as a risk management strategy. Pseudonymization under the GDPR, similar to the *limited data set* under HIPAA, helps an organization minimize the potential for data misuse and data breach by managing data volume and degree of identifiability. It should be noted, however, that under GDPR, the process of pseudonymization does not avail an organization from fulfilling all responsibilities and guaranteeing all data subject or patient rights, as if the data were within a fully identified data set, because pseudonymized data sets enable reidentification. *Reidentification* is the process of bringing back together what pseudonymization separates.

De-identification is the process of removing identifying information from a data set, with a goal of reducing risk of misuse. For this reason, experts in de-identification algorithms, the mathematical formulae for reducing risk of misuse to an acceptable level, consider the data elements in a particular data set and how likely they will lead to identification. Many organizations mistakenly assume de-identification simply means removal of a name or obvious identifiers. Compliant de-identification under HIPAA, which permits easy transfer, aggregation, or data sale of the de-identified data set without any additional patient notice or patient authorization, requires removal of nineteen identifiers. Alternatively, a certified de-identification expert, such as an actuarial scientist, can assess the data set and make an expert determination.

Organizations not subject to HIPAA may also benefit from consulting with a de-identification expert prior to relying on de-identification as a means for avoiding applicable data protection and privacy laws. For example, organizations working with data protection laws in Canada have previously accepted HIPAA-compliant de-identification procedures. Organizations operating in multiple countries should assess to what degree de-identification might be acceptable in those countries.

Anonymization as a concept is similar to de-identification in many respects, yet it sets a higher standard for compliance within most laws in that it requires removing both direct and indirect identifiers. Organizations often pursue anonymization for data sets because it eliminates the need for compliance with various data protection laws, especially for data transfer and exchange with third parties and easy data aggregation. Unfortunately, the high bar for full anonymization can also make retaining useful data for purposes of transfer, exchange, and aggregation nearly impossible. Indeed, under existing EU law, "impossibility of identification" is the current standard for anonymization procedures. At this book's writing, the EU had not yet released any acceptable procedures or guidelines for establishing a compliant anonymization program.

At this point in time, organizations may consider one of the following options when working in the EU, although no known acceptable process has been developed to date: (1) working with a reputable de-identification expert that has previously done work with DPAs to validate a de-identification procedure and documenting why the procedure is acceptable, (2) developing a procedure and working with the primary DPA to document "acceptable" anonymization procedure, (3) developing an anonymization procedure and documenting it in case of any investigation, or (4) a combination of the first three. Organizations working in the EU should instead consider alternative options for gathering broader consent, in the best case via the data subject directly or in a secondary case via contractual requirements with the data controller.

With a similar goal of obfuscation and de-identification in mind, Apple, Google, and Microsoft use *differential privacy* to protect personal information through obscuring real data with fake data. Unlike security by obscurity, differential privacy uses a proprietary algorithm to determine the precise amount of *noise*, or fake data, inserted to prevent unauthorized parties from differentiating real data from fake data. Instead, the unauthorized party will receive an approximate sense of the data without details for any one individual. Differential privacy responds to the concern that enough data, once aggregated, can eventually identify an individual within a limited area.

> Tai is the head of a four-person household that includes one adult, one young adult, and two children. In this family of four, three members of the household currently have mobile devices that connect to the Internet. If Tai receives a report about data usage on household devices, it is likely that he could determine that the data usage from 11 P.M. to 1 A.M. is his adult child, who works an overnight shift at 1 A.M. Tai also probably knows that data usage from 7 P.M. to 9 P.M. is his 12-year-old child, who he permits to use the Internet after dinner for an hour each night. Tai could also likely predict which sites visited might be each of his children, based on knowing their ages and interests.

This example, although simple, illustrates that identification of an individual is contextual. If you know enough about a set of individuals, removing a name, email address, and gender does not solve an identification problem. Differential privacy solves this problem by substituting real data (like exact times accessing the Internet) with noise in a way that does not dramatically change data trends that an organization wants to see.

Differential privacy uses a hash to create a shorter version of the message in a hash value, then data is *subsampled*, retaining only part of the data entered, finally the user's device adds noise in the form of data that essentially "flips a coin" to provide an input. The collecting organization then knows that a percentage of the data is incorrect, but because the randomized data is balanced (roughly the same amount of "yes" and "no"), a similar trend will emerge. In Tai's family's case, perhaps sometimes Tai's child's data is recorded as is, other times Tai's child appears to access the Internet at 3 A.M. or 2 P.M. The addition of incorrect data in the child's profile can potentially prevent someone accessing the data from determining that the Internet user is indeed a child. Of course, using differential privacy to reduce identifiability does not alleviate required activities under child-specific privacy laws. *See* Figure 9.4 for a description of differential privacy.

Figure 9.4 Differential Privacy

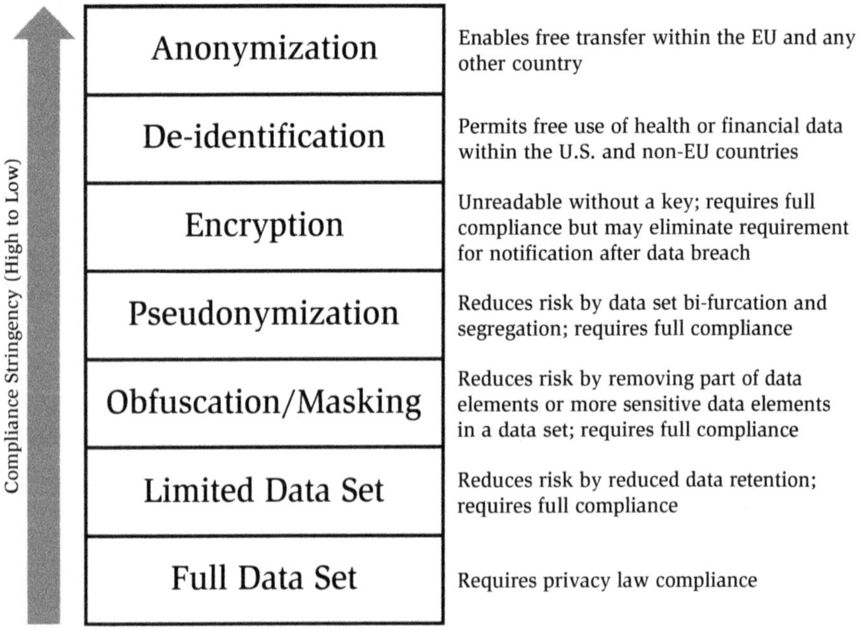

Differential privacy relies on strong statistical models and is best for organizations where approximation of aggregate information is sufficient for decision-making and substantial data volumes exist. Where individual record integrity is very important, yet data must be rendered non-identifiable in some way to exchange or transfer data, other options like de-identification or anonymization may provide a better option.

§9.03 CRYPTOGRAPHY

Cryptography is the final secrecy principle and also the most complex. The science of cryptography started with a simple concept: make messages and other information unreadable to enemies and readable to friends. The most basic cryptography started with a *private key cipher* when Julius Caesar used a *cipher* or code to transfer secret messages to be *deciphered* or decoded by the intended recipient, using the same cipher to decipher the message as was used to create the secret message. This cipher is still known as the Caesar cipher, wherein each letter in the alphabet ties to another letter in the alphabet with a prescribed shift (e.g., A is D, and so forth). Since Caesar's time, cryptography has evolved to a much more technical endeavor, but the basic concept of a cipher and a secret message are the basis of all cryptographic communications.

The word *encryption* represents the activity of converting plain-text data to encrypted, unreadable data using a cipher. A cipher today is represented by calculation mechanism, or an *algorithm.* A string of data called an *encryption key* or *cryptographic key* ("key") is used with the algorithm to create encrypted (enciphered) data. Encrypted data, if accessed, prevents an unauthorized individual who does not have the key from deciphering the underlying data. *Public encryption keys* are visible to any machine connecting to a machine with a Public encryption key. A Public Key Infrastructure (PKI) manages creation of digital certificates and procedures governing use, storage, and distribution of public keys. *Private encryption keys*, in contrast, require protection to retain their secrecy both when stored and when transferred to prevent disclosure or tampering.

Encryption can safeguard integrity, prove authenticity, and ensures secrecy. All of these security concepts depend heavily on both: (1) how difficult it is to break the encryption algorithm and (2) key management procedures, which may be strong or weak. Keys are named according to whether the key is providing authentication, encryption, or key transport (moving a key from one machine to another). Single-session or *ephemeral keys* are used once, while organizations may use *static keys* for longer periods of time. To better understand encryption's relationship to other secrecy approaches, *see* Figure 9.5 for a model of identifiability that includes the concepts previously discussed in relation to encryption.

Figure 9.5 Identifiability Model

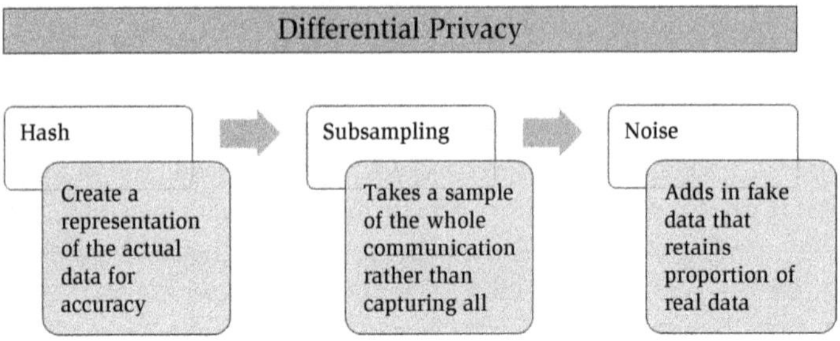

Encryption protocols are named methods using specific algorithms for encrypting data during transfer (in transmission) and in storage. To effectively manage data confidentiality and ensure secrecy, organizations must encrypt data in transmission and in storage, based on data sensitivity and risk of misuse. For data to be usable, data should be encrypted when not in use and decrypted (or plain text) when being used. To facilitate encryption and decryption, encryption keys should exist where organizations desire these activities, which means keys must be deployed to various clients, servers, and locations.

Encryption protects data insofar as it is not efficient to break. Most criminals, for example, would not spend two hundred years to access data. For this reason, organizations must balance efficiency considerations, encryption protocol performance, data sensitivity, and desirability of data compromise when deciding whether to use encryption and the strength of protocol to be used. Encryption protocols can use different types of algorithms to encrypt data: *block ciphers* and *stream ciphers*. Block ciphers encrypt data in "rounds" through repetition based on the key length. The strongest block ciphers encrypt key lengths of 256 bits. Stream ciphers use a *keystream* or a pseudo-random digit stream

Because encryption protocols use different cipher types, methods, and *bit strength* (numerical key lengths), it is not immediately evident which protocols protect data against compromise. It should not be assumed that simply because a cipher has a larger bit strength, that it is harder to break. However, longer bit length for the same encryption protocol generally makes the protocol more secure to some extent.

Symmetric encryption uses a common key for both plain text encryption and cipher text decryption in a more advanced version of the Caesar code. *Plain text* is text that is plainly readable, while *cipher text* is text as it reads after a key has encrypted it. When both parties have the same key, encryption and decryption processes may prove relatively efficient, but key management can pose challenges. Key management requires distribution and rotation of keys; distributing a new key to a remote party can prove challenging

Symmetric encryption usually refers to encryption in transmission, or protecting data when it transfers between machines, such as server to server or client to server. The most common symmetric encryption types are the Data Encryption Standard (DES) and Advanced Encryption Standard (AES). At the time of writing, 3DES, the most advanced of DES standards, is no longer a preferred encryption standard, superseded by AES protocols, notably 128-bit encryption (which is still used) and 256-bit encryption, which is the strongest symmetric encryption option today. Organizations typically use symmetric encryption for large stored data sets, such as encrypting all of the contents of a laptop or a database. *See* Figure 9.6 for an example of symmetric encryption.

Figure 9.6 Symmetric Encryption

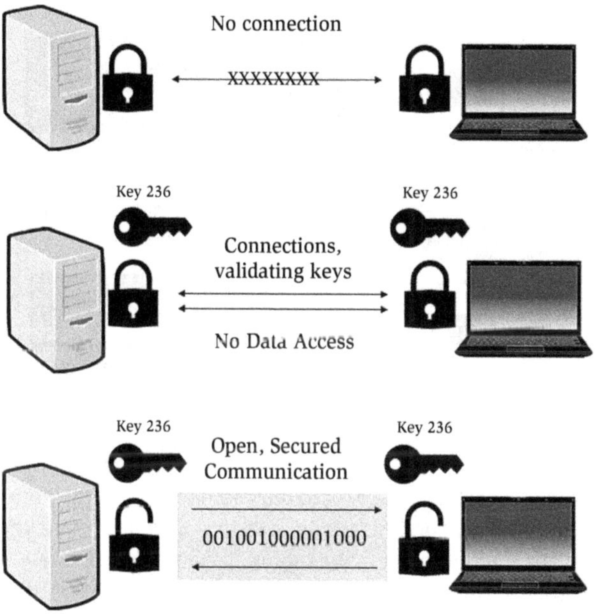

Asymmetric encryption, or public key encryption, uses two keys to facilitate encryption of plain text: a public key that is openly shared and a private key that is hidden. As described in relation to authentication, asymmetric encryption provides both authenticity and encryption. *See* Figure 9.7 for an example of asymmetric encryption. Asymmetric encryption generally provides a higher level of security than symmetric encryption but works better for shorter message encryption.

Figure 9.7 Asymmetric Encryption

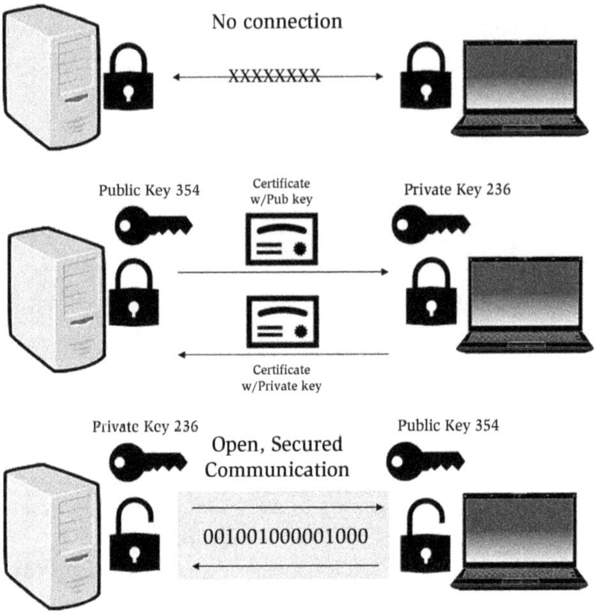

Major challenges exist for all encryption protocols, especially symmetric encryption: (1) key distribution, (2) key storage, (3) key rotation, and (4) key complexity are often culprits for poor organizational execution, yet they dramatically affect the success of encryption protocols. First, organizations need to send appropriate keys to locations where encryption and decryption activities should occur. Unfortunately, an encryption key is an incredibly sensitive piece of information and it may be impossible or undesirable to physically load an encryption key onto every device. Next, organizations must store keys using a method that enables easy key retrieval, yet secures the key and prevents only but the most privileged users, such as a *key manager* (often one or two individuals only) to access encryption keys. Further, ephemeral keys require frequent, automated rotation, whereas static keys require less frequent, more calculated rotation. Static key rotation can affect system function when systems depend on the current static key to function properly and securely. Resources like the Online Web Application Security Project (OWASP), an international association, offer excellent resources for a variety of security topics, including encryption.[207]

Key distribution requires strong encryption key transfer processes. Keys can be individually loaded onto devices, but this practice makes key rotation very difficult, unless machines are not connected to the organizational intranet or Internet. Instead,

207. Online Web Application Security Project, *Key Management Cheat Sheet* (June 6, 2016), https://www.owasp.org/index.php/Key_Management_Cheat_Sheet. OWASP also produces an excellent Vulnerability Top 10 annually or more frequently, which helps development teams and vulnerability management teams described in Chapters 11 and 12 better manage risk.

organizations usually distribute static encryption keys using strong encryption. One good method for distributing static encryption keys is through an asymmetric encryption protocol. The *Diffie-Hellman key exchange* uses ephemeral, one-time key exchange, through a strong encryption protocol like Transport Level Security (TLS) version 1.2 (version providing strong encryption at the time of writing). TLS 1.2 is the current security standard for transport over the open Web, accepted by multiple best practices. RSA and *elliptical curve encryption* also provide asymmetric data encryption.

Key storage requires a combination of strong encryption of keys at rest, including storage in a *cryptographic vault*, or physically segregated/isolated portion of the machine, and by encryption keys that are at least as complex as the key to be protected. Key rotation also can cause challenges for organizations. Strong security practices require key rotation, because over time key information can leak unauthorized persons. Rotation minimizes the risk of leaks by periodically selecting and implementing a new key. However, rotation requires: (1) knowledge of key location, (2) systems that can accommodate or automate key rotation, (3) understanding of architecture and technical dependencies, and (4) appropriately complex and randomized key generation. Many organizations that have encryption installed may not know where the key itself is stored. If an individual cannot identify the key storage location, rotation may be impossible. Further, some *legacy systems* (less modern systems may organizations still have) that accommodate encryption do not permit key rotation (have hard-coded keys) or require the highly manual process of changing keys one at a time, making key rotation quite difficult to manage.

One of the biggest challenges for key rotation involves change management considerations connected to system architecture. Because certain technologies connect and depend on other technologies within a given system, changes to one technology, e.g., a server encryption key change, can affect downstream systems, leading to operational impacts and service interruptions. For this reason, password rotation can prove challenging for complex and high-availability systems. Change management will be discussed in more detail in Chapter 11.

Encryption keys must be appropriately complex and not predictable by a would-be attacker. Encryption key complexity is determined by bit length, key rotation frequency, and degree to which key generation is randomized. Encryption keys that are not randomly generated or are generated by substandard technology require little effort to determine the key, making strong encryption protocols nearly useless. As a general rule, encryption key length should be at least as long as the bit strength of the encryption protocol: for example, AES 256 would require a 256-bit encryption key. For some encryption protocols, however, much longer keys may be required.

Randomization in key generation applies to both public keys and private keys. Public keys are created by selection of sufficiently large, random prime numbers, which are multiplied and kept secret (prime numbers, when multiplied and sufficiently large are incredibly difficult to guess). Organizations should randomly generate private keys, rather than rotate between a list of limited keys, for obvious reasons, such as compromise of the key list or predictability of key selection. Unfortunately, creating randomly generated, regularly rotated, sufficiently complex keys is quite difficult, yet these practices are integral to effective encryption.

Organizations must take great care in both key management techniques and encryption protocols selected or applying encryption may offer little to no protection at all. Because encryption provides a means for dramatically reducing potential exposure and invokes encryption safe harbors in some countries (reducing cost for expending resources notifying individuals after a data breach), organizations should strongly consider developing or reviewing encryption programs.

§9.04 IMPLEMENTING ENCRYPTION SOLUTIONS: DATA AT REST (STORAGE)

For systems with highly proprietary information or sensitive personal information, organizations should encrypt data at each of the OSI layers, both during transmission and in storage. Organizations designing system architecture will need to plan across technologies to ensure that authorized users can decrypt data when needed and encrypt data at all other times. Many encryption solutions work for specific technologies, but may require broader encryption planning to ensure no gaps exist that could be exploited. Security architects, or technical system architects focusing on security, may best develop these plans.

Organizations often use full disk encryption (FDE) for clients, especially traveling devices likely to be stolen. FDE encrypts the entire hard drive to prevent access to any data on the computer without appropriate credentials. In FDE, data is encrypted as it is created—this means that if a device is lost or stolen, the entire client's data is inaccessible.

Servers and non-laptop clients frequently use a version of AES to encrypt stored data (*data at rest*). Non-laptop clients, including mobile devices and IoT rely on manufacturer-selected encryption technologies. Many low-cost devices, such as value mobile devices and IoT, do not include encryption technologies, as these technologies tend to be quite expensive. When organizations purchase mobile devices for personnel use, future strategy should be considered, especially whether these devices support operations that provide access to, collect, process, or store personal information or SPI of any data subject.

IoT devices present a different challenge: organizations may purchase devices from a manufacturer for secondary sale, such as a heart-rate monitor that a patient will use. In this case, organizations may have an obligation to ensure the device sold has enabled adequate security controls, as a contract for sale likely exists between the business customer and the organization. If IoT devices do not adequately protect data, the organization will likely face legal action for exposed data infringing data subject rights.

Commonly, organizations must determine their encryption approach for handling large volumes of data, as these data potentially pose risk to the organization or to data subjects. When organizations purchase servers (or rent server space from a cloud provider), servers include the option for encryption technology as an "add-on" to the purchase. It is critical for organizations to remember to ask questions during the procurement process to ensure that quoted prices include encryption appropriate for the data classification of data processed and stored on the server.

Databases residing on servers also require encryption under some circumstances. Organizations implement *database encryption* in a variety of ways, such as for the entire database as a whole or for specific columns in a database, Cell Level Encryption (CLE). CLE often can perform faster because not all database queries to return data from the database require decryption and checking of authorization to view such data, but it requires more manual effort. This effort translates to better key management. However, in other circumstances, full database encryption provides more reliable protection, in case sensitive information could be stored in another cell intentionally, or by accident. Most organizations managing large collections of sensitive data (bulk encryption) prefer Transparent Data Encryption (TDE) for this reason. TDE applies encryption as data inputs and even encrypts backup copies. *See* Figure 9.8 for a summary diagram of machines requiring data in storage.

Figure 9.8 Client-Server Encryption in Storage

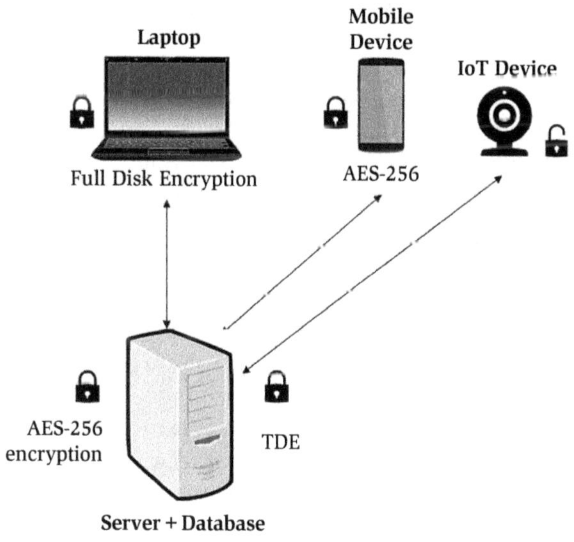

The risks associated with storing highly sensitive data include not only data exposure to malicious insiders or external parties, but also exposure to unauthorized parties, such as those in another organization. Some database solutions, as architected, store multiple customers' data sets within the same database. Organizations may prefer more control and separation by requiring data to be encrypted using a different encryption key than that used for other organizations as an additional level of protection.

Organizations required to segregate data from one customer and another, or segregate highly sensitive data from less sensitive data, may desire to employ *physical segregation* or *logical data segregation*. Physical segregation separates data sources into different self-contained database instances or to a different server altogether, while logical segregation separates access to data within a database, using identification and authorization technologies. Cloud implementations (SaaS, Platform as a Service [PaaS], Infrastructure as a Service [IaaS], database storage), providers use *multi-tenant architecture*, or shared space within a common physical server. Some providers extend this to shared databases, as well.

Logical data segregation within a common database segregates by having different user IDs, passwords, and back-end access controls that manage authorization to view only data from the user's organization. This allows a SaaS provider, for example, to easily manage one or a limited set of resources and provide timely support. Although logical data segregation both costs less and provides security controls, it can also provide a single point of failure and important target for attackers, especially with sensitive data. Primary concerns include poor identification, authorization, and authentication mechanisms wherein an unauthorized user can compromise multiple organizations' worth of data at one time. Further, encryption controls also apply to the database as an entirety, if organizations use multi-tenant architecture and TDE.

Data segregation approaches depend on four factors: (1) laws or industry requirements specifying data segregation, including whether logical segregation is sufficient, (2) the degree of control desired and security aptitude an organization has, (3) risk management concerns for data sensitivity (information classification), and (4) cost and available resources. First, laws and industry standards may require segregation to some extent in order to minimize misuse or fraud. Data isolation laws in Norway, the U.S. Sarbanes-Oxley Act, and PCI-DSS certification (described in Chapter 11) require data segregation. However, organizations leveraging cloud providers should also insist on some degree of data segregation to minimize potential exposure to other cloud customers.

§9.05 IMPLEMENTING ENCRYPTION SOLUTIONS: DATA IN TRANSIT (TRANSFER/TRANSMISSION)

A variety of encryption methodologies and solutions exist for data in transit from data transmitted over a network to data transmitted between Web applications, Websites, software, and servers receiving them. As previously discussed, typically data in transit uses asymmetric encryption involving a public and a private key. The first and most common asymmetric encryption is through a wireless connection.

Wi-Fi Protected Access (WPA2) currently provides industry-acceptable encryption for wireless connectivity, first introduced in 2006. Unfortunately, older versions of wireless Internet, such as Wired Equivalent Privacy (WEP) and WPA do not offer adequate protection for wireless transmissions. WAPs, or wireless routers, connect either directly to cable feeds or non-Wireless routers and enforce the appropriate encryption standard for data to be transmitted from a client over the Internet or within the home network. If a user on a client device attempts to connect to a wireless connection, the WAP should require a minimum level of encryption based on its internal policy. Some WAP used in the home still default to WEP, so users installing these routers should consider configuring to WPA2. When the client first connects, the WAP and the client device negotiate the agreed-upon encryption protocol to use. Then, the user enters a passcode associated with the router when first configured. Organizations that have network administrators generally configure wireless networks to approve traffic based on the identity of the device and enterprise log-in, such as when personnel log into a laptop.

When individual clients access the Internet or intranet, clients may connect to either another client (peer to peer, PTP) or to a server. End-to-end encryption (E2EE) provides secure data transmission between clients (PTP). Unlike most encryption technologies that encrypt communication between a client and a server, and a server and a client to effectively transmit a message between two clients, E2EE secures the transmission from client to client without needing to negotiate encryption keys between a client and the server. E2EE is generally considered a better encryption approach for client to client messages, because it has fewer points of encryption/decryption and key negotiation, making clients using E2EE less vulnerable to a Man-in-the-Middle Attack (described in Chapter 13). Examples of E2EE usage include some PTP messaging systems like Skype or Snapchat, Point-to-Point Encryption (P2PE), Internet Protocol Security (IPSec), and Transport Layer Security (TLS).

PTP messaging systems use E2EE for encrypted communication, which has challenged law enforcement and other government entities in a variety of countries. PTP systems allow for encrypted communication between two clients, making it tremendously difficult for a third party to access the communication at any point. This has encouraged criminals involved in terrorism or other illegal activities to share messages, prompting government entities to seek access to this technology, such as requesting an encryption key. Organizations operating services that promise secure communication resist providing encryption keys to government entities both for the reputation of services provided, but also because many organizations do not trust the government to responsibly manage the key.

P2PE provides a slightly different model. Developed to comply with PCI-DSS industry requirements for payment card processing (described in Chapter 11), P2PE completely removes a merchant receiving funds from seeing any payment information. Instead, P2PE simply sends payment card data from the point of entry, such as a petrol pump, to the bank approving payment via a third-party payment processor. The merchant getting paid for petrol, then, receives the funds in their bank account without ever having access to or seeing payment card data. This model also dramatically reduces the probability of data breach or other compromise.

IPSec also provides encryption between two clients over an open Internet network connection. IPSec is a multi-purpose framework that enables authentication, encryption, and even packet filtering to improve data integrity. IPSec is extremely flexible, providing a backbone for VPN technologies using standard data *encapsulation* described earlier in relation to asymmetric encryption (IPSec uses both asymmetric and symmetric encryption). Encapsulation ensures that a connection is made before data is transmitted, making all data within the capsule unreadable to attackers intercepting the transmission. IPSec can help to prevent Denial of Service attacks and credential theft.

TLS is perhaps the most commonly used encryption for Web traffic and is referenced by the HTTPS in a Website URL. TLS works much the same way as the other E2EE, except it uses a combination of symmetric encryption for encrypting data and asymmetric encryption for authentication purposes. Secure Sockets Layer, or SSL, preceded newer versions of TLS (at the time of writing, as high as TLS 1.3, with TLS 1.2 acceptable). However, SSL v3 vulnerabilities were exposed by the Poodle attack, which made it no longer reliable, and TLS 1.0 was exposed by BEAST).[208] Today, some practitioners still use the term SSL to mean newer versions of TLS, but some Websites and Web applications do still use SSL v3, so attorneys and practitioners inquiring about encryption protocols used should ensure that a site uses TLS 1.2 + when transferring personal information.

Organizations also transmit information via software on clients and servers. Typically, information transferred using software involves file transfer. File transfer protocols include Pretty Good Privacy (PGP), often used for e-mail, FTP or its secured version, SSH File Transfer Protocol (SFTP) used for ad-hoc file transfer between a client and a server, or between servers, and MFT used for repeat file transfers.

PGP was developed in 1991 by Philip Zimmermann, and it has quickly become the default file transfer for e-mail. PGP uses a model similar to the public-key system, as is found in asymmetric encryption, by encrypting messages using a public key but decrypting messages using a private key. Email requires fast transmission time, so Zimmerman created a novel model: use a shorter key to encrypt the e-mail, but use a longer key to encrypt the key. Therefore, the encryption key has extra protection and can be quickly decrypted, yet the message can also enjoy the same protection of a longer key. The two versions of PGP used today are RSA (proprietary) and Diffie-Hellman (open source).

FTP is one of the oldest and most reliable file transfer mechanisms, dating back to the first Internet file transfers and written by Abhay Bhushan in 1971. Organizations still use FTP today, but it does not provide encrypted transmission for sensitive data. SFTP provides the additional encryption-based security. Although organizations often use SFTP primarily for file transfers outside of an organization, organizations should also consider using SFTP over the intranet for SPI to protect SPI from malicious insiders. MFT provides an alternative to SFTP by accommodating multiple encryption methods and automating routine file transfer, amongst many other benefits. MFT is available as software and integrates with existing applications using an Application Programming Interface (API).[209]

208. Additional recent vulnerabilities of note included CRIME and Heartbleed. Perhaps because Websites and Web applications transfer a substantial amount of traffic and are open to anyone on the Internet, Website and Web application encryption is tested frequently. For this reason, organizations should ensure vulnerability management programs effectively monitor for new vulnerabilities (discussed in Chapter 12).

209. APIs are tremendously powerful tools to ensure that applications can communicate with each other. Mobile apps, in particular, make use of *open APIs*, or APIs that are available for anyone to use. This is how mobile apps can integrate data feeds from multiple sources into one app. APIs facilitate data transfer between applications that can benefit from the same data sources.

The most interesting new encryption model, especially for financial technology (FinTech) involves the blockchain. The *blockchain* is a model for data transfer that simultaneously provides identification, authentication, encryption, as well as full audit logs of transfers (financial records) completed. Because the blockchain ensures a high degree of integrity through authentication and provides a thorough transaction record, blockchain originally was created to manage cryptocurrencies like Bitcoin.[210] However, blockchain could provide substantial support for financial record-keeping (ledger management), though certainly other uses could emerge. Unlike standard record-keeping, blockchain does not require a central function to maintain records, which alleviates source of truth issues when multiple parties are transferring data.

The list of protocols described in this chapter illustrates the wide variety of protocols exist for operationalizing encryption, yet is by no means complete. By no means exhaustive, Table 9.6 summarizes these protocols for easy review and reference.

Table 9.6 Encryption Protocols (In Storage and Transit)

Name	*Description*	*Protects Data*	*Typically Used for*
WPA2	Secure wireless transmission over the internal network	Transmission	WAPs, both at home and at an organization
AES 128, AES-256	Symmetric encryption for storage	In storage	Servers, mobile devices, IoT (if available)
FDE	All information stored on a hard drive is encrypted, including software and instructions	In storage	Encrypting laptops, small client devices
TDE	Encrypts an entire database completely and backups automatically	In storage	Encrypting databases
CDE	Encrypts columns within a database and allows for greater encryption key control	In storage	Encrypting cells within a database (column-level)
End-to-end encryption	Encrypts messages completely between clients, end-to-end	Transmission	Multiple uses as described in IPSec, P2PE, TLS
P2PE	Encrypts payment card information without disclosing data to merchant systems	Transmission	Payment processing
IPSec	Encrypts traffic by encapsulation	Transmission	Multiple uses, often in VPN
TLS	Encrypts traffic from Website or Web application to the server	Transmission	Web app/Website security

210. For more details on cryptocurrencies and bitcoin, see Chapter 13.

Name	*Description*	*Protects Data*	*Typically Used for*
PGP	Encrypts files twice first the file, then the encryption key	Transmission	Email
FTP	Open file transfer protocol, no security, on-demand transfer	Transmission	Internal transfers for low-risk data
SFTP	Uses a secure channel (SSH) to securely transfer files, on-demand	Transmission	Software to server, server to server
MFT	Supports multiple transfer protocols, transfers over intranet and Internet, automates file transfer	Transmission	Multiple uses, can leverage APIs

§9.06 NETWORK SECURITY CONTROLS

Network security controls include a variety of specialized measures that defend a network's perimeter, detect unauthorized activity, and manage access to the network. The most basic network security controls include perimeter controls that manage traffic to and from the internal network. The goal of *network perimeter controls* is to separate the open Internet from the internal trusted network. Modern networks, however, complicate a clean perimeter by connecting to external sources, such as cloud storage sites, SaaS providers, and Internet sites. Common network perimeter controls include firewalls and de-militarized zones (DMZ), as described in Chapter 8, Network Access Controls (NAC), and passive and active monitoring tools.

NAC implement access control procedures with respect to the network, for example validating where users and clients can traverse on a network. Similar to client end point security, NAC policies enforce how a user and device may behave. For example, organizations that permit personnel to bring their personal mobile devices to work and access organizational resources likely would not want those same mobile devices (which may not be secure) accessing the entire organization's intranet. Instead, mobile devices likely can connect to a dedicated WAN, which permits Internet access but prevents internal access to the LAN. NAC reflect how the network itself is structured in that some NAC limit certain users and clients to a portion of the network, while other high availability resources, such as systems supporting Point of Sale (POS) systems at a large retailer, are dedicated to another part of the network. Structuring a network this way matches network performance to organizational needs. NAC, firewalls, and DMZ can support high performance networking.

From a security perspective, network segmentation ("zoning") may also reduce the impact of an incident or data breach by structurally preventing access to some zones. PCI-DSS industry standards, for example, require network segmentation of the systems processing payment card data. Organizations should strongly consider segmenting resources that process or transfer highly sensitive data and using strong NAC for that network segment.

In addition to strong NAC, organizations should monitor activities on the network regularly, both actively and passively. For example, Intrusion Detection Systems (IDS) identify events as they occur, adding to a broader picture provided by logging and monitoring controls, while Intrusion Prevention Systems (IPS) actively defend internal systems by blocking certain types of requests. These two functions elevate standard firewall functions substantially by providing substantially more sophisticated network monitoring. IDS and IPS can also send information to a common incident response tool for review (described in Chapter 13).

Logging controls ensure that information about the individual or computer that connected to an information resource is captured, including log-in time, active time, resources viewed, resources edited, and resources copied. This information helps an incident response manager and forensic investigator piece together what may have happened leading to unauthorized use, information exposure, business interruption, or data breach. Monitoring controls enable an organization to place rules and flags in place on a particular system, to automatically send information to a SIEM or incident response capability in the organization when certain situations occur (e.g., an employee logging on from an IP address in Russia at 2 AM PDT). An incident response capability, then, can dig into the details to determine what impact, if any, has occurred. Both logging and monitoring controls provide essential information to determine exactly what occurred and help an insurance company processing a claim to clearly understand where recovery services, independent forensic investigators, breach notification, or lawsuit-related services might be needed.

Networks may also make use of honeypots. *Honeypots* are resources on the internal network, usually a server or multiple servers, designed to attract attackers. Organizations may install honeypots to understand how attackers might gain access to the system, to gain information about attackers, or to stop hackers before they access real organizational resources. Honeypots can be controversial from a legal perspective. When organizations place honeypots outside of the network, it can be difficult to illustrate a form of trespass, especially criminal trespass, and honeypots can be viewed as entrapment in some jurisdictions. For jurisdictions with stronger criminal penalties, such as the United States, simply accessing the organization's network could be classified as a criminal act, so honeypots may prove less concerning for these jurisdictions.

Chapter 10
Cybersecurity Statutory Obligations

Cybersecurity law is a new and emerging area of the law that has at once drawn substantial interest and attention, yet has also caused organizational confusion through inexact requirements. Countries usually avoid incorporating specific requirements in each law because cybersecurity technologies may quickly change, setting a lower threshold than industry standards. Further, the legal field has not yet determined what cybersecurity measures are legally reasonable. Many laws increasingly identify inexact, general requirements, then provide either guidelines or conduct audits for greater definition. For this reason, Chapter 9 provided detailed technical measures generally accepted as *reasonable* in cybersecurity, and Chapters 11–13 introduce reasonable administrative measures.

Cybersecurity laws fall into three major legislation types: (1) information privacy laws including cybersecurity requirements by reference, (2) cybersecurity requirements for business, and (3) cybersecurity activities for the government. This chapter will primarily discuss types one and two.[211] Nearly all omnibus information privacy laws previously discussed in Chapters 1-5 require administrative and technical measures (measures) to protect personal information, and a few also require physical measures.[212]

Although physical measures are not discussed within this book, physical measures often include key card access, door locks, security personnel, a visitor log, CCTV (capturing video only), and procedures for limiting access to high sensitivity storage areas, such as server rooms. Other physical measures apply specifically to data centers, such as enhanced physical access, locked cages, and heating and cooling mechanisms, amongst many specialized requirements. Physical measures are usually designed by

---

211. For an excellent list of government cybersecurity strategy around the world, see NATO Cooperative Cyber Defence Centre of Excellence, *Cyber Security Strategy Documents* (3 Aug. 2015), https://ccdcoe.org/strategies-policies.html.
212. Laws may also reference "organizational" measures. Generally, this requirement is fulfilled by the same processed as administrative measures.

physical security teams, but they provide important protection against social engineering and other types of environmental interruptions and digital attacks.

§10.01 INFORMATION PRIVACY LAWS WITH CYBERSECURITY REQUIREMENTS

In addition to privacy obligations and data transfer limitations, countries increasingly require security controls surrounding consumer personal information. As most information privacy laws reference "reasonable" technical and administrative measures, these measures should reflect known best practices. While the United States has increased volume of cybersecurity laws in the United States, the Asia-Pacific (APAC) region has made considerable strides to make cybersecurity a key consideration for industry.[213]

Existing information privacy laws include cybersecurity-related considerations in the administrative, technical, and physical measures typical to most information privacy laws. These measures correspond to cybersecurity activities within an organization. *See* Table 10.1 for a mapping of cybersecurity measures with these categories. Administrative measures will be discussed in more detail in Chapters 11–13.

Table 10.1 Examples of Administrative and Technical Measures

Discipline	*Administrative Measures*	*Technical Measures*
Network Security	Network access control review, firewall rule management, network topology planning	Network access controls, intrusion detection systems, intrusion prevention systems, firewalls, DMZ, network segregation
Identity and Access Management	Access management reviews, authorization management, administrative access check-out process, granting access/terminating access review processes	Authentication methodologies, certificate management, hashing + salt algorithms, biometrics, captcha, username/password management, password requirements
Data Minimization and Obfuscation	De-identification, anonymization procedures	Differential privacy, obfuscation, masking

213. For a comprehensive compendium of E-Commerce legislation (including cybersecurity laws), see United Nations Conference on Trade and Development, *Summary of Adoption of E-Commerce Legislation Worldwide* (6 Jan. 2017), http://unctad.org/en/Pages/DTL/STI_and_ICTs/ICT4D-Legislation/eCom-Global-Legislation.aspx.

Discipline	*Administrative Measures*	*Technical Measures*
Encryption	Encryption procedures, key rotation procedures, key storage procedures	Encryption protocols (storage/transit), preferred algorithms, Public Key Infrastructure, key exchange (public, private), key complexity
Secure Development Lifecycle	Functional and non-functional security requirement build, testing procedures, change management	Security architecture planning code reviews, security testing
Incident Response and Data Breach	SIEM tool configuration, incident response procedures, incident response plan, incident response team, communication planning	Configurations for logging/monitoring systems, forensic analysis

Information Privacy laws also include other legal requirements that necessitate cybersecurity measures, such as data accuracy, data integrity, data segregation, data access, and data deletion. Data accuracy requires that data collected match actual events and that data is maintained as accurate after the point of collection. Data accuracy reflects many cybersecurity practices, but some of the most critical include: Access and Identity Management (AIM) processes and validation checks. AIM focuses on implementing tools and techniques to ensure an individual's identity and machine are validated and authenticated before permitting connectivity to a system handling data that requires a high degree of accuracy (such as health, banking, or credit data). Further, access provisioning processes ensure that when organizations grant access, it is limited to the fewest number of users (Least User Access (LUA)).

Accuracy checks often include data validation, where a system matches the user's input to an expected format; for example, data of birth should only include numbers of an expected format. Other types of input validation compare input values against expected ranges, which may apply across a population or for an individual, such as blood glucose levels or expected deposit value. Accuracy checks outside AIM processes usually aim to reduce human mistakes in the data entry process. Accuracy checks also apply during the application or software development lifecycle (described in Chapter 12), such as testing activities and change management processes, which ensure systems can also ensure accuracy.

Data integrity usually involves technical measures to ensure data is not changed downstream, while in storage, or in transfer. Similar to accuracy, AIM processes manage legitimate access by terminating unverified connections and ensuring only authenticated users access the system. Organizations use FIM or a similar technology to ensure that data transferred has not been altered during that transfer, either changing data or deleting data.

Data segregation (or data isolation) focuses on network topology, or the layout of a network, and the structure of servers and databases storing data. For some laws, segregation and isolation reduce the probability of unauthorized access by protecting part of a network or restricting access to the most sensitive data. Although strong AIM practices, properly implemented, usually protect data from unauthorized access mistakes or attacks, segregation additionally ensures that in the event data is compromised, the potential exposure or loss is reduced.

Yosef manages financial accounts for UBAK banking. A customer came into the office to talk about a new loan, and Yosef was still logged into the UBAK customer database, where he has rights to see his own customers. Yosef accidentally hit the keyboard, deleting some customer information and replacing it with "XYZ$MNDFIS" from bumping his keyboard. Assuming appropriate cybersecurity measures were implemented, the following would protect the customer's information from being inaccurate or unavailable:

- Yosef's authorization only allows him to edit his own customers' files, which reduces broad impact when a mistake occurs.
- Yosef can only change data that is not part of a financial record the bank uses for government disclosures, so the mistake is likely to occur for something else, such as contact information.
- Yosef's customer record is part of a segmented portion of a database, and only that portion can be viewed by Yosef and his colleagues at their bank's branch location, so even if Yosef has broad rights, he cannot remove data from another branch.

Rights to access, correction, transfer, and erasure also require cybersecurity and IT procedures to ensure these rights. The rights to access and correction, for example, require that an organization: (1) understand which records have been designated sources of truth and (2) have designed a system that enables efficient correction of all primary record copies. Organizations develop data inventories to understand data location within systems, but often these inventories do not accurately identify primary records and relationships between sources of truth and receiving systems. Instead, architects should determine the appropriate location for primary records and architect systems that flow from primary record-keeping systems to ensure that the most updated information resides in the primary record (and updates cascade to other systems).

Organizations should not only understand cybersecurity best practices, but should also understand cybersecurity conventions within the organization's industry. Although no information privacy law specifies, in detail, industry-specific administrative and technical measures, organizations should consider industry conventions when designing cybersecurity programs.

§10.02 APAC CYBERSECURITY LAW

Although information privacy laws usually require less specific "reasonable administrative and technical measures," some country laws have passed cybersecurity-specific laws or portions of information privacy laws specifically dedicated to cybersecurity. In the Asia-Pacific region, countries have developed relatively mature cybersecurity laws regulating private and public enterprises.[214]

[A] The Russian Federation

Although Russia has not passed any cybersecurity-specific laws, Russia's Federal Law on Personal Data (Federal Law) includes substantially more specific cybersecurity requirements than most omnibus laws. Data operators (operators) must appoint a Data Protection Officer, establish a data protection policy, and perform internal control reviews, such as risk assessments or audits, to ensure internal compliance with the data protection policy and associated rules. Operators must use certified methods to identify security threats, identify unauthorized access, adopt access rules, and maintain a data inventory to understand which media contain personal data. The Federal Law also requires that operators train employees on Federal Law legal requirements. Finally, Russia requires operators disclose their use or availability of encryption to data subjects within the privacy notice.

The Federal Law also requires operators to implement associated rules to prevent or detect a data breach and provide breach notification to data subjects, although an operator need not notify the Roskomnadzor. The Roskomanadzor, however, can investigate any complaints and fine operators for non-compliance with the Federal Law on Personal Data.

Outside of the Federal Law on Personal Data, multiple regulations apply to Russian data and personal information:

- Standard Requirements on Organizing and Providing Functioning of Cryptographic Facilities, Decree N 149/6/6-622 issued by the Federal Security Service of the Russian Federation on February 21, 2008
- Guidelines on Providing Protection for Personal Data When They are Automatically Processed, Decree N 149/54-144 issued by the Federal Security Service of the Russian Federation on February 21, 2008
- Order No. 416/489 of August 31, 2010, of the Federal Security Service and the Federal Service for Technical and Export Control of the Russian Federation *On Approval of the Requirements for Protecting Data in Public Information Systems*
- Order No. 21 of February 18, 2013, *On Approval of the Types and the Content of Organizational and Technical Measures for Personal Data Protection in the course of its Processing in Personal Data Information Systems*

A Decree is executed via presidential decree, and increasingly more often decrees apply to cybersecurity topics. For example, under Decree N 149/6/6-622, organizations must develop a threat model and apply neutralizing measures to manage threats in modeling, install encryption technologies using documentation and instructions, train

214. For a complete and routinely updated list of cyberlaw in the ASEAN region, see CYBER LAW ASIA, *Cyber Laws in Asia* (2017), http://cyberlawasia.com/cyber-laws-asia/.

operators of encryption equipment, identify violations of personal data protection, and draft opinions on such violations. For encryption technologies, organizations must keep confidential information regarding encryption keys, store primary and backup keys separately, follow appropriate key destruction techniques according to manufacturer instructions within a predefined time period. Operators must implement physical controls to store keys and encryption equipment.

The Russian government and independent hacking organizations have a reputation for advanced hacking methods. These organizations and government-sponsored organizations have increasingly demonstrated both an ability and an opportunity to engage in state-sponsored or other hacking activities. Organizations or their contractors often experience challenges when they attempt to *attribute*, or forensically determine who committed an act, so specific hacks will not be discussed here. Notable government-financed hacking organizations include Cozy Bear, Fancy Bear, APT28, and Cozy Duke.

[1] Passages of Note: Russian Federal Law

Chapter 4

Article 18

1. An operator shall be obliged, when processing data, to take or arrange for the taking of such legal, organizational and technical measures as are necessary to protect personal data against unlawful or accidental access to and destruction, alteration, blocking, copying, provision or dissemination of personal data and against other unlawful actions in relation to personal data.
   See Federal Tax Service Decree No. N MMB-7-4/959@ of the Russian Federation of 21 December 2011 concerning protection of personal data when they are processed in automated data systems of tax authorities.
2. The security of personal data shall be achieved, in particular:
   1) by identifying threats to the security of personal data while they are being processed in personal data filing systems;
   2) by applying such organizational and technical measures for ensuring the security of personal data while they are being processed in personal data filing systems as are necessary to meet the requirements relating to the protection of personal data which shall be fulfilled in order to ensure the levels of protection of personal data which are established by the Government of the Russian Federation;
   3) by applying means of data protection which have duly undergone conformity assessment procedures;
   4) by assessing the effectiveness of measures taken to ensure the security of personal data prior to the commissioning of a personal data filing system;
   5) by keeping records of media containing personal data;
   6) by detecting instances of unauthorized access to personal data and taking measures;
   7) by restoring personal data which have been modified or destroyed as a result of unauthorized access;
   8) by establishing rules for access to personal data being processed in a personal data filing system and providing for the registration and recording of all actions performed on personal data in a personal data filing system;

9) by monitoring measures taken to ensure the security of personal data and the level of protection of personal data filing systems.

3. The Government of the Russian Federation shall, taking into account potential damage to a data subject, the extent and content of personal data being processed, the type of activity in the context of which personal data are processed and the presence of threats to the security of personal data, establish:
   1) levels of protection for personal data while they are being processed in personal data filing systems based on threats to the security of those data;
   2) requirements relating to the protection of personal data while they are being processed in personal data filing systems which shall be met in order for the established levels of protection for personal data to be provided;
   3) requirements relating to physical media for the storage of biometric personal data and relating to technologies for the storage of such data outside personal data filing systems.
4. The composition and content of organizational and technical measures for ensuring the security of personal data while they are being processed in personal data filing systems which are necessary in order to fulfill the personal data protection requirements established by the Government of the Russian Federation in accordance with part 3 of this Article for each level of protection shall be established by the federal executive body in charge of security and the federal executive body in charge of technical counter-intelligence and technical protection of information within the limits of their powers.
5. Federal executive bodies which carry out functions involving the formulation of state policy and normative legal regulation in the designated sphere of activity, state government bodies of constituent entities of the Russian Federation, the Bank of Russia, bodies of state non-budgetary funds and other state bodies shall, within the limits of their powers, adopt normative legal acts in which they identify what threats to the security of personal data are present in connection with the processing of personal data in personal data filing systems used in particular types of activity, taking into account the content of personal data and the nature and methods of the processing of personal data.
6. In addition to the threats to the security of personal data which are identified in normative legal acts adopted in accordance with part 5 of this Article, associations, unions and other amalgamations of operators may issue decisions identifying further threats to the security of personal data which are present in connection with the processing of personal data in personal data filing systems used in particular types of activity by members of those associations, unions and other amalgamations of operators, taking into account the content of personal data and the nature and methods of the processing of personal data.
10. Biometric personal data may be used and stored outside personal data filing systems only on such physical data storage media and with the use of such storage technology as ensure the protection of those data against unlawful or accidental access, destruction, alteration, blocking, copying, provision and dissemination.
11. For the purposes of this Article, threats to the security of personal data shall be understood to mean the aggregate of conditions and factors which create a danger of unauthorized, including accidental, access to personal data, which may result in the destruction, alteration, blocking, copying, provision or dissemination of personal data or in other unlawful actions in connection with the processing of those personal data in a personal data filing system. The level of protection for personal data shall be understood to mean an aggregate

indicator reflecting the requirements which shall be met in order to neutralize identified threats to the security of personal data while they are being processed in personal data information systems.

[B] Indonesia

Indonesia has focused on information policy since 2008, when it passed the Law No. 11 of 2008 Concerning Electronic Information and Transactions primarily governing transactions (EIT).[215] In this law, Indonesia introduced expectations to "Business Entities" hosting an "Electronic System." Article 16 specified the obligations of business entities, some obligations referencing cybersecurity matters:

> (1) To the extent not provided otherwise by separate laws, any Electronic System Provider is required to operate Electronic Systems in compliance with the following minimal requirements:
> a. can redisplay Electronic Information and/or Electronic Records in their entirety in accordance with the retention period as provided for by Laws and Regulations;
> b. can protect the availability, entirety, authenticity, confidentiality, and accessibility of Electronic Information in the Provision of Electronic Systems.

The EIT also states that knowing and accessing electronic systems without authority by "breaching, hacking into, trespassing into, or breaking through security systems" is a prohibited and criminal act, except for research purposes.[216]

The Regulation Number 82 of 2012 Concerning Electronic System and Transaction Operation further requires security protection, including that the electronic system operator "shall ensure . . . the availability of information security agreement of services of Information Technology are used, and information security and internal communication tools are organized."[217] Further, the Regulation Number 82 requires management of secrecy, integrity, and availability of personal data and requires notification in writing when electronic system operators identify a "failure in the protection of confidential Personal Data." Part Seven details electronic system security and reference cybersecurity best practices.

215. Law No. 11 of 2008 Concerning Electronic Information and Transactions, translation available: http://www.bu.edu/bucflp/files/2012/01/Law-No.-11-Concerning-Electronic-Information-and-Transactions.pdf.
216. The research exception notated in the EIT is unique in comparison to the CFAA in the United States, which primarily relies on prosecutorial discretion, rather than a statutory exception.
217. Regulation Number 82 of 2012 Concerning Electronic System and Transaction Operation, translation available: http://www.flevin.com/id/lgso/translations/JICA%20Mirror/english/4902_PP_82_2012_e.html.

[1] Passages of Note: Regulation Number 82

Chapter II

Part Seven

Article 18

(1) The Electronic System Operator shall provide an audit trail record of all activities of the Electronic System Operation.
(2) Audit trail record as intended in paragraph (1) is used for purposes of monitoring, enforcement, dispute resolution, verification, testing, and other checking.

Article 19

Electronic System Operator shall secure the Electronic Systems components.

Article 20

(1) Electronic System Operator shall have and perform the procedures and structure for securing the Electronic Systems in avoiding disruption, failure, and loss.
(2) Electronic System Operator shall provide a security system that includes procedures and systems to prevent and solve the threats and attacks that cause disruption, failure, and loss.
(3) In case there is failure or disruption of system with seriously affected as a result of the actions of the other party to Electronic Systems, Electronic System Operator shall secure the data and immediately report at the first opportunity to the law enforcement officers or related Sector Supervisory and Regulatory Agency.
(4) Further provisions on the security system as intended in paragraph (2) are governed by Ministerial Regulation.

Article 21

Electronic System Operator shall redisplay Electronic Information and/or Electronic Documents completely in accordance with the format and retention period determined based on regulation.

Article 22

(1) Electronic System Operator shall maintain the confidentiality, integrity, authenticity, accessibility, availability, and traceability of the Electronic Information and/or Electronic Document in accordance with the provisions of the regulation.
(2) The Electronic Systems Operation purpose for Electronic Information and/or Electronic Document that are transferable, Electronic Information and/or Electronic Document must be unique and describe the acquisition and ownership.

Article 23

The Electronic System Operator shall ensure the proper functioning of Electronic Systems as it should, by keep on the interoperability and compatibility with the previous Electronic Systems and/or the related Electronic System.

Article 24

(1) The Electronic System Operator shall conduct training to Electronic Systems to Users.
(2) Training as intended in paragraph (1) at least on the rights, obligations and responsibilities of all parties involved, and the procedures for filing a complaint.

Article 25

Electronic System Operator shall submit information to the Electronic System User for at least:

a. Electronic System Operator identity;
b. objects in the transaction;
c. capability or safety of Electronic Systems;
d. procedures to use of the device;
e. terms of the contract;
f. procedures to reach an agreement; and
g. guarantee of the privacy and/or protection of Personal Data.

Article 26

(1) Electronic System Operator shall provide the features in accordance with the characteristics of the Electronic Systems are used.
(2) Features as intended in paragraph (1) at least in the form of facilities to:
    a. make corrections;
    b. cancel the order;
    c. give confirm or reconfirm;
    d. choose to continue or to stop carrying out the next activity;
    e. see the information are submitted in the form of contract or advertisement offers;
    f. check the status of success or failure of the transaction; and
    g. read the agreement before making a transaction.

Article 27

Electronic System Operator is obligated to protect its users and the public from harm caused by its operation of Electronic Systems.

Article 28

(1) Each person who works in the Electronic Systems Operation must secure and protect structure and infrastructures of Electronic Systems or information transmitted through the Electronic System.
(2) Electronic System Operator shall provide, teach, and train personnel in charge and responsible on the security and protection of structure and infrastructure of Electronic Systems.

Article 29

For the purposes of the criminal justice process, Electronic System Operator shall provide the information contained in Electronic Systems or information generated by the Electronic Systems on the legal request from investigators for certain crimes in accordance with the authority determined by regulation.

Article III

Part Two

Article 38

(1) In Electronic Agent Operation, Electronic Agent operator must consider the principles of:
   a. prudence;
   b. security and integration of Information Technology system;
   c. securing control over the Electronic Transactions activities;
   d. cost effectiveness and efficiency; and
   e. customer protection accordance with the provisions of regulation.
(2) Electronic Agent operator shall have and execute standard operating procedures that meet the user's data security control principles and Electronic Transaction.
(3) The user's data security control principles and Electronic Transactions as intended in paragraph (2) including:
   a. confidentiality;
   b. integrity;
   c. availability;
   d. authenticity;
   e. authorization; and
   f. non-repudiation.

Article 39

(1) Electronic Agent operator shall:
   a. test identity authenticity and check authorization of Electronic System User who conducting Electronic Transactions;
   b. have and implement policies and procedures to take action if there is indication of data theft;
   c. ensure control over the authorization and access right to the system, database, and application of Electronic Transactions;
   d. develop and implement methods and procedures to protect and/or keep the integrity of the data, records, and related information of Electronic Transactions;
   e. have and implement standards and controls over the use and protection of the data if the service provider has access to the data;
   f. have a business continuity plan include an effective contingency plan to ensure the availability of systems and Electronic Transaction services sustainable; and
   g. have procedures for handling unexpected events that quickly and appropriately to mitigate the impact of an incident, fraud, and failure of Electronic Systems.

Chapter V

Part One

Article 52

(1) Electronic Signature serves as an authentication and verification of:
a. Signer identity; and
b. the integrity and authenticity of Electronic Information.

(2) Electronic Signature in Electronic Transaction constitute approval Signer on Electronic Information and/or Electronic Document signed by the Electronic Signatures.
(3) In case of misuse of Electronic Signatures as intended in paragraph (2) by other parties who are not ligible, proof of abuse by the Electronic Signature is by Electronic System Operator.

Article 53

(1) Electronic Signature used in Electronic Transactions can be generated through a variety of procedures signing.
(2) Electronic Signatures as intended in paragraph (1) has valid force of law and the legal consequences if:
   a. Electronic Signature Creation Data relate only to Signer;
   b. Electronic Signature Creation Data during the signing process just to be in power Signer;
   c. any changes to the Electronic Signatures occurring after the time of the signing can be known;
   d. any changes to the Electronic Information associated with the Electronic Signature after signing time can be known;
   e. there is a certain way that is used to identify who is signer; and
   f. there is a certain way to indicate that the Signer has granted approval to the relevant Electronic Information.
(3) The provisions as intended in paragraph (2) d shall be applied if all Electronic Signatures are used to ensure the integrity of Electronic Information.

Part Five

Article 58

(1) Prior to use Electronic Signatures, Electronic Signatures Operator shall ensure identification of Signer by:
   a. Signer sends identity to the Electronic Signatures Operator;
   b. Signer registers to the Electronic Signatures Operator or Supporting Services; and
   c. If necessary, the Electronic Signature Operator may delegate signer data confidential identity to the other Electronic Signature Operator or Electronic Signature Supporting Service with the approval Signer.
(2) The mechanism used by the Electronic Signatures Operator for identity verification of Signer electronically is required to apply a combination of at least 2 (two) factors of authentication.
(3) The verification process of Electronic Information is signed can be done to check Electronic Signature Creation Data to track any changes in the data that was signed.

Chapter VI

Part One

Article 59

(1) The Electronic System for public services must have an Electronic Certificate.
(2) Electronic System Operator for non public service must have an Electronic Certificate.
(3) Electronic System Operator and Users other than as intended in paragraphs (1) and (2) may have a Electronic Certificate issued by the electronic certification operator.

(4) To have an Electronic Certificate, Electronic System Operator and Users must apply to the electronic certification operator.
(5) Further provisions on the procedure to have the Electronic Certificate are governed by Ministerial Regulation.

[C] The People's Republic of China

In 1996, China drafted its Regulations on Safeguarding Computer Information Systems (Regulations), which required organizations, both public and private, to secure computers, facilities, and peripherals; using technology best practices.[218] The Regulations focuses on protecting data and systems within Chinese borders by leveraging state-determined criticality determinations and registering any internationally connecting systems. If an incident occurs, organizations must notify the public security divisions of the government within 24 hours.

In 2000, China drafted two more cybersecurity laws, one focused on information system management, the Measures on Management of Internet Information Services, and another on network security, the Decision of the Standing Committee of the National People's Congress on Preserving Computer Network Security.[219] Then in 2012, China passed the Decision on Strengthening Network Information Protection (Decision). The Decision included limited information privacy protections.

In late 2015, President Xi Jinping and President Barack Obama signed a bilateral prohibition on state-sponsored hacking.[220] After draft reviews from 2015 to 2016, in 2017 the Chinese Cyber Security Law (CCSL) came into effect, prompting broad business concerns over potential Chinese government monitoring of business activities.[221] The CCSL focuses on Critical Information Infrastructure (CII) operators, but similar to many other international laws includes more than typical critical infrastructure sectors, such as financial and health systems. The CSL requires a national security review conducted by the Cyberspace Administration of China (CAC, 国家互联网信息办), prior to approval.

The CSL also reiterates earlier PRC decisions regarding the definition of personal information. Although the CSL does not explicitly require localization of data for all personal information, if the CAC will routinely review organizational cybersecurity

218. Regulations on Safeguarding Computer Information Systems, Feb. 1996.
219. Measures on Management of Internet Information Services, 2000. Decision of the Standing Committee of the National People's Congress on Preserving Computer Network Security, 2000.
220. Zunyou Zhou, *China's Draft Cybersecurity* Law, 15:24 CHINABRIEF (Dec. 21, 2015), https://jamestown.org/wp-content/uploads/2015/12/CB_15_24_3.pdf?x87069, at 3. For a fascinating description of language usage in Chinese, Russian, and American English and its effect on cybersecurity negotiation, *see* Keir Giles & William Hagestad II, *Divided by a Common Language: Cyber Definitions in Chinese, Russian, and English*, 2013 5TH INTERNATIONAL CONFERENCE ON CYBER CONFLICT (K. K. Podins, J. Stinissen, M. Maybaum [Eds.]). © NATO CCD COE Publications, Tallinn.
221. To comply with the CSL, early interpretations seem to anticipate approval and ongoing monitoring of proprietary systems by the CAC.

measures, pragmatically organizations may require localized servers to manage infrastructure, applications, and databases. Routine review and monitoring requires ongoing access to networked systems, which means organizations either must build redundant systems within the Chinese physical territory or provide access to systems, which likely includes proprietary data of non-Chinese customers. Localization will be discussed in more detail later in this chapter.

The CSL does include network-specific cybersecurity measures that an organization should implement as part of a network security best practices. Organizations must:

- Name a security representative and conduct regular personnel training, including technical skills training
- Develop disaster recovery, contingency, and incident response plans and test these regularly
- Implement network security authentication, network monitoring (e.g., NAC, IDS, IPS), anti-virus capabilities, testing, risk assessments, and vulnerability assessments

The CAC and other departments will provide specific requirements for implementation of these measures.

[2] The Cybersecurity Law[222]

Chapter 1 General Provisions

Article 1

This Law is formulated in order to safeguard the security of the network, safeguard cyberspace sovereignty and national security, social public interests, protect the legitimate rights and interests of citizens, legal persons and other organizations, and promote the healthy development of economic and social information.

Article 2

This Law shall apply to the supervision and administration of the construction, operation, maintenance and use of the network and the network security within the territory of the People's Republic of China.

Article 3

The State insists on both the development of network security and information management, follow the principle of active utilization, scientific development, legal obligations, ensure safety, promote the construction of network infrastructure, encourage network technology innovation and application, establish and improve the network security systems, and improve network security protection.

222. This translation was completed partially by Google Translate and Microsoft Translator, with additional edits by the Author and should not be construed as an official translation. Official copy available: http://www.npc.gov.cn/npc/xinwen/lfgz/flca/2015-07/06/content_1940614.htm. The term "organ" has been changed to "department" for readability. However, an organ under Chinese law relates to a primary function of the government, such as the NPC. Further, the Author has changed general language regarding multiple state departments' accountability in relation to managing and monitoring network security to the expected lead, the CAC.

Article 4

The State shall formulate and continuously improve the network security strategy, clearly define the basic requirements and main objectives of network security, and put forward the network security policies, tasks and measures in the key areas.

Article 5

The State shall take measures to monitor, defend and dispose of network security risks and threats arising from the territory of the People's Republic of China, protect critical information infrastructure from attack, intrusion, interference and destruction, punish the network for criminal activities, and maintain the cyber-space security and order.

Article 6

The State shall promote the network behavior of honesty and trustworthiness, health and civilization, promote the dissemination of socialist core values, and take measures to raise the awareness and level of cybersecurity in the whole society and form a favorable environment for the whole society to participate in promoting network security.

Article 7

The State shall actively carry out international exchanges and cooperation in the areas of cyberspace management, network technology research and development and standard-setting; prosecute cybercrime and promote the construction of a network of peace, security, openness and cooperation; and establish a multilateral, democratic and transparent network Governance system.

Article 8

The national network letter department is responsible for coordinating the work of network security and related supervision and management. The competent departments of telecommunications under the State Council, the public security departments and other relevant departments shall be responsible for the network security protection and supervision and administration within their respective areas of responsibility in accordance with the provisions of this Law and the relevant laws and administrative regulations.

The administrative functions of network security protection and supervision and administration of the relevant departments of the local people's governments at or above the county level shall be determined in accordance with the relevant provisions of the State.

Article 9

Network operators shall carry out their business and service activities, and must abide by the laws and administrative regulations, abide by the social morality, business ethics, honesty and credit, fulfill the obligations of network security protection, accept the supervision of the government and the public and bear social responsibility.

Article 10

The construction and operation of the network or the provision of services through the Internet shall take technical measures and other necessary measures in accordance with the provisions of laws and administrative regulations and the mandatory requirements of the national standards to ensure the safe and stable operation of the network, effectively deal with the network security incidents,

Prevent cyber criminal activities, maintain the integrity of network data, confidentiality and usability.

Article 11

The relevant organizations of the network shall, in accordance with the articles of association, strengthen the self-discipline of the industry, formulate the rules of network safety, guide the members to strengthen the network security protection, improve the level of network security protection and promote the healthy development of the industry.

Article 12

The State protects the rights of citizens, legal persons and other organizations to use the network according to law, promotes the popularization of network access, enhances the level of network services, provides safe and convenient network services for the society, and guarantees the free flow of network information according to law.

Any person and organization using the network should abide by the constitutional law, abide by public order, respect social morality, not endanger the network security, shall not use the network to endanger national security, incite subversion of state power and overthrow the socialist system, promote terrorism and extremism, National hatred and ethnic discrimination, the dissemination of violence, obscene pornography, fabricating and disseminating false information to disrupt economic order and social order, as well as violations of the reputation, privacy, intellectual property and other legitimate rights and interests of others.

Article 13

Any individual or organization shall have the right to report to the network, telecommunications, public security and other departments that are harmful to the safety of the Internet. The department that receives the report shall handle it in a timely manner and if it does not belong to the duties of the department, it shall promptly transfer the department to be handled.

Chapter 2 Network Security Support and Promotion

Article 14

The State shall establish and improve the network security standard system. The department in charge of standardization of the State Council and other relevant departments under the State Council shall, in accordance with their respective duties, organize and formulate and revise the national standards and industry standards for network security management and network products, services and operation safety.

National support enterprises, network-related industry organizations to participate in network security national standards, industry standards, and encourage enterprises to develop strict national standards, industry standards of enterprise standards.

Article 15

The State Council and the people's governments of provinces, autonomous regions and municipalities directly under the Central Government shall make overall plans, increase investment, support key network security technology industries and projects, support the research and development and application of network security technology, promote safe and reliable network products and services, Protection of network technology intellectual property rights, support enterprises, research institutions and institutions of higher learning to participate in national network security technology innovation projects.

Article 16

The State shall promote the construction of a security service system for network security and common use and encourage the relevant enterprises and institutions to carry out safety services such as network security certification, testing and risk assessment.

Article 17

The State encourages the development of network data security protection and utilization technology to promote the opening of public data resources and promote technological innovation and economic and social development.

The state supports the innovation of network security management, the use of new network technology to enhance the level of network security protection.

Article 18

The people's governments at various levels and their relevant departments shall organize regular publicity and education on cybersecurity and guide and encourage relevant units to do a good job in publicity and education of cybersecurity.

The mass media should be targeted to the community for network security publicity and education.

Article 19

State supported enterprises and institutions of higher education, vocational schools and other education, and training institutions will carry out network security-related education and training, with diverse education to train network security personnel, and promote network security in the workplace.

Chapter 3 Network Operation Safety

Section 1 General Provisions

Article 20

The State shall implement a system of network security protection. The network operator shall, in accordance with the requirements of the network security level protection system, perform the following security protection obligations to protect the network from interference, damage, unauthorized access, and to prevent the disclosure or theft of network data:

(1) Formulate internal safety management systems and operating procedures, to determine the network security responsible person, the implementation of network security protection responsibility;
(2) Take precautions against computer viruses and network attacks, network intrusion and other hazards of network security behavior of technical measures;
(3) Monitor networks, record the network running status, network security events technical measures, and keep the network log for not less than six months;
(4) Classify data, and protect availability and confidentiality through important data backup and encryption and other measures;
(5) other obligations stipulated by laws and administrative regulations.

Article 21

Network products and services shall conform to mandatory requirements of the relevant national standards. Network products and service providers may not set up malicious programs, security defects, vulnerabilities, and other risks, and should promptly inform the user and take remedial measures for such risks, and in accordance with the provisions of the relevant authorities to report.

The providers of network products and services shall provide continuous maintenance of their products and services and shall not terminate the provision of safety maintenance during the period stipulated by the parties or the parties.

Where a network product or service has the function of collecting user information, the provider shall express and obtain the consent to the user; if the personal information is collected, it shall abide by the provisions of this Law and the relevant laws and administrative regulations on the protection of personal information of citizens.

Article 22

The key equipment and network security products shall be sold in accordance with the mandatory requirements of the relevant national standards and shall be sold by qualified safety certification or safety inspection organizations. The Cyberspace Administration of China in conjunction with the relevant departments of the State Council to develop and publish network key equipment and network security products directory, and promote safety certification and safety testing results mutual recognition, to avoid duplication of certification, testing.

Article 23

The network operator shall handle the services such as network access, domain name registration service, fixed telephone and mobile telephone, or provide services such as information dissemination and instant messaging, and enter into an agreement with the user or confirm the service, the user should be asked to provide accurate identification. If the user does not provide accurate identification, the network operator shall not provide the relevant service.

The State implements a network of credible identity strategies that support research and development of safe and convenient electronic identity authentication technologies that drive mutual recognition among different electronic identities.

Article 24

The network operator shall formulate a contingency plan for the network security incident and timely handle the security risks such as system vulnerabilities, computer viruses, network attacks and network intrusion. In the event of an event that threatens network security, the emergency plan shall be initiated and the corresponding remedial measures and report to the competent authorities in accordance with the regulations.

Article 25

To carry out network security authentication, testing, risk assessment and other activities, or identify system vulnerabilities, computer viruses, network attacks, network intrusion and other network security information, should comply with the relevant provisions of the state.

Article 26

Any individual or organization may not engage in activities that invade the network of others illegally, interfere with the normal functions of others' networks, steal network data and other hazards to network security, and shall not provide special activities for engaging in intrusion network, interfering with the normal functions and protective measures of the network, network data and other activities that endanger the network security activities, tools; knowing that others engaged in activities that endanger network security, not to provide technical support, advertising, payment and settlement help.

Article 27

The network operators shall provide technical support and assistance to the public security departments and the state security departments in safeguarding the activities of national security and investigating crimes according to law.

Article 28

The State shall support cooperation between network operators in the collection, analysis, notification and emergency handling of network security information, and improve the safety and security capability of network operators.

The relevant industry organizations will establish and improve the industry's network security protection norms and collaboration mechanisms to strengthen the analysis and evaluation of network security risks, provide risk information, support and assist members to deal with network security risks.

SECTION 2: Operational safety of key information infrastructures

Article 29

The State shall, on the basis of the protection system of the network security level, carry out the protection of the key information infrastructure that has been damaged, lost function or data leakage, which may seriously endanger the national security, national economy and public interest and public interests. The specific scope and safety protection of key information infrastructure shall be formulated by the State Council.

The country encourages network operators outside key information infrastructures to participate voluntarily in critical information infrastructure protection systems.

Article 30

In accordance with the division of responsibilities stipulated by the State Council, the departments responsible for the protection of key information infrastructure shall prepare and organize the implementation of the industry, key information infrastructure security planning, guidance and supervision of key information infrastructure operations in this area.

Article 31

The construction of a key information infrastructure shall ensure that it has the performance of supporting the stable and continuous operation of the business and ensures that the safety and technical measures are synchronized.

Article 32

In addition to the provisions of Article 20 of this Law, operators of key information infrastructures shall perform the following safety and protection obligations:

(I) setting up a dedicated safety management and safety management person in charge and conducting a safety background review of the person responsible and key positions;
(2) regularly carry out network security education, technical training and skills assessment for employees;
(3) disaster recovery of critical systems and databases;

(4) the development of network security incident contingency plans, and regularly organize exercises;
(5) other obligations stipulated by laws and administrative regulations.

Article 33

Where an operator of a key information infrastructure purchases a network product and service that may affect the security of the State, it shall pass the national security review organized by the Cyberspace Administration of China in conjunction with the relevant departments of the State Council.

Article 34

Where an operator of a key information infrastructure purchases a network product and service, it shall enter into a security confidentiality agreement with the provider to clarify the obligations and responsibilities of security and confidentiality.

Article 35

Citizens' personal information and important business data collected and produced by operators of key information infrastructures in the territory of the People's Republic of China shall be stored in the territory. Due to business needs, extra-territorial services, should be in accordance with direction from the Cyberspace Administration of China in conjunction with the relevant departments of the State Council to complete a safety assessment and comply with laws and administrative regulations.

Article 36

The operator of the key infrastructure shall, at its own expense, entrust the Cyberspace Administration of China to conduct at least one annual assessment and assessment of the safety and possible risks of its network and submit the relevant assessment and assessment measures.

Article 37

The Cyberspace Administration of China shall coordinate the relevant departments to take the following measures for the protection of key information infrastructures:
(1) to carry out spot checks on the security risks of key information infrastructures and propose improvement measures to entrust the network security service agencies to carry out the testing and evaluation of the security risks of the network if necessary;
(2) Regularly organize operators of key information infrastructures to conduct cybersecurity emergency drills to improve the level and coordination capacity of network security incidents.

[D] Singapore

Although Singapore has been recognized in the APAC and ASEAN regions as a leader in cybersecurity, boosting its relationships with both German and Australian partnerships, Singapore has not passed a broad-reaching cybersecurity-specific legislation.[223]

223. At the time of writing, Singapore had drafted a cybersecurity bill, focusing on 11 critical infrastructure sectors.

Singapore first passed a law on computer misuse in 1993, revising it to include more modern references to cybersecurity in 2007.

The Computer Misuse and Cybersecurity Act primarily focuses on defining offenses for computer crimes.[224] However, it also gave broad power to the Minister to direct organizations to implement cybersecurity measures by issuing a certificate where "necessary for the purposes of preventing, detecting or countering any threat to national security, essential services, or defense." If an organization refuses, it could receive up to a USD 50,000 fine and organizational leaders up to ten years in prison. The law does not specifically notate which measures an organization must implement; rather, it gives power to the Minister to set these standards or require production of documentation or other design information for a system.

Singapore has also passed acts related to information technology activities, SPAM email and the Electronic Transactions Act (ETA) of 2010 to facilitate electronic transactions with electronic signatures.[225] The SPAM Control Act and the Consumer Protection Act of 2003, together regulate abusive practices, whether bulk SPAM email distribution or unfair or deceptive trade practices.

The Info-communications Media Development Authority (IMDA) has also developed the MDA Internet Code of Practice applicable to ISPs and Internet Content Providers (ICP) licensed under a Broadcasting (Class License) Notification (N1). The Code of Practice establishes authority of Singapore to determine prohibited material, such as pornography, and requires ISP and ICP to enact blocking to prevent transmission of prohibited material to Singapore residents.

[E] India

Although India has not yet passed a data protection law, India has focused on technology development since the early 2000s, and today has one of the largest populations of engineers in the world. In 2000, India passed the Information Technology Act, updated in 2009. The Information Technology Act includes specific security provisions for authentication purposes in online transactions, sanctions for hacking activities, and permits recovery for individuals affected by poor organizational security practices.

[1] Passages of Note: Information Technology Act

> II. DIGITAL SIGNATURE AND ELECTRONIC SIGNATURE (amended vide ITAA 2008)
>
> 3. Authentication of Electronic Records (1) Subject to the provisions of this section any subscriber may authenticate an electronic record by affixing his Digital Signature

224. THE COMPUTER MISUSE AND CYBERSECURITY ACT, Ch 50A (1993).
225. ELECTRONIC TRANSACTIONS ACT, Ch. 88 (2010), available at: http://statutes.agc.gov.sg/aol/search/display/view.w3p;query=DocId%3A294c715e-89c8-48c4-8e14-58b9ea4f1c29%20Depth%3A0%20Status%3Ainforce;rec=0.

(2) The authentication of the electronic record shall be effected by the use of asymmetric crypto system and hash function which envelop and transform the initial electronic record into another electronic record.
Explanation -
For the purposes of this sub-section, "Hash function" means an algorithm mapping or translation of one sequence of bits into another, generally smaller, set known as "Hash Result" such that an electronic record yields the same hash result every time the algorithm is executed with the same electronic record as its input making it computationally infeasible (a) to derive or reconstruct the original electronic record from the hash result produced by the algorithm; (b) that two electronic records can produce the same hash result using the algorithm.
(3) Any person by the use of a public key of the subscriber can verify the electronic record.
(4) The private key and the public key are unique to the subscriber and constitute a functioning key pair.

3A. Electronic Signature (Inserted vide ITAA 2006)
(1) Notwithstanding anything contained in section 3, but subject to the provisions of sub-section (2), a subscriber nay authenticate any electronic record by such electronic signature or electronic authentication technique which-
(a) is considered reliable; and
(b) may be specified in the Second Schedule
(2) For the purposes of this section any electronic signature or electronic authentication technique shall be considered reliable if-
(a) the signature creation data or the authentication data are, within the context in which they are used, linked to the signatory or, as the case may be, the authenticator and of no other person;
(b) the signature creation data or the authentication data were, at the time of signing, under the control of the signatory or, as the case may be,the authenticator and of no other person;
(c) any alteration to the electronic signature made after affixing such signature is detectable
(d) any alteration to the information made after its authentication by electronic signature is detectable;

VIII

42 Control of Private key
(1) Every subscriber shall exercise reasonable care to retain control of the private key corresponding to the r public key listed in his Digital Signature Certificate and take all steps to prevent its disclosure.["to a person not authorized to affix the digital signature of the subscriber".-Omitted vide amendment dated 19/09/2002]
(2) If the private key corresponding to the public key listed in the Digital Signature Certificate has been compromised, then, the subscriber shall communicate the same without any delay to the Certifying Authority in such manner as may be specified by the regulations.

Explanation - For the removal of doubts, it is hereby declared that the subscriber shall be liable till he has informed the Certifying Authority that the private key has been compromised.

IX. PENALTIES, COMPENSATION AND ADJUDICATION (Amended vide ITAA-2006/8)

43 Penalty and Compensation for damage to computer, computer system, etc (Amended vide ITAA-2008)

If any person without permission of the owner or any other person who is in charge of a computer, computer system or computer network -

(a) accesses or secures access to such computer, computer system or computer network or computer resource (ITAA2008)
(b) downloads, copies or extracts any data, computer data base or information from such computer, computer system or computer network including information or data held or stored in any removable storage medium;
(c) introduces or causes to be introduced any computer contaminant or computer virus into any computer, computer system or computer network;
(d) damages or causes to be damaged any computer, computer system or computer network, data, computer data base or any other programmes residing in such computer, computer system or computer network;
(e) disrupts or causes disruption of any computer, computer system or computer network;
(f) denies or causes the denial of access to any person authorised to access any computer, computer system or computer network by any means;
(g) provides any assistance to any person to facilitate access to a computer, computer system or computer network in contravention of the provisions of this Act, rules or regulations made thereunder,
(h) charges the services availed of by a person to the account of another person by tampering with or manipulating any computer, computer system, or computer network,
(i) destroys, deletes or alters any information residing in a computer resource or diminishes its value or utility or affects it injuriously by any means (Inserted vide ITAA-2008)
(i) Steals, conceals, destroys or alters or causes any person to steal, conceal, destroy or alter any computer source code used for a computer resource with an intention to cause damage, (Inserted vide ITAA 2008)

he shall be liable to pay damages by way of compensation not exceeding one crore rupees to the person so affected. (change vide ITAA 2008)

43 A Compensation for failure to protect data (Inserted vide ITAA 2006)

Where a body corporate, possessing, dealing or handling any sensitive personal data or information in a computer resource which it owns, controls or operates, is negligent in implementing and maintaining reasonable security practices and procedures and thereby causes wrongful loss or wrongful gain to any person, such body corporate shall be liable to pay damages by way of compensation, not exceeding five crore rupees, to the person so affected. (Change vide ITAA 2008)

Explanation: For the purposes of this section

(i) "body corporate" means any company and includes a firm, sole proprietorship or other association of individuals engaged in commercial or professional activities
(ii) "reasonable security practices and procedures" means security practices and procedures designed to protect such information from unauthorised access, damage, use, modification, disclosure or impairment, as may be specified in an agreement between the parties or as may be specified in any law for the time being in force and in the absence of such agreement or any law, such reasonable security practices and procedures, as may be prescribed by the

Central Government in consultation with such professional bodies or associations as it may deem fit.

(iii) "sensitive personal data or information" means such personal information as may be prescribed by the Central Government in consultation with such professional bodies or associations as it may deem fit.

[F] Malaysia

Malaysia has passed several cybersecurity laws and has included cybersecurity language within its omnibus information privacy law, the PDPA.[226] Under the PDPA, Security, Retention, and Data Integrity Principles apply to data users and processors collecting or processing personal data. The *Security, Retention, and Data Integrity Principles* add more cybersecurity details than are typically found in an information privacy law, but they leave some opportunity for flexibility. Data users must take "practical steps to protect personal data from any loss, misuse, modification, unauthorized or accidental access or disclosure, alteration or destruction," and data users must direct their processors to follow these instructions.

The PDPA allows for selection of measures, considering the type of data and potential resulting harm, security measures incorporated into equipment, and measures ensuring system reliability, data integrity, and personnel competency, as well as secure transfer. The Retention principle works from a similar data minimization perspective as the necessity principle, in that processors should only retain data for fulfillment of the collection purpose, then securely delete. The Data Integrity principle focuses on data accuracy and requires data users to implement technical measures and honor data subject rights for personal data correction. Malaysia also passed the Electronic Commerce Act of 2006, which establishes requirements for digital signatures and ensures effective identification and authentication of users.[227]

Malaysia's Ministry of Science, Technology and Innovation and Ministry of Finance jointly created the precursor to the CyberSecurity Malaysia Agency in 2005. Since that time, CyberSecurity Malaysia has grown to develop several impactful centers and services for the cybersecurity community, including MyCERT and Cyber999 (cybersecurity emergency response teams), a digital forensics unit, the Malaysian Vulnerability Centre (MyVAC), and an Information Security Certification Body.[228]

226. Malaysia has two computer crime acts, which will not be discussed in this chapter. Malaysia passed the The Computer Crimes Act 1997 of Malaysia and updated the Penal Code of Malaysia in 1997 to include computer crimes.
227. Electronic Commerce Act of 2006, Act 658, available at: http://www.agc.gov.my/agcportal/uploads/files/Publications/LOM/EN/Act%20658.pdf.
228. Cybersecurity Malaysia, *Corporate Overview* (2017), http://www.cybersecurity.my/en/about_us/corporate_overview/main/detail/2065/index.html.

[G] Republic of Korea

Korea passed the Act on Promotion of Information and Communication Network Utilization and Information Protection in 1986, and updated most recently in 2015.[229] Article 28 requires an internal management plan, firewall and access control mechanisms, tamperproof connection records (such as logging), encryption and security measures for personal information, and anti-virus software installation. Later articles also require service providers to secure the safety and reliability of networks and that all service providers must obtain certification from the Korea Information Security Agency to ensure quality prior to providing service. The Minister of Information and Communication may establish standards for certification.

The Republic of Korea developed a Cybersecurity Master Plan in 2011, but at the time of writing has not further developed the plan to establish cybersecurity requirements for organizations. Korea has established Cybersecurity Emergency Response Teams (KrCERT/CC and KN-CERT) for government response.

[H] The Philippines

Under the Data Privacy Act, the Philippines require greater stringency than most data privacy laws: network safeguards, a security policy describing appropriate protections for personal information, a process for identifying system vulnerabilities in order to prevent a data breach, and operational security breach monitoring. These security requirements reflect broader requirements traditional in the field of cybersecurity. We will discuss these measures in more detail in Chapters 8 through 12.

§10.03 EMEA AND CANADIAN CYBERSECURITY LAW

The GDPR has established security requirements above and beyond the more flexibly written 95/46/EC, increasing focus on risk mitigation, resilience, and recovery activities. In particular, organizations must use encryption or pseudonymization as a risk mitigation strategy and regularly test, assess, and evaluate security controls to ensure effectiveness. Organizations must be able to restore access and recover system data after a physical or technical incident. Building these capabilities after system implementation introduces significant cost and rework; therefore, organizations should incorporate privacy and security during technical strategy and system design processes. In addition to the GDPR, the EU and DPAs have enhanced direction for protecting information.

229. The Act on Promotion of Information and Communication Network Utilization and Information Protection (정보통신망 이용촉진 및 정보보호 등에 관한 법률 (1986년5월12일에 제정된 법률 제3848호는 2015 년3월27일의 법률 제13280호 개정에 이르기까지 수차례 개정이 이루어짐), Act No. 13280 of March 27, 2015, available at: http://www.wipo.int/wipolex/en/text.jsp?file_id=370834 (automated translation).

[A] Network and Information Security Directive

The European Commission adopted the Network and Information Security Directive (NIS Directive) in 2016. The NIS Directive requires member states to create a Computer Security Incident Response Team (CSIRT) team, identify a national cybersecurity authority (NIS Authority), and facilitate cooperation and information sharing between countries.[230] The Directive also identified the existence of *essential services* that require enhanced cybersecurity attention: energy, transport, water, banking, financial market infrastructures, healthcare, and digital infrastructure. Member states must ensure organizations providing essential services adopt appropriate security measures and notify the NIS Authority when serious incidents occur.

[B] Data Protection Authority Rules

Data protection authorities in a variety of EEA countries have begun to provide guidelines for cybersecurity protection. The Information Commissioner's Office (ico.) in the United Kingdom has provided a ten-step cybersecurity readiness assessment for organizations,[231] the Commission Nationale de l'Informatique et des Libertés (CNIL.) in France has created guides on training, conducting PIAs, governance, and more.[232]

[C] CSA Guidance

The Canadian Securities Administrators (CSA) recently issued a Staff Notice specific to cybersecurity concerns in the financial securities sector.[233] According to the guidance, the CSA will be re-examining recent disclosures, gathering data about cybersecurity practices via regular risk assessments, and completing desk reviews. Highlights of the guidance include:

- Establish governance and accountability for cybersecurity at the executive and board levels
- Organize and execute cybersecurity activities (develop a framework)
- Understand security considerations for technologies support business activities
- Manage third party risk
- Assess likelihood and impact of issued identified
- Improve incident response functions, such as reporting functions

---

230. Directive (EU) 2016/1148 (6 July 2016), http://eur-lex.europa.eu/legal-content/EN/TXT/?uri=uriserv:OJ.L_.2016.194.01.0001.01.ENG&toc=OJ:L:2016:194:TOC.
231. Information Commissioner's Office, *Information Security* (2017), https://ico.org.uk/for-organisations/resources-and-support/data-protection-self-assessment/information-security/.
232. Commission Nationale de l'Informatique et des Libertés, *Publications* (2017), https://www.cnil.fr/en/media.
233. Canadian Securities Administrators, *CSA Staff Notice 11-332, Cyber Security* (27 Sept. 2016), https://www.osc.gov.on.ca/documents/en/Securities-Category1/sn_20160927_11-332-cyber-security.pdf.

This Guidance begins to move the CSA closer to Financial Industry Regulatory Authority (FINRA) activity in the United States.

[D] EU Local Laws

EU member states have established requirements for appropriate security within their boundaries. Most commonly, EU local laws require organizations to conduct risk assessments, develop an information security policy, encrypt SPI in storage and transmission, use multi-factor authentication, and enforce data segregation. Most countries have a cybersecurity office and associated Computer Security Incident Response Teams (CSIRT). Regulatory authorities have also developed guidelines and sectoral approval processes for organizations. In France, for example, the ASIP Santé has established more substantial security requirements for medical device clearance, such as 2FA and encryption requirements.

[E] Switzerland

Switzerland has led many European countries in cybersecurity development activities, likely due to its well-resourced banking, technology, and scientific sectors. In 2004, Switzerland had created the Reporting and Analysis Center for Information Assurance (MELANI), which focused on public-private partnerships and information sharing.[234] In 2007, the Federal Council approved the creation of a Critical Infrastructure Protection Working Group (CIP WG), which defined critical infrastructure relatively broadly as "those infrastructures whose disruption, failure, or destruction would have a serious impact on the public health, the environment, the political affairs, the security, and the economic and social well-being of a population." These sectors included chemicals, energy, financial services, information and communication technologies, public administration, public health, public safety and rescue, transport, waste disposal, and water and food. In 2009, the CIP WG identified five considerations for organizations to reflect in risk assessments: Prevention, Preparation, Intervention, Recondition, and Reconstruction.[235] Switzerland has been working with the private sector since this time to develop standard approaches to these risk assessment considerations.

§10.04 THE UNITED STATES OF AMERICA

The United States have substantially developed cybersecurity programs, albeit in a manner similar to information privacy law: the U.S. has resisted broadly applicable and binding laws restricting business operations except for high-risk sectors. The Federal Trade Commission (FTC), however, has enforced not only law where the FTC has specific enforcement but has increasingly exercised its discretionary rights to enforce

234. MYRIAM DUNN CAVELTY, CYBERSECURITY IN SWITZERLAND (Springer: 2014), at 49.
235. *Id.*, at 58-61.

unfair and deceptive trade practices with respect to both information privacy and cybersecurity practices under Section 5 of the FTC Act.

[A] Health Cybersecurity

The Health sector has focused on developing cybersecurity laws largely out of necessity, likelihood of health care fraud, and impact to individuals. The United States Congress and administrative agencies have focused on both enhancing HIPAA security requirements in the form of regulatory audits and enhanced guidance for cybersecurity in healthcare and medical device manufacturing.

[1] HIPAA Security Rule

In contrast with the HIPAA Privacy Rule, which relies on standard privacy principles and clear rules, the HIPAA Security Rule applies risk management techniques to manage data confidentiality, integrity and availability for PHI.[236] Risk management techniques typically offer more overall flexibility for an organization to choose a particular solution to comply with the HIPAA Security Rule.

The HIPAA Security Rule organizes implementation specifications into two categories: *addressable* and *required*.[237] Unlike a required implementation specification that a CE or BA must implement, addressable specifications permit a CE or BA to choose how it satisfies the objective of the requirement. Unfortunately, organizations have often interpreted addressable requirements as optional. Satisfying the objective may include meeting the specification, finding an alternative solution, or not meeting the specification with additional documented substantiation. In all cases, the CE or BA must document its decision. When determining security measures to include, organizations must evaluate the size, complexity, and capabilities of the organization; the technical infrastructure, hardware, and software security capabilities; the costs of security measures; and the probability and criticality of potential risks to electronic PHI (ePHI).

The HIPAA Security Rule, which preceded many modern developments in digital health, requires compliance with a smattering of program-level specifications, yet does not explicitly require many cybersecurity controls.[238] Although these focus areas are

---

236. 45 C.F.R. § 160, 164; *see generally* U.S. Dep't Health & Hum. Servs., 2 HIPAA Security Series 3 (2004), https://www.hhs.gov/sites/default/files/ocr/privacy/hipaa/administrative/security rule/security101.pdf.

237. 45 C.F.R. § 164.306; What is the Difference Between Addressable and Required Implementation Specifications in the Security Rule?, U.S. Dep't Health & Hum. Servs., http://www.hhs.gov/hipaa/for-professionals/faq/2020/what-is-the-difference-between-addressable-and-required-implementation-specifications/index.html (last visited Nov. 8, 2016).

238. 45 C.F.R. § 164.400-164.414. Incorporating addressable security specifications, such as encryption using an acceptable key strength and protocol, may reduce a CE or BA's obligations for notification. *See* Breach Notification Rule, U.S. Dep't. of Health & Hum. Servs., http://www.hhs.gov/hipaa/for-professionals/breach-notification/index.html (last visited Sept. 14, 2016).

important to protect PHI from unauthorized disclosure or change and ensure availability of PHI, technical cybersecurity controls are addressable and a minor proportion of total legal requirements.[239] *See* Table 10.2 for a map of specifications and HIPAA focus on particular specifications.

Table 10.2 HIPAA Security Rule Focus Areas

Concentration	*Count*	*Measure Type*
Identity and Access Management Procedures	6	Administrative
Risk Management Overall	4	Administrative
Incident Response Process	3	Administrative
Disaster Recovery and Business Continuity	8	Administrative
Documentation	3	Administrative
Media Management	2	Administrative
Asset Management	1	Administrative
Human Resources	1	Administrative
Session Management	1	Technical
Patch Management	1	Technical
Network Management	1	Technical
Event Management	1	Technical
Data Integrity	1	Technical
Encryption	1	Technical
Physical security	4	Physical

Organizations planning for cybersecurity compliance obligations under HIPAA should review the OCR audit spreadsheet described in Chapter 3 to test and plan organizational readiness for HIPAA cybersecurity requirements. In an effort to evolve cybersecurity maturity for CEs and BAs, the OCR has also mapped applicable National Institute of Standards and Technology (NIST) specifications to the HIPAA Security Rule, the "crosswalk."[240] Unfortunately, this mapping and other NIST guidance does

239. Due to the insufficient rigor of security measures, it is worth noting that compliance with HIPAA alone would not likely protect PHI from hackers or other entities seeking to damage an organization or individual. *See* Niam Yaraghi, *Hackers, Phishers, and Disappearing Thumb Drives: Lessons Learned from Major Health Care Data Breaches,* Brookings Ctr. for Tech. Innovation 2 (May 2016), https://www.brookings.edu/wp-content/uploads/2016/07/Patient-Privacy504v3.pdf.

240. U.S. Dep't of Health & Hum. Servs., HIPAA Security Rule Crosswalk to NIST Cybersecurity Framework (Feb. 22, 2016), http://www.hhs.gov/sites/default/files/nist-csf-to-hipaa-security-rule-crosswalk-02-22-2016-final.pdf (describing the mappings between the HIPAA Security Rule and NIST specifications).

not establish mandatory requirements for CEs or BAs, and many still mistakenly believe that HIPAA compliance sufficiently protects against cybersecurity risk.[241]

HIPAA also includes a Data Breach Notification Rule, requiring CEs and BAs to notify both the Secretary of Health and Human Services via an online submission and data subjects by first-class mail within sixty days of any data breach and for ninety days via substitute notice (such as on a media platform) if data subject contact information is out of date.[242] In order to notify, organizations must have an incident response operational capability.[243] Data breach notification is required unless the organization can demonstrate a low probability that an individual's rights could be compromised, based on the following factors:

- the nature and extent of the protected health information involved, including the types of identifiers and the likelihood of re-identification;
- the unauthorized person who used the protected health information or to whom the disclosure was made;
- whether the protected health information was actually acquired or viewed; and
- the extent to which the risk to the protected health information has been mitigated.

Organizations may also avoid data breach notification when the disclosure is internal and unintentional in nature, and not an issue of poor access controls or an inadvertent disclosure to another individual within the same organization with sufficient rights to view the PHI. When the organization has a good faith belief that PHI could not have been captured by the disclosure, such as a quick flash of a computer screen, breach notification is not required.

Consistent with state data breach notification laws in the United States (described in Chapter 15), organizations should disclose data breaches when data is readable, such as data not rendered unusable or indecipherable, such as sufficiently advanced encryption technologies. To date, this requirement typically only means encrypted data under the NIST accepted encryption protocols, the "Encryption Safe Harbor." Many individual states in the U.S. have adopted an encryption safe harbor for data breach notification, as well.

241. *Id.* NIST offers helpful mappings between cybersecurity categories and relevant standards (including International Standards Organization, or ISO, a popular standard; COBIT, a popular audit standard; NIST standards; and other control sets. NIST has also created additional documents for assistance in complying with HIPAA); *see* NAT'L INST. OF STANDARDS & TECH., AN INTRODUCTORY RESOURCE GUIDE FOR IMPLEMENTING THE HEALTH INSURANCE PORTABILITY AND ACCOUNTABILITY ACT (HIPAA) SECURITY RULE (2008), http://nvlpubs.nist.gov/nistpubs/Legacy/SP/nistspecialpublication800-66r1.pdf.

242. Dept. of Health and Human Services, *Submitting a Notice of a Breach to the Secretary* (Jan. 5, 2015), https://www.hhs.gov/hipaa/for-professionals/breach-notification/breach-reporting/index.html.

243. 45 C.F.R. §§ 164.400-414.

[2] FDA Cybersecurity Guidance

The U.S. Department of Health & Human Services (HHS) Food and Drug Administration (FDA) establishes comprehensive medical device process requirements to ensure safety in the health marketplace for devices subject to the Federal Food, Drug, and Cosmetic Act (FDCA). The FDCA establishes a compliance framework for products considered medical devices under the statute. Medical devices collect, process, and store SPI, while often providing direct stimulus with a part of the physical body. Amid recent reports of potential device cybersecurity vulnerabilities, the FDA has begun considering cybersecurity threats to medical devices in the United States.

Under the FDCA, a device is broadly defined as:

> An instrument, apparatus, implement, machine, contrivance, implant . . . including any component, part, or accessory, which is . . . intended for use in the diagnosis of disease or other conditions, or in the cure, mitigation, treatment, or prevention of disease . . . or intended to affect the structure or function of the body.[244]

Coupled with case law interpretation, the FDCA defines medical devices broadly, including a large variety of devices within the digital health sector. The FDA recognizes a category of digital health medical devices involving modern technology: mHealth, IT, wearable devices, telehealth, telemedicine, and personalized medicine. The FDA further classifies devices as Class I, II, or III, and this classification determines medical device controls, including exemptions. From Class I to III, medical devices are organized from requiring least regulatory oversight to most, with Class I devices requiring only compliance with general controls in the FDCA.[245] If the FDA determines it will regulate a type of device, then reviews and approves an application, an organization's obligations do not end. Organizations must report adverse effects for cleared devices, such as safety issues and recalls, which enables the FDA to effectively share safety communications, recalls, bans, and emergency situations for the general public on its Website and via email updates.[246]

In 2014, the FDA began issuing pre- and post-release cybersecurity guidelines and issued device vulnerability notices to assist device manufacturers in producing and managing devices less likely to adversely impact consumers. The 2014 *Pre-Release Cybersecurity Guidelines* addressed incorporating cybersecurity considerations in the design and development of medical devices as part of "software validation and risk analysis . . . [in] 21 CFR 820.30(g)." [247] The FDA recommended incorporating asset

244. 21 U.S.C. § 321(h) (2009); U.S. v. Undetermined No. of Unlabeled Cases, 21 F.3d 1026, 1028 (10th Cir. 1994); JAMES T. O'REILLY & KATHARINE A. VAN TASSEL, FOOD AND DRUG ADMINISTRATION § 18.2 (4th ed. 2016) (explaining that the definition of device now includes computer software and diagnosis aids, but the device must serve a diagnostic or therapeutic purposes, "regardless of whether medical treatment will follow").
245. Paul M. Coltoff et al., *Regulation of Medical Devices*, 28 C.J.S. *Drugs and Narcotics* § 26 (2016).
246. 21 C.F.R. § 803.10.
247. U.S. FOOD & DRUG ADMIN., CONTENT OF PREMARKET SUBMISSIONS FOR MANAGEMENT OF CYBERSECURITY IN MEDICAL DEVICES 1 (2014),http://www.fda.gov/downloads/medicaldevices/deviceregulationandguidance/guidancedocuments/ucm356190.pdf.

identification, threat analysis, and vulnerability reviews into an organization's device development process, including risk assessment and analysis, to determine residual risk and apply mitigation strategies. Such processes should take into consideration the intended use and implementation of a device, such as home use. Moreover, medical device manufacturers are encouraged to specify "cybersecurity measures" in premarket submission processes, such as "hazard analysis" and "design considerations" for a medical device, and risks like device cybersecurity controls considered or implemented.

The premarket cybersecurity measures recommend asset identification, threat analysis, and vulnerability reviews, reflect a level of standardization in cybersecurity practice.[248] These standards incorporate best practice cybersecurity capabilities, such as access and identity management—the capability that bars unauthorized users from accessing a system, code validation and management, cybersecurity incident response capabilities, and business continuity—continuing function of devices even when compromised. These standards have been established by the International Electrotechnical Commission (IEC), the "world's leading organization" for electrical technologies.[249]

The FDA's *Guidance for Industry – Cybersecurity for Networked Medical Devices Containing Off-the-Shelf (OTS) Software* explicitly allocated responsibility for new cybersecurity activities under existing FDCA laws governing technology validation processes.[250] The Guidance further explained that manufacturers should work with vendors to timely receive cybersecurity updates, such as patches, and develop a "cybersecurity maintenance plan."

In January 2016, the FDA distributed the *Postmarket Management of Cybersecurity in Medical Devices* for comment purposes. This guidance document reiterated the responsibility of manufacturers to include cybersecurity considerations throughout product development and to continuously monitor for device vulnerabilities throughout each device's lifecycle. Specifically, the FDA recommends following the NIST Framework for Improving Critical Infrastructure Cybersecurity, a risk management framework, and also sharing identified cybersecurity risks and security incident data via the National Health Information Sharing & Analysis Center.[251]

The FDA also recommends monitoring for cybersecurity vulnerabilities, assessing potential vulnerability impact, and developing mitigation strategies, including

248. *See, e.g.*, Michael Muckin & Scott C. Fitch, *A Threat-Driven Approach to Cyber Security*, LOCKHEED MARTIN, http://lockheedmartin.com/content/dam/lockheed/data/isgs/documents/Threat-Driven%20Approach%20whitepaper.pdf (last visited Sept. 15, 2016), at 5 (advocating a threats-assets-controls relational model, which shifts focus from vulnerability analysis to threat analysis).

249. INT'L ELECTROTECHNICAL COMM'N, *About the IEC Vision & Mission* (2016), http://www.iec.ch/about/.

250. U.S. FOOD AND DRUG ADMIN., GUIDANCE FOR INDUSTRY - CYBERSECURITY FOR NETWORKED MEDICAL DEVICES CONTAINING OFF-THE-SHELF (OTS) SOFTWARE (May 28, 2015), http://www.fda.gov/MedicalDevices/DeviceRegulationandGuidance/GuidanceDocuments/ucm077812.htm.

251. U.S. FOOD & DRUG ADMIN., POSTMARKET MANAGEMENT OF CYBERSECURITY IN MEDICAL DEVICE 1 (Jan. 22, 2016), http://www.fda.gov/downloads/medicaldevices/deviceregulationandguidance/guidancedocuments/ucm482022.pdf.

deploying patches or remediating code to neutralize vulnerabilities. These recommendations represent industry standard vulnerability management practices, and very thoroughly explain the relationship between vulnerabilities and essential clinical performance. Although the *Postmarket Guidelines* do not establish binding rules for manufacturers, the details expressed illustrate a relatively comprehensive understanding of vulnerability management practices, which significantly affect the ability of a manufacturer to manage medical device risk.

[B] Financial Cybersecurity and Publicly Traded Companies

Similar to health cybersecurity, the United States Congress and government agencies have increasingly focused on developing and enforcing financial services cybersecurity maturity, including banking and investment businesses. U.S. businesses that are not financial services organizations, yet nevertheless are publicly traded as investment stocks, have also experienced increased oversight.

[1] GLBA Security Rule

The GLBA includes a privacy rule and separate obligation to securely protect information (safeguards):

> 15 U.S. Code § 6801
>
> (b) Financial institutions safeguards
>
> In furtherance of the policy in subsection (a), each agency or authority described in section 6805(a) of this title, other than the Bureau of Consumer Financial Protection, shall establish appropriate standards for the financial institutions subject to their jurisdiction relating to administrative, technical, and physical safeguards—
> (1) to insure the security and confidentiality of customer records and information;
> (2) to protect against any anticipated threats or hazards to the security or integrity of such records; and
> (3) to protect against unauthorized access to or use of such records or information which could result in substantial harm or inconvenience to any customer.

The OCC has issued guidelines to ensure that financial institutions meet these requirements, and these guidelines provide an important map to ensuring activities meet compliance obligations. The security guidelines require organizations to:

- Identify and assess risk internally
- Manage and control risk, such as focusing on reducing risk to customers or consumers
- Train staff through annual awareness training
- Provide appropriate oversight of service providers
- Update programs regularly to address emerging risks.

Under the GLBA, a financial institution must also establish an information security program, designed to ensure confidentiality of nonpublic personal information. In addition to the guidelines and strict GLBA requirements, Interagency Guidance on response programs requires that financial institutions establish a security breach response program, also known as an incident response program, notify affected customers when a breach occurs, and ensure third-party compliance with the same. Chapter 14 describes the incident response process in more detail.

[2] FINRA

The Financial Industry Regulatory Authority, or FINRA, has an interesting role with respect to US privacy law. FINRA works closely with the SEC and is part independent organization and government authority. FINRA members, investment organizations, must follow FINRA rules. FINRA collaborates with the SEC on information security or privacy matters including drafting rules. FINRA also assists the SEC in governing Reg S-P compliance. In addition to Reg S-P, Reg-SID covers identity theft monitoring that could occur as a result of a data breach.

Outside standard security and privacy laws, organizations must also submit a suspicious activity report under the SEC rule, which requires a report of suspicious transactions typically tied to money-laundering. However, suspicious transactions could also implicate financial fraud perpetuated through hacking or social engineering. In 2014, FINRA developed a cybersecurity initiative, which resulted in FINRA drafting examination letters and assessing securities firms' cybersecurity threat management activities. Following these enforcement activities, FINRA fined organizations, such as E*TRADE in 2016 and Morgan Stanley Smith Barney in 2015.

[3] The Sarbanes-Oxley Act

The SEC is also responsible for protecting shareholder investment, including financial record reliability. The U.S. Congress passed the Sarbanes-Oxley Act (SOX) in 2002 after the Enron scandal of 2001 to ensure financial accuracy of public financial disclosures in the United States.[252] SOX uniquely holds senior executives personally liable for the accuracy of financial information disclosed by publicly traded companies. Despite SOX focusing on financial records management, SOX requires publicly traded companies to ensure accuracy of financial records by implementing information technology controls, including security controls, which internal or external auditors validate.

[4] The Securities Exchange Commission Act

The SEC is the regulatory body for SOX and Reg-SP, but the SEC generally regulates publicly traded company operations to protect shareholder rights. The Securities Act of

252. The Sarbanes-Oxley Act of 2002, P.L. 107-204 (2002), http://www.gpo.gov/fdsys/pkg/PLAW-107publ204/pdf/PLAW-107publ204.pdf.

1933 created the SEC and first codified shareholder transparency, prohibiting in 10b-5 "[an] omission to state a material fact necessary in order to make . . . statements, in light of the circumstances under which they were made, not misleading."[253] This means that organizations must be forthcoming in information deemed material to an investment decision. Publicly traded companies owe a duty to investors with respect to information that might affect an investment decision in a material way. SEC Rule 405, passed in 1982 amended further this definition:

> When used to qualify a requirement for the furnishing of information as to any subject,
>
> [materiality] limits the information required to those matters in which there is a substantial likelihood that a reasonable investor would attach importance in determining whether to purchase a security registered.

The SEC has publicly interpreted this rule to apply to cybersecurity attacks, stating that companies must disclose these attacks to shareholders as a material matter. Corporate boards are encouraged to spend more time considering cybersecurity and selecting members with cybersecurity competency.

[C] Broadly Applicable Cybersecurity Law

A fairly large number of administrative agencies, similar to the Japanese ministries, have developed an interest in regulating cybersecurity activities. For this reason, the FTC has expanded on its role as privacy authority to incorporate cybersecurity issues demonstrating unfair or deceptive trade practices. In addition, the United States has passed laws and issued executive orders to improve cybersecurity support for key sectors and capabilities within the country, while safeguarding government systems. In sheer numbers alone, the United States has established a very active cybersecurity legislative and regulatory scheme.

[1] The Federal Trade Commission Act

Although federal regulations like HIPAA, GLBA, and Reg S-P specify some general cybersecurity requirements, few cybersecurity requirements apply to publicly traded companies outside this limited regulatory environment.

Absent specific requirements, the FTC can prosecute unfair or deceptive trade practices under Section 5 of the FTC Act, including in some cases a lack of adequate security controls. However, administrative case law so far has failed to clearly establish a baseline for cybersecurity control implementation.

Recent cases have reiterated the FTC's status for adjudicating cybersecurity-related issues. In 2015, *FTC v. Wyndham*, the Third Circuit for the United States Federal Courts determined that the FTC has the authority to adjudicate data security cases,

253. The Securities Act of 1933, 17 C.F.R. 240.15c1-2 (1933).

increasing the probability of FTC administrative decisions in the future.[254] Other cases have established that organizations operating in the U.S. should, at a minimum, implement a cybersecurity policy and conduct periodic risk assessments.

[2] Federal Information Security Management Act and Agency Requirements

The U.S. Congress passed Federal Information Security Modernization Act (FISMA) in 2002 with the original intention of establishing security requirements for government technology to match privacy obligations in the Privacy Act for state agencies.[255] However, organizations providing contract services to U.S. government agencies, such as the United States Department of Veterans Affairs, increasingly must meet FISMA requirements. FISMA provides a relatively comprehensive cybersecurity compliance framework, including requirements for annual risk assessment, incident response testing, threat sharing, breach notification, and specific technical conformance with federal standards. Importantly, some U.S. government agencies require localization of data within the U.S.

[3] Cybersecurity Information Sharing Act

The U.S. Congress passed the Cybersecurity Information Sharing Act (CISA) in 2015 to enhance information sharing and cybersecurity intel between public and private organizations.[256] The Act prohibits sharing of personal information (requires data cleansing), but grants organizations a complete legal defense when sharing data pertaining to those cybersecurity incidents.

Following CISA, the 2015 Executive Order 13691, "Promoting Private Sector Cybersecurity Information Sharing" directed the Department of Homeland Security to encourage development of Information Sharing and Analysis Organizations (ISAO), which are private cooperative organizations centered around a particular sector, designed to collect and share information with the U.S. federal government. Today, both ISAOs and Information Sharing and Analysis Centers (ISAC, also centered around a particular center, but in existence since 1999) support collaborative private and public relationships to facilitate cybersecurity information setting.

Critical infrastructure has been the focus for ISAOs and later executive orders, including not only standard critical infrastructure, such as public utilities and private energy companies, but also oil and gas, healthcare, and financial sectors.

---

254. FTC v. Wynham Worldwide Corp., 799 F.3d 236 (3d Cir. 2015). Prior to 2017, the Federal Communications Commission also exhibited interest in regulating cybersecurity, due to its regulation of Internet Service Providers (ISP).
255. The Federal Information Security Modernization Act of 2002, Pub. L. 113-283.
256. The Cybersecurity Information Sharing Act of 2015, Pub. L. 114-113, 129 Stat.694 (2015), https://grants.nhisac.org/BackgroundData/2015_CISA_Cybersecurity_Information_Sharing Act.pdf.

[4] Additional Federal Government Activities

The United States has invested substantially in developing a number of cybersecurity capabilities in the form of government offices, including the United States Computer Emergency Readiness Team (US-CERT), special cybercrime divisions in the Federal Bureau of Investigations (FBI), United States Cyber Command, the Cybersecurity Resource Center, and Department of Homeland Security's (DHS) National Cybersecurity and Communications Integration Center (NCCIC).[257]

[5] State Laws

States in the United States have also developed laws specific to cybersecurity. Increasingly more frequently, states have passed laws limiting data retention, requiring cybersecurity risk assessments, implementation of incident response processes, and liability-shifting provisions. States have also passed individual data breach notification laws. United States data breach notification laws will be discussed more in Chapter 15.

§10.05 THE LATIN AMERICA REGION

The Latin American Region (LATAM) has been somewhat slower to incorporate cybersecurity legal requirements within country laws. In 2006, the Organization of American States (OAS) agreed to unify over cybersecurity issues, yet individual Member States have been slow to adopt comprehensive cybersecurity programs and associated legislation.[258]

Although Uruguay established a Computer Security Incident Response Team (CSIRT) in 2005 and passed cybersecurity laws in 2010, few LATAM countries have followed, with the exception of fairly comprehensive legislation in Perú.

Brazil has focused on political and international law-motivated cybersecurity development, such as developing a military Cyberdefense Center (CDCiber).

[A] Uruguay

Uruguay has built a relatively comprehensive framework for cybersecurity, facilitated through presidential decree, the Information Security Direction, Article 148 of Act 18.719 (2010), and by developing a National Computer Incident Response Center and Unit for the Regulation and Control of Personal Data (Unit Reguladora Y De Control De Datos Personales). The Regulatory Framework on Cybersecurity, Decree 92/014 establishes standards, in part, such as requiring Webmail to use HTTPS, and Websites

257. Department of Homeland Security, *Cybersecurity* (2017), https://www.dhs.gov/topic/cybersecurity.
258. Council on Hemispheric Affairs, *Cyber Security and Hacktivism in Latin America: Past and Future* (July 24, 2014), http://www.coha.org/cyber-security-and-hacktivism-in-latin-america-past-and-future/.

to use TLS 1.0 or SSLv3.[259] It also focuses on standards for reliability and availability through consistent electrical connectivity and physical protection for data centers, such as heating and cooling mechanisms to ensure 24/7 operation.

[B] Perú

Perú's PDPL, in addition to providing one of the most rigorous information privacy laws in the world, also specifies a substantial amount of security requirements. Of its most restrictive language, the PDPL requires organizations (and their third parties) process data in a manner deemed "complex or critical" with respect to data subject, comply with ISO 27001, one of the frameworks illustrating cybersecurity best practices explored in Chapter 11. The PDPL also requires detailed system record-keeping in the form of logging, which assists in attribution of attackers and forensic investigation.

The Security Policy on Information Managed by Databanks of Personal Data provided an incredibly robust cybersecurity law, focusing on not only the obligation, but the method for fulfilling the obligation, including requirements for information security policies, access management, and incident response planning.[260] The guide provided by the National Authority for the Protection of Personal Data provides a detailed mapping of each requirement to criticality levels, in order demonstrate differing implementation based on risk to data subjects.

[9] Cloud Computing

Title III

Chapter IV

Article 33

Processing of personal data in "cloud computing" The processing of personal data by services, applications and infrastructure in the so-called cloud computing may be done by the data controller, provided they guarantee compliance with the provisions of the Law and this regulation.

The holder of the database or, if applicable, the data controller, may not execute the contract if the services for the processing of personal data in the computer cloud do not guarantee the due protection of such data. For the contracting for cloud computing service to be considered pursuant to the Law, it is necessary to comply with the provisions of articles 34 and 35 and this regulation.

---

259. The Regulatory Framework on Cybersecurity, Decree 92/014, available (en español) at: The Regulatory Framework on Cybersecurity, Decree 92/014. Note: TLS 1.0 and SSL v3 are no longer recommended for sensitive personal information transfer over the Web.
260. The Security Policy on Information Managed by Databanks of Personal Data enacted by Directorial Resolution (N° 019-2013-JUS/DGPDP), guide available (en español) at: https://www.minjus.gob.pe/wp-content/uploads/2014/02/Cartilla-de-Directiva-de-Seguridad.pdf.

Article 34

Obligations of the provider of cloud computing. In addition to the indications of Article 23 of this regulation, the provider of cloud computing will comply at least with the following:

1. Report with transparency the subcontracting involving the information on which the service is rendered.
2. Refrain from including conditions in the performance of the service that authorize or permit it to assume ownership or property of the information concerned by the service.
3. Keep confidentiality concerning the personal data on which it renders the service.

Article 35

Mechanisms for provision of cloud computing. The provider of the service must have the following mechanisms:

1. Inform on changes in its privacy policies or in the conditions of the service rendered to the data controller in order to obtain the consent if it means increasing its processing powers.
2. Allow the data controller to limit the type of processing of personal data on which it renders the service.
3. Establish and maintain adequate safety measures for the protection of personal data on which it renders the service.
4. Guarantee the elimination of the personal data after the service rendered to the controller is completed and the latter was able to recover them.
5. Prevent access to personal data to parties that do not have access privileges, or if it is requested by the competent authority, report this fact to the controller

[13] Security

Chapter V

Article 39

Security for the processing of digital information. The computer systems that handle databases or imply the processing of personal data must include in their operation records that keep all types of interaction with logical data, so as to identify the users, changes, consultations, starting and closing hours of a session and other actions carried out. These records will admit only the access of competent, authorized and identified personnel.

Furthermore, it is necessary to establish security measures related to the authorized accesses to the data by procedures of identification and authentication that guarantee the confidentiality and integrity of the data.

Article 40

Conservation, backup and recovery of personal data. The environments in which the information is processed, stored or transmitted must be implemented, taking into account the controls, policies, standards and recommendations related to physical and environmental security established in Peruvian Technical Standards "NTP-ISO/IEC 17799: 2007 EDI. Technology of Information. Code of Good Practice for the management of the security of the information. 2nd Edition," as well as taking into account "NTP ISO/IEC 27001: 2008 EDI Technology of Information. Security Techniques. Systems of Management of Information Security. Requisites."

Furthermore, the holders of databases will implement the necessary mechanisms for correct application of the procedures for making backup copies and recovery of the data. These mechanisms must guarantee the reconstruction in the status they had at the time of the loss or destruction.

Article 41

Logical or electronic transfer of personal data. The withdrawal or transfer of information assets containing personal data from the processing or storage environments will be done only with the authorization of the holder of the database and using the transport means authorized by it.

Any information that contains personal data must be protected in its storage and electronic transport with current encrypting algorithms. Furthermore, the electronic components that allow the transfer of information must contain security procedures and standards that protect the equipment and the information.

Article 42

Storage of non-automated documentation. The cabinets, filing cabinets and other elements where non-automated documents with personal data are stored must be in areas where access is protected with access doors with opening systems with key or other equivalent provision. Said areas must remain closed when it is not necessary to access the documents included in the database.

If, due to the characteristics of the rooms, it is established that it is not possible to comply with the provisions of the previous paragraph, alternative measures will be adopted, according to the instructions of the General Department of Personal Data Protection.

Article 43

Copy or reproduction. The generation of copies or the reproduction of documents may be done only under the control of authorized personnel.

It is necessary to destroy the copies or reproductions discarded in order to avoid access to the information contained therein or its subsequent recovery.

Article 44

Access to the documentation. The access to the documentation will be limited exclusively to the authorized personnel.

Mechanisms will be established to identify the accesses done in the case of documents that may be used by multiple users.

The access of persons not included in the previous paragraph must be adequately recorded according to the security instructions issued by the General Department of Personal Data Protection.

Article 45

Non-automated documentation transfer. Whenever the documentation contained in a database is physically transferred, it is necessary to adopt measures intended to prevent the access or handling of the information transferred.

Article 46

Provision of services without access to personal data. The controller or the processor of the information or processing will adopt adequate measures to limit the access of the personnel to personal data, to the media containing them or to the resources of the information system, to do work that does not imply the processing of personal data.

In the case of foreign personnel, the service contract will contain expressly the prohibition of accessing personal data and the secrecy obligation concerning the data that the personnel may have become aware, connected with the performance of the service.

[2] *Passages of Note: Security Policy on Information Managed by Databanks of Personal Data*[261]

1.4 Supplementary information on requirements (to be applied according to requirements table)
   1.4.1 The personal data protection policy is a formal declaration of commitment and should:
      A) Be clear and understandable, both for the personnel involved in data management and for the holders of personal data who have consented to data management.
      B) Be appropriate for the objectives of the organization.

261. This version has been translated by Google Translate with changes by the Author. The word "treatment" has been adapted to "data management" to prevent confusion with patient medical treatment laws.

C) Provide high-level organizational guidance and clear objectives that guide the implementation of appropriate conditions, requirements and safety measures.
D) Include an undertaking to comply with applicable safety requirements.
E) Include a commitment to respect the principles of Law No. 29733, Law on Protection of Personal Data.
F) Include a commitment to continuous improvement.
G) Communicate timely and clearly within the organization.

1.4.2 Implementation and maintenance of the following documented procedures must be achieved:
A) Control of documents and records.
B) Personnel records with authorized access.
C) Record of incidents and measures adopted.

1.4.3 The implementation and maintenance of the following documented procedures must be achieved
A) Control of documents and records.
B) Access records.
C) Record of audits.
D) Record of incidents and problems.

1.4.4 Documented procedures required in the Information Security Management System (SIGS), also including an access control registry, according to Article 39 of the regulation of Law No. 29733.

2. SPECIFIC PROVISIONS

A) For treatments determined as complex or critical, the appropriate controls of an information security management system must be implemented under the requirements and controls of the NTP-ISO / IEC 27001 EDI in its current edition, Incorporating the personal data banks within the scope of the ISMS, ensuring at least compliance with the measures indicated below and that the risks associated with the personal data bank are adequately managed.
B) The owner of the personal data bank must designate a security officer of the personal data bank, who will coordinate in the institution the application of this directive. The role of security officer of the personal data bank should be assigned to a person who has the necessary skills and authority to carry out their duties. When such designation does not exist, it is understood that the role of security officer of the personal data bank rests with the owner of the personal data bank.
C) References to documents or records can be in any format or type of medium (printed sheet, notebook, website, poster, video record, among others).
D) Limit the personal data banks to the data strictly necessary to fulfill the purpose for which they were collected.
E) Evaluate the possibility of implementing applicable anonymization or dissociation mechanisms.

2.3 Technical Safety Measures

2.3.1 Technical Security Measures related to unauthorized access to the personal data bank.

General measures

2.3.1.1 Management and use of passwords when processing is done by computer means.

The allocation and use of the passwords of the users of the information systems that process personal data should be controlled by adopting the following measures:

A) Require users to keep their assigned passwords secret.

B) When using an authentication server, it must store the passwords in an encrypted format.
C) Allow the user to change the assigned password when according to policy.
D) Require the use of passwords that contain at least 8 digits and are alphanumeric (uppercase, lowercase letters and numbers) and at least include a special character.
E) When access to the system is exposed in public environments (intranet, internet or similar), the user must be blocked after five (05) consecutive failed authentication attempts.

2.3.1.2 Review and manage access privileges.
It should be periodically reviewed that the privileges of access to the personal data correspond to the authorized personnel. This access review should generate a review record that evidences the accomplishment of such review.
The review period depends on the organizational policies and the type of personal data contained in the personal data bank. This must be done at least every six months.

2.3.1.3 Protect the personal data bank against unauthorized physical access by means of a physical blocking mechanism, limiting access only to those involved in the processing of duly authorized personal data (in case of unauthorized personal data bank).

2.3.1.4 When using computerized mechanisms for the processing of personal data, the personal data bank must be protected against unauthorized access by means of a logical blocking mechanism, limiting access only to those involved in the processing of duly authorized personal data.

2.3.1.5 The owner of the personal data bank, or whoever he or she designates, must authorize or withdraw access from users who process personal data. Such authorization must be registered.

2.3.1.6 Identify access made to the personal data for data management purposes (access logs).

2.3.2 Technical Security Measures related to the unauthorized alteration of the personal data bank.

2.3.2.1 Authorization for the withdrawal or transfer of personal data.
Any transfer of personal data to places outside the environments where the personal data bank is located must have the authorization of the owner of the personal data bank or whoever it designates for it.

2.3.2.2 Transfer of personal data.
All transfers of personal data should consider:
A) The physical data must be contained in a container that prevents its access and readability, as well as a mechanism to verify the non-violation of the container.
B) The data contained in a computer medium must be transported prior to encryption and an integrity verification mechanism (MD5 checksum, digital signature or similar).

2.3.2.3 Removal of information contained in removable computer media.
When removal of the information contained in a removable computer medium is required, safe removal mechanisms

should be used that include the complete erasure of information and / or destruction of the medium; In such a way that, they do not allow the recovery of the data.

The owner of the personal data bank must designate the authorized persons to remove the information of personal data contained in removable computer media.

2.3.2.4 Security in the copy or reproduction of documents.

When necessary, the owner of the personal data bank must designate the persons authorized to generate and / or delete copies or reproductions of personal data.

The following measures should be implemented to preserve the confidentiality of personal data:

A) Use printers, photocopiers, scanner or other authorized reproduction equipment.
B) Supervise the process of copying or reproduction of documents. Do not leave the equipment unattended.
C) Remove the original documents and copies of the equipment immediately after the copy or reproduction is completed.

Copies or reproductions of the documents with personal data must be recorded indicating at least:

A) Name of the person requesting the copy. B) Name of the person authorized to make copies. C) Description of the personal data copied. D) Number of copies. E) Reason. F) Name of the person receiving the copy. G) Place of destination. H) Period of validity of the copy.

The copies or reproductions of the documents must have a mark that identifies the period of validity of the same ones.

2.3.2.5 The owner of the personal data bank, or his / her designee, must assign or withdraw the privilege or privileges (data to be processed or task to be performed) for the processing of personal data to authorized users.

2.3.3 Technical Security Measures related to the loss of the personal data bank.

2.3.4 Technical Security Measures related to the unauthorized processing of the personal data bank.

General Measures

2.3.4.1 The non-automated personal data bank must keep the personal data independent in an individual way, so that it can refer univocally to a holder of personal data without exposing information of another.

2.3.4.2 The owner of the personal data bank must inform the holder of personal data of incidents that significantly affect his economic or moral rights, as soon as the fact is confirmed.

The minimum information to be provided includes:

A) Nature of the incident.
B) Personal data compromised.
C) Recommendations to the holder of personal data.
D) Corrective measures implemented.

2.3.5 Complementary measures

2.3.5.1 On loss of the personal data bank, in addition to requirement 2.3.3.1

All back-up copies of personal data must be protected by encryption techniques and stored in a safe and distant location in the main data processing environment, to ensure their availability against a disaster in the main environment (consider storing in a location Different or remote).

The frequency and the period of conservation of the backups should be in accordance with the purpose of data management to be performed and the impact of the loss on the rights of the holder of the personal data.

Where appropriate, mechanisms should be incorporated to ensure the continuity of processing of personal data, especially where the purpose has a high impact in relation to the owners of personal data or the common good.

2.3.5.2 On loss of the personal data bank, in addition to requirement 2.3.3.3

These tests must be performed at least every six months and documentation of test results including:

A) Date and time of the test.
B) Name of the person who performed the test.
C) Recovered personal data bank.
D) Recovered file and date of recovered data.
E) Recovery time.
F) Results of the tests.
G) Actions taken in case of unsatisfactory tests.

2.3.5.3 On unauthorized processing of personal data bank complement to requirement 2.3.4.6

A) Electronic transmission of personal data in encrypted form, which can be done by encrypting information before transmission or by using encrypted communication protocols (e.g., VPN, encrypted e-mail, secure FTP, among others).
B) Use of digital signatures to validate the identity of the issuer of the information.

2.3.5.4 On unauthorized processing of the personal data bank complement to requirement 2.3.4.7

The recipient or importer of personal data must implement the security measures defined by the issuer or exporter of personal data in the security document.

Acceptance of the implementation of security measures by the recipient or importer of personal data must be established in writing through contractual clauses or other legal instrument.

2.3.5.5 On unauthorized processing of personal data bank complement to requirement 2.3.4.8

It must be taken into account:

A) The provider does not have access to the information of personal data that uses its infrastructure.

B) The provider does not provide access to third parties to personal data that use their infrastructure.
C) The destruction or impossibility of recovery of the data housed in the service once the relationship with the supplier is concluded.
D) Use of secure channels for the transfer of personal data.
E) Ensure compliance with security measures in all places where the supplier's infrastructure is distributed.

2.3.5.6 On the unauthorized processing of the personal data bank complement to requirement 2.3.4.9
The person in charge of the personal data bank or whoever is designated by the owner of the personal data bank must coordinate the actions required to analyze and respond quickly and effectively to the security incidents presented.

Security incidents related to personal databases should be recorded, including at least:

A) Date and time of the incident.
B) Name of the person who reports it.
C) Nature of the incident.
D) Personal data compromised.
E) Names of the persons involved in the resolution of the incident.
F) Consequences of the incident.
G) Corrective measures implemented.
H) Recommendations for the holder of personal data. (If applicable).
I) Data recovery.
J) In case of data recovery, you must register:
   - Name of the person who performed the recovery.
   - Description and date of the restored data.
   - Description of manually restored data. (If applicable).

3. PROCEDURE

3.1 Generating the appropriate conditions provides an enabling environment for the implementation of this Directive.
3.2 Align the requirements, identify the type of processing of personal data and the applicable requirements.
3.3 When the processing of personal data corresponds to the critical type, incorporate the personal data banks within the scope of the information security management system and implement the appropriate controls.
3.4 Implement organizational safety measures according to the type of processing of personal data applicable.
3.5 Implement legal security measures according to the type of processing of personal data applicable.
3.6 Implement technical security measures according to the type of processing of personal data applicable.

4. ADDITIONAL PROVISIONS

In order to achieve the objectives of this Directive, the following provisions should also be considered:

4.1 Develop information programs in the area of responsibility, addressed to holders of personal data on "consent", "rights of the holder of personal data" and "purpose."
4.2 Those responsible for outsourcing treatment must ensure and maintain the auditing, verification and decision-making mechanisms of the contracting bank owner.

§10.06 THE MIDDLE EAST: ISRAEL

Countries in the Middle East, such as Saudi Arabia, the United Arab Emirates, and Oman have increasingly focused on criminal prosecution, rather than regulation of organizational systems. Israel, however, has led the world for some time with cybersecurity technological developments. Perhaps it is a surprise, then, that Israel has not passed a cybersecurity law. President Netanyahu, however, commissioned the creation of the Israel National Cyber Security Authority in 2014, which signed an agreement in 2016 with the United States to improve Cyber Defense Cooperation.[262] To date, the National Cyber Security Authority has developed an Israel Cybersecurity Emergency Response Training capability (CERT-IL) and released a highly informative corporate defense methodology in 2017.[263]

§10.07 DATA LOCALIZATION

Data localization, also known as data nationalism or data residency, requires data to remain in a geographic location. Unlike *data transfer restrictions*, which bar some types of data transfer due to concerns about privacy protection in receiving countries, *data localization* bars data transfer in total due to concerns about data security, desire to view data from residents and Internet traffic, or for economic protectionism. Many countries have recently passed laws barring data transfer outside geographic borders. Although countries around the world have passed these laws, the majority of localization laws have been passed in the APAC region.

The Russian Federation passed the broadest localization law currently in place, the Federal Law No. 242-FZ in 2015, requiring primary personal information record

262. Israel Foreign Affairs, *Israel and the US Sign Operative Cyber Defense Cooperation Agreement* (21 June 2016), https://israelforeignaffairs.com/2016/06/israel-and-the-us-sign-operative-cyber-defense-cooperation-agreement/.
263. National Cyber Security Authority, *The Corporate Defense Methodology* (18 Apr, 2017), https://www.gov.il/BlobFolder/policy/cyber_security_methodology_for_organizations/en/Cyber1.0_english_617_A4.pdf.

storage on Russian servers. The Roskomnadzor conducts annual audits to determine organizational compliance. Kazakhstan has employed a similarly broad data localization limitation for personal information. Other countries, though less aggressive in coverage and enforcement, have nevertheless passed localization laws that complicate international business services and infrastructure.

The People's Republic of China has passed a law limiting banking information transfer, as has South Korea. Two countries have focused on ISP and server operation, likely for economic reinvestment: Brazil and Indonesia. Nigeria has likewise focused on regulating all site data storage to improve IT investment.[264] Vietnam, in a bid to control speech on the Internet, passed the Decree on Management, Provision, and Use of Internet Services and Information Content Online (Decree 72) requiring all Internet Service Providers store a copy of information held within Vietnam.[265]

Two countries have barred transfer of population health data: China, and Australia, with the Personally Controlled Electronic Health Records Act.[266] In both these cases, it is not yet clear to what extent population health data extends to private organizations operating in these countries or providing service or products to receivers of government healthcare. Two Canadian provinces have restricted health data transfer outside of Canadian boundaries, Nova Scotia and British Columbia, although some organizations have leveraged a more involved disclosure followed by explicit data subject consent for transfer.

---

264. Anupam Chander, & Uyên P. Lê, *Data Nationalism*, 64 EMORY L.J. 677 (2015), available at: http://law.emory.edu/elj/content/volume-64/issue-3/articles/data-nationalism.html#section-42a569788a760913c2201c109f2fa7e8.

265. *Id.*

266. NATIONAL HEALTH AND FAMILY PLANNING COMMISSION OF THE PRC, *Interpretation on Population Health Information Management Measures*, http://en.nhfpc.gov.cn/2014-06/15/c_46801_2.htm; PERSONALLY CONTROLLED ELECTRONIC HEALTH RECORDS ACT 2012, No. 63, 2012, https://www.legislation.gov.au/Details/C2012A00063.

CHAPTER 11

Information Security Programs and Practical Strategies

As referenced in Chapter 8, the term "information security" is often used interchangeably with other types of risk management programs, such as information governance, although these programs serve a broader purpose than solely mitigating security risk. These functions provide a supporting role for efforts to manage safety, confidentiality, integrity, availability, and privacy. In order to effectively manage security risk, organizations must collaborate across technology and privacy teams to manage and protect assets and information. Legal counsel working in the privacy and cybersecurity practice area should understand how information security programs manage risk and how other information technology functions improve risk posture, so that it is possible to determine whether these programs fulfill legal and compliance obligations.

In addition to information governance, security programs integrate a variety of other information technology and information security disciplines to support administrative and technical measures. Table 11.1 compares the various disciplines to explain further similarities and differences.

Table 11.1 Supporting Disciplines for Information Security

Discipline	*Description*	*Impact on Security*
Asset Management, Device Management, Procurement	The discipline where decisions regarding business process, technology, or physical asset are made: including asset selection, availability and access, data reliability and records retention.	Without effective asset selection, identification, and management; organizations cannot effectively and completely apply security controls to the complete technical environment.

Discipline	*Description*	*Impact on Security*
Information Technology ITSM/SDLC/IT Governance	The discipline where issues are resolved and services are performed: including release management, change management, governance reviews and testing.	ITSM provides rigor to security programs by requiring security activities within IT development activities and other governance activities, such as review boards.
Information Governance	The discipline where decisions regarding the overall treatment of information are made: including retention schedules, data proliferation, archival strategies, and availability requirements.	Without understanding an information governance strategy, it is unknown how information should be managed to comply with both business need and legal requirements.
Business Continuity[267]	The discipline where decisions are made regarding technology availability and plans made for physical or technical impacts to business operations.	Business continuity provides mitigation solutions for cyberattacks and may create additional copies of data, requiring additional security protection.

§11.01 ASSET MANAGEMENT

The asset management discipline focuses on an asset from selection to sunset. Although most often organizations adopt an asset management team within the information technology pyramid and focus mainly on IT physical assets (such as laptops and peripherals), asset management in larger organizations may also include "virtual" assets, such as management of IT application, utility, and infrastructure lifecycles. This may include decisions regarding when to upgrade machines broadly across the company, when to retire IT tools, or when to purchase new tools.

These decisions can dramatically impact an organization's ability to mitigate risk. Without clear communication and involvement in these processes, organizations may struggle to effectively manage system security.

Organizations with procurement or third-party management teams more effectively assess and mitigate external security risks by reviewing vendors and third-party tools. However, many organizations overlook the beneficial yet often standardized processes used by procurement teams in selecting tools or vendor services, such as a request for information (RFI), request for quote (RFQ), and request for proposal (RFP). Procurement teams have more responsibility than relationship management: they also

267. Often business continuity is described with disaster recovery, as both address data availability concerns. Because business continuity often poses a more direct concern for security and privacy professionals, business continuity is described in this chapter. However, disaster recovery concepts like "emergency response procedures" are referenced in some laws, such as the Health Information Privacy and Accountability Act (HIPAA).

manage license compliance and contractual compliance issues with providers. Therefore, when a vendor or supplier does not comply with contractual security obligations, security leaders should engage procurement leadership and legal contacts to resolve issues.

Procurement teams use RFIs to solicit high-level interested parties and request basic information about a company and its products or services. An RFQ is often used interchangeably with an RFI but can be a secondary step when a shorter list or products or services is needed, also including expected cost/pricing. Procurement teams use RFPs for the last stages of a selection process, as they often require more comprehensive compilation of proposal details and include a substantial amount of questions. Naturally, RFPs provide an opportunity for more detailed review by all involved teams. *See* Figure 11.1 for an example of the procurement process and associated security risk mitigation activities.

Figure 11.1 Procurement Process and Risk Mitigation

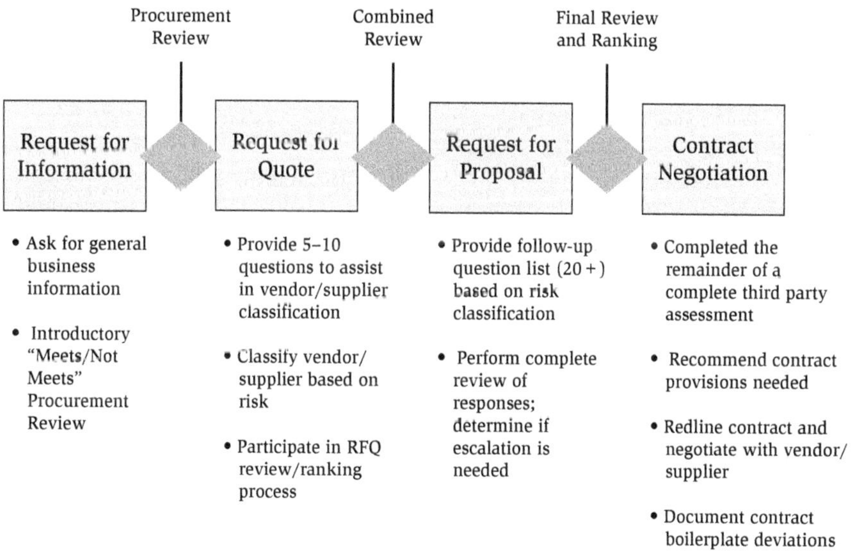

Asset management is an organizational capability that includes hardware, software, and application management. Asset management ensures that downstream IT processes, such as change management, function effectively, but also provides essential information to security and privacy practitioners. Security and privacy practitioners document business processes and IT assets to understand how assets process and transfer information. A practitioner can then create data flow diagrams (as detailed in Chapter 7). Understanding and identifying assets is central to determining whether an organization has implemented appropriate measures to manage and protect information. Figure 11.2 shows an example of an asset or data flow diagram.

Figure 11.2 Data Flow Diagram

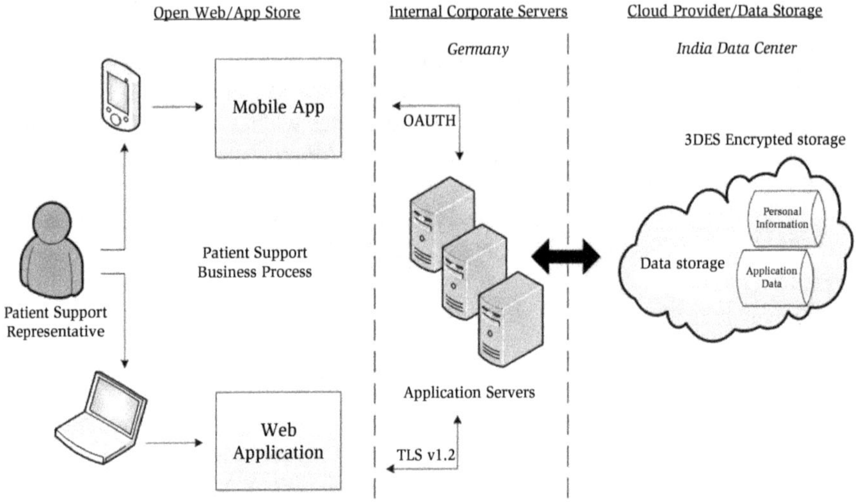

For most organizations, asset management may include device management, including management of laptops, peripherals, and mobile devices. However, increasingly more frequently, specialized teams may exist for mobile device management. Mobile device management team responsibilities involve mobile device planning, including management of corporate-owned mobile devices and personal mobile devices connected to resources on the organizational network. Due to the BYOD movement, which encourages employees to use personal computing devices for work-related activities, organizations now must manage mobile devices and associated resources.

Asset management and mobile device management teams should effectively leverage a common register for logging organizationally owned devices. The Information Technology Service Management (ITSM) capability within an organization usually manages a more comprehensive register of IT assets than most teams can create on their own, for purposes of supporting IT system support activities, such as event, incident, and problem management.[268] These asset registers, sometimes called a configuration management database (CMDB), include asset information, relationships between assets as implemented, and names of asset owners, which can provide substantial information for practitioners conducting risk assessments.

268. It should be noted here that "incident management" in ITSM is different than incident management in security. Incident management in ITSM focuses on resolving IT operability issues quickly whereas security incident management focuses on becoming aware of security incidents via a security operations center (SOC) or similar means and executing an incident response plan with the incident response team, which may include responding to a data breach scenario. An ITSM incident often ends with a fast resolution (e.g. an ITSM 'incident' could include resetting a password).

Key Takeaways:

- "Assets" include IT assets, physical assets, and business processes. All must be considered when mitigating security risk.
- Asset management provides both contacts and information about systems subject to security policy.
- Procurement teams provide existing process, such as RFP and contract review processes, which can be leveraged to manage security risk.
- Mobile device management teams are responsible for implementing mobile application management solutions and other procedures to ensure mobile security.

§11.02 INFORMATION TECHNOLOGY MANAGEMENT PROCESSES

Information Technology (IT) management processes include, in part, ITSM, the Software Development Lifecycle (SDLC), business continuity, disaster recovery, and device management. Each of these functions provides foundational components for an effective security program.

ITSM processes and an associated ITSM tool, often called a CMDB, support operational IT functions. Within a CMDB, asset owners may capture important information that improves efficiency for risk assessments and audit processes. For example, organizations often find it useful to label assets with data classification and compliance obligations. With these details, a security or privacy team may easily query the database and produce a list of assets containing sensitive personal information (SPI) or subject to the PDPA.

Organizations may also find it efficient to connect security operational processes to the ITSM service request process. The ITSM service request process supports workflow to complete an action, such as providing access to a system or other discrete tasks. Many security risk management processes require ongoing interaction with an organization's user base, so connecting to existing workflow processes improves ease of use for customers.

ITSM processes often support IT governance reviews as well. In an IT department, certain activities must pass gatekeeping functions, which ensure the organization overall follows pre-defined rules. For example, in SDLC, after developers complete coding for a product, system, or application (collectively, product), organizations need to release the product to "go live." Organizations facilitate product release through the change management and release management processes. In these processes, the IT department analyzes a product's potential impact on the IT infrastructure to validate teams have completed all required reviews and adequately tested the product.

Validation within the change and release management processes illustrate IT governance functions. IT governance functions often include upfront processes not typically considered part of ITSM. Examples of these functions involve IT funding requests, architecture reviews, software development lifecycle processes (SDLC), code reviews, and testing checkpoints. *See* an example of a product-centered IT governance process in Figure 11.3.

Figure 11.3 IT Governance Process

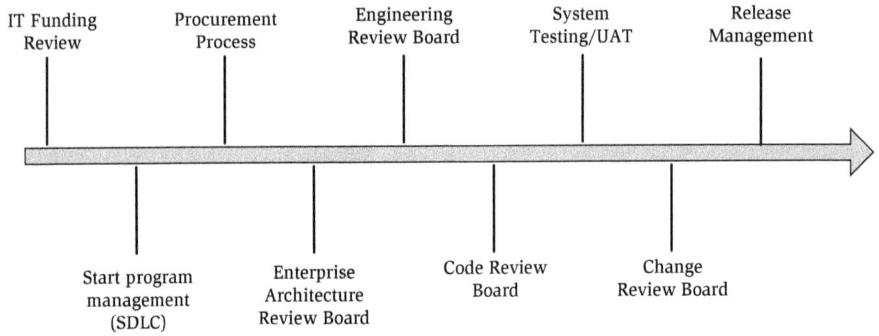

In order to build an effective information security program, attorneys and practitioners should understand an organization's existing governance processes, both related to IT and to other parts of an organization. Once governance committees have been identified, the information security organization can determine the appropriate involvement. Technical information security resources may participate in architecture and engineering reviews to ensure teams follow existing information security best practices. The Chief Information Security Officer (CISO) could participate in the IT funding request board or other central funding committees to ensure involvement in projects and compliance with security policy and legal requirements from inception. Another individual could be associated with procurement processes and vendor selection. Each of these functions provides an opportunity to ensure projects and assets meet internal organization requirements.

In addition to IT governance practices, organizations also require continuous access to data for internal operations and customer support. The business continuity capability ranks system priority to ensure system performance meets expected organizational needs. Business continuity activities include establishing procedures and technical solutions for continuous data access, drafting backup procedures, and managing data storage sites. Business continuity teams' backup data by taking periodic copies of data involved in business processes, so that if a business interruption occurs, the organization can still restore a previous version. Data site management involves the use of alternative physical or virtual locations to support operations and effectively store data backups. Ultimately, attorneys and practitioners may not require detailed knowledge of business continuity tools and technologies, but they should validate that business continuity activities apply and ascertain data transfer and storage locations.[269]

Key Takeaways:

- An organization's CMDB provides an opportunity to capture asset details that improve efficiency of creating asset inventories for compliance and review purposes.
- Information security teams can leverage existing IT governance processes to ensure the organization follows required security processes.
- Business continuity focuses on data availability, especially data backup procedures and locations.

§11.03 INFORMATION GOVERNANCE AND RECORDS INFORMATION MANAGEMENT

Information governance is an organizational capability involving broad information policy. These policies govern information collection, duplication, record-keeping, management, retention, and deletion. Although an information governance capability includes required processes and reviews, such as IT management processes or IT governance functions, organizations often adopt an information governance capability as part of a compliance or legal function. Most commonly, organizations have adopted programs in records information management (RIM), data retention, and information management. In addition to these programs, the information governance capability, in collaboration with legal departments and IT, manages and coordinates e-Discovery activities, including instituting legal holds and retrieving archival data in usable form for legal proceedings. Information management has emerged as a distinct area of focus for organizations handling large volumes of data. Out of necessity, organizations increasingly need standard models for handling formal data records, unstructured data, and combined data sets.

The information governance team, much like privacy and information security teams, manages internal organizational activities both through legal obligations and

269. In business continuity operations, organizations will likely have RTOs (recovery time objectives) and business continuity plans. Organizations use RTOs to determine the priority of an individual business capability and how fast an asset must recover after an outage (a period of resource or asset unavailability). RTOs will differ depending on the priority of the asset. For example, most organizations prioritize customer-facing assets, such as payment processing capabilities, and essential business operational tools, like e-mail. Business continuity plans describe the prioritization of specific business processes and assets, including expected backup strategies. "Hot sites" are active backup sites, ready to begin functioning after a business operation, while "cold sites" require time to support a business operation.

through internal policy. Information governance at its root seeks to enable decision-making and encourage consistency in information treatment within and organization. *See* Figure 11.4 for a diagram of information governance considerations, courtesy of Duke Law School's EDRM program.

Figure 11.4 Information Governance

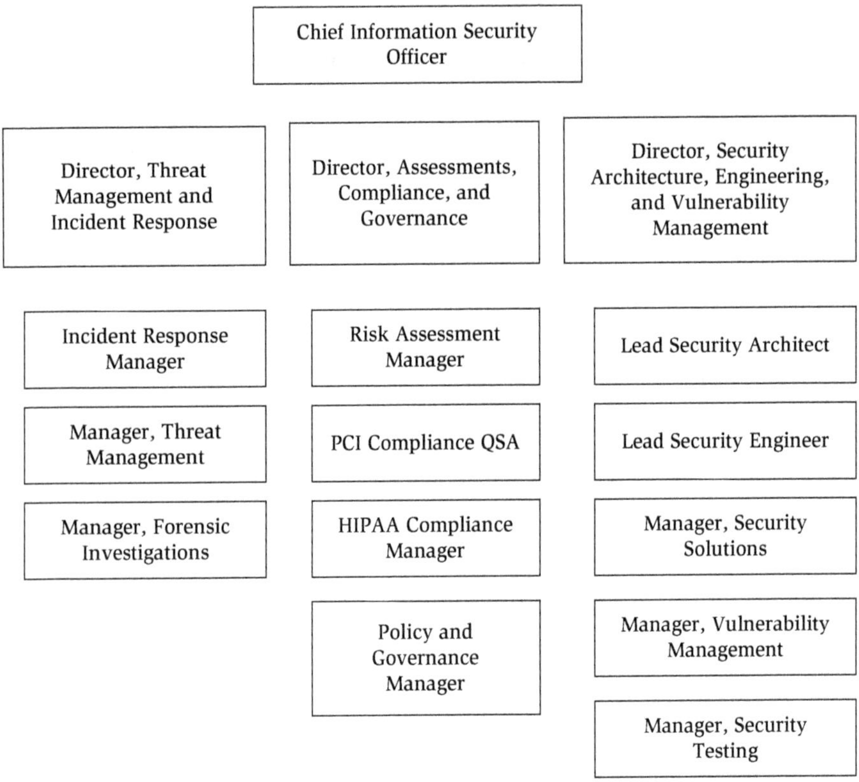

One of the key concepts in information governance is information ownership. Information ownership models inform decision-making, such as security decisions and investments, and who can make decisions under specific circumstances. Roles within an information ownership scheme include: the information owner, information steward, asset owner, asset manager, and data owner.[270] These roles provide appropriate oversight for executing and making decisions on specific security and privacy program objectives, for example expected timeline and cost commitment for resolving an

270. The terms "information owner" and "data owner" do not exactly entail ownership. In the international context, often data subjects have rights to their respective data, and organizations do not "own" data subject data. The terms, instead, are used to illustrate the role with respect to information collection, transfer, and processing for internal organizational decision-making.

identified security issue or deciding to accept the risk and not remediate a finding. Table 11.2 illustrates the accountabilities for each role.

Table 11.2 Information Ownership Roles

Role	*Description*	*Organizational Level*	*Example*
Information Owner	Individual accountable for information collected who, at a high level, makes decisions regarding business processes involving information type (such as HR info)	C-Level or upper management-usually associated with top-level business decisions	VP of Human Resources
Information Steward	Individual immediately (physically) accountable for information when it within an asset the information steward handles	Individual contributor, such as a Database Administrator (DBA)	Database Administrator (DBA)
Asset Owner	Individual accountable for an asset holistically, such as a server farm, application, or organizational laptops	Upper management	VP of IT Infrastructure
Asset Manager	Individual accountable for day-to-day management of an asset	Lower-level management	Manager, Databases
Data Owner	Individual accountable for large data schemes or databases, which may include new uses of previously collected data, such as big data solutions (may not exist in all organizations).	Mid-level to upper management	Big Data Collection Owner

Information Ownership applies to specific business processes, information included in these processes, and information governance rules. Information owners, aligned with a particular department or business area, retain top-level decision-making authority with relation to information their department or business area generates and controls. However, an asset owner and an information owner should dually decide on findings specific to a particular system, e.g., whether to remediate a security issue or when to deviate from records management standards. When individuals cannot reach consensus, or when an agreed plan of action poses substantial risk to an organization, governance processes may escalate decisions to more senior leaders or a governance committee.

Retention management is the process of identifying official information records and other data and ensuring organizations retain or delete records and data within a mandatory, legally compliant period of time.[271] Organizations adopt a retention policy and associated retention schedules, or tables capturing record and data types, that specify an organizationally determined period of time systems and business processes must retain this information.

The retention policy and schedules, with appropriate organizational adherence, also advance organizational security and privacy programs by limiting data volume. Privacy programs should provide inputs into these schedules by ensuring appropriate timeframes for retention consistently manage information described within organizational privacy notices and privacy policies. Security programs directly benefit from a retention policy and schedules largely because these programs improve official records organization, inform data classification, and implement appropriate deletion procedures. In short, retention programs not only reduce the work of attorneys and practitioners, they safeguard data subject rights.

Retention management focuses primarily on formal record-keeping, although programs should also include an assessment of non-record data and unstructured data. Formal records have a variety of legal functions and generally require a higher degree of integrity controls, due to their role in providing evidence or identification, such as financial records used to illustrate accurate financial reporting. However, RIM does not plan for standard data management or unstructured data.

Unstructured data usually are not cleanly organized in databases and do not fall into formal record-keeping functions. Personal or departmental shared drives and shared corporate solutions, such as Microsoft SharePoint or DropBox, often store large volumes of data, including employee, customer, and other sensitive data. Because unstructured data poses challenges for identification and classification, making security and privacy management goals difficult to accomplish, organizations should create plans to manage these data through asset identification and retention schedules for such data repositories.

Key Takeaways:

- Standard information governance roles include information owner, information steward, asset owner, asset manager, and data owner.
- Retention Management supports security and privacy programs by reducing overall data volume, automating data deletion, and identifying data classifications.
- Retention programs should create retention schedules and train employees on retention requirements specific to collected data.
- Unstructured data present unique challenges for retention management, privacy, and security programs.

271. Additional organizational activities influence overall data management, such as records information management. Records information management (RIM) provides an important function for organizations by determining the nature and strategy of record-keeping, such as considerations regarding e-discovery.

§11.04 RISK MANAGEMENT, ENTERPRISE GOVERNANCE, AND SECURITY LEADERSHIP

Although information governance advances information security goals, organizations must actively manage security risk to ensure organizational leadership can make informed, risk-based decisions. Risk management capabilities include determining appropriate organizational policies, reviewing identified risks, determining or influencing organizational investment priorities with respect to a particular area of focus, and apprising the Executive Committee (EC) and Board of Directors of potential organizational performance impacts.

Enterprise Risk Management (ERM) is the organizational function that compiles and compares risks across the organization. For some organizations, an audit or assurance capability fulfills ERM responsibilities. ERM provides top-level risk information by classifying risks into a risk framework, which uses multiple risk lenses to evaluate risk. One example of a risk framework used for ERM includes four risk categories. One scenario risk could pose both a legal risk and a financial risk because a certain decision does not meet a legal obligation and could likely result in a substantial fine. *See* Table 11.3 for an example enterprise risk framework.

Table 11.3 ERM Risk Types and Examples

Risk Type	*Financial Risk*	*Operational Risk*	*Reputational Risk*	*Legal Risk*
Description	Risks affecting financial future of a company, such as lost revenue, remediation costs, data breach costs, fines, lost revenue	Risk affecting business operations, such as technology outage, poor system recovery, data loss, impact to payroll or productivity	Risk affecting an organization's reputation for investors and customers, such as unsavory confidential information leaks, negative press, association with illegal activities	Risk affecting an organization's compliance and increased likelihood of legal action, such as litigation, administrative fines, injunctions, and compulsory actions
Example	Bankruptcy of a strategic customer might result in not receiving full payment for services rendered.	Influenza has increased substantially this year, causing concern for vaccine supplies.	An online retail site recommended inappropriate "Recommended for you" items for a child.	The organization failed to dispose of hazardous waste appropriately; fines could result.
Leader	CFO	COO	CMO	GC

ERM risk types, even where not officially leveraged for an ERM capability, help attorneys and practitioners effectively describe risk to leadership teams, contextualizing a risk's probability of occurrence and impact if it occurs. Risk categories also help leaders across an organization, not only security leadership, illustrate the value and risks of business strategies and investment implications. If greater consistency is desired across functional capabilities, organizations may choose to classify all identified risks using ERM categories. At a minimum, security organizations should be able to describe identified *high* or *critical* information security risks using ERM.

Information security issues will implicate all four of the ERM classifications previously described. Security issues can result in financial impacts due to fraud, expenses associated with a breach, fines, or legal decisions; operational impact through data integrity or system availability issues; reputational issues if non-public data is released to the public; and legal issues may also arise if privacy and security practices result in legal or regulatory authority action. When an ERM or audit team identifies broad risks, they rank the risks and present the highest risks to executive leadership. For some organizations, high risks identified by these teams, including privacy and security issues, require board awareness, as well. Organizations will often identify the same risk across multiple functions, requiring close coordination between teams to avoid duplicating efforts and over-reporting to the board.

Information security and privacy teams may also employ a common model for rating risks and making governance decisions. Many organizations create a Governance Risk Compliance (GRC) committee or Risk Review Committee (RRC) to review security and privacy risks. These committees include critical security and privacy leaders, such as the head of security, known as the Chief Information Security Officer (CISO), the Privacy Officer(s), legal counsel, and other rotating departmental leaders. An organization should empower the GRC Committee to make most security and privacy decisions. Although the GRC can provide reports to executive leadership, ERM, and audit teams, the GRC should make decisions within the committee meeting wherever possible.

The GRC Committee conducts programmatic strategy review, reviews investment proposals and large security or privacy plans, receives operational updates, and reviews/decides outcomes for of high risks. Strategy and investment proposal reviews involve presentation to the GRC of project details, technology purchases, and future maturity and development. The GRC provides an important role to ensure forward progress with respect to security and privacy efforts, and should expect annual strategy reviews and quarterly progress updates by both security and privacy functions. Large projects should also be presented at the GRC Committee meeting, either for investment proposal approval, which then feeds broad organizational funding or central planning processes or for informational purposes. This ensures that GRC Committee members clearly understand what might be achieved, how these projects reduce risk for the organization, and when to influence funding or effort prioritization.

Operational GRC updates include dashboards and performance metrics for key security and privacy functions. Although some GRC tools (described later in this chapter) provide metrics-based reporting for pre-determined Key Performance Indicators (KPI), many updates involve some metrics and non-metric details. Examples of updates might include the number of contracts reviewed, number of PIAs completed month over month, progress to ISO certification, average time for vulnerability remediation efforts, average incidents and time to restore, security testing results, and a list of high-risk findings. These reports provide additional update information for the executive committee or board when needed.

Security and privacy teams identify high-risk findings by conducting risk assessments; such as PIAs, DPIAs, and security risk assessments; that pose substantial risk to an organization, its customers, or its shareholders. Ideally, security and privacy teams co-present to the GRC Committee with the information owner to both provide full and complete information and to reinforce business or departmental ownership of the issue. If the information owner and asset owner or both roles have decided not to remediate a high-risk issue (risk acceptance, described in Chapter 12), both roles should attend and present the situation to the GRC Committee. In limited circumstances, the GRC Committee may elect to require the information owner and asset owner to fix the issue to protect the organization. Organizations should also consider under what conditions these decisions may require additional review by leadership, such as the EC or board.

The GRC Committee will likely meet, at most, monthly or quarterly. For this reason, organizations will likely need other governance committees to assist in specific annual activities, such as a dedicated Policy Review Committee responsible for reviewing and updating internal policies. Unlike a GRC Committee, the Policy Review Committee must include participants that can understand broader policy objectives and draft policy documents. Organizations should also include one or more legal delegates to advise on practical legal policy impacts and required language.

The Policy Review Committee is responsible for ensuring policies the organization comprehensively reviews policies within the organization's broader policy framework. For this reason, an individual involved with drafting other organizational policies, such as a general compliance attorney, often provides helpful perspective on policy conventions and normative drafting standards. Employees who understand the broader organizational policy framework also help the Policy Review Committee avoid potential collisions with other existing policies while identifying policy cross-referencing when needed.[272] A member of the CISO's team, as well as a member of the Privacy Officer's team should lead policy reviews. The CISO and Privacy Officer should formally approve all security and privacy policies, respectively.

272. The holistic policy framework for an organization should provide clear direction to organizational personnel, and developing a strong framework requires drafters to clearly understand how policies interrelate. For example, a human resources policy might reference an obligation to report any information security incidents via the incident response policy. A data classification policy owned by the information governance team might cross-reference security policies or standards for the classification applied. Privacy policies might reference data retention policies and schedules in relation to data minimization requirements.

As the reader has likely surmised through this section, the CISO and the Privacy Officer should work in very close collaboration. Some organizations have one employee fulfill CISO and the Privacy Officer roles. However, most organizations separate these capabilities into discrete teams. *See* Figure 11.5 for an example security team organizational chart or leadership diagram. Please note, some security roles will be introduced in later chapters.

Figure 11.5 Example Security Team Organizational Chart

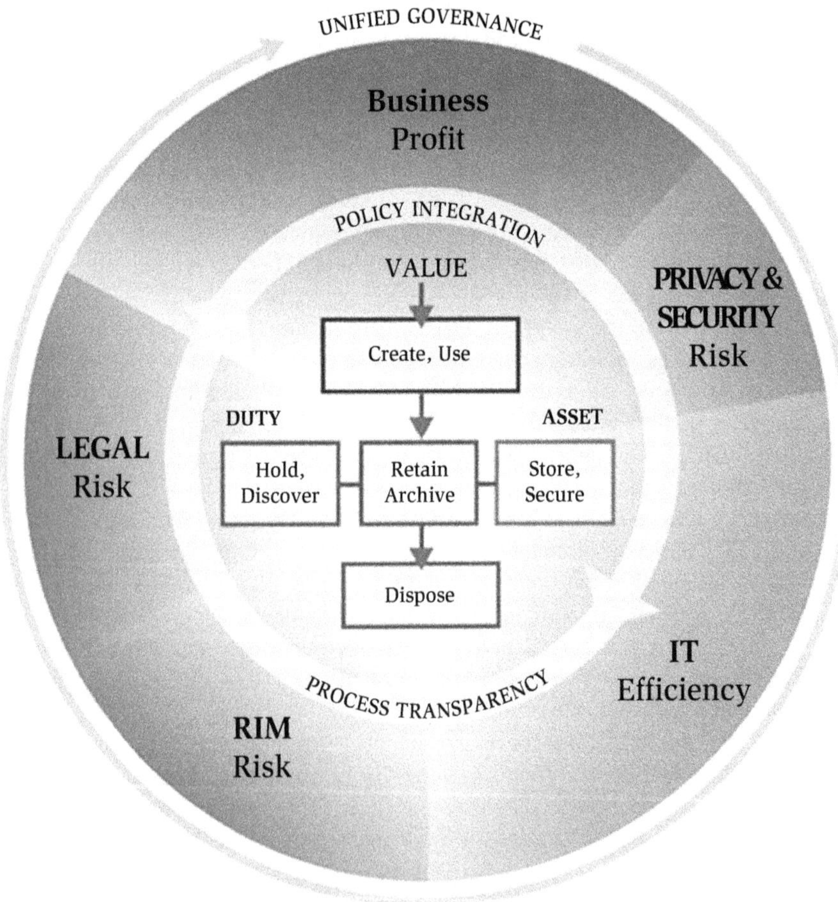

The Chief Information Officer (CIO) provides high-level IT strategy, and often security teams report through the CIO to ensure close connection with IT teams. In some organizations, security teams report through a Chief Risk Officer (CRO), Chief Data Officer (CDO), or Executive Vice President of Assurance, though less common. The CISO typically appoints leaders to manage each security capability, which ensures clear roles and enhances accountability. Security fails when any capability does not function as intended, so organizations must ensure security accountability through clear leadership. Frequently, organizations separate important operational capabilities from future project reviews and planning activities, such as risk assessments and policy reviews, although small teams may fulfill multiple roles.

One emerging topic for small organizations involves the outsourcing of security responsibilities to third party firms. Most commonly, outsourced security responsibilities include the Security Operations Center (SOC), which reviews potential security incidents and data breaches for an organization (described in more detail in Chapter 13) as a managed service. A third party holistically executes a *managed service*, usually offsite, rather than by providing personnel to an organization's team (staff augmentation).

Organizations usually augment staff when temporary assistance is needed, such as during a large project or build activity or when supporting highly specialized activities. For example, organizations do not often employ dedicated penetration testers, although having a blue team might be highly desirable to identify vulnerabilities and avoid downstream issues. Organizations often cannot afford to fund a *blue team* of penetration testers, so organizations instead employ vendor *red teams*, or Sometimes organization prefer external penetration testing (red team), as red teams usually identify different vulnerabilities and reports may be shared with business customers, as needed. When determining whether a particular team or position should be outsourced, organizations should balance the desirability of retaining knowledge and control versus potential benefits of outsourcing, such as connections within the Dark Web or benefits of broader knowledge by working with multiple clients. Organizations should avoid, whenever possible, becoming so reliant on a vendor that termination or transfer of business is unreasonably difficult.

In some cases, as above with penetration testing, organization may prefer to engage vendors, such as independent forensic investigation within an incident response process (described in Chapter 13). Although organizations may conduct initial forensic investigations internally, external investigation is highly recommended and sometimes required, such as for certain external certifications or to ensure cyberliability insurance payouts.

Although theoretically a vendor could perform any security tasks, becoming too reliant on any one vendor can spell problems for an organization. First, the CISO and Privacy Officer should be aware of any issues affecting organizational security and organizational privacy (including security issues); respectively.[273] This means that leaders need to receive ongoing information from their team(s) and provide adequate oversight. When organizations outsource too much of a security program, the CISO and

273. The engagement of the CISO and Privacy Officer individually are required by industry certifications and some laws. Outside compliance obligations, most organizations cannot run effective security and privacy programs without, at a minimum, one dedicated resource for security and privacy responsibilities. It is not advised to combine responsibilities between general IT and specialized security and privacy, as frequently general IT objectives and security/privacy requirements oppose. Between two individuals, productive friction should result; within one person, often one dominant perspective will emerge, serving neither function effectively.

Privacy Officer may miss important information about an organization's current risk status and lose a degree of operational control. Further, using vendors increases risk of potential information exposure by adding another group of systems (and people) that are vulnerable to attack. While many organizations successfully outsource security activities, an organization should carefully weigh costs, benefits, and risks of outsourcing.

§11.05 SECURITY POLICY MANAGEMENT AND RISK ASSESSMENTS

Security risk assessments focus on determining which risks affect an organization and understanding the severity of those risks. Risk assessments are considered a critical element of an effective security program and exhibit due diligence for examining security risks for an organization. Although laws may require regular risk assessments; absent legal requirements, risk assessments provide the best option for understanding organizational security risks and determining where organizations should invest in security solutions and remediation activities. Best practices and certifications often require annual internal risk assessments for an organization, and organizations conduct provide risk assessment findings as an input for other annual processes, such as IT general control audits or broader organizational risk management audits.

Mission, vision, policies, standards, and a controls library form the foundation of a risk management capability. Organizations create a mission and vision as an initial step for most capabilities to frame future goals and objectives, but for a security capability developing a mission and vision dramatically shape the risk posture of an organization. For example, one organization may prefer to operate primarily from a compliance (or legal minimum) approach, while another organization may prefer to develop a proactive risk approach, which requires substantially more risk management activities avoid risks. The overall risk point of view, reflected in mission and vision statements for a security capability, is often called *risk posture*.

An organization's risk posture informs all risk decisions for an organization, and it may change or mature with new leadership, new threats, or time and program maturity. Boards understand risk posture better than other risk concepts because risk posture provides a lens through which Boards guide organizational decisions: risk posture reflects overall risk tolerance. Organizational policies reflect the overall risk posture of an organization and establish required activities for all personnel. Organizational standards further develop details within a policy, such as encryption or access management. The organizational policies may include such common policies as a privacy policy, a security policy, a social media policy, a mobile device management policy, or a human resources policy. Some policies include policy statements reflecting a variety of organizational capabilities. For example, a social media policy may restrict sharing of confidential information, consistent with security policies, but may also include statements restricting use of social media for official organizational statements only to specific employees.

Policies are central to an organization's due diligence obligations because they notify personnel about their responsibilities, inform personnel about consequences of non-compliance, and establish internal requirements for the organization. Policies illustrate, from a legal perspective, that an organization has committed to a risk approach and have communicated requirements internally. A *control library* operationalizes policy compliance by establishing internal requirements to reduce security risk, and controls usually fall into a particular *domain*. Authoritative sources like legal requirements and industry best practices inform the policy structure, which is then represented within the control library. *See* Table 11.4 for a list of security domains and descriptions of required activities associated with these domains in line with controls.

Table 11.4 Security Domains

Domain	**Process and Procedure Examples**
Organizational Responsibility	Designate and document a management-level individual responsible for cybersecurity; implement policies and procedures; train employees.
Risk Governance	Review, document, and record risk decisions when non-compliant with internal policies and procedures.
Cryptography	Document and use processes for determining when encryption will be used and acceptable methods, protocols, and key management approaches.
Identity and Access Management	Document and use processes for determining specific identity and access technology selections appropriate to technology (e.g., biometric scanning, two-factor authentication).
Secure Development Lifecycle	Document and use a process for designing architectures and systems securely and taking into account privacy principles; develop a repository of technology-specific requirements for enterprise technologies used.
Threat and Vulnerability Management	Document and use a process for gathering threat intel to anticipate potential vulnerabilities or data exposure. Document a process for identifying vulnerabilities and appropriate remediation timeframes.
Asset Management	Implement an asset management system and include information about technologies used internally, implemented in systems or products, third party status, and configuration information.
Third Party Management	Document and use third parties providing equipment, infrastructure, or services. Routinely assess third parties are following organization processes and procedures and ensure compliance through standard contractual provisions.
Integrity Monitoring	Document and use processes and technologies for ensuring data and device function integrity, such as file integrity monitoring or similar technologies.
Incident Response/Data Breach Notification	Document, test, and use routine processes and procedures for detecting potential incidents, such as intrusion prevention or detection systems, internal forensic procedures, information sharing models, playbooks and processes, incident response team and draft notification language.

Domain	Process and Procedure Examples
Network Management	Document and implement secure network technologies and include appropriate use of firewalls, firewall management systems, DMZ, data loss prevention tools, and network segmentation.
Business Continuity and Disaster Recovery	Document, test, and use processes for determining system priority and expected uptime/downtime requirements. Document, test, and use processes for managing disaster situations, including appropriate recovery procedures, emergency operation, and storage of disaster recovery plans.
Retention, Archive, Deletion	Document, test, and use appropriate retention requirements according to data stored; archive and delete data securely. Ensure ability to ensure data can be deleted in all systems as appropriate.

In data protection laws, individual *controls*, or security measures, may be administrative (organizational or operational) or technical in nature. In security parlance, control libraries classify controls as *preventative* or *defensive*, controls that reduce security risks before they occur, and *responsive*, controls that organizations use to respond to a potential incident or data breach. Controls also can be *detective*, controls that enable efficient investigation should an incident or data breach occur. From a data protection perspective, the word "controls" reflects the same meaning as "measures," "safeguards," or "means." Language like "appropriate," "reasonable," or "risk-based" is used to communicate the expectation that some information may require advanced controls while other information should require less advanced controls: organizations should apply controls with respect to cost and expected overall benefit.

Organizations should invest heavily to build a comprehensive and representative control library. A control library not only operationalizes compliance obligations with respect to privacy and security controls but also enables assessment of such obligations with respect to any asset. Risk assessments leverage controls to determine whether an asset (such as a business process or physical asset) meets organizational policy. Security and privacy teams should draft controls to be answered affirmatively or negatively, such as "sensitive personal and personal information must adopt TLS 1.2 encryption in transfer." Each control should either map to a data classification type or incorporate that data classification into the control language.[274]

When security and privacy teams begin creating a controls library, they should compile industry standard frameworks, legal requirements, and government authority guidelines, or authoritative sources. Industry standard resources like the International Standards Organization (ISO) 27001, Payment Card Industry Data Security Standards (PCI-DSS), the European Union Agency for Network and Information Security (ENISA), and the NIST Cybersecurity framework and controls can assist organizations in developing a controls library based on industry best practices. Organizations map

274. A data classification policy lists categories of data elements with the purpose of prioritizing security control application in relation to data classification. Because security controls may be expensive to apply and may reduce system functionality, it is important to implement controls that make sense and are consistent with risk posed to data type.

the authoritative source to each control, as well as explain accepted forms of evidence, if available.[275] *See* Figure 11.6, which illustrates the relationships between policy functions in the policy framework.

Figure 11.6 Policy Functions and Framework

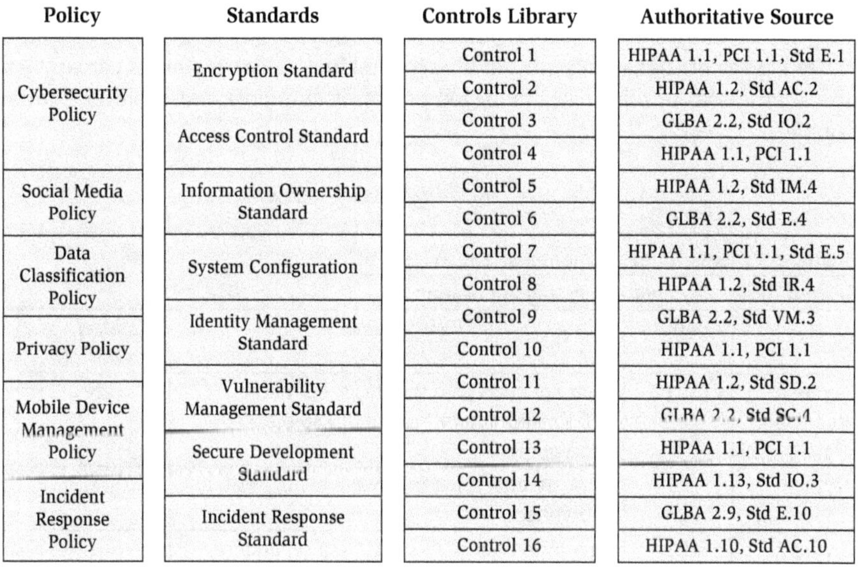

Controls in the policy framework can be leveraged by a variety of assessment types including residual risk assessments, compliance assessments, and third-party assessments. Each assessment type has a different purpose but uses a version of the common control library, and typically the organization itself conducts these reviews internally on their own assets. Organizations use enterprise risk assessments (inherent risk assessments) to determine which areas of an organization pose the most inherent risk to the organization holistically rather than assessing all controls. *Inherent risk assessments* might identify, for example, areas of a company where the most sensitive data are processed, or where critical assets support customer services. Inherent risk assessments should categorize business processes and data in relation to both business process criticality and potential risks inherent to the data classification. Usually, a security analyst catalogues all high-level business processes for an organization and reviews such processes using specific security policy statements. This high-level

275. Mature organizations limit acceptable forms of evidence to support a "yes" response to a risk assessment question. Audit best practices inform this style of assessment, though organizations may find the practice of evidence-gathering helpful for preparing organizational personnel for an authority, regulatory agency, or industry-mandated assessment or audit. Where evidence is not available, organizations may accept an *attestation*, or guarantee of compliance from the asset owner.

assessment allows for effective prioritization of future risk assessments that consider more detailed information and require significantly more time.

Residual risk assessments differ from inherent risk assessments in that they are based on controls, not policy statements, and review at a detailed level whether an asset is compliant with in-scope controls. For example, if the inherent risk assessment revealed that customer data are captured through a product sales business process, a residual risk assessment might examine the methodology for granting access, terminating access, and transferring roles pursuant to French access management guidelines reflected in the organization's control library. Residual risk assessments can apply to internal processes or third-party-managed processes and tools. *See* Table 11.5 for an example.

Table 11.5 Residual Risk Questions

Business Process Name: Customer sales payment processing			
System Asset: Payment processing application			
Asset Name	*Control #*	*Risk Statement*	*Meets Control?*
Payment Processing	1.1	Data are encrypted in transit, but uses 128-bit encryption instead of 256-bit encryption.	N
Payment Processing	1.2	Data are encrypted in storage using 256-bit encryption.	Y
Payment Processing	1.3	Encryption keys are stored in a separately managed database protected by administrative privileges and limited to two users.	Y
Payment Processing	1.4	Encryption keys are randomly generated and key generator is PCI-DSS approved.	Y

Residual risk assessments should review all controls in the control library that apply to an asset or an asset's user. For example, the customer sales payment processing asset illustrated in Table 11.2 would likely include SPI, such as credit card data, and other personal information, such as name and address for shipping a product. Because the highest classification of data involves sensitive personal information, controls required for SPI should be incorporated in the risk assessment.

Residual risk assessments differ from inherent risk assessments in that they apply specific controls then measure *residual risk* after analysis. Residual risk incorporates any mitigating factors, such as other controls (measures) that may *mitigate* or reduce risk of exploit. For example, although a system may not encrypt data in storage, data are stored on a company's internal server with limited data connections, strong physical security, limited administrative access, and staff monitors servers in real-time. These additional controls will not completely mitigate the risk of not encrypting a database storing SPI, but they may lessen the risk substantially. Residual risk assessments, then, are valuable precisely because an analyst investigates an asset more deeply and better understands the true risk a given asset poses to an organization. *See* Figure 11.7 for a process flow of steps in a residual risk assessment.

Figure 11.7 Residual Risk Assessment Process

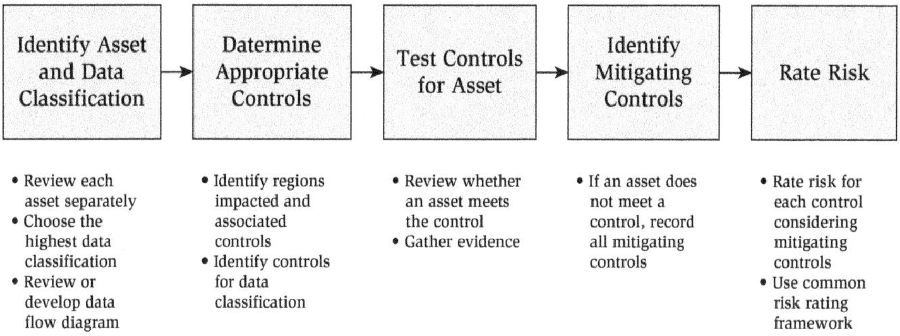

Compliance assessments do not differ from residual risk assessments in process: they also incorporate a control review for an asset, determine whether the asset meets a control, and assess residual risk. However, compliance assessments focus on compliance with a specific law or combination of laws. Because compliance assessments frequently precede external audits or assessments or follow a security incident, analysts often use a higher level of rigor for evaluation.[276] For example, during a residual risk assessment, an analyst may accept an attestation, or written guarantee that a system meets a control, rather that verifiable evidence. For a compliance assessment, analysts should require current and complete evidence with the aim of developing a process for acquiring evidence during a formal audit or external assessment. Examples of such audits or external assessments include: Payment Card Industry certification (PCI-DSS), International Standards Organization (ISO) 27001 assessment, SSAE16 SOC 2, a DPA investigation, or an OCC examination. When an organization links controls to authoritative sources and notates acceptable forms of evidence for a control in the controls library, compliance assessments may be completed easily.

Residual risk assessments take various forms, including third party assessments. Third party assessments primarily review *vendor* compliance with organizational controls. However, security and privacy experts typically use the term "third party" because organizations do business with vendors, suppliers, processors, subcontractors, partners, and affiliates, all of which could pose risk to an organization.[277] Under most privacy and cybersecurity laws, an organization must ensure downstream compliance when data flows between the organization and its third parties. Therefore,

276. Security incidents will be discussed in Chapter 13.
277. Partners and affiliates may not prefer to complete a standard third-party assessment, but some assessment of maturity should be completed prior to data transfer. Further, contractual terms should bind these third parties to the same legal requirements as the primary organization or face liability for the acts or omissions of the third party.

third party assessment activities illustrate due diligence with respect to third party compliance, in addition to binding contractual language.

Third party assessments leverage the same control library as standard internal residual risk assessments. However, the method of completing an assessment may differ from other residual risk assessments. Often, security teams leverage IT procurement relationships and contact asset owners to acquire third party contact information, then distribute a controls-based questionnaire to the third party. After the contact returns with initial responses, an analyst may need to ask follow-up questions several times to receive complete responses. Further, a third party may be unable or unwilling to provide evidence for responses, so organizations may need to schedule additional conference calls or meetings with third-party leadership. For these reasons, organizations should conduct a third party assessment whenever possible, prior to negotiating and signing a contract, as often third parties share accurate information later in the process. Due to substantial time investment simply receiving accurate information, organizations will need to prioritize the amount of time spent reviewing third parties.

Prioritization, such as "tiering," can be designed for an ongoing third-party management operational process. Tiering can include considerations of data classification, record (or data subject) volume, likelihood of misuse or fraud on the data, or criticality of the vendor's service. Figure 11.8 shows an example of a tiering structure.

Figure 11.8 Third-Party Tiering

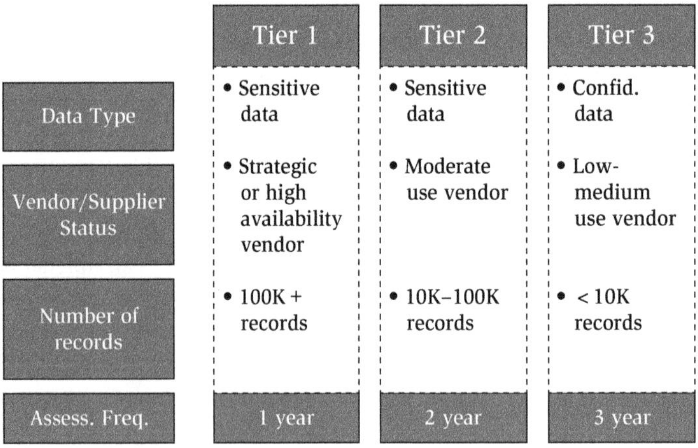

Tier one vendors should receive more frequent attention because of their role supporting the organization. Organizations may also elect to use the following "Tier One" indicators in determining Tier One vendors that should receive risk assessments annually:

- Cloud providers
- Big data plans/storage
- Over a specified financial threshold

- Significant expansion on existing contracts
- Outsourcing involving sensitive information (service or IT tools)
- Personal information storage in another inadequate jurisdiction.

Organizations operating as a third party to another organization may wish to simplify the third-party assessment process by pursuing an external certification. Because third parties often have many business customers, third parties will likely fill out hundreds of third party questionnaires unless additional actions are taken to illustrate compliance with laws or security best practices. Popular third-party certifications include PCI-DSS, ISO 27001, and SSAE16 SOC 2.

Key Takeaways:

- Risk assessment types include inherent risk assessments, residual risk assessments, compliance assessments, and third-party assessments.
- Risk assessments require a policy structure and associated controls to be conducted, and controls must reflect data classification and should map to authoritative sources.
- Inherent risk assessments enable an organization to prioritize detailed assessments, while residual risk assessments measure risk after mitigating controls have been evaluated.
- Compliance assessments may be used to measure compliance before an external audit or assessment is completed.
- Third-party risk assessments leverage existing organizational relationships in specific departments and procurement.

§11.06 THREAT ASSESSMENT, RISK DECISIONING, AND RISK GOVERNANCE

Risk assessments evaluate threats facing an organization, identify vulnerabilities associated with those threats, assess the risk systems pose to an organization, and enable organizational leadership to make informed decisions. The main idea is to determine how to make an organization aware of risks it faces and prioritize activities to reduce these risks. All practitioners and attorneys must understand the risk specific situations pose to the organization and communicate risk in a manner that executives can understand.

Attorneys must understand risks posed for an organization and counsel leadership teams to ensure organizations can make informed decisions, especially where privacy or security liability may exist, such as in administrative or authority fines or actions, regulatory non-compliance, breach of contract, or breach of other duty owed. Although often analysts conduct formal privacy and security risk assessments, attorneys must understand the probability and impact of an identified risk compromising an organization or its customer information to offer sound advice.

Organizations should evaluate risk through structured process and common risk rating criteria. Some organizations incorporate a threat assessment, or determination of threat sources and potential attack vectors, into the risk assessment process. Other organizations prefer a dedicated activity in advance of annual risk assessments, which involves reviewing new potential threats and attack vectors to determine which assets might face higher risk of compromise. A *threat source* is the origin of an attack, often a person or natural event (in the case of an earthquake or flood). The *threat* is the activity(ies) that could compromise an asset, such as a new zero-day exploit vulnerability that is being actively used to hack competitor systems. A threat is comprised of both a threat source (sometimes called a threat *agent*), and a *threat vector*, which describes the method by which the threat source will likely compromise its target (such as a system, building, or person). Threat sources are generally categorized as *inside* or *external* threat sources, insider threats or external threats.

Threat sources may come in many forms, including *malicious* and *non-malicious* sources. Malicious threat sources may reside inside or outside an organization, but a malicious threat source intends to compromise a target to misuse data or otherwise injure an organization or individual. Malicious insiders may include disgruntled employees, other personnel who take a job with the intent to access internal information or systems in an unauthorized way (e.g., corporate espionage), or insiders who have been compromised by external parties. Malicious external threat sources include script kiddies, who break or access systems for fun; hackers, who access systems for profit; hacktivists, who hack to advance a cause; organized crime, who hack as part of a larger illegal financial venture or strategy; and state-sponsored hacking, involving government-funded organizations often for geopolitical reasons. In contrast, non-malicious threat sources include an organization's personnel and natural events, which can compromise a target without intentional action. Examples of non-malicious threat sources include an employee who has greater access than needed, a system or software fault, or a tornado.[278]

A *vulnerability* is the susceptibility within an organization's asset that makes it vulnerable to compromise by a threat. Vulnerabilities include everything from a lack of encryption in a database to faulty wiring or limited perimeter controls outside a building. Generally speaking, vulnerabilities include any issues which could compromise an asset. However, the term "vulnerability" has both a general meaning, as in a system weakness, and a specific meaning, as a defined system issue, within security. We will discuss the later vulnerability type within the scope of the vulnerability management process in Chapter 12.

278. A threat source does not necessarily need to be a person. A threat source could be an earthquake, high rainfall, or out of control car. Vulnerabilities might include, for these threat sources, non-earthquake supported steel beams for a data center, failure to trench moisture-protected cabling, or failure to implement bollards outside the entrance of an operational facility. Although most frequently in security an attorney will consider the malicious or non-malicious insider or malicious outsider, it is important to remember that other threats could compromise operations, as well.

Security analysts use threat assessments identify the threat source, threat vector, and potential vulnerabilities as an input into larger risk assessment reviews. Specifically, threat assessments determine: (1) new and existing threat sources, (2) potential threats connected to threat sources, (3) attack vectors, or the specific method by which a vulnerability is compromised, (4) expected impact to systems.

Technical security experts should conduct threat assessments, especially those who regularly connect with sources of threat intelligence, such as vulnerability bulletins, the Online Web Application Security Project (OWASP) Top 11, the SANS Top 20 Security Vulnerabilities, or Verizon Data Breach Reports. Threat assessments, then, provide an input to risk calculations within the risk assessment process. For this reason, organizations should consider at least an annual deep dive threats prior to the annual risk assessment process.

In addition to technical threat assessments, organizations should consider conducting a legal appraisal annually, as well. Although not technically a "threat assessment," legal teams should advise risk assessment personnel of more frequent enforcement activities, lawsuits, audits, fine amounts, or publicized non-compliance that have caused substantial legal or financial outlay for the organization. Legal teams should provide this detail for applicable security and privacy laws to risk assessment personnel prior to conducting annual risk assessments, as this information will also influence risk rating for non-compliance with controls informed by law. Organizations with more resource availability should also leverage security and privacy-knowledgeable attorneys to prepare government affairs teams for potential legislation and clearly articulate impacts to the organization.

Threat assessments and legal appraisals provide important inputs for the risk assessment process because they ground non-compliance with internal policy in real-world impacts. Because organizations want to avoid a *realized risk*, or a vulnerability that a threat source has exploited to their benefit and the organization's detriment, organizations calculate *potential* risks in order to prioritize remediation and avoid impact. *Remediation* is the activity of closing a vulnerability to ensure a threat source cannot harm the organization. However, without clear understanding of real risk to an organization, analysts and attorneys will guess at impact and probability of circumstances. Threat assessments and legal appraisals provide risk calculations with real and reliable data.

Key Definitions:

- A security "threat" involves both a *threat source*, or the origin of the threat, and a *threat vector*, the method by which a target will be compromised.
- A *target* is an asset of the company, including physical, virtual, or personal (a human being).
- A *vulnerability* is an issue or weakness with the target that makes exploitation possible.

- *Exploitation* is the process by which a target is compromised. Sometimes an effective threat vector is called an *exploit.*

The risk assessment process integrates threat assessment with residual risk assessment to determine risk findings and rate risk. *See* Figure 11.9, for the high-level risk assessment process.

Figure 11.9 Risk Assessment Process

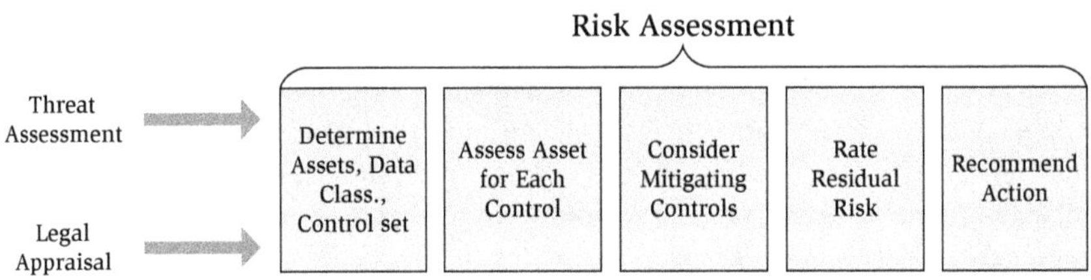

All risk can be calculated by understanding this simple equation: impact times probability equals risk (I x P = R). *Impact* represents the magnitude of what could happen if the risk is realized (i.e., a hacker exploits a vulnerability to compromise the system). *Probability* represents the likelihood of the impact occurring (e.g., the mainframe system has not encrypted the data, but it is unlikely to be compromised because a specific threat source does not compromise mainframe computers). Each *risk finding*, or an asset's non-compliance with a control, should receive a risk rating using I x P = R. Although most organizations do not have actuarial data to inform actual probabilities, dividing individual risk findings into impact and probability makes it easier to discuss the actual risk facing an organization.

Risk rating methodologies may produce *quantitative* values; or numerical, based on repeatable, objective indicators; or *qualitative* categories; such as low, medium, high, or critical. Most often, organizations incorporate aspects of both methodologies. Quantitative risk methodologies use real numbers and ratings based on actual numbers within an organization, such as financial valuation.[279] Qualitative risk methodologies use non-numerical categories like low, medium, high, and critical. Often, qualitative risk methodologies also involve a calibration step within a working group to ensure internal consistency.

Organizations may also stratify risk into categories, especially if the organization operates an ERM capability that has developed risk categories across all compliance

279. Annual loss expectancy (ALE) provides the quantitative risk measure for impact and probability in quantitative methodologies. This number takes an actual loss and annualizes the value, for example a USD 100,000 loss over two years would be an annualized USD 50,000 loss. Of course, this assumes that all losses can be verifiably reduce to a quantifiable number. Organizations may wish to begin the risk journey with less complex models until enough data can be used to support quantitative models.

functions. Risk stratification enables organizations to use a quasi-quantitative approach by considering each risk type and calculating overall organizational risk. Examples of risk types include: operational risk, financial risk, legal risk, and reputational risk.[280] Considering each category leads to a more comprehensive understanding of potential impact. Probability, then, provides the mental check on how likely it is to occur.

Organizations use a variety of tools for illustrating and prioritizing risk. Some organizations use lengthy spreadsheets and others leverage automated tools. However, organizations do not need highly engineered tracking tools to illustrate risk values and assist in prioritizing remediation. Often, a basic risk prioritization grid helps organizations visually understand potential issues for an asset and plot various risks for a given project. *See* Figure 11.10 for an example of a prioritization grid.

Figure 11.10 Risk Prioritization Grid

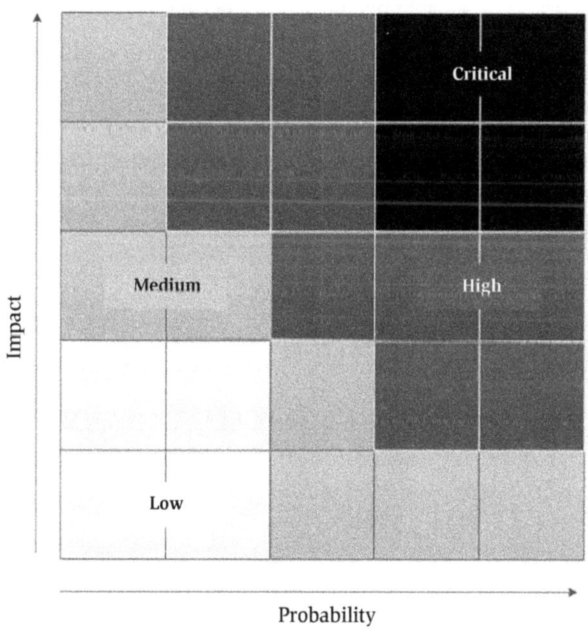

After a risk assessment is completed for each asset, the security analyst works with business contacts to determine which risk findings can be remediated, and which risk findings may require financial commitment and further consideration. After the final report is complete, the analyst should invite attendees to discuss findings,

280. Operational risk usually includes business interruption or other internal losses. Reputational risk includes damage to brand, loss of stock value, or reduction in sales or traffic. Financial risk includes non-legal fines, inability to process payment, or other direct financial losses. Legal risk includes administrative actions, authority fines, or other lawsuits resulting from non-compliance.

including the information owner and asset owner and determine the appropriate *risk treatment* option (often called the *risk decision*). Because information owners and asset owners should hold upper management titles, they can, respectively, commit personnel or financial resources to remediate risk findings. The information owner may prefer to accept the risk identified where remediation is not possible or too expensive. When risk acceptance, or not remediating a risk, is desired, a risk acceptance matrix clarifies who may accept risk in a given situation.[281] *See* Table 11.6, for an example of a risk acceptance matrix.

Table 11.6 Risk Acceptance Matrix

Risk Level	**Considerations**	**Risk Acceptance Role**	**Example**
Critical	At the critical level, additional oversight must be given, for example by a Risk Oversight Committee that includes Counsel, the CIO, the CISO, and two other representatives from business areas.	EVP in Information Ownership Area	EVP, Finance
High	At the high level, an Executive VP in the Information Ownership Functional Area can accept risk via signed agreement.	EVP in Information Ownership Area	EVP, Finance
Medium	A VP can accept risk via signed agreement.	VP (Information Owner)	VP, Accounts Receivable
Low	Individual accountable for day-to-day management of an asset	Director (Direct report of Information Owner)	Director, Strategic Relationships

In addition to the most common decisions of risk *remediation*, or closing the risk finding, and risk acceptance, organizations may also mitigate, transfer, or avoid risk as valid risk treatment options. Risk *mitigation* reduces, but does not eliminate, the risk identified. Organizations may *transfer* risk by taking out an insurance policy to shift financial accountability or engage a third party with appropriate limitation of liability provisions in the contract. Alternatively, when considering new projects investments, an organization can *avoid* risk by opting not to proceed with a particular project or technology. Organizations usually avoid risk by conducting RFPs, as described earlier in this chapter, or ensuring a secure development lifecycle is followed (described in Chapter 12).

281. Organizations can make additional decisions, such as risk transfer (risk is transferred to an insurance provider or third party protected by indemnity in contract), or risk avoidance (used when decommissioning an asset or determining not to move forward with a pilot project). Decision options include: remediate, accept, transfer, or avoid. Risk mitigation (reducing risk by applying additional controls) may be part of any or all of these decisions.

Organizations benefit by loading risk findings into a Governance, Risk, and Compliance (GRC) capability. A GRC capability serves as the hub for security (and other risk) program management. Although typically "GRC" represents a specific type of tool, GRC capabilities aggregate risks and enable effective decision-making. Usually aggregation depends on the presence of a common controls library. The controls library reflects internal policy and standards at a more granular level; therefore, organizations can aggregate to provide enterprise insights, such as top organizational risks, current and past risk posture, continuing non-compliance with specific policy statements, and progress towards organizational security goals. When providing updates to executive management, program sponsors, or an executive Board of Directors, aggregated details of all assessments can also inform program priorities and funding needs.

These insights can be aggregated using a GRC tool that supports a GRC capability. While a GRC capability may leverage a sophisticated GRC toolset, this type of aggregation can also leverage standard spreadsheet-type tools. Organizations will need to consider the breadth of GRC support, desired, automation needs, financial commitment, and internal resource commitments before selecting a GRC tool.

GRC tools are designed to support all risk management activities for an organization. These activities likely include compliance functions, such as information privacy compliance, audit or assurance functions, environmental compliance, corporate compliance, human resource compliance, financial compliance, amongst many others. Some organizations identify a benefit in using the same tool for all risk management function, for example feeding an ERM capability. Assuming a tool effectively creates a common, cross-team framework for managing and rating risk, a comprehensive GRC tool may be desirable.

GRC tools may also support a few or several security functions. Some GRC tools may specifically focus on risk assessment workflow, such as enabling risk assessment processes and storing risk assessment results, while other GRC tools may include different modules for authoritative sources (and new laws), policy management, risk assessments, risk decisioning, and processes described later in this chapter: remediation management, exception management, vulnerability management, and incident response. While implementing a fully functional security program in a GRC tool certainly is desirable, the cost and support needed to implement additional functionality may be considerable.

Organizations must also determine the degree to which teams can adapt processes to "out of the box" functionality. Mature organizations with solid processes may have great difficulty working with hard-coded GRC processes, such as workflow support. They must also balance desire for customization and ability to update tools regularly: with too much customization, tool benefits may not exist (reducing value). *See* Table 11.7 for some comparisons between GRC tool types.

Table 11.7 GRC Tool Types

Type	*Custom Development*	*Customized*	*Out of the Box*
Implementation	On premises	SaaS (Web access) or on-premises	Typically SaaS (Web access)
Benefits	- Specialized for unique programs - Supports mature process - No compromises on features	- Some customization - Lower cost - Updates - Automated upload	- Easy to implement - Lowest cost - Updates - Automated upload/transfer (e.g., API)
Drawbacks	- Higher cost - Fewer or no updates	- Sometimes tool "implementation" is expensive - Internal team support required ongoing	- Less flexibility - Changes prioritized w/other customer requests
Best For	- Highly bespoke processes and unique organizations - Orgs with more cash flow and leadership commitment	- Medium to high maturity orgs that can change process - Orgs looking for long-term relationship and investment	- Low to medium maturity - Orgs looking to begin the GRC journey - Other orgs with similar process to box

Organizations should leverage the standard procurement process, including RFI and RFP to select an appropriate GRC tool. Although this book will not recommend specific GRC tools, as they are too specific to a particular organization's needs, when reviewing GRC tools, organizations should consider costs for implementation, ability to customize and update, and cost to support the tool (including administrators or consultants). It is recommended for organizations to develop a complete requirements document prior to selection for ease of discussion and prioritization, and to ensure that GRC tools can support functional security teams and required processes.

Key Takeaways:

- Threat assessments involve review of threat source, threat, threat vectors, and likely vulnerabilities.
- Qualitative and quantitative risk rating methodologies offer different benefits for assessing risk.
- Risk treatment options include: acceptance, remediation, mitigation, transfer, and avoidance.

- Risk acceptance processes should provide effective oversight, enable escalation, and ensure business ownership of risks identified.

§11.07 EXTERNAL CERTIFICATION

External certification offers a complementary method for identifying risks to an organization and can also illustrate a level of compliance commensurate with customers' expectations. External certification can take many forms: focusing on payment processing and cardholder environments or broad reviews of business processes and systems. Business customers may require third party certification as part of a third-party contract. However, even when not mandated by business customers, organizations may wish to receive external certification to (1) identify any gaps in a security program and (2) shorten third party assessments and contract negotiations. The most popular, general use certifications include Payment Card Industry Data Security Standards (PCI-DSS) for payment processing, International Standards Organization (ISO) 27001, and the Statement on Standards for Attestation Engagement (SSAE16) System and Organization Controls 2 (SOC 2).

External certification provides many benefits to organizations. External certification can facilitate business transactions, such as payment card processing. Certification can also improve competitiveness in industries where business customers increasingly require certification, such as working with government entities or industries processing high volumes of SPI. Finally, certification illustrates to an organization's internal and external audience, such as the Board or investors, that the organization has implemented reasonably appropriate security standards.

Major international card brands, including VISA, MasterCard, American Express, Discover, and JCB established the Payment Card Industry Council to reduce payment card fraud and establish clear requirements across card brands in 2006. PCI-DSS establishes clear security requirements for an organization to follow, and compliance with these requirements must be achieved before processing payments from these card brands. Although PCI-DSS cannot directly fine a merchant, most acquiring banks can recover under contract for non-compliance with PCI-DSS.

Global credit card issuers maintain market dominance over credit services, and have banded together to establish the Payment Card Industry (PCI) security requirements for merchants and service providers, with the primary purpose of reducing expensive coverage of fraudulent charges and card reissue expenses associated with credit card fraud. Payment card Industry requirements, PCI-DSS, require merchants and service providers of a certain size to validate compliance in order to accept payment from certain branded credit cards.[282] Penalties for non-compliance can be levied by banks for the retailer or service provider, sometimes in millions for large

282. *Payment Card Industry (PCI) Data Security Standard*, PCI Security Standards Council (Nov. 2013), https://www.pcisecuritystandards.org/documents/PCI_DSS_v3.pdf.

retailers.[283] For companies processing large transaction volumes, this Author has personally observed fines amounting to EUR 11 million for an initial offense and up to EUR 1 million per month of non-compliance, although fines are specific to the acquiring bank and transaction volume.

Despite the significant industry pressure wielded from the PCI, PCI-DSS specifically applies to the management of payment card information only, not other SPI. Additionally, the degree to which PCI-DSS applies to information systems and processes depends largely on the classification of the business in question, the transaction volume, and the scope of business to which PCI-DSS is applied. As such, businesses and consumers contracting with PCI-applicable business cannot be certain that payment card information is protected without assessing the business itself.

In the U.S., some states have provided beneficial relief to organizations by incorporating PCI-DSS into statutes. These statutes often provide a waiver of liability for demonstrated and continuing compliance with PCI-DSS requirements. Other state laws offer an encryption "safe harbor," relieving notification obligations when organizations encrypt or obfuscate personal information.[284] Although not dispositive, cases have described PCI-DSS non-compliance as a factor illustrating fair warning (notice of risk) for lawsuits involving a data breach. Although PCI-DSS is not a legal statute, the substantial focus on PCI-DSS compliance commercially coupled with increasingly more frequent mentions within laws itself demonstrates that organizations required to follow PCI-DSS should treat it with the same priority.

Organizations may adopt PCI-DSS differently, depending on the type of PCI-DSS entity and the transaction volume. PCI-DSS segregates parties into two groups: merchants and service providers. *Merchants* are organizations that receive front-end payments, such as an online retailer or physical retailer. *Service providers* cover a broad spectrum of organizations, including organizations providing service to merchants. Service providers can include payment facilitators, such as vendors providing software for payment processing or enabling transfer and storage of cardholder data or suppliers enabling payment processing activities. Third parties under PCI-DSS provide service to merchants or service providers, and merchants or service providers must require third parties to follow PCI-DSS requirements via contract if such third parties provide infrastructure for a payment card environment, such as servers, databases, personnel, even ISPs under limited circumstances.[285]

283. *PCI Noncompliant Consequences*, Focus on PCI (Oct. 10, 2014), http://www.focusonpci.com/site/index.php/PCI-101/pci-noncompliant-consequences.html.

284. Although encryption safe harbors dominate U.S. state laws, increasingly more frequently updates to these laws remove safe harbors.

285. Relationships between some organizations may prove problematic for executing third-party contracts including a guarantee of PCI-DSS compliance. For example, payment processors often do not establish PCI-DSS compliance and will not guarantee compliance in contract, due to their substantial bargaining power. Other third parties may be considered borderline for PCI-DSS scope, such as Internet Service Providers that provide all Internet service, not specialized service for the payment card environment only. It is important to keep an open dialogue with your QSA about these challenges.

In the case of merchants, PCI-DSS scales diligence to the number of transactions processed, separating merchants into four tiers. For tiers two through four, merchants must complete a Self-Assessment Questionnaire (SAQ). Service Providers fall into one of two tiers, and like merchants, second-tier service providers must complete a SAQ. Merchants and service providers falling into tier one must conduct an independent assessment using a certified Qualified Service Auditor (QSA) to review the payment card environment and provide the organization a Report on Compliance (ROC). An Attestation of Compliance (AOC) certificate is also provided, which can be shared with business customers. The PCI Council maintains a list of QSAs on its Website, as well as a substantial document library to assist organizations at https://www.pcisecuritystandards.org. Some requirements, such as quarterly vulnerability scanning, require an Approved Scanning Vendor (ASV), which is also reviewed and approved by the PCI Council to provide services under PCI-DSS.

PCI-DSS assessments can cost a significant amount of money to complete, so it is critical that organizations conduct as much up-front work as possible before beginning the formal assessment. Additionally, organizations must determine the appropriate scope of assessment prior to engaging with a QSA. Organizations should consider where requests for a PCI AOC have originated and consider whether industry competitors have certified. The PCI Council includes a listing of organizations deemed PCI compliant on their Website, which is valuable both to assess competition and to verify vendor compliance for critical payment card environment activities. *See* Figure 11.11 for an example of the most stringent PCI assessment process (Tier 1 Merchants).

Figure 11.11 PCI Assessment Process (Tier 1)

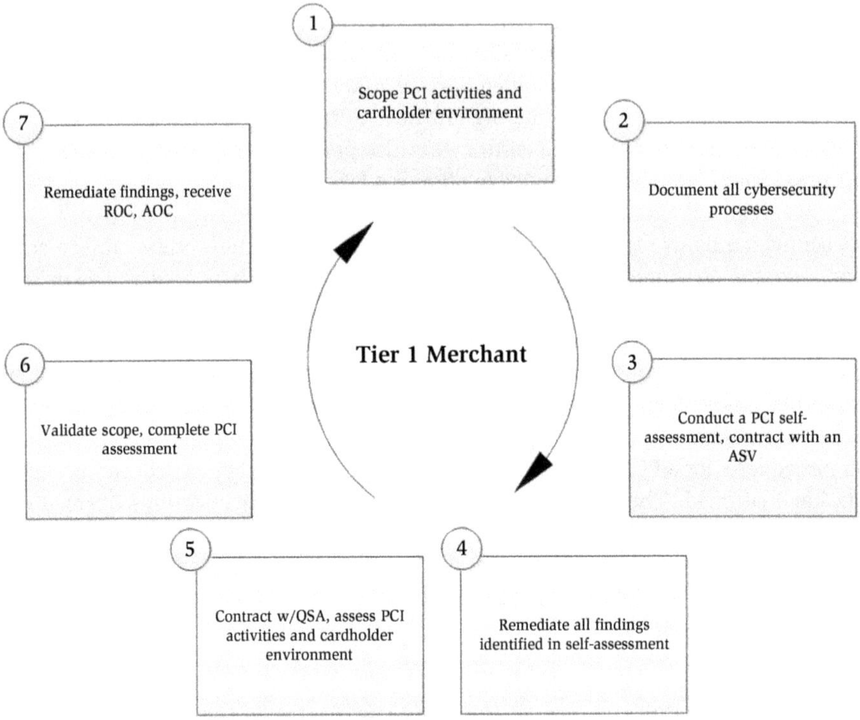

Once an organization has demonstrated its PCI-DSS compliance and received a ROC and AOC, the process does not end. Organizations have a continuing obligation to fulfill required processes under PCI-DSS, such as quarterly external network scanning.

Although PCI-DSS provides a standardized framework for the payment card industry, ISO and SSAE16 standards provide much more broadly applicable security standards. ISO, for its part, has an extremely broad compliance footprint, covering nearly every industry. The now-current ISO 27000 Information Security Management Systems began as British Standard 771111, which is likely why most international organizations pursue ISO 27001 certification over other certification models. ISO 27001 includes 14 domains, or concentrations of work, and 114 controls.[286] ISO 27001 provides a comprehensive set of security controls for most control libraries. Once an organization has established controls and has begun internally assessing for

286. The ISO 27000 series includes: 27001, requirements standard used for control libraries; 27002, the Code of Practice; 27003, guidance for 27001 implementation; 27004, guidance on metrics; 27005, the risk management standard; 27006, a guide for ISO certification; and 27007, the guide for auditing ISO 27000. Organizations seeking to be ISO-certified should purchase all standards/guidance and work on implementing required processes before pursuing certification.

non-compliance, an organization can decide whether ISO 27001 compliance is desirable. *See* Table 11.8, ISO 27001 Domains for a description of each domain.

Table 11.8 ISO 27001 Domains

Domain Name	*Description*
Information security policies	Requirements for developing an internal policy
Access Control	Managing access to systems
Communications security	Security of communications technology
Organization of information security	Roles and responsibilities
Cryptography	Encryption
System Acquisition, development, and maintenance	System development and review
Business Continuity	Ongoing business operations
Human Resource security	Managing employee security practices
Physical and Environmental Security	Buildings and physical entry
Supplier Relationships	Third party management
Compliance	Compliance with internal and external requirements
Asset Management	Asset classification, organization
Operations security	Ongoing security activities
Information Security Incident Management	Responding to potential incidents and data breaches, investigations

A non-ISO organization conducts ISO 27001 assessments by following the ISO's Committee on Conformity Assessment (CASCO) standard. ISO certification can provide a basis for contracting with business customers or government entities; therefore, organizations seeking certification should select an external organization accredited under the International Accreditation Forum. Similar to a PCI-DSS assessment, organizations interested in ISO certification should consider developing processes, determining scope, and conducting an internal self-assessment prior to ISO certification to improve the odds of a successful certification experience. Although ISO does not require annual re-certification, organizations should consider scope or process changes and ensure applicable scope is considered when presenting ISO 27001 accreditation to business customers and government entities.

The American Institute of Certified Public Accountants (AICPA) SSAE16 audits provide another avenue to prove compliance with best practices, and most frequently are used by U.S. companies, especially technology vendors. SSAE16 SOC 2 Types 1 and 2 audits provide the most comprehensive audit scheme for security. SSAE16 SOC 2, Type 1 illustrates compliance for a point in time, whereas a SOC 2, Type 2 tests ongoing compliance, usually over a period of six months. As such, SOC 2, Type 2 reports provide greater depth to illustrate compliance. SOC 2, Type 2 reports on information systems by evaluating "trust principles": security, availability, processing integrity, confidentiality, and privacy and review the areas of policies, communications, procedures, and monitoring.[287] Organizations typically engage a third-party Certified Public Accountant (CPA) to conduct SSAE16 SOC 2 audits every two years.

Regions also have a variety of country-specific certifications, and organizations would do well to consider these certifications, especially in countries where organizations conduct primary operations. In APAC, additional associations providing certification including JIPDEC, providing a PrivacyMark System and other certifications to demonstrate compliance with Japanese law related to cybersecurity. In EMEA, future developments by the Horizon 2020 initiative involve a European Security Certification Framework, which is focused on cloud computing, and EuroPriSe has offered certification for some time on privacy and related security programs, offering a seal-based program for illustrating compliance. In the Americas, the Health Information Trust Alliance (HITRUST) users a Common Security Framework (CSF) to harmonize various other certification schemes, specific to healthcare organizations. The U.S. National Institute of Standards and Technology also offers a conformity certification with respect to its comprehensive document library (NIST CSF).

Although some institutions do not provide certification per se, they offer reference documents and standards to develop security programs. The European Telecommunications Standards Institute (ETSI) has developed security standards, and Industrial control systems may seek standards and certification through IEC 62443 Conformance Certification.

Although this text does not detail all security standards applicable to services provided on behalf of, or to government entities, some countries require or prefer certification with government-associated certification bodies. Examples include IM8 in Singapore, FedRamp in the United States, or Cyber Essentials Controls in the United Kingdom. If your organization plans to provide contract services to international government entities, it may be required to meet differing standards within those countries.

Key Takeaways:

- PCI-DSS provides certification for payment card activities.
- Organizations desiring PCI-DSS certification should focus on scope of certification, process development, and self-assessment before engaging a Qualified Security Assessor to begin the assessment process.
- ISO 27001 offers a strong, internationally oriented control framework.
- SSAE16 SOC 2 provides an external audit report for third parties demonstrating compliance to business customers.
- Additional certification models exist for government entities and may require additional research.

287. SSAE-16, *SOC 2 Report – Trust Services Principles*, (2013), http://www.ssae-16.com/at-101/soc-2-report-trust-services-principles/.

Security programs require many foundational IT programs to function effectively. Strong security programs should enable asset management programs, connect with existing procurement processes, and encourage strong information governance programs. Security programs require participants from an entire organization to implement controls, participate in risk assessments, review risk assessment findings, remediate or accept risk, and to provide guidance on governance boards. Security truly is everyone's responsibility.

CHAPTER 12
Security Process Development

In Chapter 11, Security Risk Governance was introduced in reference to foundational IT programs and standard governance processes like security policy. Effectively managing security risk for an organization means understanding the degree to which different disciplines must work together to effectively manage and protect assets and information. Chapter 12 will build on concepts introduced in Chapter 11 and discuss details of specific processes required for a cybersecurity program to function effectively. Each of these processes support efforts to manage SCIAP.

§12.01 POLICY REVIEW MANAGEMENT PROCESS

A policy review management process is the most important process a security capability can have. The policy review process enables an organization to effectively review potential changes to policy on a periodic basis based on authoritative sources and desired changes to organizational risk posture. When policy changes reflect more stringent security controls, any subsequent risk assessment conducted will reflect the more stringent standard. Reviewing policy changes at least annually gives an organization the opportunity to review potential changes to policy required by changes in authoritative sources such as law or industry standards and permit additional changes according to an organization's risk posture.

Organizations should include multiple leadership levels and departments in the policy review process. Attorneys, in particular, fulfill an important role by translating how an internal policy may affect the commitments an organization makes to customers, regulatory agencies, and other entities.

A Policy Review Committee (PRC)reviews policy-level documents for an organization overall, including for other compliance functions. The PRC directly reviews policy documents before approving and posting these documents internally. The PRC may also have a review and approval role for organizational standards, procedures, or guidelines. Subject matter experts who understand the details of specific controls should draft proposed changes to standards, procedures, and control language. However, these changes may affect certain policy statements in the top-level policy framework. *See* Figure 12.1 for a high-level picture of the policy review process.

Figure 12.1 Policy Review Process

The policy review process provides the opportunity for organizations to adapt and change internal controls, consistent with authoritative sources and organizational risk posture. Common security policies include an information security policy, a data classification policy, and an incident response policy (discussed in Chapter 13). The information security policy provides a high-level map of internal commitments an organization has made. The information security policy statements should cascade through the overall policy structure from policy to controls. In addition to the Information Security Policy, the Data Classification Policy categorizes the most critical data in an organization.

Although organizations may classify data differently, most data classifications adopt between three to five-category classifications. These classifications, then, map to specific controls. For example, an encryption control likely will not apply to public data, but will apply to a secure handling or sensitive personal information designation. Although this mapping demonstrates a "risk-based" controls model, organizations should look to industry standards to inform whether individual controls are reasonable with respect to their data classification. The most specific requirements in law (e.g., the Security Law of the People's Republic of China, the Russia Data Protection Act, and U.S. HIPAA, GLBA, and Regulation S-P laws) often do not specify control-level detail, but may provide general guidance on control categories

Many non-government organizations organize data from most sensitive to least sensitive, and organizational leadership involved in policy reviews help to determine the sensitivity or importance of specific data elements in a Data Classification policy. Privacy and data protection legal counsel should collaborate with security leaders to ensure data classification includes protected data elements enumerated in applicable statutory requirements. Organizations may choose a military-inspired categorization; such as Top Secret, Secret, Classified, and Public; or a privacy-inspired categorization; such as Sensitive Personal Information, Personal Information, Internal Data, and Public Data. *See* Table 12.1 to see an example of a categorization and associated data elements.

Table 12.1 Example Data Classification

Category	*Data Elements*
Secure Handling	Mergers and acquisitions information, corporate account numbers, trade secrets, Intellectual property prior to registration/patent granted, race, national origin, national identifier or employment identifier, tax ID, location information (GPS or other), unique mobile identifier or IP address, sexual preference, religion, labor union status, political affiliation, biometric data, health data, disability information, financial data, marital status, family history
Personal	HR information (not included in secure handling category), name, address, phone, email, gender, username/password, employment appraisal details, employment history; non-secure handling information identifiable to a natural person
Business Restricted	Operational process details, vendor information, sales data prior to public release, non-personal information customer information, marketing information, pricing, proprietary product details, internal business contact information
Public	All information designed for public consumption, which is not categorized in more restrictive categories

Data classification performs an important role with respect to control libraries that provide the content for risk assessment processes. Without a data classification policy, organizations may waste financial resources applying all controls to all assets, treating all assets as if they pose equivalent risk to the organization. Organizations do well to create a clear data classification policy and map specific data classification categories to individual controls.

Key Takeaways:

- Policy provides a foundation for any privacy or security program.
- Policies stem from authoritative sources, including laws and industry standards.
- The data classification policy informs specific control sets applicable to data type.
- Controls should map to policies and standards and support the risk assessment process.

§12.02 RISK ASSESSMENT AND EXCEPTION MANAGEMENT PROCESSES

Inherent and residual risk assessments provide information, via *risk findings*, which analysts give a risk rating. Organizations should routinely assess internal policy compliance at least annually. Annual risk assessments should include an inherent enterprise risk assessment, a threat assessment, and residuals risk assessments for inherently high-risk business processes and associated assets. An annual risk assessment process will provide the most value for an organization when it closely follows any changes to policy in an annual policy review process. In this model, organizations test controls for the updated policy framework.

The third-party risk assessment process employs a slightly different process for periodic review. Unlike in internal risk assessment, third-party risk assessments may be conducted on an annual basis or every two to three years depending on the risk the third party's activities pose to the organization. Third-party *tiering* enables an organization to group third parties together to better manage assessment frequency, assessment control questions and contractual clause versions (if using multiple versions), and governance expectations. For example, a first-tier third-party likely requires an annual review, full-scale assessment questions, the most stringent contract language, and a focus on remediation prior to contracting. In comparison, second or third tier parties may require less frequent reviews, such as every two or three years. *See* Table 12.2 for an example of third party tiering and associated activities.

Table 12.2 Example Third Party Tiering

Tier	*1*	*2*	*3*	*4*
Account Value	EUR **1M** +	EUR **500K**-EUR **1M**	EUR **50**-EUR **500K**	EUR **50K** >
Operational Status	Critical	Substantial	Average	Limited

Tier	*1*	*2*	*3*	*4*
Status	Managed service	Cloud provider, SaaS	Support vendor	Consulting or other physical services
Data Classification	Secure handling	Personal	Business Restricted	Public

Organizations will likely categorize third parties using multiple tiers depending on the sub-categories. Having a common tiering strategy helps to prioritize third party reviews and ensure greater management of internal resources. Tiering also reduces impact to security programs by minimizing work for comparatively lower risk third parties.

Both internal risk assessments and third-party risk assessments produce risk findings, with future action the must be decided by appropriate individuals reflected in an information governance model. This model ensures that, in a repeatable way, individuals who accept, remediate, mitigate, transfer, or avoid risk can make and enforce decisions consistent with their roles at an organization. It also ensures that individuals who merely manage the vehicle for data transfer, such as a server farm, do not make decisions regarding the protection of information processed without input from the business leader whose team produced and owns the data.

When organizational leadership decides to accept risk, information and asset owners likely will be required to take additional steps. Risk acceptance usually requires documentation, memorialization (sign-off), reporting and escalation as needed. To handle these activities, organizations typically develop an exception management process. The *exception* management process, also called a *waiver* or *variance* management process, adds formality to risk acceptance, subsequent documentation, escalation, and reporting. *See* Figure 12.2 for an example exception management process.

Figure 12.2 Exception Management Process

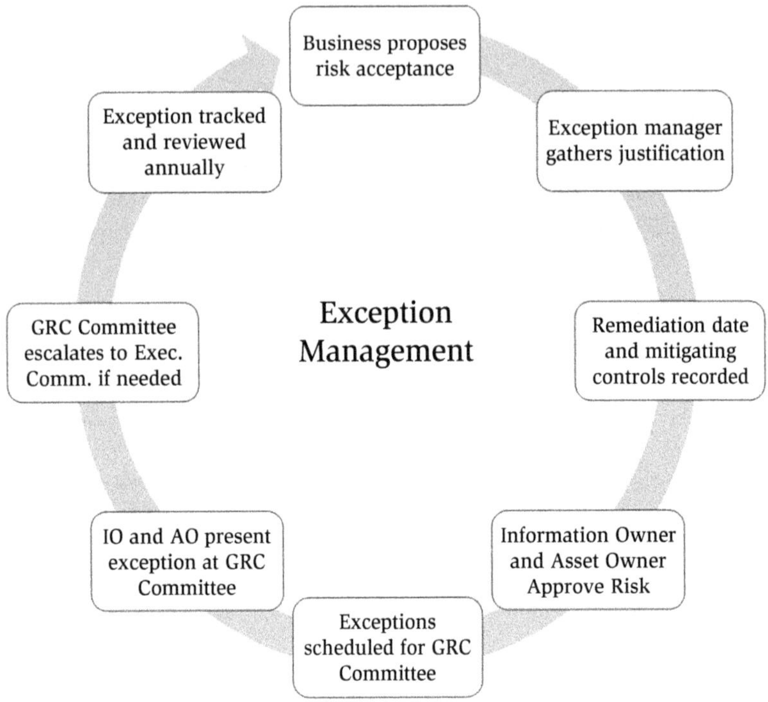

The exception management process leverages information governance concepts, including asset owner and information owner roles, to make risk acceptance decisions. The risk rating for specific findings often requires senior management review and commitment, such as a remediation deadline or financial commitment. Every organization should determine an appropriate management level to legally accept risk on behalf of the organization. In some circumstances, an asset owner and information owner's leadership team should accept risk for high or critical risk findings.

Exception management formalizes risk decisioning by requiring documentation for exception requests. Exception request documentation should include the exception requestor's information, information owner and asset owner contact details, the business process and asset name, specific control or controls evidencing non-compliance, a description of non-compliance, and any mitigating controls that reduce the risk. The exception requestor must also draft a specific business justification for accepting the risk.[288] The information owner and asset owner (or leaders of those respective teams) then review and approve (via digital or physical signature) details listed in the exception record. It should be noted that details of risk acceptance for EU GDPR reviews and findings may also require distribution to DPAs. Organizations

288. At times, the requestor has not validated the exception details with the asset owner or information owner, so it is possible that an exception might be rejected prior to signature.

should take care to ensure that documentation used within the organization can meet specific requirements for these disclosures when building programs that integrate security and privacy reporting.

Exception management may also involve escalation to additional leaders, in some cases to the EC. Organizations have great latitude in creating risk acceptance models that work for the organization's culture. However, organizations that do not provide appropriate oversight, for example permitting a manager to accept a critical risk, communicates to authorities that an organization does not take security risks seriously. A variety of committees and boards might provide useful forums for reviewing security risk, including exceptions. *See* Table 12.3 for examples and definitions of specific committee and board types.

Table 12.3 Security Committees and Boards[289]

Board	*Policy Review Committee*	*GRC Committee*	*Executive Committee*	*Board of Directors*
Members	CIO delegate, Security delegate, HR Director, Legal Counsel, Business SME	CISO[290], Sr. Legal Counsel, CRO, CPO, Business SMEs (rotating)	CEO, CFO, GC, CIO, CMO, COO, CTO[291]	Chairman of the Board, CEO, Board directors
Meeting Purpose	Review new policy and policy changes	Review security risks and operations	Discuss broadest risks for organization	Understand risks associated with organizational health
How to Leverage Expertise	Must be aware of persistent issues where additional/ enhanced policy may be needed	Could provide initial review for exceptions, can make financial commitments	Co-present pervasive risks and emerging issues; exception escalation when needed	Aggregate risks to illustrate trends; position as enterprise risks
Communication Style	Thorough and complete details	Layered information, specific approval	Headlines, immediate issues, specific request	Problem and performance trends, funding proposal

289. Please note, organizations may have different names for these levels – this example is intended to illustrate how different leadership groups can provide useful direction for security concerns.
290. CISO stands for Chief Information Security Officer, described in more detail towards the end of this chapter.
291. Chief Executive Officer, Chief Financial Officer, General Counsel, Chief Information Officer, Chief Marketing Officer, Chief Operations Officer, Chief Technology Officer.

The EC; usually consisting of General Counsel, Chief Executive Officer (CEO), Chief Financial Officer (CFO), Chief Information Officer (CIO), and any other executive Board members directly connected to security functions; provides necessary direction and prioritization of programmatic needs. The EC also provides updates and information to the organization's Board. Sometimes the CISO or an attorney provides these updates as a subject matter expert. When presenting to the Board, presenters should not provide every detail collected through program activities. Instead, presenters should consider how information may be aggregated in visual form, such as graphs, a top five list, or a proposed plan for remediation and associated investment. Although many boards do not today have security expertise, boards do clearly understand organizational risk. For this reason, presenters should describe challenges or organizational risks using common risk types. If an organization has an existing ERM framework, presenters should describe security risks within this framework. If your organization does not have an ERM framework, the audit or assurance team may use a framework of their own.

Key Takeaways:

- Risk assessments include both internal risk assessments and third party risk assessments.
- Five options exist when Information Owner and Asset Owner make a decision: accept, remediate, mitigate, avoid, or transfer risk.
- The Policy Review Committee reviews policy changes and the Governance Risk Compliance Committee (or similar name) reviews security risks.
- The exception management process supports risk acceptance through appropriate risk governance, documentation, and formal approval.

§12.03 VULNERABILITY MANAGEMENT PROCESS

In addition to risk assessment and exception management processes, other processes provide critical support to a security risk management program. Vulnerability management, for its part, focuses on detailed technical remediation for applications, software, databases, and servers an organization needs to run. Vulnerability management is different from the vulnerabilities described in Chapter 11. These vulnerabilities reflect specific changes that must be implemented a particular technology on a more granular level. For example, a Microsoft server may require routine patching. Microsoft distributes patches each month on a specific day of that month. Organizations must develop a plan to patch systems without affecting operations yet close open vulnerabilities.

Patching servers reflects just one aspect of vulnerability management. Known vulnerabilities can affect, as described prior, multiple systems. In some cases an organization may have developed an application or software ("home-grown technology")In this case, known vulnerabilities identified by cybersecurity organizations or government entities may require security teams to conduct heavy review of potential solutions to close such vulnerabilities. Vulnerabilities like Poodle, #Wannacry, Heartbleed required several changes to multiple systems to ensure these systems are not vulnerable to security attack and exploit.

Many systems require routine patching and remediation for known vulnerabilities. Security teams should develop a process and procedure for prioritizing changes, reviewing operational impact, and applying such changes. Although a vulnerability management team may manage vulnerability remediation, other teams, such as server management, database administration, application development engineering, or middleware management, actually apply changes within the systems they manage. Vulnerability management teams, then, must work collaboratively with teams to ensure timely patching or remediation of potentially vulnerable systems. Vulnerability management teams use a vulnerability management prioritization grid to determine appropriate prioritization of remediation activities.

When filling out a prioritization grid, vulnerability management teams must consider probability and impact of exploit. For example, *a zero-day vulnerability* has already been exploited by a threat source for one or more other organizations. Although a threat source has not exploited your organization, vulnerability management teams should prioritize zero-day vulnerabilities as if exploitation is forthcoming. Organizations should have the ability to quickly connect with affected teams and immediately patch or remediate these systems.

Teams should patch or remediate all other vulnerabilities based on the prioritization grid and associated timing. Remediation timing usually includes: immediate remediation, which is used for zero-day vulnerabilities and critical risk; thirty days, for high risk; sixty days, for medium risk; and ninety days for low risk. Regardless of a decision to remediate, vulnerability management teams must continue to track vulnerabilities, even if such vulnerabilities will not be patched or remediated in ninety days.

In order to effectively manage and categorize vulnerabilities, some organizations use the NIST open Common Vulnerability Scoring System (CVSS) internally as well as the CVSS Vulnerability listing.[292] Due to the CVSS scoring system's ubiquity, many global vendors have adopted CVSS scores to communicate expected patch application priority to customers, as well. This means that customers may receive patch updates or vulnerability-related information including a CVSS score reference. Organizations, then, must analyze each vulnerability with regard both to an externally determined CVSS score and to an internal risk score. *See* Table 12.4 for an example of a vulnerability prioritization grid including CVSS scores.

---

292. The CVSS calculator producing the CVSS score requires input of several details regarding the vulnerability, then uses these details to provide a score output. *See* National Institute of Standards and Technology, *National Vulnerability Database* (Jan. 23, 2017), https://nvd.nist.gov/.

Table 12.4 Example Vulnerability Prioritization Grid

Internal Risk Score	*CVSS Score*	*Remediation/Patching Timeframe*
Critical	9.0-12.0	0 days (immediate)
High	7.0-8.9	30 days
Medium	4.0-6.9	60 days
Low	0.0-3.9	90 days

As part of the vulnerability management process, the vulnerability management team should negotiate with teams remediating active vulnerabilities to determine appropriate timing for remediation or patching. For application development teams, an organization may choose to remediate certain vulnerabilities during a routine release or change process to minimize operational or customer interruptions. Likewise, certain infrastructure teams may plan system retirement (sunset) or upgrade: patching vulnerabilities during that time may avoid operational interruption at other times of the year. However, non-remediated or patched vulnerabilities do introduce risk to an organization. For example, the #Wannacry ransomware leveraged a Microsoft vulnerability. Organizations that did not patch the vulnerability experienced an operational impact to affected systems.

In addition to promotion of good security practices, laws, industry standards, and certifications may require external vulnerability or penetration testing for some assets. For example, PCI-DSS and SSAE16 (18) SOC 2, Types 1 and 2 require independent testing. Organizations should use vulnerability testing for evaluating specifically compiled vulnerabilities from third parties and other sources, penetration testing to periodically review the exploitability of systems, and secure development lifecycle processes to ensure security controls are built into internal products.

Key Takeaways:

- Vulnerability management processes ensure routine, prioritized system patching and remediation.
- Vulnerability management requires collaboration with a wide variety of IT teams.
- Zero-day vulnerabilities typically require immediate patching/remediation; other vulnerabilities will be prioritized via a prioritization matrix.
- The Common Vulnerability Scoring Systems provides pre-populated ratings for vendor products and can be leveraged for internal scoring.
- Penetration testing can identify additional vulnerabilities by routinely "hacking" organizational products.

§12.04 SOFTWARE DEVELOPMENT AND SECURE DEVELOPMENT LIFECYCLE PROCESSES

Although vulnerability management and periodic penetration testing help application and software teams ensure ongoing cybersecurity protection, teams must also build security and privacy considerations into their products. For security, organizations should employ a secure development lifecycle (SecDLC), or a complementary security engineering process included in standard software or application development lifecycles. Figure 12.3 illustrates a typical software development lifecycle.

Figure 12.3 Software Development Lifecycle

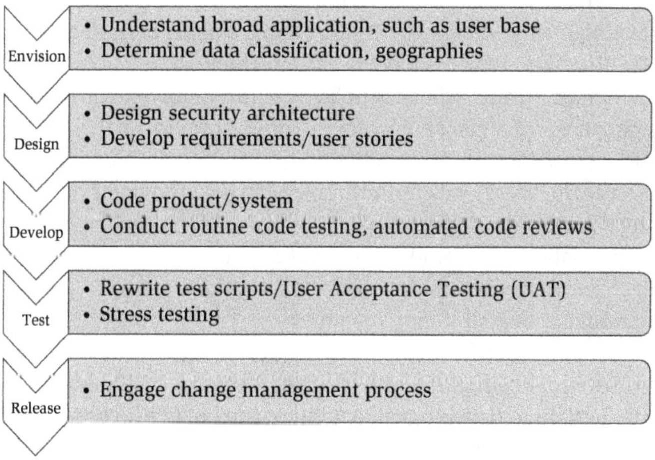

Traditional software development lifecycles include a planning process, including architecture planning and engineering strategy, followed by requirements gathering. In these three processes, teams will identify security controls applicable to the product and design defense-in-depth for the technology's architecture. Security teams often either create a requirements library for use across the enterprise or embed a security expert within the project team.

Throughout the build process, development teams should use secure testing methods, depending on the code developed, such as code scanning or peer reviews. When the development team finishes the code, testers complete testing, including system and load testing, to ensure the system can hold up to specific types of stressers, such as a cyberattack (e.g., a DDoS attack, explained in Chapter 13). The testing team will also test the specific requirements identified and ensure the product meets all requirements, for example, a log-on process and procedure.

Less traditional project development lifecycles, such as Agile, may complicate the SecDLC. Teams working with an Agile methodology should determine the best way to plan for security user stories. Agile development methodologies center around a user story; therefore, security requirements should be tied to fulfilling the needs of that user story. For example, a user story may describe an individual logging into a system. Within that user story, an agile team should also determine how the user will authenticate to the system to avoid unauthorized users connecting from unapproved locations. The team may also consider specific access roles and how to provide access to resources that are consistent and commensurate with users' business roles.

Organizations using traditional Waterfall or Iterative methodologies, as previously described, leverage functional requirements, or requirements tied to product user experience, and non-functional requirements, or underlying product functionality behind its screens, to elucidate specific security requirements. A project manager or business analyst captures these requirements during requirements gathering session(s) and continues to update requirements as changes are made throughout the project. User experience (UX) designers build these requirements into screen designs and engineers (or developers) reflect these requirements in code or system configurations. Eventually, testing teams will use these same requirements to draft test scripts, which will ensure security requirements have been implemented.

All development teams will benefit from either involvement of a cybersecurity expert in each phase of development or training specific to the engineering role. Although training provides the most valuable approach to developing secure products within a project team, security expert resources can also provide periodic oversight to ensure solutions protect the organization. Each phase of the development cycle should include security-related considerations and validations.

Organizations may use multiple tools to communicate configuration specifications or requirements overall. Some organizations create a requirements document, which is dynamic and specific to the technologies being developed. Other organizations create substantial configuration baselines. Although configuration baselines do not specifically pertain to development activities, they may provide ideas or details to inform good development choices. Additionally, organizations may use Whitepapers or guidelines to explore new technologies and provide ideas for development teams to create secure solutions. Although these documents do not reflect binding policy, they can be helpful for development teams looking for details.

Security teams must also determine how development teams will validate security requirements. Internal testing is conducted by the development team, and development teams test their code both via manual and automated testing. Examples of internal testing include *static code analysis*, but developers can leverage multiple technologies today for automated testing. These technologies reveal security issues earlier in the development process, improving both security and testing efficiency. Manual processes, such as peer code reviews, also identify issues before they arise and reduce code complexity, which can hide latent security issues.

System testing tests the system to ensure it can support expected users and operating capacity as designed. For example, system testing would measure whether a system can handle several users accessing resources simultaneously. System testing is important because even though tests may reflect standard development practices, they may also determine where inherent weaknesses lie. For example, a distributed denial of service (DDoS) attack leverages resource limitations to perpetuate the attack. If the system is inherently vulnerable to a DDoS attack because it cannot handle expected traffic, a security issue remains post-testing. For this reason, organizations may choose to conduct additional security testing specific to expected vulnerabilities for the product type and implementation.

Testing teams also conduct user acceptance testing. The purpose of user acceptance testing is to validate system requirements. Because testing teams use test scripts based on previously identified requirements, teams should ensure that test scripts accurately reflect the current requirements, including non-functional requirements. Often teams in the development lifecycle change requirements as design decisions also change, especially in Agile or iterative product development methodologies, which are designed to embrace frequent changes. Security requirements protect cybersecurity organizational interests, and when these requirements may change, teams must ensure the product continues to meet existing security requirements. For example, a policy change for encryption could define a higher-level protocol for protection of sensitive personal information. If that change is not communicated to the development team and reflected in test scripts, a product could release without meeting internal standards, causing downstream issues.

In the last phase of the development framework, a product is promoted from a testing environment into a production environment. Critically, both in security standards and for quality control, development teams must not have access to production environments. This restriction protects an organization from intentional and unintentional consequences, such as inadvertent changes that disrupt operations or malicious changes that could cause data breaches or other interruptions.

The mechanism for moving data from a testing environment to a production environment is the *change management process*. Change management is a standard operational IT process that ensures overall organizational stability. Organizations typically implement changes on various systems simultaneously or in close coordination. When multiple changes occur simultaneously without appropriate planning and review, these changes may cause major business interruption of key operational resources. Effective change management processes ensure minimum operational disruption while effectively moving a product or service into the active production environment. The change management capability should involve IT leaders, as well as a leader from the cybersecurity team. When organizations have an effective change management program, organizational risks substantially reduce. *See* Figure 12.4 for an example of a change management process.

Figure 12.4 Change Management Process

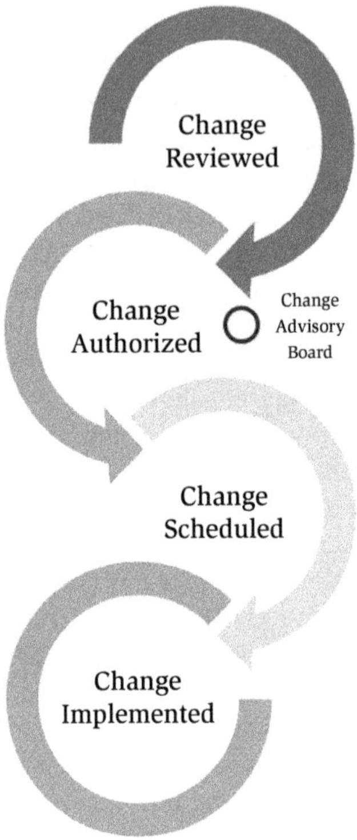

Each step in the secure development process seeks to implement security controls and validate that they are effective. However, organizations providing applications, software, or other products to business customers or consumers should additionally consider targeted penetration testing to validate the effectiveness of security controls in production (live product). Unlike security testing conducted before deployment to production, penetration testing, as described in Chapter 11, simulates an incident or data breach to identify additional security vulnerabilities a threat source might exploit. Organizations should conduct penetration testing on externally facing applications, software, or products containing SPI, e.g., health care systems, law enforcement records, or biometrics databases.

The Secure Development Lifecycle illustrates one of many ongoing processes to reduce risk for an organization. Identity and Access Management, however, provides a critical combination of technical and administrative controls, managing both the identity of an entity and what and to what extent the entity may access resources.

Key Takeaways:

- The Secure Development Lifecycle can adapt to a variety of methodologies, including Waterfall, Iterative, and Agile.
- Security requirements should be integrated into functional and non-functional requirements or notated in user stories.
- Products should fit accepted security architectures.
- Development and engineering teams must automate or conduct secure code reviews.
- The change management process ensures required security processes have been fulfilled and operations are not interrupted.

§12.05 IDENTITY AND ACCESS MANAGEMENT

Identity and Access Management (AIM) provides a foundation for secure systems. Identity and access management represent two different sides of the same goal: preventing unauthorized access and restricting access to the minimum necessary. *See* Table 12.5 for a description of identity and access management as security disciplines.

Table 12.5 Identity and Access Management

	Identity Management	*Access Management*
Purpose	Verify that an entity is who/what it purports to be	Ensure an entity only accesses the systems and resources it has been approved to access
Goal	Prevent unauthorized access	Prevent unauthorized access and restrict access to minimum necessary
Applies to	Systems connecting to systems; people connecting to systems	Systems connecting to systems; people connecting to systems
Examples	- Access allowed only from particular IP addresses - Federated Access ("Circle of Trust") - Multi-factor authentication	- Username/password - Role-based access - Password complexity requirements - Biometrics

Identity management seeks to ensure an entity is authentic and principally ensures this through various technical solutions. Technical solutions for identity management usually include one of the following: certificate exchange, federated access, or MFA. Unlike what most individual users might associate with standard username and password controls, identity management provides an extra layer of verification and protection. Today, usernames and passwords often are easily guessable by malicious external parties. For this reason, a secondary verification is needed. Organizations manage this verification process any number of ways. First, in its most basic form, firewall rules are used to limit access to specific IP addresses. For example, if only a Chinese company's personnel use a Chinese company's payroll system, which is hosted in a Chinese data center, the Chinese company should block IP addresses from locations outside a limited geographic area, from ever connecting to the payroll system. It might also consider only permitting IP addresses specifically owned by the Chinese company. In order to block "spoofed" IP addresses, it will also require additional steps to gain access, such as a username and password or second authentication measure (e.g., multi-factor authentication).

Many organizations today use Federated Access for organizational resources. *Federated Access* is access connected to a central authentication step, such as gaining access to the internal network. Most personnel log into a computer at their desk or remotely, which then permits them to access additional resources without having to log-in another time. This type of authentication, which places the security burden on the log-in process, manages authentication on the back end. One example of federated access is called single sign-on (SSO). SSO groups resources together to simplify the authentication and access management processes.

MFA uses two or more methods for verifying identity: what you are, what you know, or what you have. By validating two or more methods, these systems dramatically reduce the frequency of unauthorized access. Examples of authentication methods include: soft tokens, or software on a machine that creates a session-specific code coupled with Federated Access; hard tokens, or hard key-chain-style fobs generating session-specific codes that are combined with a user-specific personal identification number (PIN); or a combination of username and password with a one-time use code displayed on a Website, sent to an e-mail address, or provided by text message or call. Increasingly more frequently, organizations use biometric inputs, such as fingerprint, as one of the two factors. Although biometric inputs provide a high level of authentication, they also produce a data set that must be protected under many data protection laws.

Access management processes began with privacy and security concepts of least user access (LUA). LUA reflects the access version of data minimization: only individuals with a "need to know" should have access to systems, access specific data within those systems, and ability to view, edit, delete, or copy within those systems. Building LUA processes into systems ensures that users do not have access to more than they need, reducing the probability of malicious or non-malicious insider threat sources affecting data. LUA also reduces potential exposure, should a malicious external threat source gain access to a system using stolen credentials.

Access management capabilities usually include administrative controls, such as access provisioning, access reviews, and access termination. *Access provisioning* is an approval procedure completed prior to a user receiving access to a system. *Access review* is the process of periodically reviewing all access and removing access for individuals who no longer have a business need to know. *Access termination* is the process of revoking access after an individual leaves an organization or accepts a new role. Each of these processes requires action by a member of the management team and action by support staff or system administrators.

For users requesting access to databases containing sensitive personal information or administrative access to a system, additional levels of approval should be required. *Administrative access* (or *root*) is access that permits an individual user to change system behavior, view large stores of data, delete large data sets, and potentially copy data to an external location. Because administrative access carries with it substantial risk of misuse or mistake, organizations should only provide administrative access when absolutely necessary, and then with multi-layered approvals and review by an individual experienced in the system. Administrative access to an individual workstation may prove damaging: organizations that permit workstation administrative access also open themselves to malware and viruses hiding in applications and other executables downloaded by individuals on their home networks. When organizations choose to permit administrative access, check-out (or temporary) IDs can be used, or organizations may condition access on dual reviews from the asset owner and the user's upper management, such as a vice president.

Organizations conduct access reviews to remove unused access for active users and reduce current access to LUA, if no longer needed. These access reviews generally occur annually, or more frequently (such as quarterly access reviews (QAR)) for systems including highly sensitive or critical data. Organizational management conducts access reviews by reviewing access for all personnel reporting to them at every level of the organization: a supervisor reviews his direct reports, his manager reviews her direct reports, and so forth up to the CEO or president of an organization.

Unlike provisioning and review processes, access termination processes may require substantially more procedure development. Employment termination generally is not desired by an employee, so organizations should exhibit due diligence in access termination processes to avoid potential for a disgruntled former employee to cause damage or steal data.[293] Required procedures include timely engagement of Human Resources termination processes and immediate revocation of Federated or corporate computer access (no longer than 24 hours, but sooner if possible). Managers should also revoke all other system access. Although revocation of Federated Access will dramatically reduce the risk of damage by a malicious former employee, under certain circumstances, an employee can access other systems, especially some third-party systems.

293. Disgruntled former employees can turn into malicious insider threat sources quite quickly. Legal counsel should ensure compliance with local laws regarding surveillance notice, but an organization may best protect itself by saving business emails and monitoring system use for systems storing sensitive personal information, trade secrets, or other high-value data.

The access review lifecycle should support every stage of employment from start of employment to termination or departure. However, many organizations cannot support the complexity of access reviews without additional management tools. Today, IAM tools automate access provisioning, reviews, and termination, including security-specific management tools and workflow management through service management tools connecting to a CMDB asset database. Figure 12.5 shows the complete access review lifecycle that one or more tools can support.

Figure 12.5 Access Review Lifecycle

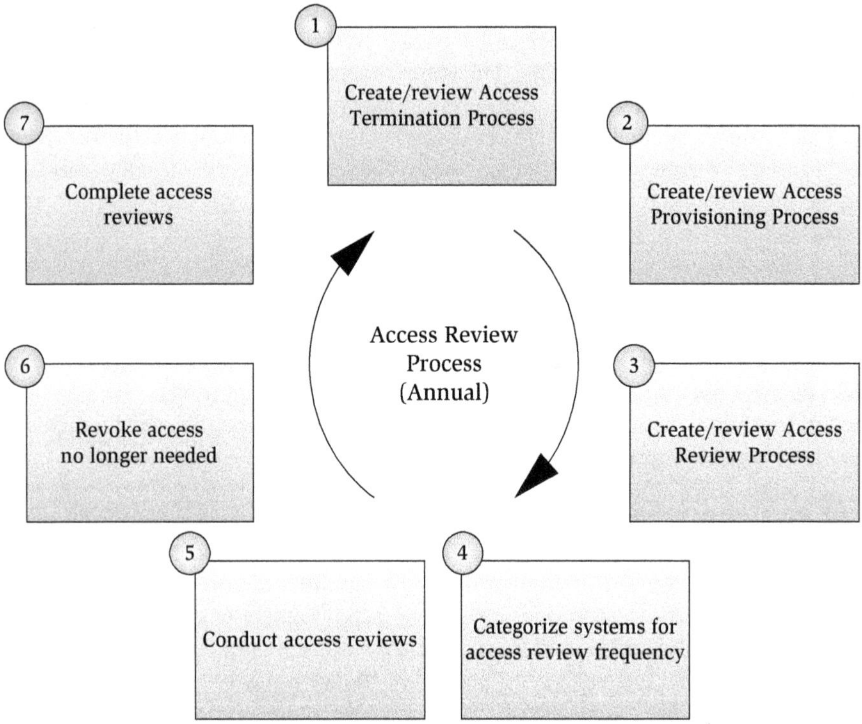

Identity and Access Management processes, when executed properly, provide a strong line of defense against security threats.

Key Takeaways:

- Identity management includes various technologies for managing identity, such as federated access and multi-factor authentication.
- Multi-factor authentication includes two or more types of information reflecting: who a user is, what the user knows, or what the user has.

- Access management includes access provisioning, access termination, and access reviews.
- Access management processes are easier to implement when they are supported by a workflow tool.

§12.06 TRAINING AND AWARENESS PROCESSES

Like many compliance topics, organizations communicate privacy and security topics to their personnel. Training and awareness activities provide an administrative control for protecting an organization because they communicate good privacy and security practices directly to personnel. Many laws require regular training and where laws do not apply, annual training represents a baseline industry minimum, a reasonable administrative control expected under most data protection regimes. More frequently, training is not considered a "check the box" activity; training must be *effective* and *measurable*. Creating truly effective training and validating that personnel have been trained requires more effort than organizations characteristically expend on training activities.

Organizations do, however, have many options when they determine how to develop and deliver content: they may conduct virtual training via a Learning Management System (LMS) or in-person training, and third parties or organizational resources may develop content. When determining the appropriate training strategy, organizations should also consider training scope, training obligations, and personnel roles to be trained. *See* Table 12.6 as an example of a training roadmap.

Table 12.6 Example Training Roadmap: Global Healthcare

Timing	*Activities*	*Audience*	*Vehicle*
Q1 following policy update, new hire process	Annual Training	All personnel	LMS
Q1	Phishing test 1, Annual Training Review	All personnel	E-mail, LMS
Q2 following annual training, new hire process	Secure Development Training	Development, Engineering, Architecture teams	In-Person, to be recorded for later viewing
Q3, new hire process	Caller Validation and Data Handling	Health Support Line teams	LMS
Q3, new hire process	Privacy Notice, Consent, and Authorization	Physicians, Nurses, Hospital staff	LMS

Timing	*Activities*	*Audience*	*Vehicle*
Q3	Phishing test 2, Annual Training Review	All personnel	E-mail, LMS
Q4	Policy Reviews	N/A	N/A

When designing privacy and security training or selecting packaged training from a third party, organizations should spend substantial time developing or validating content and effectiveness. From a risk management perspective, training is a security and privacy control, yet it also enhances additional internal requirements by communicating them in a consumable format. Although some organizations rely primarily on personnel reading policy documents on an internal Website or providing attestation to having read these documents, this approach does not effectively communicate internal expectations. Effective training requires applying learning strategies for adult learners: content prioritization, content summarization, contextual scenarios, integrated exercises, content review, and testing.

Content prioritization and summarization focus on choosing topics and content most relevant to the audience and presenting this information in short form. Personnel often cannot retain all the information security and privacy teams wish to share. Therefore, organizations must display the most crucial content, such as policy changes and substantial risk areas where individuals have the power to reduce security and privacy risk with training effort that will capture attention.

Contextual, individualized scenarios and integrated exercises help personnel understand how content applies to situations they may encounter. Organizations with more flexibility may choose contextual scenarios and integrated exercises that reflect the background of personnel such as managers, IT workers, contact center personnel, executives, or contractors. When personnel can practice what they have learned specific to their roles, better retention results. Integrated exercises take these scenarios and put them into practice, providing dynamic if/then experiences to test knowledge and provide feedback.

Content review and testing focus on retention and evaluation of retained knowledge. Content reviews summarize information presented after an individual has completed a particular training chapter. This summary helps an individual remember key points in preparation for an exam at the end of training. Testing focuses on evaluation of retention by requiring personnel to successfully pass with a particular percentage. When testing works well, it evaluates key points of summary from each training chapter. Dynamic training may require an individual to re-train one or more chapters without a passing score. *See* Table 12.7 for an example design or order of a standard annual training.

Table 12.7 Annual Training Design Example

Chapter 1: Understanding Risk		
Slide #	*Topic*	*Takeaway*
1	Why Does Security Matter?	Understand risks to organization
2	What Do We Owe Our Customers?	Understand why privacy and security are important to customers
3	What Data are Valuable?	Understand data classification
4	What Is the Risk?	Understand how individuals and the organization can be harmed
5	Summary of previous topics	
6	Vignette1: Widmer and Annabelle	Understand risks in this scenario
7	Vignette Quiz	Respond and learn
8	Vignette 2: Cheng and Ivan	Understand risks in this scenario
9	Vignette Quiz	Respond and learn
10	Chapter 1 Review	Remember Content
11	Final Exam, all Chapters	Passing Score/Examination

Scores and training completion statistics provide useful documentation for illustrating program maturity for assessments, audits, authority investigations, and legal proceedings. For example, during a trade secret misappropriation case, illustrating that annual training reminded personnel of their confidentiality obligations, and the individual accused of misappropriation completed and passed the training each year, could help establish one prong of a successful case. For its part, PCI-DSS requires reporting of participation percentages for training. In other situations, strong, complete, and individualized training demonstrates an internal commitment to strong privacy and security practices. Overall, training along with a policy framework and risk assessment processes form foundational program components for any privacy or security program.

Other role-specific training may help personnel fulfilling specialized roles also understand specific processes and procedures required by internal policy. Development, engineering, and architecture teams often require specialized training in SecDLC, especially when security representatives cannot participate in all development projects. Call centers handling SPI should receive specialized caller validation training to minimize the probability of social engineering or data loss. Other personnel in specialized roles who work directly with customers, handle personal information, or manage highly sensitive organizational information (e.g., Legal) should also receive specialized training. Although all personnel could receive role-based training, organizations should evaluate where a complaint or incident would likely occur and focus on these departments first.

Awareness activities provide frequent reminders of personnel obligations and connect personnel to privacy and security activities. Activities can include a cybersecurity or privacy day, week, or month out of the year where teams provide more details and communication on these topics. Designation of a specific day can accompany special food, prizes, recognition, or internal sharing of accomplishments. Security and privacy leaders may choose to give presentations, write blog posts, or send e-mails to personnel on an ongoing basis either as part of a specific celebration or throughout the year. Organizations should work with internal communications teams to determine the best approach for ongoing sharing of security and privacy information.

Key Takeaways:

- Effective and measurable annual training is generally required for "reasonable" administrative controls, and some laws and industry standards require annual training.
- Role-based training be especially beneficial for call center teams, development teams, and consumer/patient-facing teams.
- Awareness activities enable organizations to continue educating personnel after annual training.

Security and privacy programs require operational processes to effectively manage risk and meet legal obligations. Organizations must focus on developing repeatable processes that manage internal policy compliance, effective risk management, support organizational governance, workforce education, and incident and data breach response activities.

CHAPTER 13

Incident Response and Attack Types

Incident response management provides a critical function in today's privacy and cybersecurity environment. Although controls can dramatically reduce the risk of an incident or data breach occurring, organizations now must prepare for potential data breaches by developing *resiliency*, or an ability to respond and return to normal operations following an incident or data breach. Resiliency requires exceptional planning, exercise, preparation, and lessons learned following execution.

§13.01 INCIDENT RESPONSE MANAGEMENT

Incident response management is the capability of effectively preparing for and responding to an incident. An *incident* differs from a data breach in that an incident has not yet confirmed data loss, misuse, or other business interruption. An incident, therefore, must be investigated, prior to any notification of affected parties or complete remediation. Organizations should use the term "incident" to connote when an event that could have compromised data *may* have occurred. Because many legal obligations, such as statutory duties or contractual obligations, tie to data breaches (indeed, laws explicitly define *data breach*), organizations should exhibit due diligence in validating that a data breach has indeed occurred before labeling the situation.

Organizations use the term "incident" for all security-related situations involving loss, interruption or misuse, so incidents may be any size or severity.[294] Security practitioners often call incidents *realized risks*, or a previously identified or unidentified risk that has been exploited. Incidents may include lost or stolen laptops, phishing events, unauthorized access to the internal network, individual employee-related

294. Organizations may decide to use severity ratings related to incidents. However, because most incidents display at a severity different from later severities when all information has been collected, it may prove difficult to drive specific incident response activities from a severity value. Instead, organizations often categorize the type of incident and execute response activities accordingly.

issues (such as accessing a medical record without legitimate purpose), as well as large incidents. To effectively manage this breadth of incidents within an organization, organizations should use a formal incident response process. The incident response process usually consists of seven steps: preparation, identification, containment, investigation, eradication, and recovery. *See* Figure 13.1 for the six steps and associated activities.

Figure 13.1 Incident Response Process and Activities

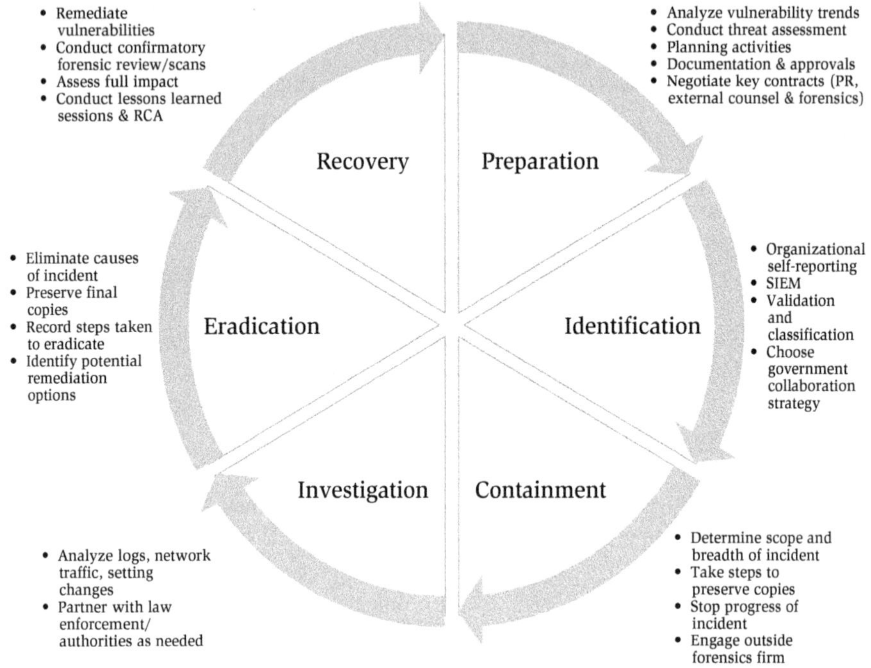

In the Incident Response Process's first step of *Preparation*, an organization develops key plans, documentation, and steps to ensure effective responsiveness. In addition to analyzing vulnerability trends, described earlier in this chapter, and conducting threat assessments, organizations must plan for future incidents and data breaches. Primary planning activities include: developing a Security Operations Center (SOC); creating an incident response plan and associated incident response team; and designing incident response procedure, playbooks, and testing plans.

The SOC is the operational component of an incident response capability, including Security Incident and Event Management (SIEM) tool use and proactive incident response activities. The SOC monitors active network traffic, events, and other data provided by the SIEM tool. When data seems to indicate a potential incident, the incident response process begins.[295] Although some organizations may integrate SOC functions with other IT support activities, organizations should strongly consider having a dedicated person, team, or managed service to focus on incident identification, as SOC monitoring activities tend to differ dramatically from traditional service-type IT tasks, such as problem management.

A functional SOC includes toolsets and dependencies on tool configuration. Toolsets may include both preventative toolsets and reactive toolsets. Reactive toolsets focus on data aggregation, processing of security alerts, and fast response. The SIEM tool, for example, works by pulling or receiving information from multiple internal systems, applying advanced analytics, and in more advanced implementations may leverage artificial intelligence to determine patterns indicating potential compromise. It gathers network data to identify problematic or suspicious traffic.

Proactive tools include configuration of applications, infrastructure, and utilities, which log and send information, such as log-on time stamps, user behavior during and after log-on (e.g., missed password attempts), and resources accessed in a consolidated format. For example, a hacker could have used a few different passwords before gaining access to the internal network, then use credentials with guessable passwords to access an application with personal information inside. In this case, effective logging would enable a forensic investigator to determine how a breach occurred by determining which potential passwords the hacker used, signaling how the hacker guessed or obtained the password. Resources accessed inform an incident's size (and potential data breach), useful to determine, if needed, legally defensible data breach size and scope.

Effective logging records ensure that a system can transfer information about credentials used and resources accessed to a common repository for review. If a SIEM tool connects to the application and read log files, it can routinely pull information, aggregate data, and dynamically analyze. This makes real-time or near real-time monitoring possible, as well as pattern recognition to spot certain threat vectors. Therefore, if an external malicious person accesses personal information using credentials at a time the legitimate user would not access this information based on previous behavior (e.g., in a different time zone), the SIEM tool would send an alert for SOC review. If reviewed in real-time, a data breach could be avoided.

SIEM tools rely on system-generated *events*, which are rules or flags in a system. When a series of circumstances match a system-configured rule, the system transmits data to the SIEM tool for review, such as a user hits the threshold for incorrect log-on attempts. Effective event configuration not only improves incident responsiveness, it also provides information necessary to determine typical or normal traffic and data versus abnormal and unauthorized data access or use. The newest utilities now mine historical data collected over time from systems to determine the appropriate indicators

295. It should be noted that the incident response process does not only investigate potential incidents resulting from the SIEM tool. For example, an incident can result from improper destruction of paper documents or on authorized access to a building. In both of these cases, information about the incident would not likely appear in the SIEM tool.

of incident or data breach. For this reason, many security frameworks require logging and monitoring controls to improve data sets feeding incident response capabilities.

Although the SOC uses the SIEM to identify potential incidents, a wide variety of incidents also require organizational involvement. Organizations should broadly train their workforce to report suspicious activities through an incident inbox or helpline. In addition to creating a method for reporting incidents, organizations must also create a culture where individuals do not fear reporting issues, such as clicking on a phishing email. Incident response capabilities also include proactive measures to protect the business. When personnel report incidents through an alternative source, the Incident Response Manager should log and manage the potential incident as if the SOC had reported it.

Third parties may also experience incidents or data breaches. Organizations should focus on developing strong contract language that provides rights with respect to third parties. When a third party reports a confirmed incident or data breach, organizations may prefer to receive regular progress reports, control media communications, designate a forensic investigation company, require penetration testing activities, approve remediation plans, or perform confirmatory audits after remediation. However, absent contractual language, organizations often have little control over third party activity during an incident or data breach.

Incidents and data breaches require a multi-functional team to handle internal and external activities. The team must be able to handle business-associated incident response activities, such as designing media strategy and message, determining appropriate legal strategy, and devoting resources to remediate any cause of injury. The Incident Response Team (IRT) performs much of the incident response process. The IRT usually consists of an attorney; the Chief Information Security Officer (CISO, CIO if a CISO is not named); the Incident Response Manager; and a Public Relations (PR), Communications, or Marketing department contact. However, the IRT may also include other leaders, depending on the nature of the incident. *See* Table 13.1 for a list and description of IRT roles.

Table 13.1 Incident Response Team

Title	*Activities*	*Required?*
Incident Response Manager	- Not usually a rotating role (dedicated resource) - Manages day-to-day incident response activities - May manage the SOC (depending on organization) - Coordinates external forensics team, internal technology teams	Yes
CISO (CIO if no CISO)	- Manages upwards executive communication about incident - Supervises all information security activities	Yes

Title	*Activities*	*Required?*
Internal Legal Counsel	- Proposes legal strategy - Advises of notification/monitoring obligations - Advises on communication strategy (business customers, partners, investors, consumers) - Manages external legal partners	Yes
External Legal	- Consults on specific issues and strategy	Auxiliary
Marketing, Communications, or PR	- Develops internal and external communication strategy - Executes strategy, manages external PR partners	Yes
External PR	- Consults on specific issues and strategy	Auxiliary
Compliance Officer	- Included for compliance issues that may involve managing relationships with regulatory authorities	Auxiliary
Technical expert	- Included for specific knowledge about a technology affected	Auxiliary
Experts required by cyberliability insurers or industry associations	- Insurers may require engagement prior to filing claim - Industry standards, such as PCI-DSS require qualified forensics and scanning vendors be used	Yes

The IRT provides guidance and direction for the EC to approve. Early in the incident response process, the IRT may discuss proposed approach if the incident is confirmed as a data breach. As the incident is confirmed, the IRT may determine how to fund remediation activities or notification letter dissemination. For all activities, the CISO and the legal representative must provide a direct line of communication with the EC, especially the General Counsel.

Internal counsel perform several lead roles in the IRT but also provides a crucial advisory role by providing risk-based advice for the organization, not only pure legal advice. As a crucial legal advisor, meetings established under attorney-client privilege and communications notated as privileged legal communication can protect an organization, should a legal action, such as a lawsuit, result. For this reason, internal counsel should participate in all IRT calls as a required IRT team member.

The Incident Response Plan (IRP) formalizes the activities of the IRT and documents the incident response process. The IRP should be reviewed and approved by executive management, as the IRT will use this document for every incident. Although some organizations draft lengthy IRPs, shorter IRPs improve repeatability and minimize questions. The IRP generally includes sections on IRT members and roles and responsibilities, the process for notifying IRT members and the organization's EC, incident types and definitions, details on how to determine a data breach has occurred, and required steps for specific types of incidents. Permanent IRT members should provide both business and personal contact information, and this information will be used to notify IRT members of an incident. Due to the prevalence of mobile devices in the workplace, an organization may leverage text messaging capabilities to alert the IRT.

Incident types and information about data breaches provide clear direction for an IRT trying to determine whether to categorize an incident as a "data breach." Data breach status triggers several obligations for organizations, and these obligations should be listed and details in the IRT. For payment card data breaches, PCI-DSS and individual card brands require notification. An organization's bank and processor may also require notification via contractual obligation. For data breaches including personal information, laws may require notification within a specific time period, such as notification to a regulator or agency, notification to credit monitoring agencies, or notification directly to a data subject.

For data breaches involving a business customer's data, many business customers contractually require notification requirements for both reasonably suspected incidents and data breaches. Even where business customers may not require notification, organizations should include appropriate timing for business customer notification, as hearing about a breach concerning your data via news media could easily end a business relationship. Including incident details and notification steps will simplify downstream processes.

The IRT will also need to develop an approach to working with law enforcement and other authorities (government entities). When an incident is not yet a data breach, organizations need not engage government entities. However, involving government entities sooner in the incident response process may provide some benefits: (1) government entities have relationships and expertise, such as forensics experts, which can assist an organization; (2) cyberliability policies (described in Chapter 12) may require legally enforceable reporting of an incident prior to any claim filing or insurance resource utilization; (3) organizations working with administrative agencies often receive more beneficial treatment if investigations determine non-compliance with specific legal requirements.

Alternatively, working with government entities earlier in the process may not be desirable for some organizations: (1) government entities may seek to manage the incident response process and associated investigations, which reduces the amount of control an organization has; (2) organizations have comparatively less discretion regarding breach notification, as the government entity will likely determine affected persons and scope; and (3) organizations with business customers outside their countries may be restricted from sharing information with government entities without first notifying the customer. The IRT, in documenting planned engagement of government entities, must consider both legal obligations and business impact. Internal legal counsel should directly lead strategy for data breach notification and government entity involvement and may choose to engage external legal counsel on these topics. *See* Table 13.2 for a list of advantages and disadvantages for including government entities sooner in the incident response process.

Table 13.2 Including Government Entities in Incident Response

Advantages	*Disadvantages*
- Officials may be able to "connect the dots" across other information sources - Early assistance with correct forensic procedures - May reduce damage with more complete, efficient response - Benefit of the doubt if administrative action taken - Better positioned to stop a particular actor from attacking again - Future partnership and information sharing	- Once engaged, the government will typically take control to manage a situation - Administrative agency notification may be required sooner than an organization might feel comfortable - Disclosing information to the government may necessitate involvement of external counsel earlier in the process

In addition to the IRP, organizations may seek to develop Incident Response Playbooks (Playbooks) for specific incident types. Playbooks serve three purposes for an organization: (1) playbooks force an organization to review and apply threat assessment findings to prioritize which playbooks should be developed; (2) playbooks require the IRT determine how the organizations *should* respond in a circumstance, providing practice for the internal team; and (3) playbooks guide the IRT in actual response activities when an incident occurs. The incident response manager develops Playbooks in collaboration with the IRT and threat and vulnerability personnel. The incident response manager should draft Playbooks with specific scenarios in mind, focused on assets that seem most likely targets.

Organizations may develop communications plans and pre-prepared statements within the IRP and Playbooks or as stand-alone collateral. In both circumstances, organizations will reduce stress during an incident by preparing communication for internal and external use in advance. External communications organizations routinely develop include a *holding statement*, or a common communication given to media outlets, EC members, and other internal leadership acknowledging that an incident has occurred. A holding statement communicates to the public that the organization is aware of an incident without directly taking responsibility or speculating about the scope or impact of the incident. Holding statements often use the term "incident," rather than data breach. Organization CEOs and Presidents should approve any holding statement in consultation with PR contacts, well in advance of an incident or data breach occurring.

Organizations also create draft press releases that require little review during an incident, other than inclusion of incident-specific details, and predefined data breach notification documents. Organizations should use previously developed press release documents as templates and discuss overall disclosure strategy with legal counsel and executive leadership. If the organization prefers to provide more transparency and disclose an incident or data breach sooner, consumers may have greater opportunity to protect themselves, but an organization also risks disclosing incorrect information. If the organization prefers a more conservative approach, consumers may experience greater impact (and fines or other legal action could be more expensive), but information disclosed could be more accurate. Organizations should determine, in advance, their relative risk tolerance for communicating information and document any communication policies.

Organizations should also prepare for internal communication to personnel. Although organizations typically focus on external communications, personnel can dramatically impact the success of external communications by posting incorrect, misleading, or confidential information on social media or by sharing information with friends and family members. The internal communication plan should not only remind personnel of their organizational confidentiality obligations but also provide personnel with accurate information regarding the incident or data breach and instructions for responding to formal or informal inquiries. Incidents and data breaches should be considered events involving potential legal impact. As such, it is incredibly important that information shared by personnel is accurate, not speculative.

Although developing holding statements, press releases, incident and data breach notification, and internal communications will simplify the incident response process during an active incident, many organizations have not prepared for when a government entity or news source identifies an incident or data breach first. When a government entity brings an incident or data breach to the attention of an organization, an organization often has very little time to respond before a non-government entity, such as a hacking organization or media source, shares this information publicly. Several organizations have received a call from a government entity, sharing information of a breach prior to the organization having detected any anomaly. Although the circumstance can feel daunting, organizations with an IRP in place can kick-off the incident response process immediately. When a government entity has alerted an organization, it will likely be involved in the rest of the process. Legal counsel and the CISO should prepare the EC for this possibility.

In addition to government entities, media contacts and Dark Web insiders, like American reporter Brian Krebs, Wikileaks, or Anonymous may break a story before an organization knows an incident or data breach has even occurred. Organizations must prepare for this possibility and quickly execute the IRP upon notice. Dark Web insiders may trade on "exclusive" media deals to not publish a story for a limited time. However, organizations should think carefully about exclusive deals, especially to contemplate the appropriateness of the media source for the organization's message, and the degree of preparation an organization has to quickly publish a press release. Regardless of an organization's preference regarding media exclusivity, organizations should seek to provide information to news outlets before other sources, to minimize inconsistent stories and control the message.

With previously discussed considerations in mind, the security team should test the IRP and associated documents at least annually to ensure the IRP can effectively support the organization during an incident or data breach. Organizations ensure IRP effectiveness with incident response simulations, such as an incident response tabletops, standard incident response tests, or blind incident response tests. An incident response tabletop involves creating a data breach scenario, inviting the IRT to work through the scenario and using the IRP and associated documents. During the tabletop, the IRT simulates an incident by working together as they would during a typical incident. Usually incident response tabletops include one to two days of simulation, followed by a "lessons learned" session to identify IRP updates.

The incident response test simulates an active incident, usually by hiring an internal or external penetration testing company to break into an organization's system. In the standard incident response test, the IRT knows a red team will conduct a test and actively participates during the demonstration. More mature organizations may instead conduct an unrehearsed incident response test, where only the CISO and Executive Committee know a test will occur. A "real" incident most effectively tests responsiveness and effectiveness of the IRT and the IRP, Playbooks, and communication collateral.

In incident response test simulations and when actively working an incident, organizations may identify a third-party need. The Incident Response Manager and CISO should work with the IRT to negotiate key contracts, and legal counsel should plan to recommend external legal counsel. Organizations should evaluate external public relations companies, external forensics companies, and external legal counsel with enough time to review multiple options, conduct an RFP process, and gather competitive bids. Often, organizations wait until an incident occurs requiring external services, and do not always find external partners that can provide knowledgeable support during the incident response process at a reasonable cost. Further, some cyberliability plans may require engagement of a limited subset of providers while industry standards, like PCI-DSS, only permit pre-approved forensic investigators to conduct reviews acceptable to the PCI Council.

The *Plan* phase of the incident response process requires substantial time investment to prepare for a potential incident or data breach. However, the IRT will use the IRP, Playbooks, and communication collateral throughout the incident response process, so it is critically important that planning documents created reflect how the organization chooses to handle incidents every time. The Incident Response Manager should lead review of the incident response policy and associated documents at least annually during routine policy review activities and update with any changes. An IRP and associated documents have failed when an organization no longer uses them during an active incident or data breach. An IRP should contain, at a minimum:Mission, strategies, and goals statements:

- Organizational approach
- Details of senior leadership involvement and approval
- Approach for communication within and outside the organization
- References to procedures (which then include checklists, technical processes, forms, or playbooks)
- Effectiveness metrics
- Maturity Roadmap

IRPs, to ensure maximum efficacy, should be tested at least annually to ensure they support an organization's incident response capabilities and IRT.

The *Detect* phase is not a step in a process, per se, but is rather an ongoing capability in which potential incidents are reported. The SOC and individual reporting typically result in incident reviews and validation to determine that an incident has actually occurred. *See* Figure 13.2 for an example incident response process flow.

Figure 13.2 Incident Response Process

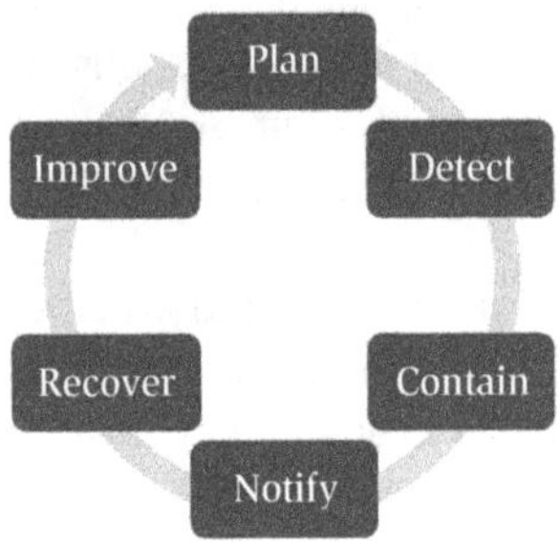

The remaining incident response process steps involve determining whether an incident has resulted in a data breach and who, what, when, and why an asset has been compromised. In the *Identification* phase, the SOC and Incident Response Manager (and internal forensics team, as applicable) work to determine whether an incident has occurred, and whether that incident has progressed to a data breach. In the *Contain* phase, external forensic experts and other technical experts take steps to preserve copies of the system and halt incident progress. In the *Investigation* phase, organizations determine to what degree law enforcement partnership is necessary as external forensics analyze all data available to determine the threat source, threat vectors, and compromised data.

In *Contain*, organizations take steps to stop exposure and remediate vulnerabilities, while preserving final copies of system and data that could be needed for administrative actions, authority investigations, or lawsuits. Strong organizational e-Discovery practices will complement these activities by providing an associated trail of supporting information. The *Notify* phase, if applicable, supports legal obligations for notification after an incident has been designated a data breach. In this phase, the IRT determines the best approach for delivering notification, to which regions, and to whom. Many organizations will not only need to notify consumer-type customers, but in many cases will be obligated to notify business customers due to contractual obligations.

Data breach notification, once confirmed as a data breach, may require specific information, such as data breach volume, data type, affected geographies, and brief description of the compromise. Government entities, industry organizations, credit monitoring agencies, or customers may require submission of specific templates and information. This may require developing a strategy for substitute notice, or notice when direct data breach notification to customers exceeds a specific volume, such as selecting preferred media outlets. For expected notification activities, organizations should compile all required templates and fill in known information as part of the communication strategy.

The *Recover* phase focuses on validating appropriate investigations and eradication are complete, full impact has been determined, and the organization can learn from the recent incident. Recovery allows the organization to take time and record what was done, fully document lessons learned, preserve details of the investigation, and identify what an organization should change about its practices. For this reason, incidents can drive both policy changes and identify new personnel training topics.

Key Takeaways:

- The Incident Response process includes the following phases: Preparation, Identification, Containment, Investigation, Eradication, and Recovery.
- The Incident Response Plan designates the members of the Incident Response Team (IRT), incident types, and notification processes for the IRT.
- The Incident Response Team, at a minimum consists of an Incident Response Manager, the CISO, internal Legal Counsel, and Marketing/Communications/ Public Relations.
- The Security Operations Center reviews potential incidents by examining data pulled into a Security Incident and Event Management (SIEM) tool.
- Logging and monitoring capabilities enable effective security operations that maximize incident responsiveness.

§13.02 SOCIAL ENGINEERING AND MALWARE ATTACKS

Threat sources perpetuate cyberattacks in any number of ways. It is important for both practitioners and attorneys to understand the basic types of cyberattacks, both to understand how cyberattacks can be prevented, understand the degree of complicity in the attack, and to adequately explain how an incident occurred to regulatory authorities or in other legal proceedings. This section focuses on the most common cyberattacks.

Many attacks begin with *social engineering*. Social engineering tactics involve non-technical means: essentially fooling or defrauding a person, rather than taking advantage of a system. Social engineering can include physical entry, such as *piggybacking*, or following an individual in a locked door; *shoulder surfing*, or gaining credentials and sensitive information from looking over someone's shoulder; or otherwise taking advantage of unlocked private facilities. Social engineering may also include using broad tactics to gain introductory information to later seem credible. For example, a social engineer may call an IT service desk or contact center to ask for an employee's contact information or may seek to connect with an individual on a social networking site to appear legitimate to another connection (the real target). Social engineering, therefore, can either be the attack (if directly soliciting information, when gaining information is the objective) or a means to a more advanced attack.

The most common social engineering tactic used today is phishing. *Phishing* is social engineering by e-mail or other electronic means and attackers design emails to include links, attachments, or executables that either solicit sensitive information or convince an individual to introduce malware into the internal network. Often emails will include a URL link that is different from the link when clicked (often exposed by hovering over the link, displaying the actual link's URL). Attackers design the e-mail to convince the receiver of the legitimacy of the sender, encouraging the receiver to click the link, open the file, or execute the application. More advanced phishing attacks provide personal references and use strong e-mail design to appear legitimate. However, because phishing schemes usually involve convincing spam e-mails, e-mail recipients may have difficulty identifying a phishing email. *See* Figure 13.3 for an example phishing e-mail.

Figure 13.3 Spam Phishing E-mail

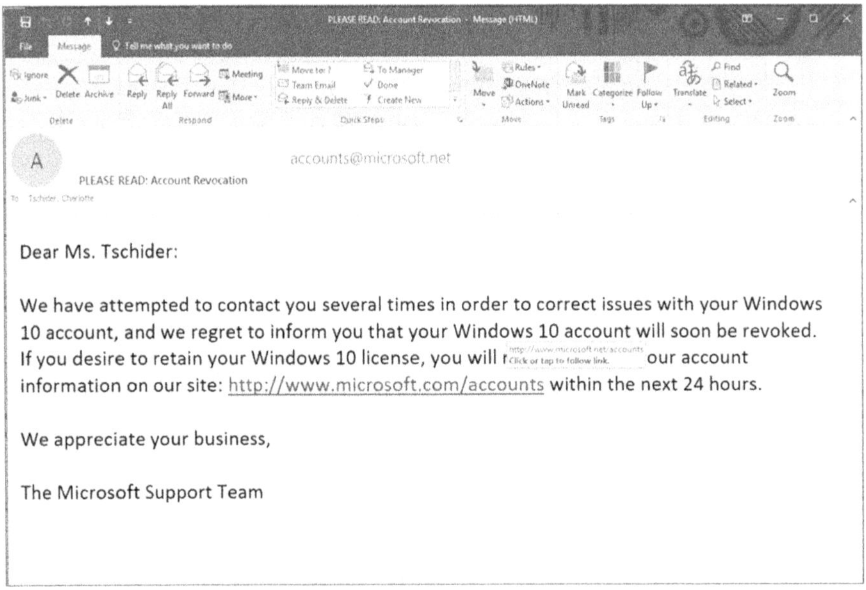

Organizations can usually minimize standard Phishing attacks through spam filtering, phishing training, and timely reporting. Spam filtering within email can eliminate a portion of phishing emails sent to personnel by moving these files to folders, blocking them entirely, or flagging them as "potential spam." Training can also assist individuals in spotting phishing e-mails and validating whether senders, links, and documents appear to be legitimate. Many organizations encourage teams to send questionable e-mails to a protected e-mail box, where a forensics or incident response team can review the e-mail on a machine that does not infect the internal network.

Organizations also request timely reporting of phishing attempts, successful or unsuccessful, with no penalty to the individual reporting. Timely reporting can facilitate fast blocking of e-mails from a particular e-mail address before other individuals are compromised. Despite these tactics, organizations should prepare for some proportion of all individuals to click on phishing e-mail links and ensure appropriate anti-virus technologies have been installed.

Pharming borrows concepts of phishing, in that it presents a legitimate-looking Website after an individual clicks on a legitimate link. Instead of connecting the individual to the appropriate Website, however, the individual connects to a substitute Website designed to look like the original. Most URLs for pharming sites also take advantage of an issue with the server that resolves the domain name of a computer, such as http://www.tesco.com, to the actual IP address (location) of the Web server hosting the Website on the Internet. In a pharming attack, instead of sending the http://www.tesco.com link to the appropriate IP address that has the legitimate site, it instead sends it to another, legitimate-looking site at another IP address (another Web server). Then the attacker uses the fake site to gather credentials from users. Usually, attackers focus on vulnerabilities on individual home computers and routers for this attack, making it incredibly important for users to only access protected Websites, such as those encrypting using HTTPS and using valid certificates. Web browsers, such as Google Chrome, notify the user when a site does not use these two features.

Highly personal e-mails used to target a particular person are called *spear phishing* attacks. Spear phishing attacks generally provide recognizable references, use appropriate terminology, and otherwise appear highly legitimate. Many spear phishing attacks involve impersonation of an individual in power. A popular attack involves sending a spear phishing e-mail to a *target* (the individual to be exploited) while impersonating an individual, such as someone on the person's upper management team. When information about the individual in upper management can be collected from a social network, such as when the person is on vacation, an email can be sent from an illegitimate "personal" email. Examples include a Vice President claiming to be on vacation and asking an analyst or manager to complete a task while they are out of the office. Successful spear phishing attacks include references to real information, increasing the appearance of legitimacy because the stakes are higher than a typical phishing email. These high stakes usually include wiring money or sending confidential information of value; spear phishers leverage power differentials to put the recipient in a position not to say "no."

Spear phishing attacks focused solely on individuals in a position of power, such as the executive team, are called *whaling* attacks. Whaling attacks often use similar techniques to phishing attacks, but may also include additional measures of legitimacy, such as the whaler sending an e-mail followed with a phone call, sometimes even with a caller-ID name that appears legitimate. Similar to spear phishing attacks, which leverage impersonation, whaling attacks may involve references to other executives the target knows, and may couple correct information, such as the name of a vendor and information about an account, with incorrect information, such as the need to settle an account. High-pressure tactics are also used, such as the whaler stating that she will terminate an organization's system functionality for a critical operational system unless the balance due is paid in full within 48 hours. The executive, then, sends an e-mail down the chain, directing an individual to take some action. When the request comes from the executive, an individual may not challenge the legitimacy of the request.

Clearly, spear phishing and whaling attacks require substantial information about an organization, the individual, the individual's work, and the individual's relationships to successfully complete a more advanced attack. Social engineers prey on human elements to facilitate a successful attack: ego, fear, loyalty, a sense of responsibility, sense of belonging, and desire for advancement. However, in many cases, the target often feels unsure before human elements overtake any insecurity. Defense against spear phishing and whaling usually involves training to pause and consider the implications of activities that do not "feel right." Organizations taking these attacks seriously train personnel to challenge upper management when a request seems outside standard process. Executives should ask their teams to challenge them on requests and hold them accountable, as well. Finally, executives should be required to complete training, as well as teams, to ensure all personnel can better identify phishing attacks.

Many cybersecurity attacks involve malicious software. *Malicious software*, as the name entails, is software intended to compromise a system by allowing an attacker to gain unauthorized access to an intranet and gather identification credentials. Malicious software, or *malware*, includes many different types of software, defined by their behavior and purpose. *See* Table 13.3 for descriptions of common malware.

Table 13.3 Common Malware

Name	*Description*
Virus	Viruses are designed to spread within a client by self-replication followed by software modification. They often prevent files, software, and hardware from being used by modifying their code and replacing with its own. Viruses require access to active software in order to replicate and function. Mostly, viruses require a user to download code, and they usually do not
Worm	Worms, like viruses, replicate through a system, often using a network to spread. However, unlike viruses, worms do not require access to software programs to spread, as they are standalone software.
Spyware	Spyware is software specifically installed to gather information about the user, and includes system monitoring activities; keyloggers, which gather information about key strokes; tracking cookies, which track Websites visited and information provided; and rootkits, or installed software allowing an attacker to access administrative capabilities of the system.

Name	*Description*
Trojan	Trojans are software that appear to be legitimate but actually contain malicious code. Trojans can perpetuate any number of behaviors, such as annoying window pop-ups. They can also create backdoors that attackers can use to access the internal network. Trojans do not self-replicate and require an individual to download a trojan, such as from a phishing e-mail.
Bot	Bots are automated, self-contained software that are deposited across the Internet to complete certain tasks. With broad, automated bots, an attacker can launch a far-reaching attack. Bots' versatility allow them to change and evolve, so they are difficult to identify and stop. Bots can do many of the things worms and trojans can do, including opening backdoors for attackers on the Internal network.

Malware can be the attack itself or a gateway to a larger attack. Many types of malware delivered after an individual clicks on a link, opens a file, or installs software, usually compromise the client and sometimes transmit to other servers and clients. Malware transferred from individual users is usually deployed when the user downloads software from an untrusted source; opens an unknown Word, PDF, Excel, or.EXE file; or clicking on a phishing email. The landscape for malware deployment methods constantly changes, and organizations must continue to stay abreast of malware updates.

Anti-malware products do improve malware containment and faster recovery. Anti-malware products include definition files, which enable broad scanning of clients, servers, and the intranet. If the anti-malware locates infected files, it contains these files until a security team can review them. Anti-malware products, like anti-virus, require updated malware definition files to match and contain malware, so organizations should purchase well-known products that update malware definitions regularly. Although malware and anti-virus capabilities often do not eliminate all malware and viruses infecting an individual laptop or mobile device, they identify files on a network, match these files against known malware and virus definitions, and *quarantine* or separate files into a safe area for analysis. Anti-malware products dramatically improve network security by reducing internal exposure. These functions prevent spread of malware and viruses that often serve as a stepping stone to more extensive data breaches. For this reason, the quarantine and review of files serve two functions: alerting to attempted organizational exploitation and halting the spread of malware and viruses causing damage.

In addition, effective vulnerability management procedures that include client OS updates should patch systems on a routine basis, which will minimize malware using vulnerabilities to access the internal network. Usually patches extend the life of software until a new *release*, or version, of software is available. For example, Microsoft releases a variety of patches: *software updates* for clients, *patches* for Microsoft-based servers, and *service packs* for more comprehensive updates. Apple also provides patches in the form of *updates*, which include security changes and GUI changes for clients, with new OS *versions* released annually. Although frequently technologists criticize the frequency and function of patching (and may argue that software providers should invest more heavily in security initially, rather than issuing frequent patches after release), patches do perform an important role. Without patches, organizations would likely not close recently exploited vulnerabilities (zero-day exploits) without substantial effort.

Key Takeaways:

- Social engineering involves tactics that leverage human vulnerabilities to perpetuate or as a first step in attacks.
- Phishing, spear phishing, and whaling all involve e-mail or phone-based social engineering.
- Phishing often includes clicking on a link, opening a file attachment, or downloading software that includes malware.
- Malware is a very large group of malicious software, including viruses, worms, trojans, and bots.

§13.03 SYSTEM AND DATA AVAILABILITY ATTACKS

Some attacks primarily focus on system availability. Attackers use ransomware, denial of service, and brute force to prevent a system from functioning to receive payment or punish the recipient organization. *Ransomware* is an attack type with a variety of threat vectors that focuses on making a system unavailable for a period of time, by using malware to access a system then encrypting its contents with the attacker's key, with expectation of a payment. Organizations have a limited timeframe to pay ransomware attackers, or attackers will erase data or permanently disable a system. Attackers often demand high, yet reasonable, payments victims will pay and make money on simultaneously deployed attacks.

Attackers collect payments in *cryptocurrency* (such as *Bitcoin*), currency that can be exchanged for goods on the Dark Web or exchanged for actual currency.[296] Most attackers using ransomware adopt a reasonably trustworthy business model: pay the ransom, unlock the data. Because ransomware attackers generally are motivated by

296. The blockchain was originally created to manage cryptocurrencies like Bitcoin. *Cryptocurrencies* are pieces of code that have established value in their transfer. Bitcoins were originally created by hiding pieces of code throughout the Internet. After a period of time, enough individuals were interested in finding bitcoin that bitcoin came into demand. Eventually, those who did not have bitcoin exchanged it for standard currency. Once standard currency could be traded for bitcoin, many models emerged: the ability for those desiring privacy to use an untraceable model for financing activities, without using offshore financial managers. The combination of Dark Web activities coupled with untraceable currency like bitcoin (and other cryptocurrencies) enabled individuals to purchase almost anything without a financial trial, whether innocuous like pizza or criminal like drugs.

financial gain, failing to unlock data would result in fewer organizations paying ransom, reducing income. Although attackers often honor this agreement, organizations may have additional concerns with paying ransom (*see* Inset).

> A Word on Ransomware:
>
> Organizations suffering a ransomware attack may be tempted to pay ransom, especially when critical systems, such as those managing patient records or bank accounts, are at risk. Although organizations should employ regular backups for systems, separated from the primary system, some organizations have not completed these activities at the time a ransomware attack hits. Although every organization must make its own determination of risks in paying a ransom, organizations should consider that (1) if attackers have accessed the system, they likely have other information or data and (2) many ransomware attackers will install a backdoor or other mechanism for facilitating a later ransomware attack. Organizations should consult with a reputable forensic investigation partner immediately and determine whether recovery without ransom payment is possible before paying a ransom.

Readers may recognize attacks like Petya and Wannacrypt (#Wannacry) as examples of widespread ransomware attacks that propagated over networks using worm malware then encrypted systems, making them unusable. The same strategies for avoiding malware and updating systems with patches apply to ransomware. In addition to technical solutions, organizations should also mature business processes, such as business continuity and disaster recovery practices for critical operational systems. These practices ensure an organization need not pay a ransom to recover data because data can be restored when needed from other sources.

More than just ransomware makes data unavailable. A Denial of Service (DOS) attack also compromises system availability. A DOS attack focuses on denying access for authorized system users by overwhelming a machine with a high frequency of requests. A Distributed Denial of Service (DDOS/DDoS) attack is the most common form of a DOS attack, in which attackers use different IP addresses (different machines) to simultaneously sent requests to one machine, diversifying the attack. Although an organization can stop a DOS attack by blocking a particular requestor, a DDOS attack continues, even after one or many machines are blocked. Most attackers perpetuating a DDOS attack seek disruption as retribution, such as recently terminated employees, hacktivists, or criminals for purpose of extortion. DDOS extortion is similar to a ransomware attack, except that organizations may pay ransom to stop the DDOS attack rather than decrypt files. E-Commerce sites and SaaS solutions supporting critical business operations are especially at-risk for DDOS attacks, because a DDOS attack can result in substantial business impact through lost sales or customers.

Often attackers use botnets of zombie computers to perpetuate a DDOS attack. A *botnet* is a collection of bots, which take control of machines in order to user them to perpetuate a DDOS attack. A *zombie* is usually a client machine that is taken over by the bot and used to make requests to a Website or Web application for purposes of a DDOS attack. Of note, attackers will also sell access to pre-established botnets to other attackers, as the owner or operator of the client may not know they have downloaded malware containing a bot, so often a bot can reside on a client (mobile device, Internet of Things device, PC, or laptop) for a long period of time without detection. Common attacks following a DDOS model include a Christmas Tree attack, Smurf attack, and Brute Force attack.

Application Layer (OSI Layer 7) DDOS attacks have increased substantially over the past four years, likely because they target the user interface layer, which requires fewer resources than deeper layer attacks. Organizations can prevent attacks by reviewing Internet traffic in a traffic-scrubbing methodology, which pulls in various inputs from traffic and validates them, for example through a *traffic-scrubbing filter*. Some cloud providers also offer distributed site offerings, which allow traffic to flow through multiple connections, rather than one.

Key Takeaways:

- Ransomware involves accessing internal networks using malware, then holding data or systems hostage by encrypting important data unless an organization pays the ransom.
- Organizations may be tempted to pay a ransom, but they should also consider potential impacts associated with an attacker's previous access to the system.
- DDOS attacks make use of bots in zombie computers (forming a botnet), to overwhelm Website or Web applications, making them unusable.

§13.04 DATA CONFIDENTIALITY ATTACKS

Although attackers do perpetuate attacks affecting the availability of information, successful attacks affecting the confidentiality of data tend to be most lucrative, whether personal information or confidential business information, such as trade secrets. One common attack, Cross-Site Scripting (XSS/CSS) focuses on Web applications at the Application Layer, similar to a DDOS attack. However, XSS works by pasting malicious code (a *payload*) into a Web form, where the form does not use input validation. Input validation ensures that data input, such as a phone number, meets expected phone number length and breakdown for a particular geographic region.[297] When Web applications do not use input validation, an attacker can paste code in a Web form's field, such as a product review or a comment field, which then is presented as code, infecting the Web browser.

297. *Code injection* or *command injection*, attack types perpetuated through Web applications, also can be prevented with input validation measures.

Although XSS on its own may seem less dangerous than other attacks, attackers may use certain code used in Web browsers to execute a more sophisticated attack by impersonating the user through cookie theft, or accessing a user's Web cam or microphone. Organizations can, however, prevent these attacks by vulnerability scanning their Websites.

SQL Injections (SQLi) are commonly used attacks compromising data confidentiality. SQLi preys on SQL databases connected to a Web application, which often store substantial volumes of data collected from the application. In a SQLi, an attacker delivers a payload to an Internet-connected SQL server by inputting specific SQL code into a Web application using specific types of code. This code enables the attacker to access, modify, or delete data in the database, bypassing identification, authorization, and authentication controls. Preventing SQL injections requires more advanced techniques to structure code appropriately, a field often called *AppSec*, or Application Security.

Some attacks focus on guessing log-in passwords, such as *Dictionary attacks.* Dictionary attacks take advantage of weak passwords, or those incorporating full words or short-length passwords, rather than a sufficient number of random letters, numbers, and special characters. Organizations can prevent most dictionary by requiring sufficiently complex and lengthy password requirements or additional authentication factors, i.e., MFA. Similar to the automated analysis of short words in a dictionary attack, hashes used for authentication purposes can be similarly aggregated and attempted as a sort-of hash dictionary, called a *rainbow table.* Organizations can prevent attacks involving a rainbow table simply by including salt in each hash.

A brute force attack is another common method for compromising confidentiality. *Brute force attacks* work by using substantial computing power to attempt to determine a password by guessing each sequentially. Because this process can take a substantial amount of time and computing power, attackers perpetuate successful brute force attacks when attempting to guess shorter sequences. Similar to dictionary attacks, more random, longer passwords and encryption keys prove substantially more difficult to crack using these attacks. Therefore, effective encryption key management and effective password policies can stop brute force attacks.

Another example of username and password misuse is credential stuffing. *Credential stuffing* is an emerging attack involving purchase of a large volume of breached usernames and passwords on the Dark Web, then using an *account checker*, or automated software that checks the loaded usernames and passwords against many common sites on the Internet, such as social media, e-Commerce sites, and other highly used sites. When the attacker successfully gains access to a site, the attacker takes information for future sales or fraud, such as personal information or credit card details. Individual users can avoid compromise by using different passwords for sites, minimizing the cascading effect of one breach leading to another. Organizations can prevent mass-breach of usernames and passwords leading to credential stuffing by following standard security practices, especially encrypting usernames and passwords in storage and encouraging personnel to use different passwords for organizational resources than passwords used at home.

Attacks involving network connectivity also affect the confidentiality of messages. The most common attack methods include *Man-in-the-Middle attacks* (or session hijacking, active eavesdropping) and *packet sniffing* (application sniffing). In a Man-in-the-Middle attack, the attacker can view, siphon, or change data flowing between two machines. This situation leads to unintentional disclosure of confidential information to an outside party or the "man in the middle" altering messages, which instruct a person or machine to do something that is inaccurate and potentially damaging. Organizations can prevent man-in-the-middle attacks with better Intranet protection and encouraging personnel not to use unprotected Internet access for organizational work outside the organization (such as an Internet café or coffee shop). One relatively easy defense for Man-in-the-Middle attacks involves designing an encrypted VPN solution. Because a VPN creates an encrypted, authenticated channel between an individual client and the internal servers, an attacker cannot understand the information transferred, unless the VPN uses poor encryption techniques.

Similar to the Man-in-the-Middle attack, packet sniffing is a more passive attack type wherein an attacker intercepts and views packets sent of data in transmission, including in some cases usernames and passwords passed in clear text within the network. Malicious insiders commonly packet sniff using a network monitor, as packet sniffing requires access to a trusted network. When functioning normally, network monitors identify irregularities in data transfer and monitor network performance. However, in *promiscuous mode*, network monitors enables a malicious insider to intercept all, not just some, traffic for purposes of harvesting credentials. If organizations use tools to detect monitors in this mode, they can prevent packet sniffing attacks.

Attack types specific to Bluetooth technologies can send unauthorized messages and compromise confidential information. With the increased use of Bluetooth technologies, increasingly more often attacks like bluejacking and bluesnarfing compromise Bluetooth technologies. *Bluejacking* allows an attacker to send anonymous messages within a limited geographic space to another Bluetooth-enabled device. Although relatively innocuous compared to other attack types, bluejacking can be used with social engineering tactics to distract an individual for various other purposes. Bluesnarfing, in comparison, can view messages and information on devices using Bluetooth technology. In both cases, these attacks leverage devices set to "discoverable" in Bluetooth-managing programs and take advantage of autoconnectivity for Bluetooth-enabled devices. Individuals can protect themselves by turning off Bluetooth connections when not in use or rendering devices temporarily undiscoverable.

Key Takeaways:

- XSS and SQLi both take advantage of Websites and Web applications by allowing for code to be input into open fields.
- Implementing data validation can dramatically reduce potential impacts through XSS and SQLi.
- Dictionary attacks more easily crack longer passwords, and brute force attacks more easily crack shorter passwords. Complex (non-dictionary

worded) passwords, preferably with 2FA, reduce both dictionary and brute force attacks.
- Bluetooth is vulnerable to attack and users should turn off Bluetooth when not in use.

§13.05 ATTACKS AND TECHNOLOGY IN PRACTICE: THE ADVANCED PERSISTENT THREAT

Attacks are often combined to ensure data or system compromise is all but inevitable. One of the most challenging situations today involves the Advanced Persistent Threat (APT). APT requires substantial resources and a relatively longer period of time. For these reasons, most typically APT pertains to state-sponsored hackers or other organized hacking groups focused on an individual organization for an extended period without being discovered. In an APT, attackers usually follow five steps to successfully fulfill their objectives: (1) Reconnaissance, (2) Incursion, (3) Discovery, (4) Capture, and (5) Exfiltration.

In *Reconnaissance*, the attackers get to know the victim organization, gathering information, including researching potential insiders to assist with the attack and finding as much information about the systems as possible. In *Incursion*, the attackers access the network, usually by using malware installed after social engineering. In *Discovery* attackers identify and document security controls applicable to the network and assets within the system, which enables them to form an approach and plan for exploiting vulnerabilities. *Capture* involves actually gathering sensitive information from systems and compiling it for fraud or espionage purposes. When the attackers reach the *Exfiltration* phase, data has been collated, but the data must be transferred outside of the victim organization's system without detection. APT attackers can execute these phases over several months or years without detection by internal experts because many of the actions mimic legitimate activities within an organization. Organizations can prevent APTs by implementing anti-malware technologies, patching vulnerabilities as soon as possible and on a recurring basis, and instituting firewall application white listing. Unlike blacklisting, which bars access to known malicious sites, white listing permits access only to known uninfected sites.

APTs are famous for substantially large data breaches around the world. Although many APTs first focused on government systems, APTs today also affect large organizations. In 2006, Sykipot used spear-phishing e-mails with malware and zero-day exploits to access U.S. and United Kingdom organizations' intellectual property, trade secrets, design documents, and other sensitive information in telecommunications, defense, computing, chemicals, energy, and others. A later analysis determined that Chinese servers had been used for the attacks. In 2007, APT kits started to emerge, including most famously *Zeus*, which hundreds of hackers used to exfiltrate financial data. Zeus is still used today and continues to be leveraged by crime networks to exploit financial institutions globally.

In 2009, an APT called GhostNet, loosely tied to China and rumored to have been created by the U.S. government compromised computers with political and economic ties in over 100 countries. It used phishing e-mails delivering trojan horses to gain access to systems. Another APT involving a trojan horse, Operation Aurora, was used in 2009 as well to compromise private entities, including Google, which dramatically improved implementation of security controls for Google and other large companies. Another global company, Sony Pictures, experienced an APT in 2014, which compromised substantial employee personal information and revealed embarrassing e-mails. When assessed by a security firm, the security firm explained that the attack was so advanced and specific, that it could not have been prevented using standard security controls.

Today, APTs pose the biggest concern for larger organizations because threat vectors used are tremendously difficult to combat. Although organizations may have relatively strong security controls, APTs use the benefit of research and time to perpetuate an attack that leverages any vulnerability. Organizations, therefore, must not only focus on implementation of security controls, but also improve resilience and security maturity over time to respond quickly once an incident or data breach is detected.

Organizations today, especially government entities, have increasingly considered a more aggressive approach to data protection, sometimes called active defense. *Active defense* (or Active Cyber Defense—ACD) is the activity of launching attacks to prevent damage to an organization's assets and customers. Commentators in the information security consider active defense highly controversial because clearly articulating when true defense ends and retribution begins is tremendously difficult. This may mean that organizations involved in active defense activities (sometimes called *gray hat* activities) may actually face legal issues by accessing and potentially damaging another individual's or organization's assets and personal property. Governments engaged in these activities could elicit cyber aggression from another government with geopolitical fallout. The rules of active defense are still being defined, which means that organizations today are safe focusing on stopping attackers within systems and preventing attackers from accessing systems through true defensive strategies.

Key Takeaways:

- The five steps of an APT are (1) Reconnaissance, (2) Incursion, (3) Discovery, (4) Capture, and (5) Exfiltration.
- APT increasingly affects private organizations, but has affected government entities at least since 2006.
- APT involve highly complex, dedicated attacks over long period of time, but they also can result in substantial compromise and losses.

Part III Managing Privacy and Security Legal Risk

CHAPTER 14

Managing Legal Risk

§14.01 CONTRACT MANAGEMENT

Organizations rely on third parties to manage many activities on behalf of the organization. As previously referenced, third parties (including processors, affiliates, partners, and true third parties) can pose substantial risk to an organization. Although third-party assessments can help identify security issues with third parties, contracts provide a reliable, legally binding method to ensure third-party compliance or legal recovery, should a third-party not honor its commitments. Contract law provides a useful tool for organizations doing business with third parties across various geographical regions, including between states, countries, or regions. Indeed, contracts are usually enforced internationally.

Increasingly more so today, organizations include a security and privacy addendum to contracts. Under some laws, in particular when transferring personal data to inadequate recipient countries or when transferring data pursuant to a CE/BA relationship (under HIPAA), privacy addendums are required, such as MCCs or a Business Associate Agreement (BAA).[298]

Despite the legal focus on privacy language in contracts, attorneys serve best interests of an organization by executing security and privacy language within third-party contracts, regardless of legal requirements to do so. Contracts provide two benefits for organizations working with third parties: (1) they put the third-party on notice about their obligations and (2) contracts provide recovery following financial damage.

Although organizations should expect honesty in negotiations and reviews with third parties, organizations often react to privacy and security terms by agreeing to all

298. BAAs enforce HIPAA obligations on BAs that would not otherwise be obligated to follow HIPAA requirements, including organizations outside of the United States. MCCs work in a similar way for the EU, and alternative contractual clauses may be used in other parts of the world.

terms without reviewing them, replace terms with their own boilerplate, or conscientiously redline the document. In the best case, when third parties observe privacy and security terms, they may observe their own practices more closely. Often, organizations will not commit to actions in a contract they may otherwise claim to have in place during an assessment. For this reason, it is central that teams conducting assessments and negotiating contracts work closely together on third party reviews.

Contracts usually have existing boilerplate outside privacy and security obligations that could make certain security and privacy situations more challenging. Legal teams should review general-purpose boilerplate in light of potential enforcement and recovery issues. *See* Table 14.1 for explanations of each standard boilerplate term.

Contracts provide recovery for organizations when they experience financial damage following a data breach or privacy violation. Indemnification clauses provide the ability to recover from a third-party if an organization suffers damage because of the third-party's actions. However, sometimes indemnification terms only reference provisions in the contract that do not implicate confidentiality, privacy, or security obligations. In some contracts, indemnification amounts may be capped at the annual contract cost or six months of the contract. Unfortunately, this amount may not come close to covering the cost of a data breach.

Table 14.1 General Purpose Clauses

Clause Name	*Why It Should/Could Change*
General confidentiality clause	Should reference additional data classifications
Applicability to Affiliates/Partners	Obligations should extend to affiliates or other legally connected parties or restrict transfer
Sub-contractors or sub-processor responsibilities	Vendors must ensure obligations are included in subsequent sub-contractor or sub-processor contract[299]
Insurance coverage	Errors & Omissions insurance does not cover cyberliability (usually); cyberliability coverage should cover data breach cost if records exposed
Financial viability	Solvency terms critical, especially without cyberliability coverage; 80 percent of small businesses go out of business following a data breach financial
Third party beneficiaries	The organization may want to reserve rights for customers, affiliates, partners, or others who might be harmed
Applicability after service (continuing obligations	Third parties must continue security obligations after termination for data maintained
Severability and modification clauses	Privacy and information security clauses should persist and be explicitly referenced as surviving

299. The Author calls this term "sub-privity," where third parties of third parties must obligate the next, ad infinitum, to ensure the controller meets legal obligations and adequately protects personal information.

Clause Name	*Why It Should/Could Change*
Integration clause	Privacy and information security clauses must be added with the Master Services Agreement (MSA) at the time integration clause executed

Organizations, whether on the third party or customer side, should ensure that legal provisions governing the contract, such as definitions and applicable laws, are well-defined. For example, applicable laws could define personal information more or less favorably, depending on the jurisdiction, if the contract does not include an alternative. Contracts should also clearly communicate applicable laws, as well as choice of law provisions at the beginning of the contract, so all parties must abide by the provisions, regardless of the third party's home laws and location.[300]

§14.02 PRIVACY CLAUSES

Organizations may be tempted to paste in EU MCCs for example, and execute the contract without additional details included. However, additional information may assist organizations in clearly articulating transferred obligations, cost allocation, and various steps should personal information exposure occur. Some organizations may, as part of processing responsibilities, require third parties to execute obligations on their behalf, for example providing notice or collecting consent. Organizations should clearly communicate these obligations within the contract to ensure a right of recovery if a processor's failure triggers a regulatory fine or other legal action.

When a data breach or other event occurs, compromising personal information, various activities will require funding, such as data breach notification or credit monitoring activities, which can run as much as EUR 2 per notice and EUR 14 per month of credit monitoring. For large breaches, organizations may pay millions in notification and credit monitoring fees. When the third party has caused the breach, a controller may want to ensure the third party pays for these activities. Further, controllers will likely prefer to "control" the message following a data breach. Contractual terms requiring a processor to alert the controller as soon as possible and before other parties might enable a controller to obtain a protective order, lessening the probability of public relations issues before the organization can properly investigate.

§14.03 SECURITY CLAUSES

Security clauses should balance specificity and flexibility. Where possible, organizations should find mutually acceptable indicia for appropriate measurements, such as "best practices as specified under ISO 27001" or "the processor must conduct an annual SSAE16 SOC 2, Type II review and provide a report to the controller not more than two

300. Challenges often result when two parties reside in jurisdictions exhibiting radically different data protection expectations. Often under these circumstances, a customer might need to explain to a third party the repercussions of the third party not following the law.

months after completion." These agreements tend to lessen the challenges associated with heavy and lengthy security reviews, yet also provide a high degree of stringency.

Organizations should clearly describe the scope of such requirements. For example, a processor may conduct a PCI-DSS assessment, but narrowly scope its application to systems that do not fully cover the controller's services. Other vendors might provide assurances as to security controls, yet the price quoted and listed in the Statement of Work might apply only to basic offerings. When controllers do not clearly describe the scope of services and how security requirements might apply within the contract, controllers may not receive expected services. Some controllers explicitly specify data elements or data classification for planned processing within the applicable law section to underscore the data processed and avoid confusion.

Security requirements, when articulated in the contract, should be written in a straightforward manner, referencing external standards where possible:

- Annual policy updates, and annual or more frequent training of personnel on internal policies/standards
- Current existence of a formal security program and primary security contact
- Current and regularly exercised/tested incident response process
- Clearly articulated data breach disclosure process and controller rights with respect to data breach, such as rights to involvement in the investigation, notification timeframe, rights to audit, and rights to terminate
- Regular audit/assessment rights (e.g., quarterly, annually, bi-annually; nature of the audit or assessment, such as on-premises or based on a questionnaire)
- Current vulnerability management program and common vulnerability scoring
- Secure architecture planning and secure development practices
- Existing virus/malware scanning processes
- Standard network security controls, such as IDS/IPS and NAC
- Remote access procedures if processor stores controller data, or planned access to controller systems via remote access
- Identity and access management procedures for personnel with access to controller data
- Physical security requirements, such as CCTV, visitor sign-in and escort, key-card locked doors
- Data destruction procedures ensuring secure and complete deletion
- Business continuity/disaster recovery processes
- Personnel background checks and contents of those checks.

§14.04 CHALLENGES

By far, the biggest challenge to ensuring privacy and security obligations involves contract efficiency. Routine service providers frequently acting as a processor or third party may have great difficulty managing diverse obligations for themselves and for their sub-processors or sub-contractors.

The business customer's terms and conditions in a first contract frequently require a service provider to bind its third parties to the same or similar terms *vis-à-vis* a second contract, causing a domino effect of reduced contract efficiency. When a third party manages personal information, it also requires data centers, data storage services, additional backend software, hardware, infrastructure, or subcontractors. Therefore, organizational data are managed by sub-contractors of the third party, complicating oversight.[301] To meet sub-privity terms and provide some evidence of due diligence, the service provider must subsequently negotiate with all applicable third parties in each contract.[302] If the service provider agrees to hold its third parties to the same data protection terms, the service provider likely engages in protracted contract negotiations and renegotiations to ensure all of a service provider's third parties can adhere to the original business customer's terms or exerts tremendous effort in finding a replacement third party that will agree to these terms in entirety. This results in a cascading and sometimes circuitous effect from a business customer and its service provider to the third parties of the service provider.[303] In particularly complex scenarios, one business arm of a customer could require the service provider to hold its third parties to the same data protection terms, while the same customer as a third-party vendor refuses to include the same data protection terms.

Service providers serving as processors or third parties can work to provide fair, balanced, and specific boilerplate terms for most engagements, ensuring consistency across multiple contracts. When service providers, then, work with very large organizations that have comparatively high negotiating power, the service provider can weigh the costs and benefits of efficiency impacts of unique contract terms or alternative support models to streamline potential downstream impacts.

However, if a third party uses sub-contractors and cannot effectively negotiate to a similar boilerplate agreement, it must ensure multiple sets of different obligations from each of the controllers are reflected in the third party's sub-contracting agreement. For this reason, processors handling several controller accounts often create boilerplate contracts to ensure consistency across contracting arrangements. *See* Figure 14.1 for a visual diagram of contracting complexities between controllers and processors.

301. *Security Concerns in Licensing Agreements, Part Two: Negotiating Security Provisions*, SYMANTEC (Nov. 2, 2010), http://www.symantec.com/connect/articles/security-concerns-licensing-agreements-part-two-negotiating-security-provisions.

302. *Guidance on Managing Risks from Third-Party Relationships*, FED. BANKING L. REP. P 35-522 (C.C.H.) (2013).

303. As an example, many technology companies provide base technology capabilities or data storage to businesses that support storage or processing of personal information. However, these companies also rely on business process vendors for specific services; e.g. accounting, HR, insurance, recruiting, IT consulting, payment processing; and often demand protection of personal information through these processes. Both organizations could be relying on each other as customers and as vendors, complicating contractual negotiation.

Figure 14.1 Controller and Processor Contracts

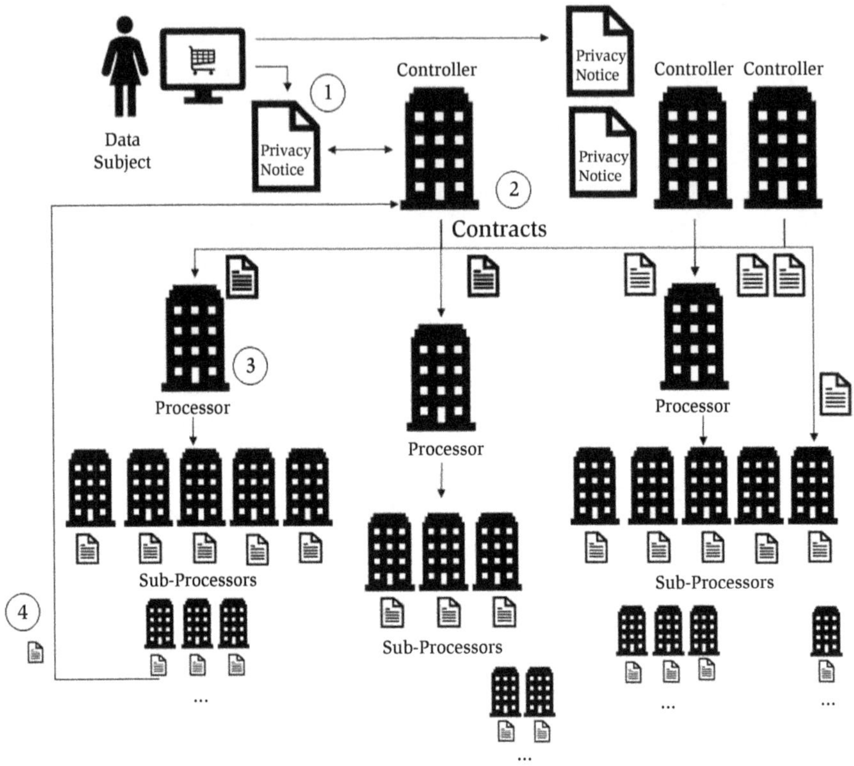

In Step 1, the controller has made data handling commitments to the data subject, and the data subject has multiple relationships with multiple controllers, as they sell her various products and services. In Step 2, each controller has passed its respective data handling commitments and other legally required clauses, to the processor. In Step 3, each processor passes down these commitments to its sub-processors, who pass it down to their sub-processors. In Step 4, a sub-processor passes the commitment down to its sub-sub processor, which happens to be the processor for the controller for other services. Of note, in Step 2, a processor receives three different contracts from three different controllers with respect to the same data subject. Reviewing this figure, it should be clear how complex contract management might be with respect to providing goods or services to a data subject.

Boilerplate language assists both organizations as controllers and processors in streamlining and managing obligations to other parties, and privacy and data protection (security) terms help to ensure commitments made to data subjects are honored through all processing activities. However, boilerplate language can prove challenging when a processor is faced with different boilerplate from multiple controllers, or when two parties switch positions.[304]

§14.05 CYBERLIABILITY INSURANCE

Prior to negotiating cyberliability or cyberrisk insurance, organizations should focus on developing, formalizing, and communicating strong security policies, processes, and procedures. Although highly regulated organizations may in some cases review security maturity with respect to compliance obligations, the cybersecurity industry may require more at policy issuance or during claims processing. Meaningfully reducing risk to merit lower premiums, qualify for cyberrisk insurance, or recover cost requires a "compliance plus" approach to building a better security program.

Strong security programs accomplish more than baseline compliance with a specific regulation. They also draw awareness to risks facing an organization and enable effective prioritization of remediation tasks and security technology investments. Organizations must implement security programs to determine the amount of coverage, appropriate premium/deductible, and type of cyberrisk or cyberliability policies that make most sense for the risk profile of an organization. Ultimately, the best cyberrisk or cyberliability policy rarely needs to be used.

Cyberrisk as a term is often adopted in modern insurance discussions instead of *cyberliability* because of its applicability to a broader set of business operations and potential impacts. In some circumstances, for example, cyberrisk insurance may apply to events involving service interruption or compromise by non-malicious individuals (e.g., not a hacker or malicious insider, like a disgruntled employee) that nevertheless require funding to recover. Examples of such interruptions could stem from an IT employee's mistake in an active (production) version of a software application or a natural disaster. In contrast, cyberliability is often used to describe activities leading to or probable to invoke liability, whether it includes failure to meet contractual obligations for a customer resulting in breach of contract or an actual legal action following a consumer data breach. Other names for this type of insurance include privacy or information security liability insurance. Despite these distinctions, insurance providers

304. For example, technology vendors often will be both consumers and providers of certain services, such as Microsoft, Apple, Oracle, or SAP. Microsoft provides services to individual data subjects, so it is a controller with respect to that data subject. However, Microsoft also provides services to organizations in the form of enterprise services, e.g. servers, databases, operating systems. Microsoft may look to a supplier to provide services to a data subject, such as helpline support. However, the helpline support company likely also uses Microsoft products to store helpline call information. In this circumstance, the helpline is required to meet certain obligations from Microsoft according to the contract it has with Microsoft, and Microsoft is a sub-processor for the helpline. Microsoft, in this example, would be both controller and downstream sub-processor for itself. On its face, this might not prove challenging, except that many organizations have different boilerplate and commitments they will make depending on the role of the organization as controller or processor, making it almost impossible to ensure that the controller-as-sub-processor meets the obligations it has set for processors.

intermix these terms; *cyberliability* insurance will be used here, as insurers most frequently use this name to describe this product.

Cyberliability coverage may cover a variety of activities necessary in the event of a data breach, such as immediate recovery for business operation, engagement of third party experts, setting up call centers to handle inquiries, data breach notification, credit monitoring offerings, litigation expenses, acts and omissions of third parties, and sometimes remediation activities. Most cyberliability policies, like any other insurance policy, include events limiting claim payout and may restrict payout for certain types of data breach effects, but not others. For example, most cyberliability policies do not extend coverage to physical injury or property damage, even though cybersecurity attacks could harm the physical operation of machinery. Increasingly more frequently, cyberliability insurers have found opportunities to deny claims for organizations suffering data breaches.

Organizations should have a formal privacy and security program(s), including a security official that is accountable and monitors security risk and compliance. A security program should also have one or more security policies and associated standards or procedures for implementing policy requirements, which will also feed workforce training and management functions. Organizations should provide appropriate supervision and training for personnel who work with SPI; however, organizations should also train based on internal policy and associated security procedures. Employment agreements combined with internally posted policy and personnel training, then, may permit downstream sanctions when personnel violate policies and procedures, depending on local laws.

Security assessments conducted annually or more frequently help an organization determine where the organization has not followed internal policy. Assessments consider threats facing certain business processes, systems, and the sensitivity of data elements. Assessment results, then, help an organization effectively prioritize mitigation and remediation activities that collectively reduce risk for an organization. Security assessments reveal non-compliance with internal policies and procedures, which enables an organization to determine potential risks to the data and appropriate security measures to mitigate or remediate risks. Conducting assessments across the organization will also identify how well security policies, procedures, and training appropriate reduce risk of unauthorized use, exposure, fraud, and data breaches.

Security assessment results and associated mitigation or remediation strategies must be documented, which improves auditability if needed for cyberliability insurance. However, security remediation and mitigation documentation also can illustrate relative progress and maturity for a security program, which may substantiate a request for lower deductible or broader/higher ceiling insurance coverage, as well as streamline any applicable regulatory audit.

When implementing a program, regulatory authorities generally do not dictate specific measures, but permit organizations to consider size, complexity, and capabilities; technical, hardware, and software infrastructure; security measure cost; and the likelihood and impact of potential risks to electronic protected health information. However, flexibility under the law does not necessarily match the relative inflexibility of insurance policies. This means that although an organization may benefit from implementing flexible measures, failing to understand what measures must be implemented under a cyberliability policy will likely lead to less coverage in the event of a data breach or similar interruption. For this reason, it is prudent to implement industry best practices when developing a security program, as it will most likely reduce the risk of a data breach and also improve the likelihood of successfully submitting a claim when cyberliability insurance payout is needed.

Administrative controls provide organizations with "self-help" mechanisms for reducing the occurrence of situations that will require cyberliability insurance. These safeguards often also reduce the extent of damage by employing a risk-based approach to control application and by creating high-resilience and high-responsiveness procedures for recovery. These two benefits should mean lower premiums and fewer issues successfully submitting insurance claims.

Some insurers require an organization to provide evidence of risk mitigation strategies and program formalities prior to underwriting a policy, such as distributing a questionnaire or requiring submission of documentation. In other circumstances, insurers may not require such evidence, but may be amenable to organizations demonstrating improved security maturity to negotiate a lower deductible. Developing and continuously improving an information security program enables an organization to demonstrate its security maturity.

An information security program includes processes needed to submit cyberliability claims. For example, without intrusion detection systems (IDS), which identify when an intrusion has occurred and alert a security team, or a security incident and event monitoring (SIEM) tool, which helps a security team manage and monitor systems, an organization might not know that a data breach has occurred. Similarly, an incident response plan and associated procedures help an organization manage what could be a crisis situation. During an incident, security personnel will follow procedures for maintaining accurate copies of affected systems, conducting early investigations, and understanding when the business legitimately needs third party services like an external forensic investigator to draft a court admissible report. This illustrates but one example of where an organization's information security program can ensure cyberliability insurance policies work effectively, charge an acceptable premium and deductible, and do not deny reasonable claims.

Organizations face a variety of statutory, regulatory, and industry requirements for compliance purposes. However, appropriately managing risk to adequately leverage cyberliability insurance may require implementation of additional industry best practices. Organizations should seriously consider building out security programs to include additional organizational and technical controls and monitor compliance to internal policy to reduce data breach probability, substantiate insurance resource utilization (e.g., forensic services), and avoid claim denial.

CHAPTER 15

Data Breach Notification

Data breach notification is a hot topic in cybersecurity and privacy law, with the new GDPR requiring data breach notification to data subjects, and several other countries in the world already requiring the same notification.

Data breach notification has become increasingly important. Among ever-increasing cyberattacks and data breaches, timely notice may assist a data subject in facilitating self-help, such as canceling payment cards, placing a notice on credit report, or other protective activities. Further, considering the concept of information privacy in the consumer sphere hinges on consumer choice, lack of awareness to data breaches prevents consumers from making an informed decision regarding their privacy rights. The move towards notification, then, is a permanent and increasingly important obligation.

Data breach notification may include any of these considerations:

- How quickly notification must be delivered after discovering a data breach
- Data compromised requiring notification
- Contents of the notification
- Who may disseminate notification (e.g., controller, processor)
- Whether an organization must notify a data subject, regulatory authority, credit agencies, or all
- Whether substitute notice is available instead of individually mailing letters.

Most international data breach notification laws do not include many specific details for notification today. According to the World Law Group, as of 2016, only thirteen countries outside of the EU require data breach notification either explicitly within data protection laws (eight countries) or through other mechanisms (five countries). *See* Table 15.1 for a list of countries and details of data breach notification activity.

Table 15.1 International Data Breach Notification[305]

Country	*Law or Other Obligation*
EU	General Data Protection Regulation
United States	GLBA, Reg-SP, HIPAA, non-HIPAA health, state laws
Canada	PIPEDA, provincial laws
México	Federal Law for the Protection of Personal Data in Possession of Private Parties
Uruguay	Uruguayan Data Protection Law
Costa Rica	Art. 38 of the regulation for the Data Protection Law
Japan	Act on the Protection of Personal Information (APPI)
South Korea	Personal Information Protection Act ("PIPA") and the Act on Promotion of Information and Communications Network Utilisation and Information Protection
Taiwan	Personal Information Protection Act ("PIPA")
Russia	None, required to take "necessary measures to remedy;" notification required if remediation cannot occur
Indonesia	Government Regulation No. 82 of 2012 requires operators to protect CIA, failure requires notification
China	Consumer Rights Protection Law, requires "remedial measures" by operator, notification is "remedial"
Philippines	Republic Act No. 10173 (Data Privacy Act of 2012), Section 20(f), only with SPI with real risk of harm

Although most data breach requirements do not specify required contents, the more comprehensive requirements include:

- Identity of the data controller/database owner
- Basic information about the breach (information potentially compromised, number affected, dates of compromise, cause if known)
- Contact information for more information or questions
- Additional information, such as availability of credit or identity theft monitoring
- In some cases notification to the regulatory authority (highly recommended where not mandated for large data breaches)

Data breach notification proves challenging for organizations with operations in multiple locations. In some countries such as South Korea and the U.S., organizations must notify data subjects in the event of a data breach. However, some countries require multiple parties be notified, such as data subject, regulators, and credit agencies. Typically, the organization with a direct relationship to the data subject (the

305. World Law Group, *Global Guide to Data Breach Notifications, 2016* (2016), http://www.theworldlawgroup.com/Document.asp?DocID=115509.

controller) distributes the notification, although under some contractual arrangements the processor may distribute or pay for a notification service.

To date, no country overall requires that organizations pay for credit monitoring services. In the U.S, a small proportion of states do require provision of credit monitoring services. The question of whether to offer such services usually turns on the degree to which fraud or other misuse might occur. When the probability of fraud or misuse is high, organizations should consider providing credit monitoring services, if for no other reason than to minimize potential injury and damages recoverable under some laws. Although countries that provide an explicit private right of action often include both economic and moral damages in recovery, it is much less likely that organizations will pay a substantial amount of money in a court of law absent financial injury.

Organizations can easily spend millions of Euro covering credit monitoring activities, but many organizations voluntarily opt to purchase credit monitoring or fraud monitoring services for affected data subjects to maximize goodwill and minimize personal damages. Depending on the market, this can cost anywhere from USD 10 to USD 12 a month per subject for a reasonable time period for monitoring purposes (usually twelve to twenty-four months, depending on the type of loss). Monitoring activities reduce the probability of fraud or other injury affecting a data subject, while simultaneously protecting an organization from paying more money should injury occur.

When a data breach occurs, the organization should prepare for some type of legal activity. This may include regulatory authority investigation, litigation, or fines. For this reason, organizations should retain all records under a legal hold so that proof of activities up to and including the data breach can be preserved for discovery or investigation purposes. During incident response activities and subsequent data breach conversations, external counsel should be engaged to ensure attorney-client privilege.

§15.01 U.S. DATA BREACH NOTIFICATION

As a result of the U.S. federal government's sectoral regulations with limited, embedded information privacy provisions, data breach notification has never been so complicated. States have opted to regulate broad usage of personal information for their residents. At the time of writing, forty-eight U.S. states enacted a data breach notification statute.[306] Most states regulate corporations operating within state borders (either by reaching consumers or physical presence), requiring data breach notification within a specific time period and procedures for less expensive, broader dissemination for large breaches (e.g., television or newspaper).[307] In 2002, California was the first state to enact a data breach notification statute, but more recent statutes passed by Massachusetts and Florida reflect some of the most broadly applied and restrictive

306. National Conference on State Legislatures (12 Apr. 2014), http://www.ncsl.org/research/telecommunications-and-information-technology/security-breach-notification-laws.aspx.

307. *Data Breach Charts*, BakerHostetler (2014), http://www.bakerlaw.com/files/Uploads/Documents/Data%20Breach%20documents/Data_Breach_Charts.pdf.

requirements to date, for example requiring businesses to adopt a comprehensive security program if doing business with state residents and encouraging techniques to render information indecipherable, such as encryption.[308] International businesses handling U.S. consumer information also face a difficult situation: how to effectively comply with forty-eight variations on data breach notification and data protection requirements, especially when these laws fundamentally differ from many other countries' data protection laws and data breach notification obligations.[309]

In the United States, around 31% of statutes employed highly specific language, limiting statutes to non-government organizations incorporated or doing business in the state, while 57% employed broader language, including any organization handling personal information of state residents or including commercial and non-commercial entities, as well as state agencies.[310] This definition of statutory application extended to extraterritorial effect: after 2007, extraterritorial provisions increased dramatically, to 54% of statutes adopting overt extraterritorial provisions. This movement towards extraterritorial effect means that likely organizations outside of the United States will need to understand the individual complexities of U.S. data breach notification laws.

Despite broad and increasing application of statutes, however, the breadth of information covered by the majority of states did not increase as dramatically. Forty-seven percent of statutes used just six information types or less, while 53% included more than six information types.[311] The most common information types, at 100% of all statutes, included financial information like credit card, debit card, and financial account number (combined with required security passcodes, PINs, or access codes); social security number; and state identification numbers. Health information, health insurance, and biometric information were classified in a moderate number of states, suggesting that these information types have emerged as sources of consumer concern or potential fraud. For the most part, this type of data would likely be recognized as personal information under international laws, as well. *See* Figure 15.1 for percentages of data types requiring data breach notification.

---

308. Timothy K. Skinner, *California's Database Breach Notification Security Act: The First State Breach Notification Law Is Not Yet a Suitable Template for National Identity Theft Legislation*, RICH. J. LAW & TECH. (2003), *available at* http://jolt.richmond.edu/v10i1/article1.pdf; Mac McMillan, *Data breach notification and data protection law: Will Florida Lead?* INFORMATION-WEEK (Jul. 16, 2014); Steven A. Meyerowitz & Craig Komanecki, *The Move Towards Mandatory Encryption of Sensitive Personal Information*, PRIVACY & DATA SECURITY L. 2009.03-6 (2009). Nevada law also requires encryption of sensitive personal information.
309. *See* Steven Bellman, Eric J. Johnson, Stephen J. Kobrin, & Gerald L. Lohse, *International Differences in Information Privacy Concerns: A Global Survey of Consumers*, THE INFORMATION SOCIETY (2004), https://www8.gsb.columbia.edu/sites/decisionsciences/files/files/1172.pdf. States have surfaced highly specific and relatively taxing requirements for businesses including: incorporating PCI by reference in state law (Texas), assigning retailers liability for costs during a data breach including credit monitoring and bank compensation (New Jersey, Illinois, Connecticut, Massachusetts), and imposing restrictions higher than the PCI standard (California).
310. Charlotte A. Tschider, *Experimenting with Privacy: Driving Efficiency Through a State-Informed Federal Data Breach Notification and Data Protection Law*, 18 TUL. J. TECH. & INTELL. PROP. 45 (2015).
311. Information types were counted twice for statutes that included language like "credit cards with or without passcodes."

Figure 15.1 Data Types Requiring Notification

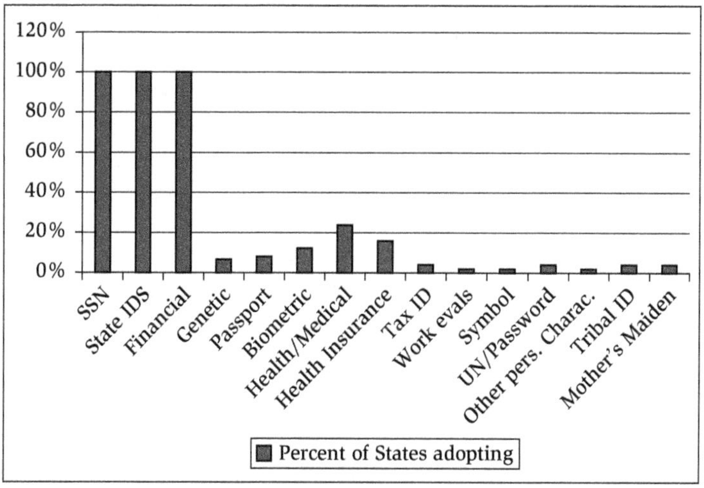

Despite the broad extraterritorial reach, states have heavily leveraged a data manipulation safe harbor. A data manipulation safe harbor involves obscuring, encrypting, masking, or otherwise making personal information unreadable. When manipulated and later exposed, in most states organizations will not need to provide notification of a data breach, as the risk of fraud or misuse is simply too low. One hundred percent of statutes reference a safe harbor for manipulated data, whether referencing actual encryption technologies or other methods rendering information partially or completely unreadable, such as redaction, and presumably including obfuscation, tokenization, or masking.

States varied to what degree waivers were deemed voidable and unenforceable. Waivers, as in any statutory context, typically involve contractual agreements to waive some right an individual is otherwise entitled to enforce. Likely due to a concern around consumers not reading terms of use and other online contracts used to provision services, many states incorporated language limiting the use of waivers to disclaim data breach notification responsibilities. Thirty-seven percent of statutes today include explicit no-waiver language, and the use of statutes that do has decreased over the past three years.

When entities have not successfully avoided compliance with a data security breach statute, they must actually notify individuals impacted by a data security breach. However, the speed of the communication can matter very much for a consumer. Because fraudsters and identity thieves know a limited window exists before someone discovers the issue, most criminals act quickly to maximize gains. Most statutes, however, employ flexible language subject to interpretation, the most popular "without unreasonable delay" (76% of statutes), while other states opt to specify a time requirement (17%).

The contents of data breach notifications, along with the method of delivery, can play a significant role in whether consumers receive helpful information from an entity and the likelihood of that communication reaching a resident of that state. When required, content of such communications often includes a description of the data breach, contact information for the entity breached, what information it stores about the person affected, and contact information for the Federal Trade Commission (FTC), the state Attorney General, or consumer credit reporting agencies. Despite the helpfulness of the information, the vast majority of statutes do not require specific content in notifications.

When large breaches affect many customers, most states allow substitute notice to communicate a data breach with residents. Instead of communicating directly with residents; over a certain threshold of notification, cost, or residents affected; organizations do not need to communicate directly with residents but instead typically must e-mail residents if an e-mail address is available, conspicuously post a notice on a website, and (or, depending on the statute) notify major local or state-wide media. These steps reduce financial burden for organizations, while using common communication channels, even though residents may not know if they individually have been affected by a breach. About 65% of statutes set a limit at around 150,000 dollars.

Some statutes also require an entity to notify the Attorney General's office, the major Consumer Credit Reporting Agencies, or other state agencies. For statutes that do require notification to the Attorney General or Consumer Credit Reporting Agencies, often a threshold must be met, most commonly 1,000 residents affected or more. Over time, requiring reporting to the Consumer Credit Reporting Agencies has become increasingly common at around 53%, while Attorney General notice has decreased in popularity, at 37%.

§15.02 ADMINISTRATIVE ACTIONS AND FINES

Regulatory authorities today provide the greatest percentage of oversight for privacy and cybersecurity legal concerns. Regulatory authorities in many countries act as a custodian for the general public and have considerable power to pursue legal action and levy fines for consumer privacy harms. One or more of six steps usually result from a data breach or finding of non-compliance: (1) Investigate, (2) Notify, (3) Audit, (4) Decide, (5) Settle, and (6) Pursue Legal Action.

For the regulatory authority to begin to *Investigate*, the authority has either received a complaint from a data subject or has independently observed non-compliance, for example like CNIL cookie enforcement activities, which started with an independent CNIL review. During *Investigation*, the regulatory authority seeks to gather information about reported non-compliance and formally document details using internal processes. During the *Notice* phase, if the investigation indicates that an organization has engaged in non-compliant activities and the authority decides to pursue an action against the organization, the authority will notify the organization using a formal letter, document request, or audit request.

In the *Audit* phase, the authority performs a formal review of an organization's policies, procedures, training, and systems. Although some authorities conduct routine audits with clearly articulated controls that are publicly available, others may use an internal process that involves document requests, reviews, and follow-up questions. In the *Decide* phase, after an audit has been conducted and investigation has concluded, the authority must decide how to proceed, depending on the gravity of non-compliance. Most frequently, one of four decisions will be made: no action, for minor infractions; agreement to legally binding action, for first-time offenders; or a fine, for substantial or repeat offenses. Some countries may prefer to collect fines, even small fines, as a warning to other organizations. Legally binding action at this stage typically involves voluntary cooperation by an organization and authority supervision for a period of time, in a form that is contractually binding. For some countries, voluntary cooperation can provide an alternative path to fines and public disclosure, and for this reason is desirable.

Fines can vary considerably from jurisdiction to jurisdiction, and a fine in one jurisdiction often does not satisfy a fine in another jurisdiction. Broad international organizations should consider potential financial outlay across jurisdictions when pursuing non-compliant activities. However, jurisdictions may vary greatly by the fine amount and fine aggregation. For example, the GDPR may fine four percent of revenue at the top end, the South African PPI may fine up to 100,000 Rand (EUR 650,000 at time of writing), and the TCPA in the United States fines USD 1,500 per violation. These differing models are described in Table 15.2.

Table 15.2 Fine Models

Fine Type	*Percent Base*	*Variable Range*	*Incident*
Description	Takes a percentage of revenue	Discretionary choice with a ceiling, or a range of fine values	Cost per data subject or incident affected
Advantages	Adjustable, based on size of the company	Discretionary leaves authority ability to punish bad actors at higher level	Good for jurisdictions that use fines as compensation for data subjects, at least a minimum fine
Disadvantages	Can appear heavy-handed in relation to the non-compliant act	Lower end ranges do not provide needed incentive to be compliant	Difficult to determine how an incident is identified—the whole event, or each person affected
Examples	EU's GDPR	México's PPDPP, Canada's PIPEDA, South African PPI	U.S.' TCPA, Russian No. 242-FZ

Organizations may never experience the last two phases of *Pursue Legal Action* and *Settle*, if they agree earlier to compulsory activities or pay a fine. However, organizations that question the accuracy of findings, clarity of legal requirement, or actual authority of the regulatory authority, may prefer to pursue legal action in some jurisdictions. At any point in the legal process, organizations may prefer to arrange some other alternative contractual agreement, a settlement, which is contractually binding on the parties.

Internationally, many countries provide a private right of action for individuals directly injured and occasionally special interest groups representing these individuals, by non-compliance with data protection laws. A private right of action allows for an individual person the ability to independently bring a legal proceeding against an organization for privacy or cybersecurity compliance violations. *See* Table 15.3 for a short list of International, non-U.S. statutes.

Table 15.3 Country-Level Privacy Statutes

Country/Region	*Law*	*Private Right?*
Canada	Personal Information Protection and Electronic Documents Act (PIPEDA)	N
Canada	Canada's Anti-Spam Legislation (CASL)	Y, suspended
European Union	General Data Protection Regulation	Y
México	Law on Protection of Personal Data	Y
Argentina	Personal Data Protection Law	Y
Brazil	Civil Rights Framework for the Internet	Y
Russian Federation	Russian Federal Law of July 27, 2006 N 152-FZ	Y
Chile	Law 19.628	Y, for data access
People's Republic of China	NPC Decision on Network Information Protection	Y
Malaysia	Personal Data Protection Act	N
Indonesia	Electronic Information and Transactions	N
Colombia	Law 1581 + Decree 1377	Y, Constitutional only
Costa Rica	Law No. 8968, *Protection in the Handling of the Personal Data of Individuals*	N, only to regulatory body
México	Federal Law on the Protection of Personal Data	Y, ARCO rights
Perú	The Personal Data Protection Law No. 29733	N
Uruguay	Data Protection Act Law No. 18.331	N
Australia	The Privacy Act	N
New Zealand	The Privacy Act	N
Singapore	Personal Data Protection Act	Y, but binding regulatory decisions apply

Country/Region	*Law*	*Private Right?*
Republic of Korea	Personal Information Protection Act	Y, and with punitive
Hong Kong	Personal Data (Privacy) Ordinance	Y
Taiwan	Personal Data Protection Law	Y, collective action allowed
UAE-Dubai	DIFC Law/Data Protection Law	N
Israel	Protection of Privacy Law, 5741-1981	Y
Angola	Data Protection Law No. 22/11	N
Ghana	Data Protection Act, 2012 (Act 842)	Y
South Africa	Protection of Personal Information Act	Y
Zimbabwe	Access to Information and Protection of Privacy Act	N

Although the United States may have a litigious reputation, an individual in the U.S. generally cannot pursue a private right of action statutorily without specific right to do. *See* Tables 15.4 and 15.5 for a list of U.S. statutes and associated private rights.

Table 15.4 U.S. Federal Privacy Statutes

Statute	*Enforcement*	*Private Right?*
Health Information Portability and Accountability Act (HIPAA)	Office for Civil Rights (OCR)	N
Gramm-Leach Bliley Act (GLBA)	Office of the Comptroller of Currency (OCC)	N
Regulation S-P (Reg S-P)	Securities Exchange Commission (SEC)	N
Children's Online Privacy Protection Act (COPPA)	Federal Trade Commission (FTC)	N
Family Educational Rights and Privacy Act (FERPA)	Family Policy Compliance Office (FPCO)	N
Telephone Consumer Protection Act (TCPA)	Federal Communications Commission (FCC) + FTC	Y
CAN-SPAM	FCC (+ FTC)	ISPs, Government
Federal Wiretapping Act, Electronic Communications Privacy Act, Stored Communications Act (SCA)	Department of Justice (DOJ)	Y

Table 15.5 U.S. Federal Cybersecurity Statutes

Statute	*Enforcement*	*Private Right?*
Food, Drug, and Cosmetics Act (FDCA)	Food & Drug Administration (FDA)	N
Computer Fraud and Abuse Act (CFAA)	Department of Justice (DOJ)	Y
Cybersecurity Information Sharing Act (CISA)	National Security Agency (NSA)	N
Federal Trade Commission Act (FTC Act)	Federal Trade Commission (FTC)	N

CHAPTER 16
Synthesizing Information Privacy and Cybersecurity

Organizations of the future will have multi-dimensional concerns regarding the collection, retention, use, transfer, and processing of a wide variety of data. The data managed will include personal information and non-personal information of significant value to organizations. Although some organizations have begun collaborating across functions, teams will need to dramatically improve collective efforts to successfully manage new technology and resulting business and compliance challenges.

§16.01 PRIVACY AND CYBERSECURITY COLLABORATION

Organizations increasingly plan for privacy and cybersecurity together, and mature organizations consider how data obligations might connect from a management perspective. At the highest level, organizations can map all information to high-level business processes as part of information governance. Some organizations may have stronger privacy concerns or stronger security concerns depending on the information collected and processed, but these concerns usually connect back to how information is collected, processed, and managed. When organizations begin conducting risk assessments and assembling information about assets, usually organizations find that privacy and security disciplines review common assets and may under some circumstances provide conflicting direction. Organizations find it easier to conduct inherent and residual risk assessments that include both privacy and security questions. For example, the security team may prefer to retain biometric data for MFA purposes and for forensic analyses, yet the privacy team may resist long-term storage of biometric data, due to increased work when handling data breach notification. Organizations that manage or, at the very least, discuss these topics together often find a balanced and collaborative approach to problem-solving and internal policy.

Privacy and security obligations often fall within common organizational processes, such as policy development, governance, assessment, and incident or data breach response. Although security often becomes more technical, security practitioners should understand privacy considerations and vice-versa. Attorneys advising either capability should also understand both to some extent, due to frequent and considerable overlap. At the same time, certain situations may demand more attention paid from one capability or the other. Security teams, for example, may show greater concern for key operational capabilities that do not handle personal information, such as manufacturing or customer management capabilities. Information privacy teams may similarly be more concerned with large volumes of data collected under circumstances that do not meet legal obligations for notice or consent or where the organization intends to transfer data to inadequate jurisdictions. Although security teams may care very much about how data transfer and storage, including the integrity, availability, confidentiality, and safety concerns associated with this information; information privacy teams necessarily focus on civil rights concerns and statutory compliance. Unfortunately, when teams do not collaborate through similar priorities, business process and projects may receive attention from one, but not both, teams.

Some strategies do exist, however, for building selectively collaborative teams. Clear partnerships include governance activities. Governance responsibilities include decision-making and oversight of risk decisions, such as the GRC committee and EC or Board updates, as well as audit activities that evaluate the efficacy of both teams or capabilities. Additionally, teams can streamline assessment protocol and delivery turnaround for an organization by considering both privacy and security obligations together, and in engineering or upfront activities, such as SecDLC and PbD. When privacy and security work closely together and present requirements and standards as one team, the organization often benefits. Organizations increasingly have combined these teams together for more cohesive and collaborative work efforts. It is essential that organizations considering this path prioritize relationship management with both IT and Legal departments, regardless of reporting lines.

§16.02 EMERGING TOPICS

Emerging topics do bring information privacy and cybersecurity teams together to solve challenges for the organization. Teams working on emerging topics should find new and innovative ways to collaborate while balancing organizational goals and business financial success. Some of the biggest topics today include cloud services (Cloud), big data storage and mining (Big Data), Internet of Things (IoT), and Artificial Intelligence (AI).

[A] Cloud Computing

Cloud services, or shared technology resources, are a cornerstone of enabling organizational services and emerging technology, like IoT. While in the past, organizations often operated their own data centers or leased dedicated rack space in others, cloud services capitalize on resource sharing and redundancy within vendor systems to provide scalable, reliable, and often inexpensive services for an organization.[312] Cloud implementations can include Infrastructure as a Service (IaaS), Software as a Service (SaaS), Platform as a Service (PaaS, or storage, database, and application implementations.[313] Each of these cloud service types, implemented as public, private, hybrid, or community clouds, pose unique security challenges.[314] The privacy of data in the cloud, as well as integrity and availability of IoT services, depends in large part on the cloud vendor security controls implemented.[315]

Public and private cloud implementations each pose security challenges. Manufacturers offering public cloud services may not encrypt databases, may not protect source code for IoT applications, and may loosely manage administrative accounts providing support. When security controls are in place, often data is only logically segregated, which increases the probability of vulnerability to cyberattack.[316] However, public cloud implementations often are most cost-effective, scalable, and have the best performance, so manufacturers focused on margin and performance first may not insist on appropriate security controls. Organizations should request third party reports, such as the SSAE16 SOC 2, Type 2, which provides substantially more details than the typically executed SSAE16 SOC 1 or SOC 2, Type 1. Providers may have alternative or different cloud security certification, as well.

Data transfer, given its challenges in contract negotiation, business operations (Binding Corporate Rules), adequacy standards, and localization requirements, also present unique and important challenges for IoT architecture. As part of a cost, convenience, and extensibility strategy, organizations increasingly look to cloud service providers with associated big data mining tools to host IoT infrastructure. These organizations may use low-cost support models in locations not deemed adequate or substantially similar by the EU or other countries. Organizations should clearly understand (and stipulate in contract) cloud data centers' geographic location.

The concept of big data has led to concerns both in the security and privacy spaces. Big data is defined as quite simply large, functional data sets, which enable more robust data science and reporting. Of course, the concept of big data and the reality of implementing big data solutions are very different. The precursor to big data sets involves, in many cases, ubiquitous data collection. Ubiquitous data collection involves data gathering from a variety of sources. This may mean organizations collect data directly from a consumer or patient, but they may also purchase data sets about those same consumers or patients and collect ancillary data via IOT devices. For these reasons, ubiquitous data collection for big data implementation can cause challenges in

---

312. Kai Hwang, Jack Dongarra & Geoffrey C. Fox, Distributed and Cloud Computing (Waltham: 2012), at 77, 95-96.
313. Goran Čandrlić, *Cloud Computing – Types of Cloud*, GlobalDots Website (Mar. 19, 2013), http://www.globaldots.com/cloud-computing-types-of-cloud/.
314. Jaydip Sen, *Security and Privacy Issues in Cloud Computing*, Semantic Scholar (last accessed: Feb. 2, 2017), https://pdfs.semanticscholar.org/4dc3/70d253020947a8e66b701e12dd0233161229.pdf (describing the various security concerns for cloud computing).
315. *Id.*
316. Online Web Application Security Project, *Cloud-10 Multi-Tenancy and Physical Security* (Aug. 30, 2010), https://www.owasp.org/index.php/Cloud-10_Multi_Tenancy_and_Physical_Security.

notice prior to data collection, appropriately informative privacy notices, and transparency of other operations, such as automated processing. In fact, the addition of an ability to object to automated processing in the GDPR illustrates an acknowledgment that ubiquitous data collection coupled with automation data, IOT, and automated processing, could potentially impact data subjects' rights.

Professor David Vladeck has identified three risks associated with data collection generally: ubiquitous data collection, data breach, and identity theft; unrestrained collection of sensitive, personal data; and the use of algorithmic decision-making to make consequential decisions.[317] IoT consumer privacy concerns involve variations on these three risks, as well as impact to consumer safety and potential property damage. Substantial volumes of data make data stores a potential target for data breach and identity theft, depending on the data type. Financially motivated hackers may target data involving traditional types of SPI, such as health data, financial data, biometric information, insurance information, ID numbers, or employment information. However, other hackers could benefit from a high probability of re-identification in some data sets to disclose embarrassing or sensitive information consumers may believe is anonymized.[318]

The World Economic Forum has criticized traditional approaches for privacy protection in the global big data and big data use context. Data use disclosure, a primary component of most modern privacy and data protection laws, ignores the potential for future beneficial data use and adds complexity with additional notice and consent procedure requirements. Data use change fluidity also complicates previously static exchanges: changing and beneficial consumer-oriented uses can be developed and deployed on-the-fly, making consent complicated and onerous. Data localization and transfer limitations have increased as countries pursue economic protection agendas and information privacy goals, increase overall cost for data storage. This vast amount of data stored, especially significantly high volumes of data projected to be generated by IoT, makes it nearly impossible for an individual user or data subject to intelligently manage data use in available daily time. In short, the user or data subject may no longer want to make every decision regarding their data, even though the law has promoted notice and consent as a cornerstone of choice, both in the context of consumer products and information privacy.

[B] The Internet of Things

Although precursors to the Internet of Things (IoT) laid foundational elements, such as developments in radio frequency identifiers (RFID) and wearable computers, Chana Schoenberger and Bruce Upbin first published an article introducing the "Internet of

317. *See* Janice Phaik Lin Goh, *Privacy, Security, and Wearable Technology*, 8 No. 2 LANDSLIDE 30, 31 (2015). Wearable technologies, as a subset of Internet of Things technologies, collect a continuous stream of data about an individual. Please note: Phaik Lin Goh defines wearables in much the same way as IoT are defined within this article, including both implanted and "wearable" devices in this definition.

318. Mark van Rijmenam, *The Re-Identification of Anonymous People with Big Data*, DATAFLOQ (Feb. 10, 2016), https://datafloq.com/read/re-identifying-anonymous-people-with-big-data/228.

Things" in 2002.[319] The IoT recognized today represents a far-evolved version of those first developments, including consumer, industrial, or medical products that are designed with a primary purpose enhanced by Internet connectivity, such as a network-enabled washing machine. Oxford Dictionaries defines the Internet of Things as "the interconnection via the Internet of computing devices embedded in everyday objects, enabling them to send and receive data," illustrating the fascinating and legally challenging core of IoT: how to regulate consumer devices with new technical capabilities and new consumer risks.[320]

The complementary nature of Internet connectivity in IoT devices is revolutionizing the product manufacturing ecosystem, creating a competitive environment that differentiates connected IoT devices from analog products.[321] Due to enhanced convenience and extensibility, including higher utilization and increased reliability of devices, IoT devices are poised to dominate the consumer device market. IoT devices (rather than analog devices) are now the choice *du jour* of consumers with mobile devices: baby monitors, children's learning games, refrigerators, cars, and even hair brushes connect to the Internet.[322]

IoT household devices introduce a unique value proposition of convenience through remote monitoring. IoT devices enable a user to monitor and direct activities remotely, such as reviewing your grocery list from your connected refrigerator or unlocking your door remotely for a weekend guest. Internet connectivity drives a significant convenience factor through remote direction and information gathering.[323]

IoT devices also dynamically increase service optimization with better access to broadband technologies.[324] IoT devices including network-enabled children's toys, cleaning robots, and multi-purpose virtual assistants benefit from connectivity with a manufacturer's systems. The ability to download new content or capabilities provide more or improved services beyond those hard-wired or initially programmed into the

319. Gil Press, *A Very Short History of the Internet of Things*, FORBES (June 18, 2014), http://www.forbes.com/sites/gilpress/2014/06/18/a-very-short-history-of-the-internet-of-things/2/#b596e1c63437.

320. Karen Rose, Scott Eldridge & Lyman Chapin, *The Internet of Things: An Overview*, INTERNET SOCIETY (Oct. 2015), https://www.internetsociety.org/sites/default/files/ISOC-IoT-Overview-20151014_0.pdf.

321. Michael E. Porter & James E. Heppelmann, *How Smart, Connected Products Are Transforming Competition*, HARVARD BUSINESS REVIEW (Nov. 2014), available at https://hbr.org/2014/11/how-smart-connected-products-are-transforming-competition. The use of the term "analog" devices by the Author is meant to illustrate a distinct difference between consumer devices that may have embedded software, but are not networked, and those properly considered consumer IoT devices.

322. *See* Matt Burgess, *We've reached peak IoT. There's now a smart hairbrush.* WIRED (Jan. 4, 2017).

323. Darla Scott, *ISTR Insights: The Internet of Things (IoT) and the Concerns of Convenience*, SYMANTEC BLOG (Sept. 14, 2016), https://www.symantec.com/connect/blogs/istr-insights-the-internet-of-things-iot-and-the-concerns-of-convenience. Although convenience drives much of IoT adoption, risks accompany such convenience.

324. Organisation for Economic Co-Operation and Development, *The Internet of Things: Seizing the Benefits and Addressing the Challenges* (May 24, 2016), http://www.oecd.org/officialdocuments/publicdisplaydocumentpdf/?cote=DSTI/ICCP/CISP(2015)3/FINAL&docLanguage=En, at 5.

device out of the box.[325] When combined with other technologies, such as big data, cloud services, artificial intelligence and machine learning, such devices benefit from access to backend systems collecting, processing, and transferring substantial, nearly real-time data across all devices while they are connected.[326]

Although data collection enables business to provide near real-time service to consumers, the amount of data transmitted, processed, stored, and mined may also pose substantial privacy challenges. Because IoT devices are connected, often pervasively passing data in real-time to the product cloud and other backend systems, IoT devices provide a significant volume of data about individuals, including geolocation information and other personal information.[327] Potential data elements include location information (such as geolocation), health information, biometric data, home usage "smart" technology, and other personal information like name or credit card data.[328] Children's devices may collect and transmit data specific to children, which could include images (as in connected baby monitors), location information, audio, communication details like text, or biometric data. This data can be stored in the product cloud or backend systems, or reside on the device itself. Each storage location has its own unique challenge with regard to specific threats.[329]

Although IoT devices will likely collect and transfer personal information to the product cloud and other backend systems, a wide variety of other data may also be transferred, which could also cause physical damage or safety issues for users. Data stored regarding IoT devices may include a variety of data, some of which could directly compromise an individual's personal information, while unauthorized changes to other data or device configurations could change the integrity of code transmitted to an IoT device, causing it to function incorrectly. Such application or configuration data alteration could cause a device to shut down, start up, operate at a higher or lower temperature than configured, change other operating protocol, or alter artificial intelligence rules and algorithms.

In addition to data use for purposes of service improvement and sales strategy, IoT data combined with other consumer data has the potential for external data sale,

---

325. Gatis Paeglis, *Over-the-Air Updates, Part 1: Introduction*, QT BLOG (May 31, 2016), https://blog.qt.io/blog/2016/05/31/over-the-air-updates-part-1-introduction/.
326. Tim Allen, *How to Solve IoT's Big Challenge with Machine Learning*, FORBES (Feb. 2, 2017), http://www.forbes.com/sites/sap/2017/02/02/how-to-solve-iots-big-data-challenge-with-machine-learning/#3bb9237f4337; Daniel Gutierrez, *Unlock the Potential of IoT with Real-Time Data*, INSIDEBIGDATA (Sept. 26, 2016), http://insidebigdata.com/2016/09/26/unlock-the-potential-of-iot-with-real-time-data/.
327. David C. Vladeck, *Consumer Protection in an Era of Big Data Analytics*, 42 OHIO N.U. L. REV. 493, 498 (2016).
328. *See supra* Phaik Lin Goh, note 317, at 31-32; Vassiliki Andronikou, Dionysios S. Dementis & Theodora Varvarigou, *Biometric Implementations and the Implications for Security and Privacy*, (Jan. 2007), http://www.fidis.net/fileadmin/journal/issues/1-2007/Biometric_Implementations_and_the_Implications_for_Security_and_Privacy.pdf; Greg Lindsay, Beau Woods & Joshua Corman, *Smart Homes and the Internet of Things*, ATLANTIC COUNCIL (Mar. 2016), https://otalliance.org/system/files/files/initiative/documents/smart_homes_0317_web.pdf (describing security and privacy protections for smart home technologies); Stacey Higginbotham, Companies need to share how they use our data. Here are some ideas.
329. Ashwin Pal, *The Internet of Things (IoT) – Threats and Countermeasures*, CSO (2017), http://www.cso.com.au/article/575407/internet-things-iot-threats-countermeasures/.

transfer, or exchange.[330] Unlike Web form data or basic consumer sales or demographic data, IoT's high volume of data points combined with other data sources has the potential to map an individual's behaviors through most of her life, which could prove highly lucrative for organizations seeking to better market and sell to consumers. However, because data collection often occurs ubiquitously, consumers may not be aware of data transferred.

Although more data, or big data, could increase business market share by providing more tailored or personalized IoT devices and associated services, this aggregation of data across platforms and organizations also increases the probability of re-identification even when individual data points might not independently be classified as personal information.[331] Substantial data volume is already collected by data aggregators. Acxiom, for example, stores around 3,000 data points on a given individual, and data points will only increase with IoT devices capturing real-time data.[332]

Recent vulnerability analyses conducted by ethical hackers over smart home products and other consumer products have also raised concerns over the potential of risks to personal safety and physical damages, in addition to unauthorized access and exposure of personal information.[333] Potential results of exploiting such vulnerabilities have so far included: unlocked door locks and padlocks, compromising the safety of a home; wheelchairs remotely controlled by an attacker, potentially causing injury to the occupant; thermostats used to cause excessive heating, frozen pipes, and furnace failures, causing substantial damage to property and potentially home owners.

IoT devices pose significant risks through ubiquitous data collection, data breach risk, and identity theft; unrestrained collection of sensitive, personal data; the use of algorithmic decision-making to make consequential decisions; impacts to consumer physical safety; and property damage. Existing and planned legal solutions do not yet cover all aspects of IoT devices and leave significant gaps, especially for consumer IoT devices without especially sensitive status.

[C] Artificial Intelligence

In recent years, the uptick in artificial intelligence technologies within big data systems has revolutionized data analytics and automated decision-making, and is poised to

330. *See, e.g.*, Johannes Deichmann, Kersten Heineke, Thomas Reinbacher & Dominik Wee, *Creating a successful Internet of Things data marketplace*, McKinsey & Company (Oct. 2016), http://www.mckinsey.com/business-functions/digital-mckinsey/our-insights/creating-a-successful-internet-of-things-data-marketplace (describing monetization strategies for IoT data).
331. Joseph Jerome, *Big Data: Catalyst for a Privacy Conversation*, 48 Ind. L. Rev. 213 (2014) (highlighting challenges in consumer autonomy for making decision regarding how an individual's data is used).
332. Federal Trade Commission, *Data Brokers: A Call for Transparency and Accountability* (May 2014), https://www.ftc.gov/system/files/documents/reports/data-brokers-call-transparency-accountability-report-federal-trade-commission-may-2014/140527databrokerreport.pdf, at 8.
333. Lucian Constantin, *Hackers found 47 new vulnerabilities in 23 IoT devices at DEF CON*, CSO (Sept. 13, 2016), http://www.csoonline.com/article/3119765/security/hackers-found-47-new-vulnerabilities-in-23-iot-devices-at-def-con.html.

revolutionize IoT. *Machine learning* is a foundational capability for artificial intelligence and includes a variety of techniques including data mining, learning models, and algorithm creation. These techniques present a vast quantity of data, which is then organized and future decision-making algorithms created by computer resources finding trends and patterns in the data itself. Machine learning and, by extension, artificial intelligence, involves computerized decision-making that may present ethical challenges. *Unsupervised learning*, or machine learning that occurs without human intervention, may provide macro data that, when coupled with automated decision-making, marginalizes specific groups or demographics.[334]

[D] Digital Health

The global digital health market has grown exponentially in the past five years, fueled by Internet of Things (IoT) development, increased mobile device adoption, and Big Data investment. Historically, the medical device industry focused on device implants and direct therapies, but future medical technologies also leverage network connectivity and data aggregation, necessitating comprehensive cybersecurity activities to protect consumers. Market leaders in digital health have recently invested heavily in technologies that simultaneously improve patient connectedness and convenience, yet increase the probability of cybersecurity threats compromising system vulnerabilities.

While digital health technologies offer several benefits to patients and healthcare providers, connected technologies attract new threats, potentially resulting in both health data loss and compromise of patient physical safety. The combination of technology connectivity with increasingly common third-party involvement via the cloud, SaaS, and big data, multiplies the probability of harm, due to the presence of high-volume data sets for multiple customers, often connected over the public Internet or home networks with unknown settings. *See* Table 16.1 for examples of Digital Health technology and associated cybersecurity risks.

Table 16.1 Digital Health Technology Cybersecurity Risks

Device Type	*Inherent Risk*	*Risk Description*
Implanted Device	Critical	Network-enabled devices are open to malware or viruses impeding or changing function. Unauthorized users can also launch attacks altering data, commands, or configurations remotely. Loss of personal could also result via remote data storage capabilities.

334. Stephen Gardner, *Artificial Intelligence Poses Data Privacy Challenges*, Bloomberg BNA (Oct. 26, 2016), https://www.bna.com/artificial-intelligence-poses-n57982079158/.

Device Type	*Inherent Risk*	*Risk Description*
Non-Implanted Device	High	Network-enabled non-implanted devices are open to malware, viruses, or attacks, many of which would likely result in device inoperability, which could cause patient safety hazards. Loss of personal information could also result remote via data storage capabilities if healthcare providers store medical record numbers or other identifying information in the device.
Wearables	Medium	Network-enabled wearables are open to malware, viruses, or attacks that could result in device inoperability. Attacks could alter data reliability, causing unnecessary concern or treatment. Wearables also pose significant concern for loss of personal information due to the connectivity with mobile devices.
Mobile App	Medium	Network-enabled mobile devices are open to malware, viruses, or attacks that could result in device inoperability and personal information loss. Thick client mobile apps often function offline, which means that significant data volumes can be stored on a mobile device.
Web Application	Low	Web Applications are subject to well-known threats and vulnerabilities, in particular identity and encryption concerns, leading primarily to organizational risk (e.g., site defacing), personal information loss, and potential malware/virus infection from an organization to a consumer's computer.
General Admin. IT	Medium	Administrative software can process and store significant volumes of personal information for employees and patients, which can be subject to personal information loss, data integrity issues (such as deletion, addition, or change of critical patient information) resulting in incorrect patient treatment. Ransomware and other data availability attacks could cause patient data to be unavailable during critical treatments

Future healthcare models embrace new healthcare technologies that enhance patient convenience, enable remote monitoring, and improve health outcomes. Patients in clinical trials, after recovery from surgery, or older adults desiring to reside at home, benefit tremendously from remote monitoring. Remote monitoring requires internet connectivity for monitoring equipment used, interoperability with consumer health Internet of Things devices (such as an IoT weight scale, FitBit, glucose meter, etc.), and big data capabilities to store substantially higher data volumes. This model complicates consent and relationships because effective remote monitoring requires commingled data from many sources and third-party data sharing, such as data from consumer IoT devices. A patient faced with consent for data sharing for all IoT devices, consent for data sharing with multiple medical device companies, and consent for one or more healthcare providers to access this data, again demonstrates the incredibly complex and relatively untenable nature of managing consent for healthcare of the future.

Value-based healthcare presents the most challenging scenario for healthcare provider notice and consent. The purpose of value-based healthcare is to leverage big data solutions to commingle data from several sources, including IoT devices and across geographies and determine appropriate recommendations to improve health outcomes. This model will be used by pharmaceutical companies, medical device manufacturers, healthcare providers, and medical researchers. Mining substantial data also requires flexibility in the business use justification for data, as artificial intelligence technologies like machine learning create algorithms based on large data sets. These algorithms then identify new uses and insights, leveraging data to improve health outcomes not previously defined or contemplated. The power of these technologies to improve population health around the world is undeniable. However, notice and consent in this scenario is nearly impossible using the traditional notice and consent model.

Organizations creating these emerging technologies aim to dramatically improve human convenience, effectiveness, health, and productivity. Attorneys choosing to practice in information privacy and cybersecurity embrace an increasingly global environment with growing regulatory considerations and new technologies pushing the barriers of accepted models and methods for managing information privacy and cybersecurity.

Index

D

E

Q

R

T

U

V

W